Voice of the Heart

Voice of the Heart

⌒

Songs of Devotion
from the Mystics

Radha Soami Satsang Beas

Translated by Mewa Singh from the Hindi edition: 'Binati Aur Praarthna Ke Shabd'
© Radha Soami Satsang Beas

Published by:
J. C. Sethi, Secretary
Radha Soami Satsang Beas
Dera Baba Jaimal Singh
Punjab 143 204, India

First edition 2013

20 19 18 17 16 15 14 13   8 7 6 5 4 3 2 1

ISBN 978-81-8466-236-8

Printed in India by: Lakshmi Offset Printers

Table of Contents

Preface

Originally published in the Indian languages as *Binati aur Prarthana ke Shabd*, this anthology brings together heartfelt prayers or shabds by twenty-eight mystics who lived in the Indian subcontinent between the thirteenth and nineteenth centuries. Although the mystics came from different spiritual traditions and walks of life, their voice is one because it is a universal voice of longing for the Lord.

The Great Master, Baba Sawan Singh Ji, when explaining the meaning of prayer in his book *Philosophy of the Masters*, refers to the Persian word *dua* meaning 'call' – calling on the Lord for help. Prayer, he said, "should come from the heart. Our heart, head and tongue should agree. Pray in such a manner that your inner feelings are aroused, every pore begins to weep, and all your veins become like the strings of a violin. The feeling of love should pour forth, and you should become absorbed in your prayer."[1]

The living Masters of Beas have taught the way to fulfil this longing of the heart for over one hundred years. Wherever a saint serves others, people gather. Like bees attracted to flowers, seekers are drawn irresistibly into the circle of the saint, for they sense that through the mystic, they will find what they seek. The shabds in this book have been sung day after day over the years before satsang by seekers of God wanting to become receptive to the divine.

For this new edition, English translations of the shabds are presented along with the original text in Hindi script as well as transliteration for those who are familiar with the original language but cannot read the script. It is our hope that this three-language format will serve well the ever-growing community of devotees wherever they live in the world.

Many of the English translations have been published by us earlier. While we appreciate that no poetic expression can convey the same in translation as it does in the original, for this new translation our endeavour has been to stay as close as possible to the meaning of the original while rendering the verses in natural contemporary English and avoiding expanded interpretation. Line numbers have been given in the Hindi text as well as the translation for cross-reference. Brief footnotes and a glossary are provided to give the meaning of terms and concepts that may be unfamiliar to the reader. For those who wish to find the English translation of particular shabds, an index of first lines in transliteration as well as translation is given.

It is our hope that this anthology will serve to remind us of the mystic teachings and renew the spirit of the teachings in ourselves, inspiring us to live in the Lord's will through the life of devotion praised so highly by the saints in these shabds.

J. C. Sethi
Secretary
Radha Soami Satsang Beas

पाठकों से निवेदन

बानी का सही उच्चारण

गुरबानी

अकसर देखने में आया है कि हिंदी पाठक श्री गुरु ग्रन्थ साहिब की बानी (गुरबानी) का शुद्ध उच्चारण नहीं कर पाते हैं। गुरबानी मूल रूप में गुरुमुखी लिपि में लिखी गई है। इसमें कई शब्दों के अंत में ह्रस्व इ (ि) और ह्रस्व उ (ु) की मात्राओं का प्रयोग किया गया है। यह प्रयोग केवल व्याकरण दृष्टि से है; बानी पढ़ते समय इन मात्राओं का आमतौर पर उच्चारण नहीं किया जाता। हिंदी पाठक बड़े प्रेम से गुरबानी का पाठ या गायन करने का यत्न करते हैं, लेकिन इन मात्राओं और कुछ अन्य अपरिचित हिज्जों (स्पेलिंग) के कारण अनजाने में उच्चारण ग़लत हो जाता है। हम श्री गुरु ग्रन्थ साहिब का पूरा सम्मान करते हैं। हम चाहते हैं कि पाठक बानी का उच्चारण ग़लत न करें। इसलिए गुरबानी का रूपांतर देवनागरी लिपि में करते समय ये ह्रस्व मात्राएँ हटा दी गई हैं और अन्य कुछ परिवर्तन कर दिए गए हैं ताकि हिंदी भाषा के पाठक गुरबानी का सही उच्चारण कर सकें।

उदाहरण के रूप में :

मूल रूप : कुदरति पउणु पाणी बैसंतरु कुदरति धरती खाकु॥
सभ तेरी कुदरति तूं कादिरु करता पाकी नाई पाकु॥
नानक हुकमै अंदरि वेखै वरतै ताको ताकु॥

उच्चारण रूप : कुदरत पउण पाणी बैसंतर कुदरत धरती खाक॥
सभ तेरी कुदरत तूं कादिर करता पाकी नाई पाक॥
नानक हुकमै अंदर वेखै वरतै ताको ताक॥

यहाँ यह बात स्पष्ट कर देना आवश्यक है कि इन मात्राओं का प्रयोग पढ़ने में भले ही नहीं होता, लेकिन गुरबानी में इन मात्राओं का व्याकरण और अर्थ की दृष्टि से विशेष महत्त्व है। गुरु साहिबान के संदेश को अधिक गहराई से समझने के इच्छुक गुरबानी का मूल रूप में अध्ययन कर सकते हैं।

हिंदी बानी

हिंदी बानी में कहीं-कहीं 'ख' वर्ण को 'ष' लिखा जाता है – जैसे देषि, मूरिष, पंषी। लेकिन इन शब्दों का उच्चारण देखि, मूरिख, पंखी किया जाता है। इसलिये सही उच्चारण की दृष्टि से इस पुस्तक में आवश्यकतानुसार 'ष' के स्थान पर 'ख' वर्ण का प्रयोग किया गया है।

प्रकाशक

Note to the reader:
The transliteration of Hindi script into English script is always an approximation because the Hindi language has more letters than the English language. RSSB publications use simplified transliteration for easier reading in preference to the more comprehensive academic style. Readers are therefore advised to refer to the original script to ensure they do not mispronounce any words.

Voice of the Heart

बानी सन्त नामदेव जी

Bani Sant Namdev Ji

राग बसंत बाणी नामदेउ जी की

लोभ लहर अत नीझर बाजै॥
काइआ डूबै केसवा॥१॥
संसार समुंदे तार गोबिंदे॥
तार लै बाप बीठुला॥१॥ रहाउ॥
अनिल बेड़ा हउ खेव न साकउ॥
तेरा पार न पाइआ बीठुला॥२॥
होह दइआल सतगुर मेल तू मो कउ॥
पार उतारे केसवा॥३॥
नामा कहै हउ तर भी न जानउ॥
मो कउ बाह देह
बाह देह बीठुला॥४॥

Raag Basant Baani Naamdeo Ji ki

1 lobh lahar at neejhar baajai.
   kaaya doobai kesava.
2 sansaar samunde taar gobinde.
   taar lai baap beethula. rahaa'o.
3 anil berra hau khev na saakau.
   tera paar na paaya beethula.
4 hoh dayaal satgur mel tu mo kau.
   paar utaare kesava.
5 naama kahai hau tar bhi na jaanau.
   mo kau baah deh
   baah deh beethula.[1]

राग तिलंग बाणी भगता की नामदेव जी

मै अंधुले की टेक
तेरा नाम खुंदकारा॥
मै गरीब मै मसकीन
तेरा नाम है अधारा॥१॥ रहाउ॥
करीमां रहीमां अलाह तू गनीं॥
हाजरा हजूर दर पेस तूं मनीं॥१॥
दरीआउ तू दिहंद तू
बिसीआर तू धनी॥
देह लेह एक तूं दिगर को नही॥२॥

Raag Tilang Baani Bhagtaan ki Naamdev Ji

1 main andhule ki tek
   tera naam khundkaara.
2 main gareeb main maskeen
   tera naam hai adhaara. rahaa'o.
3 kareema raheema allaah tu gani.
   haajara hajoor dar pes toon mani.
4 dareeyaa'o tu dihand tu
   biseeyaar tu dhani.
5 deh leh ek toon digar ko nahi.

---

[1] The selections in this book that are taken from the Adi Granth, as this one is, begin with a header line giving the name of the raga (the musical measure of the hymn) and the Saint who composed the hymn. It sometimes also includes the verse form of the hymn.

Sant Namdev Ji

Raga Basant, Namdev Ji*

In constantly resounding waves of greed   1
   I am drowning, O Lord!

Ferry me across this ocean of existence,†   2
   O Father, please ferry me across.

Unable to steer my boat against this windstorm,   3
   O Beloved, I cannot reach your shore.

Be merciful, O Lord,   4
   and bless me with the company of the Satguru,
   who will ferry me across.

Says Namdev: I do not even know how to swim –   5
   give me your hand, O Lord, give me your hand.‡

Raga Tilang, Namdev Ji

Your Nam is the mainstay of this blind one;   1–2
   O Lord, poor and helpless as I am,
   your Nam is my only support.

You are the benevolent,   3
   merciful and compassionate Lord,
   all-pervading and ever-present before me.

You are the ocean, you are the giver,   4
   you are the infinitely bountiful Lord.

You alone give, you alone take back –   5
   other than you, no one can do so.

---

† See the Glossary for explanations of Indian-language terms or terms with unusual usage that are not footnoted.

‡ For sources, see the endnotes referenced in the transliteration on the opposite page.

तूं दानां तूं बीनां

मैं बीचार किआ करी॥

नामे चे सुआमी

बखसंद तूं हरी॥३॥

6 toon daana toon beena

main beechaar kya kari.

7 naame che suaami

bakhsand toon hari.[2]

राग गोंड बाणी नामदेउ जी की

घर १

मो कउ तार ले रामा तार ले॥

मैं अजान जन तरिबे न जानउ

बाप बीठुला बाह दे॥१॥रहाउ॥

नर ते सुर होए जात निमख मैं

सतगुर बुध सिखलाई॥

नर ते उपज सुरग कउ जीतिओ

सो अवखध मैं पाई॥१॥

जहा जहा धूअ नारद टेके

नैक टिकावहो मोहे॥

तेरे नाम अविलंब बहुत जन उधरे

नामे की निज मत एह॥२॥

Raag Gond Baani Naamdeo Ji Ki

Ghar Pahila

1 mo kau taar le raama taar le.

2 main ajaan jan taribe na jaanau

baap beethula baah de. rahaa'o.

3 nar te sur hoye jaat nimakh main

satgur budh sikhlaa'i.

4 nar te upaj surag kau jeetyo

so avkhadh main paa'i.

5 jaha jaha dhu naarad teke

naik tikaavho mohe.

6 tere naam avilamb bahut jan udhre

naame ki nij mat eh.[3]

पतितपावन माधऊ विरदु तेरा॥

धनि ते वै मुनिजन धिआइउ

हरि प्रभु मेरा॥

1 patit-paavan maadhau virad tera.

2 dhani te vai munijan dhiaayo

hari prabhu mera.

---

[*]**Dhruva** was the son of a mythological king. When he realized that he had no chance to succeed to the throne, he decided to leave home and follow the path of devotion, seeking no honour except that which his own actions would bring him. **Narad** was a sage

You are all-knowing and all-seeing –   6–7
  how can I comprehend you,
    O ever-forgiving Lord of Namdev?

Raga Gond, Namdev Ji

Ferry me across, O Lord, ferry me across!   1
I am ignorant and do not know how to swim;   2
  O Father, give me your hand.
The wisdom imparted by my Satguru   3
  instantly transformed me
  from a human into a divine being.
Although born human, I have triumphed over the heavens   4
  through the medicine you have given me.
Place me, O Lord, where you have placed   5
  devotees like Dhruva and Narad,*
  be it only for a short while.
With the support of your Nam, many are liberated;   6
  such is Namdev's own perception.

O Lord, your intrinsic nature is to redeem the fallen.   1
Blessed indeed are the Saints who meditate upon my Lord.   2

---

celebrated for his devotion who travelled through the worldly and higher realms playing the veena, singing God's Name and giving advice to gods and human beings.

मेरे माथै लागीले	3 mere maathai laageele
धूरी गोविंद चरणन की॥	dhoori govind charnan ki.
सुर नर मुनि जन तिनहु ते दूरी॥	sur nar muni jan tinahu te doori.
दीन का दइआलु माधो	4 deen ka dayaalu maadho
गरब परिहारी॥	garab parihaari.
चरण सरन नामा बलि तिहारी॥	5 charan saran naama bali tihaari.[4]

तुझ बिन क्यूं जीऊं रे	1 tujh bin kyoon jee'oon re
तुझ बिन क्यूं जीऊं।	tujh bin kyoon jee'oon,
तू मंझा प्रांन अधार	2 tu manjha praan adhaar
तुझ बिन क्यूं जीऊं॥ टेक॥	tujh bin kyoon jee'oon. tek.
सार तुम्हारा नांव है	3 saar tumhaara naanv hai
झूठा सब संसार।	jhootha sab sansaar,
मनसा बाचा कर्मना	4 mansa baacha karmana
कलि केवल नांव अधार॥	kali keval naanv adhaar.
दुनियां मैं दोजग घनां	5 duniyaan main dojag ghana
दारन दुख अधिक अपार।	daaran dukh adhik apaar,
चरन कंवल की मौज मैं	6 charan kanval ki mauj main
मोहि राखौ सिरजन हार॥	mohe raakhau sirjan haar.
मो तो बिचि पडदा किसा	7 mo to bich parrda kisa
लोभ बडाई काम।	lobh badaa'i kaam,
कोई एक हरिजन ऊबरे	8 koi ek harijan oobare,
जिनि सुमिरया निहचल रांम॥	jini sumirya nihchal raam.
लोग वेद कै संगि बह्यौ	9 log ved kai sangi bahyau
सलिल मोह की धार।	salil moh ki dhaar,
जन नांमा स्वामी बीठला,	10 jan naama swaami beethala
मोहि खेइ उतारौ पार॥	mohe khe'i utaarau paar.[5]

---

[*] The present and fourth age in the current cycle of time is known as **Kaliyuga**, the Dark or Iron Age.

The dust from the Lord's holy feet –   3
   beyond the reach of human beings, sages and even gods –
   adorns my forehead.
The Lord is merciful to the meek;   4
   he is the destroyer of pride.
Namdev takes refuge at your feet and sacrifices himself to you.   5

*H*ow could I live without you, O Lord,   1
   how could I live without you?
You are the support of my life –   2
   how could I live without you?
The whole world is false;   3
   your Nam alone is the true essence.
In thought, word and deed,   4
   only Nam is of any help in Kaliyuga.*
The world is a hell,   5
   full of dreadful suffering and immense misery.
Keep me, O Creator,   6
   under the blissful shelter of your lotus feet.†
The veil between you and me   7
   is made of greed, ego and lust.
Only that rare devotee is saved   8
   who remembers the eternal Lord.
Acting on legends, the people of the world   9
   are drifting in the current of attachments.
Says Namdev: O Lord, ferry me, your servant,   10
   across the ocean of existence.

---

† In the bhakti tradition, the expression **lotus feet** refers to the inner vision of the Lord, an experience which indicates a highly advanced state of inner revelation. Keeping under the shelter of the lotus feet means keeping constantly absorbed in the presence of the Lord.

बानी सन्त तुकाराम जी

Bani Sant Tukaram Ji

चित्ता ऐसी नको देऊं आठवण।
जेणें देवाचे चरण अंतरे तें॥

1 chitta aisi nako de'oon aathvan,
jene devaache charan antare tein.

आलिया वचनें रामनामध्वनि।
ऐकावीं कानीं ऐसीं गोडें॥

2 aaliya vachane raam-naam-dhvani,
ekaaveen kaani aiseen goden.

मत्सराचा ठाव शरीरीं नसावा।
लाभेंविण जीवा दुःख देतो॥

3 matsaraacha thaav shareereen nasaava,
laabhenvin jeeva dukh deto.

तुका म्हणे राहे अंतर शीतल।
शांतीचें तें बल क्षमा अंगीं॥

4 tuka mhane raahe antar sheetal,
shaanteechen tein bal kshama angeen.[1]

जीवनावांचूनि तलमली मासा।
प्रकार हा तैसा होतो जीवा॥

1 jeevanaa-vaanchooni talmali maasa,
prakaar ha taisa hoto jeeva.

न संपडे जालें भूमिगत धन।
चरफडी मन तयापरी॥

2 na sampade jaalen bhoomigat dhan,
charphadi man tayaapari.

मातेचा वियोग जालिया हो बाला।
तो कलवला जाणा देवा॥

3 maatecha viyog jaaliya ho baala,
to kalvala jaana deva.

सांगावे ते किती तुम्हांसी प्रकार।
सकलांचें सार पाय दावीं॥

4 saangaave te kiti tumhaansi prakaar,
saklaanchen saar paaye daaveen.

येचि चिंते माझा करपला भीतर।
कां नेनों विसर पडिला माझा॥

5 yechi chinte maajha karpala bheetar,
kaan nenon visar padila maajha.

तुका म्हणें तूं हें जाणसी सकल।
यावरि कृपाल होई देवा॥

6 tuka mhane toon hein jaanasi sakal,
yaavari kripaal ho'een deva.[2]

कृपालू सज्जन तुम्ही संतजन।
हेंचि कृपादान तुमचें मज॥

1 kripaalu sajjan tumhi santjan,
henchi kripaadaan tumchen maj.

आठवण तुम्ही द्यावी पांडुरंगा।
कींव माझी सांगा काकुलती॥

2 aathvan tumhi dyaavi paanduranga,
keenv maajhi saanga kaakulati.

Sant Tukaram Ji

O mind, let me not cherish any remembrance   *1*
   that would take me away from the Lord's divine feet.
May my tongue repeat only the Lord's Nam   *2*
   and my ears hear only the divine melody of Nam.
Let me not bear ill will towards anyone –   *3*
   it benefits no one and causes misery.
Let my mind always be calm, says Tuka –   *4*
   through forgiveness and peace one gains inner strength.

*J*ust as a fish writhes in agony when out of water,   *1*
   so my soul suffers in agony without you.
Just as a person's mind becomes agitated   *2–3*
   when he cannot find his buried treasure
   even after a thorough search,
   and a child becomes distraught
   when separated from its mother,
   O Lord, please know that this separation from you
   is causing the same anguish in my heart.
In how many ways can I tell you of my pain?   *4*
Refuge at your feet is the only remedy for my affliction.
Gripping my heart is a gnawing fear   *5*
   that you may have forgotten me.
Says Tuka: you know my condition, O Lord!   *6*
Shower your mercy on me now.

*S*aints, you are ever gracious and merciful –   *1–2*
   pray, grant me one boon:
   remind the Lord about me, plead for me
   and tell him about my deplorable condition.

अनाथ अपराधी पतिताआगला।
परि पायांवेगला नका करूँ॥

3 *anaath apraadhi patitaa-aagala,*
    pari paayaanvegla naka karoon.

तुका म्हणे तुम्हीं निरविल्यावरि।
मग मज हरि उपेक्षीना॥

4 *tuka mhane tumhi nirvilyaavari,*
    mag maj hari upeksheena.[3]

माझा तंव खुंटला उपाव।
जेणें तुझे आतुडती पाव॥

1 *maajha tanv khuntala upaav,*
    jene tujhe aatudati paav.

करूं भक्ति तरि नाहीं भाव।
नाहीं हातीं जीव कवणेविशीं॥

2 *karoon bhakti tari naaheen bhaav,*
    naaheen haateen jeev kavnevisheen.

धर्म करूं तरि नाहीं चित्त।
दान देऊं तरि नाहीं वित्त॥

3 *dharm karoon tari naaheen chitt,*
    daan de'oon tari naaheen vitt.

नेणें पुजों ब्राह्मण अतीत।
नाहीं भूतदया पोटा हातीं॥

4 *nene pujon braahman ateet,*
    naaheen bhootdaya pota haateen.

नेणें गुरुदास्य संतसेवन।
जप तप अनुष्ठान॥

5 *nene gurudaasya santsevan,*
    jap tap anushthaan.

नव्हे वैराग्य वनसेवन।
नव्हे दमन इंद्रियांसी॥

6 *navhe vairaagya vansevan,*
    navhe daman indriyaansi.

तीर्थ करूं तरि मन नये सवें।
व्रत करूं तरि विधि
नेणें स्वभावें॥

7 *teerth karoon tari man naye saven,*
    vrat karoon tari vidhi
    nene svabhaaven.

देव जरि आहे म्हणों मजसवें।
तरि आपपरावें न वंचे॥

8 *dev jari aahe mhano majhsaven,*
    tari aap-paraaven na vanche.

I am an orphan, immoral and a notorious sinner,   3
   the worst among the fallen;
   yet I beg you: please implore the Lord on my behalf
   not to separate me from his divine feet.
Says Tuka: if you entrust me to his care   4
   the Lord will not ignore me.

I failed to do anything   1
   that would have helped me reach your blessed feet.
I want to devote myself to you, but I lack love   2
   and am unable to restrain my mind by any means.
When I wish to perform a righteous act, my mind is not willing;   3
   when I wish to give in charity, I do not possess the money.
I do not know how to honour priests or guests;   4
   I have neither compassion in my heart
   nor mercy for living beings.
I do not know how to surrender to the Master,   5
   nor how to serve the Saints,
   nor how to perform religious rites, rituals or penances.
Feeling no detachment, I cannot renounce all   6
   and go to the forest, nor can I subdue my senses.
If I want to go on a pilgrimage,   7
   my mind does not cooperate with me;
   if I wish to observe a fast, I do not know how to do so.
I understand that the Lord resides within me;   8
   nevertheless, the feelings of mine and thine
   have not yet been eliminated.

म्हणोनि जालों शरणागत।
तुझा दास मी अंकित॥
यास कांहीं न लगे संचित।
जालों निश्चिंत तुका म्हणे॥

9 mhanoni jaalon sharanaagat,
tujha daas mi ankit.
10 yaas kaanheen na lage sanchit,
jaalon nishchint tuka mhane.[4]

नर नारी बालें अवघा नारायण।
ऐसें माझें मन करीं देवा॥
न यो काम क्रोध द्वेष निंदा द्वद्व।
अवघा गोविंद निःसंदेह॥
असावें म्यां सदा विषयी विरक्त।
काया वाचा चित्त तुझे पायीं॥
करोनियां साह्य
पुरवीं मनोरथ।
व्हावें कृपावंत तुका म्हणे॥

1 nar naari baalen avgha naaraayan,
aisen maajhen man kareen deva.
2 na yo kaam krodh dvesh ninda dvadv,
avagha govind nihsandeh.
3 asaaven myaan sada vishayi virakt,
kaaya vaacha chitt tujhe paayeen.
4 karoniyaan saahya
puraveen manorath,
vhaaven kripaavant tuka mhane.[5]

नरस्तुति आणि कथेचा विकरा।
हें नको दातारा घडों देऊं॥
ऐसिये कृपेची भाकितों करुणा।
आहेसि तूं राणा उदारांचा॥
पराविया नारी आणि परधना।
नको देऊं मनावरी येऊं॥
भूतांचा मत्सर आणि संतनिंदा।
हें नको गोविंदा घडों देऊं॥

1 narstuti aani kathecha vikra,
hein nako daataara ghadon de'oon.
2 aisiye kripechi bhaakiton karuna,
aahesi toon raana udaaraancha.
3 paraaviya naari aani pardhana,
nako de'oon manaavari ye'oon.
4 bhootaancha matsar aani sant-ninda,
hein nako govinda ghadon de'oon.

It is for these reasons that I have come to you for refuge.　　　*9–10*
Now that I am marked as your slave,
　my worries have ended.
Says Tuka: I am convinced that
　there is no need for my past merits anymore.

O Lord, bring my mind to such a state　　　*1*
　that in all people – men, women and children –
　I perceive only you.
May lust, anger, malice, slander and conflict　　　*2*
　never find a place within me;
　without any doubt, O Lord,
　only you should reside in my heart.
May I always remain detached from sensual pleasures,　　　*3*
　offering my mind, body and speech at your blessed feet.
O Lord, says Tuka, shower your mercy;　　　*4*
　help me, and fulfil these desires of my heart.

*Y*ou, O benevolent giver, are the paragon of generosity;　　　*1–3*
　I beg for your grace, O Lord,
　that I may praise no one but you
　and never indulge in trading spirituality for worldly gain.
O Lord, never let me be deficient in your devotion,
　never let me forsake your Nam,
　and let not the desire for women
　or others' wealth ever enter my mind.
O Lord, never let me indulge in the slander of Saints　　　*4*
　nor feel jealous of others.

देहअभिमान नको
देऊं शरीरीं।
चढों कांही परी एक देऊं॥
तुका ह्मणे तुझ्या पायांचा विसर।
नको वारंवार पडों देऊं॥

5   deh-abhimaan nako
de'oon shareereen,
chadhon kaanhi pari ek de'oon.

6   tuka hamne tujhya paayaancha visar,
nako vaaramvaar padon de'oon.[6]

तुजविण वाणीं आणिकांची थोरी।
तरी माझी हरी जिव्हा झडो॥
तुजविण चित्ता आवडे आणीक।
तरी हा मस्तक भंगो माझा॥
नेत्रीं आणिकांसि पाहीन आवडी।
जातु तेचि घडी चांडाल हे॥
कथामृतपान न करिती श्रवण।
काय प्रयोजन मन यांचे॥
तुका ह्मणे काय वांचून कारण।
तुज एक क्षण विसंबता॥

1   tujvin vaani aanikaanchi thori,
tari maajhi hari jivha jhado.

2   tujhvin chitta aavade aaneek,
tari ha mastak bhango maajha.

3   netreen aanikaansi paaheen aavadi,
jaatu techi ghadi chaandaal he.

4   kathaamritpaan na kariti shravan,
kaaye prayojan man yaanche.

5   tuka mhane kaaye vaanchoon kaaran,
tuj ek kshan visambata.[7]

विश्वास धरूनि राहिलों निवांत।
ठेवूनियां चित्त तुझे पायीं॥
तरावें बुडावें तुझिया वचनें।
निर्धार हा मनें केला माझ्या॥
न कळें हें मज साच चालविलें।
देसी तें उगलें घेइन देवा॥
मागणें तें सरे ऐसें करीं देवा।
नाहीं तरी सेवा सांगा पुढें॥
करावें कांहीं कीं
पाहावें उगलें।
तुका ह्मणे बोलें पांडुरंगा॥

1   vishvaas dharooni raahilon nivaant,
thevooniyaan chitt tujhe paayeen.

2   taraaven budaaven tujhiya vachane,
nirdhaar ha mane kela maajhya.

3   na kalen hein maj saach chaalvilen,
desi tein ugalen ghe'in deva.

4   maagane tein sare aisen kareen deva,
naaheen tari seva saanga pudhen.

5   karaaven kaanheen keen
paahaaven ugalen,
tuka mhane bolen paanduranga.[8]

Never let me become conceited about my physical attributes;   5
    never let such flaws become a part of me.
O Lord, says Tuka, this is my entreaty: 6
    may I never forget your lotus feet.

Let this tongue of mine wither away, O Lord,   1
    if it ever praises anyone but you.
Let my head split open if I even think fondly of another.   2
If my eyes look with longing at anyone but you,   3
    may they be blinded that very instant.
If my ears do not hear the nectar-sweet melody of the Lord,   4
    of what use are they?
My life would be worthless, says Tuka,   5
    if I forgot you even for a moment.

With firm trust in you   1
    I have surrendered my mind at your divine feet
    and have become free from all worries.
I have made a firm resolve in my mind: 2
    whether you ferry me across or drown me,
    I shall always remain in your will.
I do not know, O Lord, how you pulled me towards the truth,   3
    but I will gladly accept whatever you give me.
Please, O Lord, grant me the boon   4
    that I should not ask for anything from you,
    or at least explain to me how I may serve you.
Should I strive for something   5
    or just observe what comes to pass?
O Lord, says Tuka, please guide me!

बानी सन्त कबीर जी

Bani Sant Kabir Ji

अब तोहि जाँन न देहूँ राम पियारे,
ज्यूँ भावै त्यूँ होह हमारे॥ टेक॥

बहुत दिनन के बिछुरे हरि पाये,
भाग बड़े घरि बैठे आये॥

चरननि लागि करौं बरियायी,
प्रेम प्रीति राखौं उरझाई।

इत मन मंदिर रहौ नित चोखै,
कहै कबीर परहु मति धौखै॥

1 ab tohe jaan na dehoon raam pyaare,
jyoon bhaavai tyoon hoh hamaare. tek.

2 bahut dinan ke bichhure hari paaye,
bhaag barre ghari baithe aaye.

3 charnani laagi karaun bariyaa'i,
prem preet raakhaun urjhaa'i.

4 it man mandir rahau nit chokhai,
kahai Kabir parho mati dhaukhai.[1]

बाप राँम सुनि बीनती मोरी,
तुम्ह सूँ प्रगट
लोगन सूँ चोरीं॥ टेक॥

पहलैं काँम मुगध मति कीया,
ता भै कंपै मेरा जीया॥

राँम राइ मेरा कह्ना सुनींजै,
पहले बकसि अब लेखा लीजै॥

कहै कबीर बाप राँम राया,
कबहूँ सरनि तुम्हारी आया॥

1 baap raam suni beenati mori,
tumh soon pragat
logan soon choreen. tek.

2 pahlain kaam mugadh mati keeya,
ta bhai kampai mera jeeya.

3 raam raaye mera kahiya suneejai,
pahle bakasi ab lekha leejai.

4 kahai Kabir baap raam raaya,
kabahoon sarani tumhaari aaya.[2]

राग बिलावल बाणी भगता की॥
कबीर जीउ की

दरमादे ठाढे दरबार॥

तुझ बिन सुरत करै को मेरी
दरसन दीजै खोल्हकिवार॥ १॥ रहाउ॥

तुम धन धनी उदार तिआगी
स्रवनन्ह सुनीअत सुजस तुम्हार॥

Raag Bilaawal Bani Bhagta Ki
Kabir Jee'o Ki

1 darmaade thaadhe darbaar.

2 tujh bin surat karai ko meri
darsan deejai khol kivaar. rahaa'o.

3 tum dhan dhani udaar tyaagi
sravanan suniyat sujas tumhaar.

Sant Kabir Ji

I will not let you go now, my beloved Lord – *1*
    pray become mine in whatever way pleases you.

After endless days of separation, I have at last met you; *2*
    I am fortunate indeed,
    for you have revealed yourself within me.

Keenly devoting myself to your lotus feet, I sing your glory, *3*
    and I will keep you captivated with my love and devotion.

O Lord, dwell forever within the temple of my heart *4*
    and do not be enticed elsewhere, begs Kabir.

*H*ear my plea, O Lord, my Father! *1*
All my actions are known to you,
    even though I concealed them from the world.

My heart shudders when I think of the misdeeds *2*
    I have committed under the sway of my foolish mind.

O Lord, hear my supplication: *3*
    first forgive me, then take my deeds into account.

Says Kabir: O supreme Father, *4*
    now I have come to take refuge with you.

Raga Bilawal, Kabir Ji

*H*umbled and worn down, I stand at your doorstep, O Lord – *1–2*
    who other than you would take care of me?

Please open the door and grant me your darshan.

You are the wealthiest of the wealthy, *3*
    benevolent and detached, and I listen to your praise.

मागउ काहे रंक सभ देखउ
तुम्ह ही ते मेरो निसतार ॥ ९ ॥
जैदेउ नामा बिप सुदामा
तिन कउ क्रिपा भई है अपार ॥
कह कबीर तुम संम्रथ दाते
चार पदारथ देत न बार ॥ २ ॥

4   *maangau kaahe rank sabh dekhau*
      tum hi te mero nistaar.

5   *jaideo naama bip sudaama*
      tin kau kripa bhayi hai apaar.

6   *kah Kabir tum samrath daate*
      chaar padaarath det na baar.[3]

दरसन दीजे नाम सनेही।
तुम बिन दुख पावे मेरी देही ॥ टेक ॥
दुखित तुम बिन रटत निसि दिन,
प्रगट दरसन दीजिये।
बिनती सुन प्रिय स्वामियाँ,
बलि जाउँ बिलँब न कीजिये ॥
अन्न न भावे नींद न आवे।
बार बार मोहिं बिरह सतावे ॥
बिबिधि बिध हम भई ब्याकुल,
बिन देखे जिव न रहे।
तपत तन जिव उठत झाला,
कठिन दुख अब को सहे ॥
नैनन चलत सजल जल धारा।
निसि दिन पंथ निहारौं तुम्हारा ॥
गुन अवगुन अपराध छिमाकर,
औगुन कछु न बिचारिये।
पतित-पावन राख परमति,
अपना पन न बिसारिये ॥

1   *darsan deeje naam sanehi,*
      tum bin dukh paave meri dehi. tek.

2   *dukhit tum bin ratat nisi din,*
      pragat darsan deejiye;

3   *binati sun priy swaamiyaan,*
      bali jaa'un bilamb na keejiye.

4   *ann na bhaave neend na aave,*
      baar baar mohen birah sataave.

5   *bibidhi bidh ham bhayi byaakul,*
      bin dekhe jiv na rahe.

6   *tapat tan jiv uthat jhaala,*
      kathin dukh ab ko sahe.

7   *nainan chalat sajal jal dhaara,*
      nisi din panth nihaaraun tumhaara.

8   *gun avgun apraadh chhimaakar,*
      augun kachhu na bichaariye;

9   *patit-paavan raakh parmati,*
      apna pan na bisaariye.

---

* **Jaidev** was a devotee and poet with immense determination to love nothing but God. In the thirteenth century he wrote the *Gita Govinda*, which describes the relationship between Krishna and his devotees. **Sudama Brahmin** was a childhood friend and great devotee of Krishna.

From whom shall I beg, O Lord,   4
   when I find everyone a pauper?
In you alone lies my redemption.
To Jaidev, Namdev and Sudama Brahmin*   5
   you have shown boundless grace.
Says Kabir: O Lord, you are the all-powerful giver, 6
   and you bestow the four boons without delay.†

Grant me your darshan, O lover of Nam –   1
   without you, my whole being is racked with pain.
Distraught without you, I incessantly call out: 2
   reveal your true form to me!
Listen to my plea, O beloved Master;   3
   I sacrifice everything to you – pray do not delay!
Food does not appeal to me and sleep eludes me; 4
   the pangs of separation cause me relentless agony.
I am tormented in countless ways   5
   and cannot live without seeing you.
My body burns and my entire being is in agony – 6
   how can I endure this painful suffering?
A constant stream of tears flows from my eyes;   7
   day and night, I gaze your way, awaiting your arrival.
Forgive my sins and transgressions   8
   and do not consider my faults.
O redeemer of the fallen, uphold your intrinsic nature – 9
   do not forget your promise.

---

† The **four boons** are *dharma* (righteous living), *arth* (material blessings), *kaam* (satisfaction of bodily needs) and *moksha* (salvation). These are given to all human beings to use to realize one's true self.

गृह आँगन मोहिं कछु न सोहाई।
बज्र भई और फिरयो न जाई॥

10 grih aangan mohen kachhu na sohaa'i,
bajr bhayi aur phiryo na jaa'i.

नैन भरि भरि रहे निरखत,
निमिख नेह न तोड़ाइये।

11 nain bhari bhari rahe nirkhat,
nimikh neh na torraa'iye;

बाँह दीजे बंदी छोड़ा,
अब के बंद छोड़ाइये॥

12 baanh deeje bandi chhorra,
ab ke band chhorraa'iye.

मीन मरै जैसे बिन नीरा।
ऐसे तुम बिन दुखित सरीरा।

13 meen marai jaise bin neera,
aise tum bin dukhit sareera.

दास कबीर यह करत बिनती,
महा पुरुष अब मानिये।

14 daas Kabir yah karat binati,
maha purush ab maaniye;

दया कीजे दरस दीजे,
अपना कर मोहिं जानिये॥

15 daya keeje daras deeje,
apna kar mohen jaaniye.[4]

कब देखूँ मेरे राम सनेही,
जा बिन दुख पावै मेरी देही॥ टेक॥

1 kab dekhoon mere raam sanehi,
ja bin dukh paavai meri dehi. tek.

हूँ तेरा पंथ निहारूँ स्वाँमी,
कबरे मिलहुगे अंतरजाँमी।

2 hoon tera panth nihaaroon swaami,
kabare milohge antarjaami.

जैसैं जल बिन मीन तलपै,
ऐसै हरि बिन मेरा जियरा कलपै।

3 jaisain jal bin meen talpai,
aisai hari bin mera jiyara kalpai.

निस दिन हरि बिन नींद न आवै,
दरस पियासी राँम क्यूँ सचु पावै।

4 nis din hari bin neend na aavai,
daras pyaasi raam kyoon sach paavai.

कहै कबीर अब बिलंब न कीजै,
अपनौं जाँनि मोहि दरसन दीजै॥

5 kahai Kabir ab bilamb na keejai,
apnau jaani mohe darsan deejai.[5]

राग आसा श्री कबीर जीउ

Raag Aasa Sri Kabir Jee'o

करवत भला न करवट तेरी॥
लाग गले सुन बिनती मेरी॥१॥

1 karvat bhala na karvat teri.
laag gale sun binati meri.

Nothing in hearth and home interests me;   *10*
  I have become like a stone and cannot move.

Brimming with tears, my eyes constantly seek you –   *11*
  do not let me stop loving you even for a moment.

Give me your hand, O liberator of captives,   *12*
  and this time rescue me from bondage.

Just as a fish dies without water,   *13*
  without you, my body writhes in pain.

Kabir, your slave, offers this supplication: *14–15*
  almighty Lord, have mercy on me
  and bless me with your darshan,
  considering me your very own.

When will I behold you, my beloved Lord?   *1*
Without you, my entire being
  suffers from the pain of separation.

Gazing your way, I constantly await you, O Lord –   *2*
  when will you meet me, O knower of all hearts?

Just as a fish writhes in agony when removed from the water,   *3*
  my heart is in torment without the Lord.

Without the Lord, I am sleepless day and night;   *4*
  thirsty for a glimpse of you, O Lord,
  how can I perceive your true form?

Pleads Kabir: do not delay, O Lord –   *5*
  consider me your own and grant me your darshan.

Raga Asa, Sri Kabir Ji

O Lord, I would rather be sawn alive   *1*
  than see you turn your back on me.

हउ वारी मुख फेर पिआरे॥

क़रवट दे मो कउ

काहे कउ मारे॥१॥ रहाउ॥

जउ तन चीरह अंग न मोरउ॥

पिंड परै तउ प्रीत न तोरउ॥२॥

हम तुम बीच भइओ नही कोई॥

तुमह सो कंत नार हम सोई॥३॥

कहत कबीर सुनहो रे लोई॥

अब तुमरी परतीत न होई॥४॥

2 hau vaari mukh pher pyaare.

karvat de mo kau

kaahe kau maare. rahaa'o.

3 jau tan cheerah ang na morau.

pind parai tau preet na torau.

4 ham tum beech bhayo nahi koi.

tumah so kant naar ham soi.

5 kahat Kabir sunho re loi.

ab tumri parteet na hoi.[6]

प्रीत लगी तुम नाम की,

पल बिसरै नाहीं।

नजर करो अब मिहर की,

मोहिं मिलो गुसाईं॥

बिरह सतावै मोहिं को,

जिव तड़पै मेरा।

तुम देखन की चाव है,

प्रभु मिलो सवेरा॥

नैना तरसै दरस को,

पल पलक न लागै।

दर्दवंत दीदार का,

निसि बासर जागै॥

जो अब के प्रीतम मिलैं,

करूँ निमिख न न्यारा।

अब कबीर गुरु पाइया,

मिला प्रान पियारा॥

1 preet lagi tum naam ki,

pal bisrai naahi;

2 najar karo ab mehar ki,

mohen milo gusaa'een.

3 birah sataavai mohen ko,

jiv tarrpai mera;

4 tum dekhan ki chaav hai,

prabhu milo savera.

5 naina tarsai daras ko,

pal palak na laagai;

6 daradvant deedaar ka,

nisi baasar jaagai.

7 jo ab ke preetam milain,

karoon nimikh na nyaara;

8 ab Kabir guru paaya,

mila praan pyaara.[7]

Listen to my supplication, O Lord,
 and hold me in your arms.
I sacrifice myself to you, O Beloved;   2
 please turn your face to me –
 why kill me by turning away from me?
If you rip my body apart,   3
 I shall not move a limb,
 and even as my body collapses,
 I shall not break off my love.
You are my husband and I am your wife –   4
 no one stands between you and me.
Listen, O people of the world, says Kabir: 5
 I trust you no more.

I am deeply in love with your Nam   1
 and constantly remain absorbed in it.
Cast your merciful glance on me now, O Lord –   2
 please meet me!
I am agonized by this separation;   3
 my whole being is tormented.
I yearn for just a glimpse of you, O Lord –   4
 please hurry to meet me.
My eyes thirst for your darshan   5
 and do not rest even for a moment.
Afflicted with longing for a glimpse of you,   6
 I remain awake day and night.
This time, if the Beloved comes,   7
 not for even a fleeting moment will I let him part from me.
Now Kabir has met his Master, the beloved of his heart.   8

राग बिलावल बाणी भगता की ॥
कबीर जीउ की

राख लेहो हम ते बिगरी ॥
सील धरम जप भगति न कीनी
हउ अभिमान टेढ पगरी ॥ ९ ॥ रहाउ ॥
अमर जान संची इह काइआ
इह मिथिआ काची गगरी ॥
जिनह निवाज साज हम कीए
तिसह बिसार अवर लगरी ॥ ९ ॥
संधिक तोहे साध नही कहीअउ
सरन परे तुमरी पगरी ॥
कहे कबीर इह बिनती सुनीअहो
मत घालहो जम की खबरी ॥ २ ॥

Raag Bilaawal Bani Bhagta Ki
Kabir Jee'o Ki

1 raakh leho ham te bigari.
2 seel dharam jap bhagti na keeni
   hau abhimaan tedh pagari. rahaa'o.
3 amar jaan sanchi eh kaaya
   eh mithia kaachi gagari.
4 jinah nivaaj saaj ham keeye
   tisah bisaar avar lagari.
5 sandhik tohe saadh nahi kahee'au
   saran pare tumri pagari.
6 kahe Kabir eh binati sunee'ho
   mat ghaalho jam ki khabari.[8]

राग गउड़ी पूरबी कबीर जी

राम जपउ जीअ ऐसे ऐसे ॥
ध्रू प्रहिलाद जपिओ हर जैसे ॥ ९ ॥
दीन दइआल भरोसे तेरे ॥
सभ परवार चड़इआ बेड़े ॥ ९ ॥ रहाउ ॥
जा तिस भावै ता हुकम मनावै ॥
इस बेड़े कउ पार लघावै ॥ २ ॥
गुर परसाद ऐसी बुध समानी ॥
चूक गई फिर आवन जानी ॥ ३ ॥
कहो कबीर भज सारिगपानी ॥
उरवार पार सभ एको दानी ॥ ४ ॥

Raag Gaurri Poorbi Kabir Ji

1 raam japau jee'a aise aise.
   dhru prahilaad japio har jaise.
2 deen dayaal bharose tere.
   sabh parvaar charraaya berre. rahaa'o.
3 ja tis bhaavai ta hukam manaavai.
   is berre kau paar laghaavai.
4 gur parsaad aisi budh samaani.
   chook gayi phir aavan jaani.
5 kaho Kabir bhaj saarigpaani.
   urvaar paar sabh eko daani.[9]

---

* **Yama** is the lord of justice who takes charge of the soul at the time of death and administers reward or punishment according to that soul's actions during life.

† **Dhruva** was the son of a mythological king. When he realized that he had no chance to succeed to the throne, he decided to leave home and follow the path of devotion,

Raga Bilawal, Kabir Ji

Save me, O Lord, I confess my transgressions: 1–2
    I have not practised piety, righteous conduct,
    devotion or remembrance of your Nam;
    ego-bound, I have followed a crooked path.
Frail like an unbaked pitcher of clay is my body, 3
    but I nourished it as if it were everlasting.
Forsaking the One who created and adorned me, 4
    I attached myself to duality.
I am your thief and should not be called a Saint, O Lord; 5
    I surrender at your feet, seeking your shelter.
Says Kabir: listen to my supplication, O Lord – 6
    let me not be summoned to Yama's court.*

Raga Gauri Poorbi, Kabir Ji

Repeat God's Nam, O my soul, as did Dhruva and Prahlad.† 1
You are merciful to the meek, O Lord; 2
    putting my trust in you,
    I have made my whole family board your ship.
If it be God's will, he enforces obedience to his command 3
    and propels this ship to the far shore.
Such insight has been instilled in me by the Guru's grace 4
    that my coming and going in transmigration has ended.
Says Kabir: meditate on the Lord, 5
    for in this world and the world beyond he is the sole provider.

---

seeking no honour except that which his own actions would bring him. **Prahlad** was known for his great devotion, despite the opposition of his father. The Puranas contain many stories about his loving devotion to Vishnu and he is mentioned in the Adi Granth.

राग मारू बाणी कबीर जीउ की

Raag Maaru Bani Kabir Jee'o Ki

राम सिमर पछुताहिगा मन॥	1 raam simar pachhutaahega man.
पापी जीअरा लोभ करत है	2 paapi jeeyara lobh karat hai
आज काल उठ जाहिगा॥१॥ रहाउ॥	aaj kaal uth jaahega. rahaa'o.
लालच लागे जनम गवाइआ	3 laalach laage janam gavaaya
माइआ भरम भुलाहिगा॥	maaya bharam bhulaahega.
धन जोबन का गरब न कीजै	4 dhan joban ka garab na keejai
कागद जिउ गल जाहिगा॥१॥	kaagad jyon gal jaahega.
जउ जम आए केस गह पटकै	5 jau jam aaye kes gah patakai
ता दिन किछु न बसाहिगा॥	ta din kichhu na basaahega.
सिमरन भजन दइआ नही कीनी	6 simran bhajan daya nahi keeni
तउ मुख चोटा खाहिगा॥२॥	tau mukh chota khaahega.
धरम राए जब लेखा मागै	7 dharam raaye jab lekha maangai
किआ मुख लै कै जाहिगा॥	kya mukh lai kai jaahega.
कहत कबीर सुनहो रे संतहो	8 kahat Kabir sunho re santo
साधसंगत तर जांहिगा॥३॥१॥	saadh-sangat tar jaanhega.[10]

साचा साहिब एक तू,	1 saacha saahib ek tu,
बंदा आसिक तेरा॥ टेक॥	banda aasik tera. tek.
निसदिन जप तुझ नाम का,	2 nisdin jap tujh naam ka,
पल बिसरै नाहीं।	pal bisrai naahi;
हर दम राख हजूर में,	3 har dam raakh hajoor mein,
तू साचा साई॥	tu saacha saa'een.

Raga Maru, Kabir Ji

Repeat God's Nam, O my mind,   1
    or you will repent in the end.

You are given to avarice, O my sinful mind;   2
    know that tomorrow – if not today –
    you will depart from this world.

Beguiled by the illusion of maya,   3
    you squander your life in greed.

Take no pride in your wealth and youth –   4
    you will, one day, crumble like a piece of paper.

The day Yama comes, grabs you by the hair   5
    and dashes you to the ground
    you will find yourself utterly helpless.

If you do not practise simran and meditation   6
    nor show compassion to others,
    you will be struck in the face.

With what face will you go before Dharmrai,*   7
    the divine judge, when he calls you to account?

Listen, O holy people, says Kabir: 8
    through the company of Saints
    you will sail across the ocean of existence.

You alone are true, O Lord –   1
    this slave has fallen in love with you.

May I repeat your Nam day and night,   2
    without forgetting it even for a moment!

You are the true Lord –   3
    always keep me in your presence.

---

*Dharmrai is the lord of judgement, also called Yama.

गफलत मेरी मेटि के,
मोहिं कर हुसियारा।

भगति भाव बिस्वास में,
देखौं दरस तुम्हारा॥

सिफत तुम्हारी क्या करौं,
तुम गहिर गँभीरा।

सूरत में मूरत बसै,
सोइ निरख कबीरा॥

4   *gaflat meri meti ke,*
    mohen kar husiyaara;

5   *bhagti bhaav bisvaas mein,*
    dekhaun daras tumhaara.

6   *sifat tumhaari kya karaun,*
    tum gahir gambheera;

7   *soorat mein moorat basai,*
    soi nirakh kabeera.[11]

साँई बिन दरद करेजे होय॥ टेक॥

दिन नहिं चैन रात नहिं निंदिया,
कासे कहूँ दुख रोय॥

आधी रतियाँ पिछले पहरवाँ,
साँई बिन तरस तरस रही सोय॥

पाँचो मारि पचीसो बस करि,
इन में चहै कोइ होय॥

कहत कबीर सुनो भाई साधो,
सतगुरु मिले सुख होय॥

1   *saa'een bin darad kareje hoye. tek.*

2   *din nahin chain raat nahin nindiya,*
    kaase kahoon dukh roye.

3   *aadhi ratiyaan pichhale paharvaan,*
    saa'een bin taras taras rahi soye.

4   *paancho maari pacheeso bas kari,*
    in mein chahai koi hoye.

5   *kahat Kabir suno bhaa'i saadho,*
    satguru mile sukh hoye.[12]

सतगुरु मोरी चूक सँभारो।

हौं अधीन हीन मति मोरी,
चरनन तें जिन टारो॥ टेक॥

मन कठोर कछु कहा न माने,
बहु वा को कहि हारो॥

1   *satguru mori chook sambhaaro.*

2   *haun adheen heen mati mori,*
    charnan tein jin taaro. tek.

3   *man kathor, kachhu kaha na maane,*
    bahu va ko kahi haaro.

---

[*] The night was divided into four watches because a city guard could not stand watch all night. The **last watch** was just before dawn.

[†] In Hindu metaphysics, interactions between the **five passions** – lust, anger, greed, attachment and pride or ego – produce **twenty-five tendencies** in the human being.

Put an end to my oblivion   4–5
   and elevate me to divine consciousness,
   so that with unwavering faith and true devotion
   I may have your darshan.
How can I describe your qualities, O Lord?   6–7
You are profound and unfathomable –
   your divine form dwells within,
   and that is what Kabir beholds.

Without the Lord, my heart aches!   1
I am restless during the day and sleepless throughout the night –   2
   to whom should I narrate my tale of woe?
In the wee hours of the morning, during the last watch,*   3
   sleep overcomes me as I pine for the Lord.
Only a rare one indeed   4
   is able to control the five passions
   and subdue the twenty-five tendencies.†
Says Kabir: hear me, O Saints,‡   5
   only upon meeting the Satguru can bliss be obtained.

O Satguru, forgive my transgressions!   1
I am lowly and my thoughts are impure,   2
   but do not push me away from your lotus feet.
My wayward and intractable mind does not pay heed to me;   3
   after countless attempts, I am utterly defeated.

---

‡ Mystics such as Kabir often address their audience as **Saints** (*santo*) because of the potential which they see in all human beings to become true God-realized Saints through love and devotion.

तुम हीं तें सब होत गुसाँई,
या को बेग सँवारो ॥

अब दीजे संगत सतगुर की,
जा तें होय निस्तारो ॥

और सकल संगी सब बिसरैं,
होउ तुम एक पियारो ॥

कर देख्यो हित सारे जग से,
कोइ न मिल्यो पुनि भारो ॥

कहैं कबीर सुनो प्रभु मेरे,
भवसागर से तारो ॥

4   tum heen tein sab hot gusaa'een,
ya ko beg samvaaro.

5   ab deeje sangat satgur ki,
ja tein hoye nistaaro.

6   aur sakal sangi sab bisrain,
ho'u tum ek pyaaro.

7   kar dekhyo hit saare jag se,
koi na milyo puni bhaaro.

8   kahain Kabir suno prabhu mere,
bhavsaagar se taaro.[13]

तुम्ह बिन राँम कवन सौं कहिये,
लागी चोट बहुत दुख सहिये ॥ टेक ॥

बेध्यौ जीव बिरह कै भालै,
राति दिवस मेरे उर सालैं ॥

को जाँनै मेरे तन की पीरा,
सतगुर सबद बहि गयौ सरीरा ॥

तुम्ह से बैद न हमसे रोगी,
उपजी बिथा कैसैं जींवैं बियोगी ॥

निस बासुरि मोहि चितवत जाई,
अजहूँ न आइ मिले राँम राई ॥

कहत कबीर हमकौं दुख भारी,
बिन दरसन क्यूँ जीवहि मुरारी ॥

1   tumh bin raam kavan saun kahiye,
laagi chot bahut dukh sahiye. tek.

2   bedhyau jeev birah kai bhaalai,
raati divas mere ur saalain.

3   ko jaanai mere tan ki peera,
satgur sabad bahi gayau sareera.

4   tumh se baid na hamse rogi,
upaji bitha kaisain jeevain biyogi.

5   nis baasuri mohe chitvat jaa'i,
ajahoon na aa'i mile raam raa'i.

6   kahat Kabir hamkaun dukh bhaari,
bin darsan kyoon jeevahi muraari.[14]

Everything happens according to your will, O Lord – 4
    pray, quickly reform my mind.
Now please grant me the company of the Satguru, 5
    through whom I may attain salvation.
May I forget all my companions 6
    and may you become the sole object of my affection.
I showed affection to the whole world, 7
    but found no one who would care for me.
Says Kabir: listen to my entreaty, O Lord – 8
    take me across the ocean of existence.

O Lord, I am deeply hurt and suffer immense pain – 1
    to whom but you can I tell my tale of woe?
I have been pierced by the spear of separation – 2
    day and night my heart throbs in agony.
The Satguru's Shabd has permeated my entire being – 3
    who can comprehend my pain?
There is no physician as great as you 4
    nor any patient as helpless as me –
    I am tormented in separation and cannot bear to stay alive.
Day and night my gaze is fixed, O supreme Lord, 5
    yet you have not come to meet me.
Says Kabir: my agony is beyond measure – 6
    without your darshan, how can I live, O Lord?

दोहे

बिनवत हौं कर जोरि कै,
सुनिये कृपा-निधान।
साध सँगति सुख दीजिये,
दया गरीबी दान॥

जो अब के सतगुरु मिलैं,
सब दुख आखौं रोय।
चरनों ऊपर सीस धरि,
कहौं जो कहना होय॥

मेरे सतगुरु मिलैंगे,
पूछैंगे कुसलात।
आदि अंत की सब कहौं,
उर अंतर की बात॥

सुरति करौ मेरे साइयाँ,
हम हैं भवजल माहिं।
आपे ही बहि जायँगे,
जो नहिं पकरौ बाहिं॥

क्या मुख लै बिनती करौं,
लाज आवत है मोहिं।
तुम देखत औगुन करौं,
कैसे भावौं तोहिं॥

Dohe

1 binvant haun kar jori kai,
   suniye kripa-nidhaan;
2 saadh sangati sukh deejiye,
   daya gareebi daan.

1 jo ab ke satguru milain,
   sab dukh aakhaun roye;
2 charnon oopar sees dhari,
   kahaun jo kahna hoye.

1 mere satguru milainge,
   poochhainge kuslaat;
2 aadi ant ki sab kahaun,
   ur antar ki baat.

1 surati karau mere saa'eeyaan,
   ham hain bhavjal maahen;
2 aape hi bahi jaayenge,
   jo nahin pakrau baahen.

1 kya mukh lai binati karaun,
   laaj aavat hai mohen;
2 tum dekhat augun karaun,
   kaise bhaavaun tohen.

Dohas[*]

With folded hands I pray to you –   1
   hear me, O fountainhead of mercy!
Grant me the blissful company of Saints   2
   and the gifts of compassion and humility.

When my Master meets me this time,   1
   I will cry my heart out to him.
Putting my head at his feet,   2
   I will say what I have always longed to say.

My Master will meet me   1
   and ask about my well-being.
I will tell him the tale from beginning to end   2
   and convey all that is in my heart.

Pay attention to me, O Master –   1
   I am tossing about in the ocean of existence.
Left by myself, I will be swept away   2
   if you do not take hold of my hand.

With what face do I pray?   1
I am ashamed of myself.
You see me sinning all the time –   2
   how then can I win your approval?

---

[*] A **doha** is a verse form. Some of the selections from the Adi Granth begin with a header giving the name of the verse form of the composition. See the Glossary for descriptions of the various verse forms.

मैं अपराधी जनम का,
नख सिख भरा बिकार।
तुम दाता दुख-भंजना,
मेरी करो सम्हार॥

1   *main apraadhi janam ka,*
      nakh sikh bhara bikaar;
2   *tum daata dukh-bhanjana,*
      meri karo samhaar.

अवगुन मेरे बाप जी,
बकस गरीब निवाज।
जो मैं पूत कपूत हौं,
तऊ पिता को लाज॥

1   *avgun mere baap ji,*
      bakas gareeb nivaaj;
2   *jo main poot kapoot haun,*
      tau pita ko laaj.

औगुन किये तो बहु किये,
करत न मानी हार।
भावै बंदा बकसिये,
भावै गरदन मार॥

1   *augun kiye to bahu kiye,*
      karat na maani haar;
2   *bhaavai banda baksiye,*
      bhaavai gardan maar.

जो मैं भूल बिगाड़िया,
ना करु मैला चित्त।
साहिब गरुआ लोड़िये,
नफर बिगाड़ै नित्त॥

1   *jo main bhool bigaarriya,*
      na karu maila chitt;
2   *saahib garua lorriye,*
      nafar bigaarrai nitt.

साहिब तुम जनि बीसरो,
लाख लोग लगि जाहिं।
हम से तुमरे बहुत हैं,
तुम सम हमरे नाहिं॥

1   *saahib tum jani beesro,*
      laakh log lagi jaahen;
2   *ham se tumre bahut hain,*
      tum sam hamre naahen.

कर जोरे बिनती करौं,
भवसागर आपार।
बंदा ऊपर मिहर करि,
आवागवन निवार॥

1   *kar jore binati karaun,*
      bhavsaagar aapaar;
2   *banda oopar mihar kar,*
      aavaagavan nivaar.

I am a born sinner   1
   and am filled with vices from head to toe.
You are the beneficent giver, the destroyer of misery –   2
   please take me under your care.

O Father, you are merciful to the meek –   1
   forgive my faults.
I am an unworthy son;   2
   only you, O Father, can hide my shame.

I have indulged in countless vices;   1
   never did I tire of committing misdeeds.
Punish me or forgive me;   2
   do with this slave as you please.

Please do not take to heart   1
   what I have spoiled due to my blunders.
The Master in his greatness always forgives,   2
   even if a servant constantly errs.

O Lord, do not ever forget me   1
   even if millions are devoted to you.
For you, there are countless people like me;   2
   for me, there is no one like you.

With folded hands I pray to you –   1
   boundless is this ocean of existence.
Shower your grace on this servant, O Lord,   2
   and liberate me from the cycle of transmigration.

अंतरजामी एक तुम,
आतम के आधार।
जो तुम छोड़ौ हाथ तें,
कौन उतारै पार॥

1 *antarjaami ek tum,*
aatam ke aadhaar;
2 *jo tum chhorrau haath tein,*
kaun utaarai paar.

भवसागर भारी महा,
गहिरा अगम अगाह।
तुम दयाल दाया करो,
तब पाओं कछु थाह॥

1 *bhavsaagar bhaari maha,*
gahira agam agaah;
2 *tum dayaal daaya karo,*
tab paa'on kachhu thaah.

साहिब तुमहिं दयाल हौ,
तुम लगि मेरी दौर।
जैसे काग जहाज को,
सूझै और न ठौर॥

1 *saahib tumhen dayaal hau,*
tum lagi meri daur;
2 *jaise kaag jahaaj ko,*
soojhai aur na thaur.

मन परतीत न प्रेम रस,
ना कछु तन में ढंग।
ना जानौं उस पीव से,
क्योंकर रहसी रंग॥

1 *man parteet na prem ras,*
na kachhu tan mein dhang;
2 *na jaanau us peev se,*
kyonkar rahsi rang.

जिन को साई रँगि दिया,
कबहुँ न होहिं कुरंग।
दिन दिन बानी आगरी,
चढ़ै सवाया रंग॥

1 *jin ko saa'een rang diya,*
kabahun na hohen kurang;
2 *din din baani aagri,*
charrhai savaaya rang.

मेरा मुझ में कछु नहीं,
जो कछु है सो तुज्झ।
तेरा तुझ को सौंपते,
का लागत है मुज्झ॥

1 *mera mujh mein kacchu nahi,*
jo kacchu hai so tujjh;
2 *tera tujh ko saumpte,*
ka laagat hai mujjh.

You alone are all-knowing   *1*
  and you are the support of the soul.
If you let go of my hand, O Lord,   *2*
  who will ferry me across?

The ocean of existence is vast,   *1*
  deep, impassable and unfathomable.
O Compassionate One, shower your grace –   *2*
  only then can I hope to fathom its mystery.

O Master, you alone are merciful;   *1–2*
  it is only to you that I can run for shelter,
  just as a crow flying across the vast seas
  finds no refuge other than a sailing ship.

I have no idea how to get dyed   *1–2*
  in the colour of the Beloved's love.
My mind has no faith or sweet love,
  nor do I have any charm or grace.

Those whom the Lord dyes in the colour of his love   *1*
  never lose their hue.
Day by day, as Shabd takes hold,   *2*
  its effect becomes more profound.

There is nothing in me that is mine;   *1*
  whatever there is – it is all yours.
What do I lose by surrendering to you   *2*
  that which already belongs to you?

औगुनहारा गुन नहीं,
मन का बड़ा कठोर।
ऐसे समरथ सतगुरू,
ताहि लगावैं ठौर॥

तुम तो समरथ साइयाँ,
दृढ़ कर पकरो बाहिं।
धुरही लै पहुँचाइयो,
जनि छाड़ो मग माहिं॥

कबीर करत है बीनती,
सुनो संत चित लाय।
मारग सिरजनहार का,
दीजै मोहिं बताय॥

सतगुरु बड़े दयाल हैं,
संतन के आधार।
भवसागरहि अथाह से,
खेइ उतारैं पार॥

भक्ति दान मोहिं दीजिये,
गुरु देवन के देव।
और नहीं कछु चाहिये,
निसु दिन तेरी सेव॥

1 augun-haara gun nahi,
  man ka barra kathor;
2 aise samrath satguru,
  taahe lagaavain thaur.

1 tum to samrath saa'eeyaan,
  drirrh kar pakro baahen;
2 dhur-hi lai pahunchaa'iyo,
  jani chhaarro mag maahen.

1 Kabir karat hai beenati,
  suno sant chit laaye;
2 maarag sirjan-haar ka,
  deejai mohen bataaye.

1 satguru barre dayaal hain,
  santan ke aadhaar;
2 bhavsaagarhi athaah se,
  khe'i utaarain paar.

1 bhakti daan mohe deejiye,
  guru devan ke dev;
2 aur nahi kachhu chaahiye,
  nisu din teri sev.[15]

I am a sinner bereft of virtues –
    totally cold-hearted am I.   *1*

Truly mighty is the Satguru,
    who ferries even this sinner to the eternal abode.   *2*

Truly powerful are you, O Master –
    firmly hold my arm.   *1*

Take me to the eternal abode,
    and do not abandon me on the way.   *2*

Entreats Kabir: O Master,
    listen carefully!   *1*

Show me the path
    that leads to the almighty Creator.   *2*

Merciful is the Satguru,
    the support of the Saints.   *1*

He ferries souls across
    the unfathomable ocean of existence.   *2*

Bestow on me the gift of devotion, O Master,
    Lord of all the gods.   *1*

Nothing else do I seek
    except to serve you day and night.   *2*

बानी धनी धरमदास जी

बंदी-छोर बिनती सुनि लीजै॥ टेक॥

कपट कुटिल अपराधी द्रोही,
ठहरावो मन निस्चै।

नाम तुम्हारा अधम उधारन,
ता की दिच्छा दीजै॥

पाप पुन्न नहिं जाँचन कीजै,
काटि फंद अब दीजै।

माँगूँ अपन सुभाव दयानिधि,
सुनि अनुमान न कीजै॥

बिषे बिनास रहूँ निसु बासर,
यह तन छिन छिन छीजै।

साठ जन्म को हौं अपराधी,
अबकी छिमा प्रभु कीजै॥

सतगुरु नाम मुनींद्र कहाये,
साहेब कबीर सुनि लीजै।

धरमदास बिनवै कर जोरी,
काटि चौरीसी दीजै॥

Bani Dhani Dharamdas Ji

1 *bandi-chhor binati suni leejai. tek.*

2 *kapat kutil apraadhi drohi,*
thahraavo man nischai;

3 *naam tumhaara adham udhaaran,*
ta ki dicchha deejai.

4 *paap punn nahin jaanchan keejai,*
kaati phand ab deejai;

5 *maangoon apan subhaav daya-nidhi,*
suni anumaan na keejai.

6 *bishe binaas rahoon nisu baasar,*
yah tan chhin chhin chheejai;

7 *saath janam ko haun apraadhi,*
abki chhima prabhu keejai.

8 *satguru naam muneendr kahaaye,*
saaheb kabir suni leejai;

9 *Dharamdas binavai kar jori,*
kaat chauraasi deejai.[1]

भक्ति दान गुरु दीजिये
देवन के देवा हो।

चरन कँवल बिसरौं नहीं
करिहौं पद सेवा हो॥

तिरथ बरत मैं ना करौं
ना देवल पूजा हो।

तुमहिं ओर निरखत रहौं
मेरे और न दूजा हो॥

1 *bhakti daan guru deejiye*
devan ke deva ho,

2 *charan kanval bisraun nahi*
karihaun pad seva ho.

3 *tirath barat main na karaun*
na deval pooja ho,

4 *tumhin or nirkhat rahaun*
mere aur na dooja ho.

Dhani Dharamdas Ji

*H*ear my prayer, O liberator of captives!   1

Subdue this mind of mine once and for all;   2

  it is deceitful, cunning, sinful and rebellious.

Grant me the initiation of your Nam,   3

  for it is the redeemer of sinners.

Do not evaluate my sins or good deeds –   4

  cut the noose of my attachments now.

Be true to your nature, O treasure trove of mercy –   5

  do not consider the extent of my sins.

Night and day I am immersed in deadly sensual pleasures;   6

  this body is waning with every passing moment.

For numerous lifetimes have I sinned, O Lord –   7

  forgive me this time.

You were also known as Satguru Munindra;*   8

  Kabir, my Master – pray listen to me.

Dharamdas pleads with folded hands: 9

  free me from the cycle of transmigration.

*G*rant me the gift of devotion, O Master, Lord of all gods!   1

May I never part from your lotus feet   2

  and may I always remain in your service.

Keep me from going on pilgrimages   3

  and from observing fasts and worshipping in temples.

Let me keep my gaze fixed only on you –   4

  except you, there is no one else for me.

---

*When Kabir appeared in Tretayuga, the Silver Age, he was known as **Munindra**.

आठ सिद्धि नौ निद्धि हैं
बैकंठु निवासा हो।
सो मैं ना कछु माँगहूँ
मेरे समरथ दाता हो॥
सुख सम्पति परिवार धन
सुन्दर बर नारी हो।
सुपनेहु इच्छा ना उठै
गुरु आन तुम्हारी हो॥
धरमदास की बीनती
साहेब सुनि लीजै हो।
दरसन देहु पट खोलि कै
आपन करि लीजै हो॥

5 aath sidhi nau nidhi hain
baikunth nivaasa ho,
6 so main na kachhu maangahoon
mere samrath daata ho.
7 sukh sampati parivaar dhan
sundar bar naari ho,
8 supnehu icchha na uthai
guru aan tumhaari ho.
9 Dharamdas ki beenati
saaheb suni leejai ho.
10 darsan dehu pat kholi kai
aapan kari leejai ho.[2]

बिन दरसन भइ बावरी,
गुरु ग्यो दीदार॥ टेक॥
ठाढ़ि जोहौं तोरी बाट में,
साहेब चलि आवो।
इतनी दया हम पर करो,
निज छबि दरसावो॥
कोठरी रतन जड़ाव की,
हीरा लागे किवार।
ताला कुन्जी प्रेम की,
गुरु खोलि दिखावो॥
बंदा भूला बंदगी,
तुम बकसनहार।
धरमदास अरजी सुनो,
भव पार करावो॥

1 bin darsan bhayi baavari,
guru dyo deedaar. tek.
2 thaarrhi jo-haun tori baat mein,
saaheb chali aavo;
3 itni daya ham par karo,
nij chhabi darsaavo.
4 kothri ratan jarraav ki,
heera laage kivaar;
5 taala kunji prem ki,
guru kholi dikhaavo.
6 banda bhoola bandagi,
tum baksan-haar;
7 Dharamdas arji suno,
bhav paar karaavo.[3]

---

* The **eight supernatural powers** (*siddhis*) include the ability to shrink and expand one's size, to reduce and increase one's weight, to have access to all places, to realize one's desires, to control nature and to control others. The **nine treasures** refer to material wealth, possessions and skills of all kinds.

The eight supernatural powers, the nine treasures,*   5–6
  a place in the heavens – for none of these I ask,
  O Master, my all-powerful benefactor!
Happiness, property, family, wealth, a beautiful spouse –   7–8
  may I never desire these even in my dreams, O Master;
  I long only for you.
Hear Dharamdas's plea, O Master!   9
Lift the veil, bless me with your vision,   10
  make me your very own.

𝒲ithout your darshan I am distraught, O Master;   1
  grant me your vision.
I stand here in anticipation – come, O Lord!   2
Bestow at least this much grace on me: 3
  reveal your true form.
The chamber is bejewelled with precious gems,   4
  its door studded with diamonds.†
With the key of love, O Master,   5
  open the lock and reveal its mystery.
Although this devotee has forsaken devotion,   6
  you are ever forgiving.
Hear Dharamdas's plea, O Master: 7
  ferry him across the ocean of existence.

---

† A reference to the inner treasure found in the chamber of the spiritual heart, the eye centre.

मिहरबान है साहेब मेरा।
दिल भर दरसन पाऊँ तेरा॥
तुम दाता मैं सदा भिखारी।
देव दीदार जाऊँ बलिहारी॥
करूँ बंदगी खिजमत दीजै।
बकसो चूक दया बहु कीजै॥
सेवक तें बिगरै सौ बारा।
सतगुरु साहेब लेव उबारा॥
औगुन सेवक साहेब जानै।
साहेब मन में ना गिल्यानै॥
धर्मदास लइ तुम्हरि पनाह।
अगले पछिले बकस गुनाह॥

1 meharbaan hai saaheb mera,
  dil bhar darsan paa'oon tera.
2 tum daata main sada bhikhaari,
  dev deedaar jaa'un balihaari.
3 karoon bandagi khijmat deejai,
  bakso chook daya bahu keejai.
4 sevak tein bigrai sau baara,
  satguru saaheb lev ubaara.
5 augun sevak saaheb jaanai,
  saaheb man mein na gilyaanai.
6 Dharamdas layi tumhri panaah,
  agale pachhile bakas gunaah. [4]

साहेब दीनबंधु हितकारी॥ टेक॥
कोटिन ऐगुन बालक करई,
मात पिता चित एक न धारी॥
तुम गुरु मात पिता जीवन के,
मैं अति दीन दुखारी॥
प्रनत-पाल करूना-निधान प्रभु,
हमरी ओर निहारी॥
जुगन जुगन से तुम चलि आये,
जीवन के हितकारी॥
सदा भरोसे रहूँ तुम्हारे,
तुम प्रतिपाल हमारी॥
मोरे तुम हीं सत्त सुकृत हौ,
अंतर और न धारी॥
जानत हौ जन के तन मन की,
अब कस मोहिं बिसारी॥

1 saaheb deen-bandhu hitkaari. tek.
2 kotin aigun baalak karayi,
  maat pita chit ek na dhaari.
3 tum guru maat pita jeevan ke,
  main ati deen dukhaari.
4 pranat-paal karoona-nidhaan prabhu,
  hamri or nihaari.
5 jugan jugan se tum chali aaye,
  jeevan ke hitkaari.
6 sada bharose rahoon tumhaare,
  tum pratipaal hamaari.
7 more tum hi satt sukrit hau,
  antar aur na dhaari.
8 jaanat hau jan ke tan man ki,
  ab kas mohen bisaari.

My Master, you are gracious indeed –   1
   let me behold you to my heart's content!
You are the giver, and ever a beggar am I –   2
   grant me your darshan; I sacrifice everything unto you.
I pray to you for the opportunity to serve you –   3
   forgive my faults, O Master,
   and shower me with abundant grace.
A disciple may err a hundred times;   4
   the benevolent Master saves him every time.
The Master is aware of the disciple's faults,   5
   yet the Master does not take them to heart.
Dharamdas has taken refuge with you –   6
   please forgive all his sins.

O benevolent Master, you are the benefactor of the meek.   1
A child commits innumerable transgressions,   2
   but the parents overlook them all.
You, O Master, are mother and father to all beings –   3
   I am utterly destitute and distressed.
You are the guardian of those who come to you for refuge;   4
   O fountainhead of mercy, cast your glance at me.
You have been coming in all the ages, O Master;   5
   you are the benefactor of all life.
You are my sole guardian and I always rely on you.   6
You are my very own Sat Sukrit;*   7
   I have turned to no one else within.
You are aware of the condition of your devotee's mind and body –   8
   how could you forsake me now?

---

* Kabir was known as **Sat Sukrit** in Satyuga, the Golden Age.

को कहि सकै तुम्हारी महिमा,
केहि न दिह्यो पद भारी॥
धरमदास पर दाया कीन्हीं,
सेवक अहौं तुम्हारी॥

9   *ko kahi sakai tumhaari mahima,*
     kehi na dihyo pad bhaari.
10   *Dharamdas par daaya keenhi,*
     sevak ahaun tumhaari.[5]

साहेब मोरी ओर निहारो।
परजा पुत्र अहौं मैं साहेब,
बहुत बात मैं टारो॥
हौं मैं कोटि जनम को पापी,
मन बच करम असारो।
एकौ कर्म छुटे ना कबहूँ,
बहु बिधि बात बिगारो॥
हौं अपराधी बहुत जुगन को,
नइया मोर उबारो;
बंदीछोर सकल सुख-दाता,
करुनामय करत पुकारो॥
सीस चढ़ाइ पाप की मोटरी,
आयो तुम्हरे द्वारो।
को अस हमरे भार उतारै,
तुमहीं हेतु हमारो॥
धरमदास यह बिनती बिनवै,
सतगुरु मो को तारो।
साहेब कबीर हंस के राजा,
अमर लोक पहुँचावो॥

1   *saaheb mori or nihaaro,*
2   *parja putr ahaun main saaheb,*
     bahut baat main taaro.
3   *haun main koti janam ko paapi,*
     man bach karam asaaro;
4   *ekau karm chhute na kabahoon,*
     bahu bidhi baat bigaaro.
5   *haun apraadhi bahut jugan ko,*
     nayya mor ubaaro;
6   *bandee-chhor sakal sukh-daata,*
     karunaamay karat pukaaro.
7   *sees charrhaaye paap ki motri,*
     aayo tumhre dvaaro;
8   *ko as hamre bhaar utaarai,*
     tumhi hetu hamaaro.
9   *Dharamdas yah binati binavai,*
     satguru mo ko taaro;
10   *saaheb kabir hans ke raaja,*
     amar lok pahunchaavo.[6]

Who can extol your glory, O Master –   9
   is there anyone whom you have not elevated
   to the supreme state?
You have showered your mercy on Dharamdas   10
   and he has become your devotee.

O Master, bless me with your merciful glance!   1
I am your offspring, your son, O Lord,   2
   countless times have I disregarded your commands.
I have been a sinner for countless lifetimes   3
   and am worthless in thought, word and deed.
Not from a single vice have I abstained   4
   and all my actions have been disastrous in so many ways.
I have been a sinner for many ages – ferry my boat across.   5
O liberator of captives   6
   and bestower of all bliss and happiness,
   you have also been called Karunamay.*
With a bundle of sins on my head,   7
   I have come to your door.
You are my sole benefactor –   8
   who else can relieve me of my load?
Dharamdas submits this earnest prayer: 9
   O Satguru, please take me across.
O Kabir, my Master, Lord of my soul,   10
   take me to the eternal realm.

---

* **Karunamay** was Kabir's name when he incarnated in Dwaparyuga, the Copper Age.

सतगुरु आवो हमरे देस,
निहारौं बाट खड़ी॥ टेक॥

वाहि देस की बतियाँ रे,
लावैं संत सुजान।

उन संतन के चरन पखारौं,
तन मन करौं कुरबान॥

वाहि देस की बतियाँ हम से,
सतगुरु आन कही।

आठ पहर के निरखत हमरे,
नैन की नींद गई॥

भूल गई तन मन धन सारा,
ब्याकुल भया सरीर।

बिरह पुकारै बिरहनी,
ढरकत नैनन नीर॥

धरमदास के दाता सतगुरु,
पल में कियो निहाल।

आवागवन की डोरी कट गई,
मिटैं भरम जंजाल॥

1 satguru aavo hamre des,
   nihaaraun baat kharri. tek.

2 vaahi des ki batiyaan re,
   laavain sant sujaan;

3 un santan ke charan pakhaaraun,
   tan man karaun kurbaan.

4 vaahi des ki batiyaan ham se,
   satguru aan kahi;

5 aath pahar ke nirkhat hamre,
   nain ki neend gayi.

6 bhool gayi tan man dhan saara,
   byaakul bhaya sareer;

7 birah pukaarai birhani,
   dharkat nainan neer.

8 Dharamdas ke daata satguru,
   pal mein kiyo nihaal;

9 aavaagavan ki dori kat gayi,
   mitein bharam janjaal.[7]

I stand gazing your way, O Master –   1
  come to my abode within; reveal yourself.

The wise Saints bring tidings of that supreme realm;   2–3
  I would wash their feet
  and sacrifice my mind and body in their service.

The Master came and narrated to me   4
  his account of that supreme realm.

Gazing at him day and night,   5
  sleep has vanished from my eyes.

My entire being is restless   6
  and I have become oblivious to all –
  body, mind and wealth.

Tormented by separation, my yearning soul cries out   7
  and my eyes shed tears constantly.

The benevolent Satguru of Dharamdas has filled him   8
  with bliss in an instant.

The bonds of transmigration are severed   9
  and the web of delusion is destroyed forever.

बानी गुरु रविदास जी

अब कैसे छूटै नाम रट लागी॥ टेक॥

प्रभु जी तुम चंदन हम पानी,
जाकी बास अंग अंग समानी।

प्रभु जी तुम घन बन हम मोरा,
जैसे चितवत चंद चकोरा॥

प्रभु जी तुम दीपक हम बाती,
जाकी जोति जरै दिन राती।

प्रभु जी तुम मोती हम धागा,
जैसे सोनहिं मिलत सोहागा॥

प्रभु जी तुम स्वामी हम दासा,
ऐसी भगति करै 'रविदासा'।

Bani Guru Ravidas Ji

1 ab kaise chhootai naam rat laagi. tek.

2 prabhu ji tum chandan ham paani,
   jaaki baas ang ang samaani;

3 prabhu ji tum ghan ban ham mora,
   jaise chitvat chand chakora.

4 prabhu ji tum deepak ham baati,
   jaaki joti jarai din raati;

5 prabhu ji tum moti ham dhaaga,
   jaise sonhi milat sohaaga.

6 prabhu ji tum swaami ham daasa,
   aisi bhagti karai 'ravidaasa'.[1]

राग मारू
बाणी रविदास जीउ की

ऐसी लाल तुझ बिन कउन करै॥

गरीब निवाज गुसईआ मेरा
माथै छत्र धरै॥ १॥ रहाउ॥

जा की छोत जगत कउ लागै
ता पर तुहीं धरै।

नीचह ऊच करै मेरा गोबिंद
काहू ते न डरै॥ १॥

Raag Maaru
Baani Ravidaas Jee'o Ki

1 aisi laal tujh bin kaun karai.

2 gareeb nivaaj gusa'eeya mera
   maathai chhatr dharai. rahaa'o.

3 ja ki chhot jagat kau laagai
   ta par tuheen dharai.

4 neechah ooch karai mera gobind
   kaahu te na darai.

---

*The **moonbird** is a legendary bird that is in love with the moon. It watches the moon with such absorption that as the moon moves across the sky the moonbird keeps bending its head backwards until it touches its tail.

Guru Ravidas Ji

Incessant is the repetition of Nam –   *1*
  how can it be stopped now?
Lord, you are the sandalwood and I am the water   *2*
  whose every drop is permeated with your fragrance.
Lord, you are the rain cloud   *3*
  and I am the peacock in the forest;
  just as the moonbird gazes at the moon, I gaze at you.*
Lord, you are the lamp and I am the wick;   *4*
  in me burns your flame day and night.
Lord, you are the pearl and I am the thread that strings it;   *5*
  just as borax merges in gold, I merge in you.
Lord, you are the Master and I am your slave;   *6*
  such is the devotion of Ravidas.

Raga Maru, Ravidas Ji
Who other than you   *1*
  can do such a wonderful thing, O Lord?
O my beloved Lord, merciful to the poor,   *2*
  you have installed over my head the canopy of your grace.
You alone can show compassion to the one   *3*
  whose touch defiles others.†
My Lord exalts the lowly and fears no one.   *4*

---

† During Ravidas's time, the touch of those of low birth was considered to be defiling.

नामदेव कबीर तिलोचन

सधना सैन तरै॥

कह रविदास सुनहो रे संतहो

हर जीउ ते सभै सरै॥ २॥

5 namdev kabir tilochan

sadhna sain tarai.

6 kah Ravidas sunho re santo

har jee'o te sabhai sarai.[2]

दरसन दीजै राम दरसन दीजै।

दरसन दीजै हो बिलंब न कीजै॥ टेक।

दरसन तोरा जीवनि मोरा,

बिन दरसन क्यूं जीवै हो चकोरा।

माधउ सतगुर सब जग चेला,

अबकैं बिछुरैं मिलन दुहेला।

धन जोबन की झूठी आसा,

सति सति भाखै जन 'रविदासा'॥

1 darsan deejai raam darsan deejai,

darsan deejai ho bilamb na keejai. tek.

2 darsan tora jeevani mora,

bin darsan kyoon jeevai ho chakora.

3 maadhau satgur sab jag chela,

abkain bichhurain milan duhela.

4 dhan joban ki jhoothi aasa,

sati sati bhaakhai jan 'ravidaasa'.[3]

राग धनासरी

भगत रविदास जी की

Raag Dhanaasari

Bhagat Ravidaas Ji Ki

हम सर दीन दइआल न तुम सर

अब पतीआर किआ कीजै॥

बचनी तोर मोर मन मानै

जन कउ पूरन दीजै॥ १॥

हउ बल बल जाउ रमईआ कारने॥

कारन कवन अबोल॥ रहाउ॥

1 ham sar deen dayaal na tum sar

ab pateeyaar kya keejai.

2 bachni tor mor man maanai

jan kau pooran deejai.

3 hau bal bal jaa'u rama'eeya kaarne.

kaaran kavan abol. rahaa'o.

Namdev, Kabir, Trilochan, Sadhana and Sain[*] –   5
   all of them swam across the ocean of existence.
Listen, O Saints, says Ravidas: 6
   all is accomplished by the Lord.

Grant me your darshan, O Lord; reveal yourself to me;   1
   without delay, bless me with your vision.
Your darshan sustains my life;   2
   without seeing the moon, how can the moonbird survive?
The Lord and Satguru are one –   3
   before them the whole world stands as disciple.
If one should remain separated from God this time,
   it would indeed be difficult
   to get another chance to meet him.
Ravidas, the Lord's devotee, speaks the truth;   4
   false is the hope of wealth and youth!

Raga Dhanasari, Ravidas Ji
No one is as poor as me,   1
   no one as compassionate as you, O Lord;
   where then is the need to test my devotion?
Grant this devotee the perfect wisdom   2
   to make his mind submit to your teaching.
Forever and ever I sacrifice myself to you, O Lord;   3
   why do you not speak with me?

---

[*] Great devotees whose writings are preserved in the Adi Granth, these Saints were all of humble origin.

बहुत जनम बिछुरे थे माधउ

इह जनम तुम्हारे लेखे॥

कह रविदास आस लग जीवउ

चिर भइओ दरसन देखे॥ २॥

4 *bahut janam bichhure the maadhau*

eh janam tumhaare lekhe.

5 *kah Ravidas aas lag jeevau*

chir bhayo darsan dekhe.[4]

राग सोरठ

बाणी भगत रविदास जी की

Raag Sorath

Baani Bhagat Ravidaas Ji Ki

जउ तुम गिरिवर तउ हम मोरा॥

जउ तुम चंद

तउ हम भए है चकोरा॥१॥

माधवे तुम न तोरहो

तउ हम नही तोरह॥

तुम सिउ तोर

कवन सिउ जोरह॥१॥रहाउ॥

जउ तुम दीवरा तउ हम बाती॥

जउ तुम तीरथ तउ हम जाती॥२॥

साची प्रीत हम तुम सिउ जोरी॥

तुम सिउ जोर अवर संग तोरी॥३॥

जह जह जाउ तहा तेरी सेवा॥

तुम सो ठाकुर अउर न देवा॥४॥

तुमरे भजन कटह जम फांसा॥

भगति हेत गावै रविदासा॥५॥

1 *jau tum girivar tau ham mora.*

jau tum chand

tau ham bhaye hain chakora.

2 *maadhave tum na torho*

tau ham nahi torah.

tum sio tor

kavan sio jorah. rahaa'o.

3 *jau tum deevara tau ham baati.*

jau tum teerath tau ham jaati.

4 *saachi preet ham tum sio jori.*

tum sio jor avar sang tori.

5 *jah jah jaa'u taha teri seva.*

tum so thaakur aur na deva.

6 *tumre bhajan kattah jam phaansa.*

bhagti het gaavai ravidaasa.[5]

For numerous lifetimes   4
    have I remained separated from you, O Lord –
    this life I dedicate to you.
Says Ravidas: I live on hope, O Lord;   5
    long has it been since I had your darshan.

Raga Sorath, Ravidas Ji

If you are the mountain, O Lord, I am the peacock;   1
    if you are the moon, I am the moonbird.
If you do not break your ties with me, O Lord,   2
    I shall never break away from you,
    for if I broke this bond of love,
    to whom would I attach myself?
If you are the lamp, I am the wick;   3
    if you are the holy shrine, I am the pilgrim.
In true love am I attached to you, O Lord,   4
    and having fallen in love with you,
    I have broken away from all else.
Wherever I go I remain in your service, O Lord;   5
    there is no other Master like you.
By meditation on you, O Lord,   6
    the noose of death is cut;
    in loving devotion Ravidas sings your praises.

जो तुम तोरो राम मैं नहिं तोरौं।	1
तुम से तोरि कवन से जोरौं॥ टेक॥	
तीरथ बरत न करौं अँदेसा।	2
तुम्हरे चरन कमल के भरोसा॥	
जहँ जहँ जाओं तुम्हरी पूजा।	3
तुम सा देव और नहिं दूजा॥	
मैं अपनो मन हरि से जोर्यो।	4
हरि से जोरि सबन से तोर्यों॥	
सबही पहर तुम्हारी आसा।	5
मन क्रम बचन कहै रैदासा॥	

1 jo tum toro raam main nahin toraun,
  tum se tori kavan se joraun. tek.
2 teerath barat na karaun andesa,
  tumhre charan kamal ke bharosa.
3 jahan jahan jaa'on tumhri pooja,
  tum sa dev aur nahin dooja.
4 main apno man hari se joryo,
  hari se jori saban se toryon.
5 sabahi pahar tumhaari aasa,
  man kram bachan kahai raidaasa.[6]

माधौ! मुहि इकु सहारौ तोरा॥ टेक॥	1
तुम्हहि मात पित प्रभ मेरो,	2
हौं मसकीन अति भोरा।	
तुम जउ तजौ कवन मोहि राखे,	3
सहिहै कौनु निहोरा॥	
बाहाडंबर	4
हौं कबहुं न जान्यौ,	
तुम चरनन चित मोरा।	
अगुन स्रगुन दौ समकरि जान्यौ,	5
चहुं दिस दरसन तोरा॥	
पारस मनि मुहि रतु नहिं भावै,	6
जग जंजार न थोरा।	
कहि 'रविदास' तजि सभ त्रिस्ना,	7
इकु राम चरन चित मोरा॥	

1 maadhau! mohe iku sahaarau tora. tek.
2 tumhi maat pit prabh mero,
  haun maskeen ati bhora;
3 tum jau tajau kavan mohe raakhe,
  sahihai kaunu nihora.
4 baahaadambar
  haun kabahun na jaanyau,
  tum charnan chit mora;
5 agun sragun dau samkari jaanyau,
  chahun dis darsan tora.
6 paaras mani mohe ratu nahin bhaavai,
  jag janjaar na thora;
7 kahi 'Ravidas', taji sabh trisna,
  iku raam charan chit mora.[7]

---

*Different traditions in India consider the true form of the Lord to be **manifest**, with attributes (*saguna*), or **unmanifest**, without attributes (*nirguna*). Ravidas sees both as the Lord.

O Lord, even if you break the bond of love with me,   *1*
    I will not let go of you –
    without you, who else could I love?
I have no interest in pilgrimages or penances;   *2*
    I trust only in your lotus feet.
Wherever I go, only your devotion is in my heart;   *3*
    there is no one to compare with you, O Lord!
I have attached my mind to the Lord;   *4*
    having devoted it to him, I have detached it from all else.
Ravidas says: at all times, I pine only for you   *5*
    in thought, word and deed.

You are my only support, O Lord!   *1*
You alone are my mother, my father and my Master;   *2*
    I am helpless and extremely ignorant.
If you abandoned me, who would protect me   *3*
    and who else would consider my entreaties?
Outward appearances I do not understand;   *4*
    my attention is fixed only at your lotus feet.
I know that both your manifest and unmanifest forms   *5*
    are the same, O Lord;*
    I perceive you everywhere, in all directions.
I do not care in the least for the philosopher's stone;†   *6*
    my worldly entanglements are already too many.
Says Ravidas: I have forsaken all desires   *7*
    and my mind is focused solely at the Lord's holy feet.

---

† The mythical **philosopher's stone** was much sought after by alchemists, who believed it had the power to turn base metals into gold and to grant eternal youth.

राग गउड़ी रविदास जी के पदे
गउड़ी गुआरेरी

Raag Gaurri Ravidaas Ji Ke Pade
Gaurri Guaareri

मेरी संगत पोच सोच दिन राती॥	1
मेरा करम कुटिलता जनम कुभांती॥९॥	
राम गुसईआ जीअ के जीवना॥	2
मोहे न बिसारहो	
मै जन तेरा॥१॥ रहाउ॥	
मेरी हरहो बिपत जन करहो सुभाई॥	3
चरण न छाडउ सरीर कल जाई॥२॥	
कहो रविदास परउ तेरी साभा॥	4
बेग मिलहो जन कर न बिलांबा॥३॥	

1 *meri sangat poch soch din raati.*
mera karam kutilta janam kubhaanti.
2 *raam gusa'eeyaan jee'a ke jeevana.*
mohe na bisaarho
main jan tera. rahaa'o.
3 *meri harho bipat jan karho subhaa'i.*
charan na chhaadaun sareer kal jaa'i.
4 *kaho Ravidas parau teri saabha.*
beg milho jan kar na bilaamba.[8]

प्रभु जी संगति सरनि तिहारी।	1
जग जीवन राम मुरारी॥ टेक॥	
गली गली कौ नीर बहि आयो,	2
सुरसरी जाइ समायो।	
संगति कै परताप महातम,	
नांव गंगोदिक पायो॥	
स्वांति बूंद बरषै फनि ऊपर,	3
सीस विषै विष होइ।	
वाही बूंद को मोती निपजै,	
संगति की अधिकाई॥	
तुम चंदन हम इरंड बापुरे,	4
निकटि तुम्हारे बासा।	
नीच ब्रिख तै ऊंच भए हैं,	
तुम्हरी बास सुबासा॥	

1 *prabhu ji sangati saran tihaari.*
jag jeevan raam muraari. tek.
2 *gali gali kau neer bahi aayo,*
sursari jaaye samaayo;
sangati kai partaap mahaatam,
naanv gangodik paayo.
3 *svaanti boond barshai phani oopar,*
sees vishai vish hoi;
vaahi boond ko moti nipjai,
sangati ki adhikaa'i.
4 *tum chandan ham irand baapure,*
nikat tumhaare baasa;
neech brikh tai oonch bhaye hain,
tumhri baas subaasa.

---

[*] According to legend, when the moon passes through the **Swati Constellation**, very special raindrops fall. When they fall into an oyster shell, a pearl is formed.

Raga Gauri, Ravidas Ji, Gauri Guareri

Day and night I am troubled by the thought   1
   that my company is deemed to be degrading,
   for humble is my occupation, low is my birth.

O Lord, life of my soul, do not forsake me –   2
   I am your humble servant.

Take away my suffering and grant me your love –   3
   I shall not leave your feet even if my body collapses.

Says Ravidas: I put myself under your shelter;   4
   meet your servant without delay, O Lord;
   please do not procrastinate.

I seek refuge in your company, O Lord;   1
   you are the sustainer and protector of the world.

When the water flowing from alleys merges into the Ganges,   2
   it also bears the name 'water of the holy Ganges' –
   so great is the glory of association!

During the time of the Swati Constellation, the drop of rain   3
   that falls on the head of a serpent adds to its venom,
   but the same drop, if it falls into an oyster shell, creates a pearl* –
   such is the greatness of association!

You are the sandalwood tree, O Lord,   4
   and I am a lowly castor plant that has grown in your vicinity;†
   from a lowly shrub I have attained this lofty status
   because your fragrance now abides in me.

---

† The **castor plant** is considered a weed in India because it seeds itself and grows rampantly in most conditions.

जाति भी ओछी पांति भी ओछी,
ओछा कसब हमारा।
तुम्हरी क्रिपा तैं ऊंच भए हैं,
कहै 'रविदास' चमारा॥

5 *jaati bhi ochhi paanti bhi ochhi,*
ochha kasab hamaara;
tumhri kripa tain oonch bhaye hain,
kahai 'Ravidas' chamaara.[9]

प्रभु जी तुम औगन बकसन हार।
हऊं बहु नीच उधरौ पातकी,
मूरिख निपट गंवार॥ टेक॥
मो सम पतित अधम नहीं कोउ,
क्षीन दुखी विसयार।
नांम सुनहि नरकु भजै है,
तुम्ह बिन कवन हमार॥
पतित पावन विड़द तिहारौ,
आई परौं तोहि दुवार।
कहि रविदास इहु मन आसा,
निज कर लेहू उबार॥

1 *prabhu ji tum augun baksan haar,*
haun bahu neech udharau paataki,
moorikh nipat ganvaar. tek.
2 *mo sam patit adham nahi ko'u,*
ksheen dukhi visyaar;
3 *naam sunahi naraku bhajai hvai,*
tum bin kavan hamaar.
4 *patit paavan virrad tihaarau,*
aa'i paraun tohe duvaar;
5 *kahi Ravidas ehu man aasa,*
nij kar lehu ubaar.[10]

राग आसा
बाणी श्री रविदास जीउ की
तुम चंदन हम इरंड बापुरे
संग तुमारे बासा॥
नीच रूख ते ऊच भए है
गंध सुगंध निवासा॥१॥
माधउ सतसंगत सरन तुम्हारी॥
हउ अउगन तुम्ह उपकारी॥१॥ रहाउ॥
तुम मखतूल सुपेद सपीअल
हम बपुरे जस कीरा॥

Raag Aasa
Baani Sri Ravidas Jee'o ki
1 *tum chandan ham irand baapure*
sang tumaare baasa.
2 *neech rookh te ooch bhaye hai*
gandh sugandh nivaasa.
3 *maadhau satsangat saran tumhaari.*
hau augan tumh upkaari. rahaa'o.
4 *tum makhtool suped sapee'al*
ham bapure jas keera.

I was born in a low caste – low is my lineage and occupation.   5
It is only by your grace that I have attained
   this exalted status, says Ravidas, the cobbler.

O Lord, you are the forgiver of sins;   1
   I am a worthless and shameless sinner,
   utterly foolish and ignorant.
There is none as fallen and base as me;   2
   I am weak, corrupt and prone to sensual indulgence.
Even hell would refuse to accept me –   3
   other than you, who else is mine?
Your glory is in redeeming the fallen;   4
   I submit myself at your door, O Lord.
Says Ravidas: it is my only hope   5
   that you will accept me as your own and liberate me.

Raga Asa, Sri Ravidas Ji
You are the sandalwood tree, O Lord,   1
   and I am a poor castor plant near you.
With your fragrance pervading me,   2
   from a lowly shrub I have become exalted.
I am a sinner and you are the benevolent Lord;   3
   I seek refuge in the company of your Saints.
You are like yellow-white silk   4
   while I am a poor worm.

सतसंगत मिल रहीऐ माधउ
जैसे मधुप मखीरा ॥ २ ॥
जाती ओछा पाती ओछा
ओछा जनम हमारा ॥
राजा राम की सेव न कीन्ही
कह रविदास चमारा ॥ ३ ॥

5 satsangat mil raheeyai maadhau
jaise madhup makheera.
6 jaati ochha paati ochha
ochha janam hamaara.
7 raaja raam ki sev na keenhi
kah Ravidas chamaara.[11]

तुम्ह करहु क्रिपा मुहि साईं ॥ टेक ॥
स्वांस–स्वांस तुझ नाम संभारउ,
तुम्हहि भेंटि ममु मन हरसाई ।
तुमहु दयाल क्रिपाल करुणानिध,
तुम्हहि दीनबंधु रघुराई ॥
तुम्हरी सरन रहौं निसवासर,
भरमत फिरौं न हौं हरि राई ।
तुम्हरी अनुकम्प मान मदु छूटै,
राम रसाइन अम्रितु पाई ॥
ऐसो बुध जाचिहुं करुनामैं,
तुझ चरन तजि कितहु न जाई ।
चरण–सरन 'रविदास' रावरी,
अपनो जान लेहु उर लाई ॥

1 tumh karoh kripa muhe saa'een. tek.
2 svaans-svaans tujh naam sambhaarau,
tumahen bhenti mamu man harsaa'i;
3 tumho dayaal kripaal karunaa-nidh,
tumhi deen-bandhu raghuraa'i.
4 tumhri saran rahaun nisvaasar,
bharmat phiraun na haun hari raa'i;
5 tumhri anukamp maan madu chootai,
raam rasaayan amritu paa'i.
6 aiso budh jaachihun karunaa-mai,
tujh charan taji kitahu na jaa'i;
7 charan-saran 'Ravidas' raavri,
apno jaan leho ur laa'i.[12]

Just as a honeybee yearns for honey,   5
   I long for the company of your Saints, O Lord.
Says Ravidas, the cobbler: 6–7
   low is my caste, low is my social standing,
   low is my birth.
Alas, I have failed to serve my supreme King!

*H*ave mercy on me, O Lord!   1
With every breath I meditate on your Nam;   2
   my mind will attain bliss only on meeting you.
You are merciful, benevolent   3
   and the ocean of compassion;
   you are the companion of the meek, O supreme Lord!
Day and night may I remain under your shelter   4
   so that I do not wander in delusion, O almighty Lord.
By your grace, vanity and pride are eliminated   5
   and the nectar of Nam is obtained.
O Merciful One, grant me such wisdom   6
   that my mind does not stray from your lotus feet.
Ravidas has taken refuge at your feet;   7
   consider him as your own
   and hold him within your heart.

बानी मीराबाई जी

Bani Mirabai Ji

अब मैं सरण तिहारी जी,	1	*ab main saran tihaari ji,*
मोहिं राखो कृपानिधान॥ टेक॥		*mohen raakho kripaa-nidhaan. tek.*
अजामील अपराधी तारे,	2	*ajaameel apraadhi taare,*
तारे नीच सदान।		*taare neech sadaan;*
जल डूबत गजराज उबारे,	3	*jal doobat gajraaj ubaare,*
गणिका चढ़ी बिमान॥		*ganika charrhi bimaan.*
और अधम तारे बहुतेरे,	4	*aur adham taare bahutere,*
भाखत संत सुजान।		*bhaakhat sant sujaan;*
कुबजा नीच भीलनी तारी,	5	*kubja neech bheelani taari,*
जानै सकल जहान॥		*jaanai sakal jahaan.*
कहँ लगि कहूँ गिनत नहिं आवै,	6	*kahan lag kahoon ginat nahin aavai,*
थकि रहे बेद पुरान।		*thaki rahe bed puraan;*
मीरा कहै मैं सरण रावली,	7	*Mira kahai main saran raavali,*
सुनियो दोनों कान॥		*suniyo dono kaan.* [1]

अब तो निभायाँ सरेगी,	1	*ab to nibhaayaan saregi,*
बाँह गहे की लाज॥		*baanh gahe ki laaj.*
समरथ सरन तुम्हारी सइयाँ,	2	*samrath saran tumhaari sayyaan,*
सरब सुधारण काज॥		*sarab sudhaaran kaaj.*

---

* **Ajamil** was a brahmin who sinned his whole life but was saved in the end by calling out his son's name, Narayan, which is also a name of the Lord.

† Although he was a butcher, **Sadhana** constantly repeated the name of the Lord throughout many misfortunes and achieved inner peace.

‡ **Gajraj** was an elephant who cried out to the Lord and was saved from a crocodile's attack.

§ **Ganika** was a prostitute who attained liberation through the practice of the Lord's Name.

Mirabai Ji

Now I have taken refuge with you –   *1*
   protect me, O merciful Lord!
You redeemed sinners like Ajamil*   *2*
   and also ferried across ignoble ones like Sadhana.†
You saved Gajraj from drowning‡   *3*
   and you exalted Ganika.§
Many sinners have you liberated –   *4*
   so the wise Saints say.
The whole world knows how you emancipated Kubja¶   *5*
   and the lowly tribal woman.**
Of how many should I tell –   *6*
   I can hardly keep a count;
   even the Vedas and the Puranas have failed to do so.
Says Mira: lend your ears to my entreaty, O Lord –   *7*
   I have taken refuge in you.

Now that you have taken hold of my hand,   *1*
   you are honour bound to keep your promise.
My almighty Beloved,   *2*
   under your shelter all objectives are accomplished.

¶ In the Mahabharata, **Kubja** was a physically deformed servant of the king of Mathura. When she met Krishna she gave him sandalwood paste intended for the king. Krishna then transformed her into a beautiful maiden, reflecting her inner state.

** The **lowly tribal woman** is Shabri, whose story is told by Tulsidas in *Ramcharitmanas*. When Shabri met Ram and his brother Lakshman in the forest, she offered them wild fruits that she had tasted to determine which were the sweet ones. Despite the fact that they were considered defiled because she had tasted them, Ram took them and declared that these fruits offered with such devotion were excellent. He then gave a famous discourse on nine kinds of devotion.

भवसागर संसार अपरबल,
जामें तुम हो जहाज॥

निरधाराँ आधार जगत गुरू,
तुम बिन होय अकाज॥

जुग जुग भीर हरी भक्तन की,
दीनी मोक्ष समाज॥

मीराँ सरण गही चरणन की,
लाज रखो महाराज॥

3 *bhavsaagar sansaar aparbal,*
jaamein tum ho jahaaj.

4 *nirdhaaraan aadhaar jagat guru,*
tum bin hoye akaaj.

5 *jug jug bheer hari bhaktan ki,*
deeni moksh samaaj.

6 *meeraan saran gahi charnan ki,*
laaj rakho mahaaraaj.[2]

छोड़ मत जाज्योजी महाराज॥

में अबला बल नायँ गुसाई
तुम ही मेरे सिरताज॥

में गुणहीन गुण नायँ गुसाई
तुम समरथ महाराज॥

थाँरी होय के किनरे जाउँ
तुम ही हिवड़ा रो साज॥

मीराँ के प्रभु और न कोई
राखो अब के लाज॥

1 *chhorr mat jaajyo ji mahaaraaj.*

2 *mein abla bal naayen gusaa'een*
tum hi mere sirtaaj.

3 *mein gun-heen gun naayen gusaa'een*
tum samrath mahaaraaj.

4 *thaanri hoye ke kinare jaa'un*
tum hi hivrra ro saaj.

5 *meeraan ke prabhu aur na koi*
raakho ab ke laaj.[3]

दरस बिन दुखन लागे नैन॥ टेक॥

जब से तुम बिछरे मेरे प्रभु जी,
कबहुँ न पायों चैन।

सबद सुनत मेरी छतियाँ कंपै,
मीठे लगे तुम बैन॥

एक टकटकी पंथ निहारूँ,
भई छमासी रैन॥

बिरह बिथा कासूँ कहूँ सजनी,
बह गइ करवत ऐन॥

मीरा के प्रभु कब रे मिलोगे,
दुख मेटन सुख देन॥

1 *daras bin dukhan laage nain. tek.*

2 *jab se tum bichhre mere prabhu ji,*
kabahun na paayon chain;

3 *sabad sunat meri chhatiyaan kampai,*
meethe lage tum bain.

4 *ek taktaki panth nihaaroon,*
bhayi chhamaasi rain.

5 *birah bitha kaasoon kahoon sajani,*
bah gayi karvat ain.

6 *Mira ke prabhu kab re miloge,*
dukh metan sukh den.[4]

You are the ship in this dreadful ocean of worldly existence.   3

O Master of the universe, the support of the helpless: 4
   without you, all pursuits are futile.

Throughout the ages   5
   you have eliminated your devotees' suffering
   and brought salvation to the world.

Mira has taken refuge at your feet –   6
   please uphold my honour, O Master!

*D*o not abandon me, O Master!   1

I am helpless and weak;   2
   dear Master, you are my sovereign Lord.

I am worthless, without merit,   3
   but you are all-powerful.

Now that I belong only to you, where else can I go –   4
   you alone are the rhythm of my heart.

O Mira's Lord! Except for you, there is none other;   5
   uphold my honour now.

*M*y eyes are aching without your darshan!   1

Never have I been at peace   2
   since you parted from me, my Lord.

My body trembles when I hear the Shabd –   3
   sweet indeed is your voice.

Intently I look for you;   4
   a night without you seems like months.

To whom shall I tell my woes of separation, dear Friend –   5
   it is as if I have been sliced with a saw.

When will you meet me, O Mira's Lord,   6
   to bestow bliss and remove this pain?

हरि मने पार उतार,
नमी नमी विनती करूं छुं॥

जगत मां जन्मीने
बहु दुःख देख्या,
संसार शोक निवार॥

कष्ट आपे मने कर्म ना बंधन,
दूर तुं कर किर्तार॥

आ संसार वह्यो वह्यो जाय छे,
लख चोराशी धार॥

मीराँ कहे प्रभु गिरधर नागर,
आवागमन निवार॥

1 hari mane paar utaar,
nami nami vinati karoon chhun.

2 jagat maan janmeene
bahu dukh dekhya,
sansaar shok nivaar.

3 kasht aape mane karm na bandhan,
door tu kar kirtaar.

4 aa sansaar vahyo vahyo jaaye chhe,
lakh choraashi dhaar.

5 meeraan kahe prabhu girdhar naagar,
aavaa-gaman nivaar.[5]

हे री मैं तो प्रेम दिवानी,
मेरा दरद न जाणे कोय॥ टेक॥

सूली ऊपर सेज हमारी,
किस बिध सोणा होय।

गगन मँडल पै सेज पिया की,
किस बिध मिलणा होय॥

घायल की गत घायल जानै,
की जिन लाई होय।

जौहरी की गत जौहरी जानै,
की जिन जौहर होय॥

दरद की मारी बन बन डोलूँ,
बैद मिल्या नहिं कोय।

मीरा की प्रभु पीर मिटैगी,
जब बैद साँवलिया होय॥

1 he ri main to prem divaani,
mera darad na jaane koye. tek.

2 sooli oopar sej hamaari,
kis bidh sona hoye;

3 gagan mandal pai sej piya ki,
kis bidh milna hoye.

4 ghaayal ki gat ghaayal jaanai,
ki jin laa'i hoye;

5 jauhari ki gat jauhari jaanai,
ki jin jauhar hoye.

6 darad ki maari ban ban doloon,
baid milya nahin koye;

7 Mira ki prabhu peer mitaigi,
jab baid saanvaliya hoye.[6]

---

*currents of eighty-four: A reference to the cycle of 8,400,000 life forms into which beings keep reincarnating.

Bowing down to you again and again, I implore you,   *1*
   O Lord, please ferry me across.

Since my birth in this world, I have seen great suffering –   *2*
   liberate me from worldly sorrows.

I am distressed by the fetters of my own karmas –   *3*
   free me from them, O Lord.

The whole world is drifting   *4*
   in the currents of eighty-four.*

Prays Mira: O supreme Lord,   *5*
   deliver me from the cycle of transmigration.

O friend, I am madly in love; no one knows my agony.   *1*

How can I get any sleep on a bed of nails?   *2*

In higher realms is my Beloved's seat –   *3*
   alas, how can I meet him?

Only the wounded know the agony of the wounded.   *4*

Only one who has committed *jauhar* herself   *5*
   can know the state of a *jauhari*.[†]

Tormented by pain, I wander in the wilderness   *6*
   unable to find a physician who can cure my affliction.

O Lord, Mira will be relieved of her suffering   *7*
   only when the Lord himself becomes her healer.

---

† See **jauhar** in the Glossary.

कोई कहियौ रे प्रभु आवन की,
आवन की मन भावन की। टेर।

आप न आवै लिख नहिं भेजै,
बाँण पड़ी ललचावन की॥

ए दोई नैन कह्यो नहिं मानैं,
नदियाँ बहै जैसे सावन की॥

कहा करूँ कछु नहिं बस मेरो,
पाँख नहीं उड़ जावन की॥

मीरां कहै प्रभु कब रै मिलोगे,
चेरी भई हूँ तेरे दावन की॥

1 koi kahiyau re prabhu aavan ki,
   aavan ki man bhaavan ki; ter.

2 aap na aavai likh nahin bhejai,
   baan parri lalchaavan ki.

3 e doyi nain kahyo nahin maanai,
   nadiyaan bahai jaise saavan ki.

4 kaha karoon kachhu nahin bas mero,
   paankh nahi urr jaavan ki.

5 meeraan kahai prabhu kab rai miloge,
   cheri bhayi hoon tere daavan ki.[7]

मैं हरि बिन क्यों जिउँ री माइ॥टेक॥

पिब कारण बौरी भई
ज्यूँ काठहि घुन खाइ।

ओखद मूल न सँचरै
मोहि लाग्यो बौराइ॥

कमठ दादुर बसत जल में
जलहि ते उपजाइ।

मीन जल के बीछुरै
तन तलफि करि मरि जाइ॥

पिव ढूँढ़ण बन–बन गई
कहुँ मुरली धुनि पाइ।

मीराँ के प्रभु लाल गिरधर
मिलि गये सुखदाइ॥

1 main hari bin kyon jiyun ri maa'i. tek.

2 pib kaaran bauri bhayi
   jyoon kaathahi ghun khaa'i;
   aukhad mool na sancharai
   mohe laagyo bauraa'i.

3 kamath daadur basat jal mein
   jalahi te upjaa'i;
   meen jal ke beechhurai
   tan talafi kari mari jaa'i.

4 piv dhoondhan ban-ban gayi
   kahun murli dhuni paa'i.
   meeraan ke prabhu laal girdhar
   mili gaye sukhdaa'i.[8]

$\mathcal{W}$ill someone bring me tidings of my Lord's coming –   *1*
   the coming of the one who delights my heart?
He comes not himself, nor does he send a letter –   *2*
   it has become his habit to make me pine for him.
These two eyes do not listen to me;   *3*
   they overflow like rivers during the monsoon.
What can I do? I am utterly helpless   *4*
   and have no wings to fly to him.
O Lord, when will you meet me, asks Mira –   *5*
   I am entirely dependent upon you.

$\mathcal{H}$ow do I live without the Lord, O mother?   *1*
Without the Beloved, I have lost my sanity;   *2*
   I am like wood being eaten away by termites
   and there is no remedy for my affliction –
   I have gone insane.
The turtle and the frog are born in water and live in water –   *3*
   it is only the fish that dies in agony
   when taken out of water.
I wandered the woods in search of my Beloved,   *4*
   hoping to hear the sound of his flute,*
   but Mira's beloved Lord, the bestower of all bliss,
   revealed himself within her.

---

* Esoterically, the **sound of his flute** refers to the unstruck music, the inner spiritual sound or Shabd with which the devotee yearns to make contact during meditation.

मैं वारी जाऊँ राम,
तुम आवो गली हमारी।
तुम देख्यां बिन कल न परत है,
जोऊँ बाट तुम्हारी॥
कौन सखीसों तुम रंगराते,
हमते अधिक पियारी।
किरपा कर मोहे दरशन दीजो,
सब तकसीर बिसारी॥
मैं शरनागत तुम हो दयाला,
भव से तार मुरारी।
मीराँ दासी तुम चरनन की
बार बार बलिहारी॥

1   main vaari jaa'oon raam,
     tum aavo gali hamaari;
2   tum dekhyaan bin kal na parat hai,
     jo'oon baat tumhaari.
3   kaun sakheeson tum rang-raate,
     hamte adhik pyaari;
4   kirpa kar mohe darshan deejo,
     sab takseer bisaari.
5   main sharanaagat tum ho dayaala,
     bhav se taar muraari;
6   meeraan daasi tum charnan ki
     baar baar balihaari.[9]

मन माने जब तार प्रभुजी॥
नदिया गहरी नाव पुरानी।
किस विध उतरूँ पार॥
वेद पुरान बखानी महिमा।
लगे न गुण को पार॥
योग याग जप तप नहीं जानूं।
नाम निरन्तर सार॥
बाट तकत हौं कबकी ठाड़ी।
त्रिभुवन पालन हार॥
मीराँ के प्रभु गिरधर नागर।
चरण कमल बलिहार॥

1   man maane jab taar prabhu ji.
2   nadiya gahri naav puraani,
     kis vidh utaroon paar.
3   ved puraan bakhaani mahima,
     lage na gun ko paar.
4   yog yaag jap tap nahi jaanu,
     naam nirantar saar.
5   baat takat haun kabki thaarri,
     tribhuvan paalan haar.
6   meeraan ke prabhu girdhar naagar,
     charan kamal balihaar.[10]

I would sacrifice everything to you, O Lord –   *1*
  please come to my lane.
Without seeing you, I am restless and on edge;   *2*
  I constantly gaze your way.
Who is that friend, dearer than me,   *3*
  whose love has so enchanted you?
Pray have mercy on me, forget all my transgressions   *4*
  and bless me with your darshan.
I seek refuge in you, O merciful Lord –   *5*
  ferry me across the ocean of existence.
Mira, your slave, offers herself again and again   *6*
  as a sacrifice at your feet.

Ferry me across whenever you will, O Lord!   *1*
Deep is the river and old is my boat –   *2*
  how can I get to the other shore?
The Vedas and the Puranas extol your glory   *3*
  but have no idea of your true greatness.
I know not any penances   *4*
  nor do I practise yoga or devotion –
  for me, Nam is the true eternal Essence.
O sustainer of the three realms,*   *5*
  long have I stood gazing your way.
I sacrifice everything at your lotus feet,   *6*
  O Mira's beloved Lord!

---

*The **three realms** are the physical, astral and causal worlds below the region of pure spirit.

म्हाँरो जनम मरन को साथी,
थाँ ने नहिं बिसरूँ दिन राती॥ टेक॥

तुम देख्याँ बिन कल न पड़त है,
जानत मेरी छाती।

ऊँची चढ़ चढ़ पंथ निहारूँ,
रोय रोय अँखियाँ राती॥

यो संसार सकल जग झूँठो,
झूँठा कुल रा नाती।

दोउ कर जोड़याँ अरज करत हूँ,
सुण लीज्यो मेरी बाती॥

यो मन मेरो बड़ो हरामी,
ज्यूँ मद मातो हाथी।

सतगुरु दस्त धर्यो सिर ऊपर,
आँकुस दे समझाती॥

पल पल तेरा रूप निहारूँ,
निरख निरख सुख पाती।

मीरा के प्रभु गिरधर नागर,
हरि चरणाँ चित राती॥

1 mhaanro janam maran ko saathi,
thaan ne nahin bisroon din raati. tek.

2 tum dekhyaan bin kal na parrat hai,
jaanat meri chhaati;

3 oonchi charrh charrh panth nihaaroon,
roye roye ankhiyaan raati.

4 yo sansaar sakal jag jhoontho,
jhoontha kul ra naati;

5 do'u kar jorryaan araj karat hoon,
sun leejyo meri baati.

6 yo man mero barro haraami,
jyoon mad maato haathi;

7 satguru dast dharyo sir oopar,
aankus de samjhaati.

8 pal pal tera roop nihaaroon,
nirakh nirakh sukh paati;

9 Mira ke prabhu girdhar naagar,
hari charna chit raati.[11]

म्हारी सुध ज्यूँ जानो
ज्यूँ लीजो जी॥ टेक॥

पल पल भीतर पंथ निहारूँ,
दरसण म्हाँने दीजो जी॥

मैं तो हूँ बहु औगणहारी,
औगण चित्त मत दीजो जी॥

मैं तो दासी
थारे चरण–जनाँ की,
मिल बिछुरन मत कीजो जी॥

मीराँ तो सतगुरु के सरणे,
हरिचरणाँ चित दीजो जी॥

1 mhaari sudh jyoon jaano
jyoon leejo ji. tek.

2 pal pal bheetar panth nihaaroon,
darsan mhaane deejo ji.

3 main to hoon bahu augan-haari,
augan chitt mat deejo ji.

4 main to daasi
thaare charan-janaan ki,
mil bichhuran mat keejo ji.

5 meeraan to satguru ke sarne,
hari-charna chit deejo ji.[12]

O companion of my life and death,   *1*
    I shall not forget you day or night.
Without seeing you, only my heart knows   *2*
    how restless I am.
I climb higher and higher to gaze at your path;   *3*
    my constant crying has left my eyes red.
This world and all the people in it are ephemeral;   *4*
    false are family and all relations.
O Master, I pray to you with folded hands –   *5*
    kindly listen to my entreaty.
My wicked mind is like an intoxicated elephant, O Satguru –   *6–7*
    place your hand on my head like a goad
    and tame this wayward mind.
I am absorbed each moment in seeing your beautiful form,   *8*
    and I experience bliss through this continuous contemplation.
The almighty Lord is Mira's Beloved;   *9*
    her attention is ever absorbed in his lotus feet.

O Master, take care of me as you deem fit.   *1*
I eagerly wait for you within at every moment –   *2*
    pray come and bless me with your darshan!
I am full of countless vices –   *3*
    do not take my transgressions to heart.
I am but a slave of your slaves;   *4*
    after meeting me, do not forsake me.
Mira has taken refuge with you, beloved Master –   *5*
    turn her attention towards the Lord's feet.

मोहे लागी लगन
गुरु–चरनन की॥ टेक॥
चरन बिना कछुवै नहिं भावै,
जग–माया सब सपनन की॥
भवसागर सब सूखि गयौ है,
फिकर नहीं मोहि तरनन की॥
मीराँ के प्रभु गिरधरनागर,
आस वही गुरु–सरनन की॥

1   mohe laagi lagan
     guru-charnan ki. tek.

2   charan bina kachhuvai nahin bhaavai,
     jag-maaya sab sapnan ki.

3   bhavsaagar sab sookhi gayau hai,
     phikar nahin mohe tarnan ki.

4   meeraan ke prabhu girdhar-naagar,
     aas vahi guru-sarnan ki.[13]

प्यारे दर्शन दीजो आय,
तुम बिन रह्यो न जाय। टेर।
जल बिन कमल चंद बिन रजनी,
ऐसे तुम देख्यां बिन सजनी।
आकुल ब्याकुल फिरूं रैन दिन,
विरह कलेजा खाय॥
दिवस न भूख नींद नहिं रैनां,
मुख से कथन न आवै बैनां।
कहा करूं कुछ कहत न आवै,
मिल कर तपत बुझाय॥
क्यों तरसाओ अंतरजामी,
आय मिलो किरपा कर स्वामी।
मीराँ दासी जनम जनम की,
परी तुमारे पांय॥

1   pyaare darshan deejo aaye,
     tum bin rahiyo na jaaye. ter.

2   jal bin kamal chand bin rajani,
     aise tum dekhyaan bin sajani;

3   aakul byaakul phiroon rain din,
     virah kaleja khaaye.

4   divas na bhookh neend nahin raina,
     mukh se kathan na avai baina;

5   kaha karoon kuchh kahat na aavai,
     mil kar tapat bujhaaye.

6   kyon tarsaa'o antarjaami,
     aaye milo kirpa kar swaami;

7   meeraan daasi janam janam ki,
     pari tumaare paanye.[14]

री मेरे पार निकस गया
सतगुरू मार्या तीर।
विरह भाल लगी उर अंदर
व्याकुल भया सरीर॥

1   ri mere paar nikas gaya
     satguru maarya teer,

2   virah bhaal lagi ur andar
     vyaakul bhaya sareer.

I have an intense longing for the feet of my Master. *1*

Nothing pleases me except his lotus feet; *2*
 to me this world is but an illusory dream.

This dreadful ocean of existence has dried up for me; *3*
 I no longer worry about swimming across.

Says Mira: O almighty Lord, *4*
 I yearn only for my Master's refuge.

O Beloved, come and grant me your darshan – *1*
 I cannot live without you.

Without a glimpse of you, your dear one is like *2*
 a lotus without water, or a night without the moon.

Agonized and restless, I wander day and night; *3*
 pangs of separation keep gnawing at my heart.

I pass my days without hunger and my nights without sleep; *4*
 I am unable to voice my anguish.

What can I do? I have no words to express myself; *5*
 come douse the fire searing my heart.

Why do you torment me so, O knower of all hearts? *6*

Pray, have mercy, come and meet me.

Mira, your slave of countless births, falls at your feet. *7*

Ah, Satguru's arrow has pierced me right through! *1*

The spear of longing is lodged deep within me, *2*
 and restless is my body.

इत उत चित चलै नहिं कबहूँ,
डारी प्रेम-जंजीर।
कै जाणे मेरो प्रीतम प्यारो,
और न जाणै पीर॥
कहा करूँ मेरो बस नहिं सजनी,
नैन झरत दोउ नीर।
मीराँ कहै प्रभु
तुम मिलियाँ बिन
प्राण धरत नहीं धीर॥

3 it ut chit chalai nahin kabahoon,
  daari prem-janjeer;
4 kai jaane mero preetam pyaaro,
  aur na jaanai peer.
5 kaha karoon mero bas nahin sajani,
  nain jharat do'u neer;
6 meeraan kahai prabhu
  tum miliyaan bin
  praan dharat nahi dheer.[15]

तनक हरि चितवौ जी मोरी ओर॥
हम चितवत तुम चितवत नाहीं
दिल के बड़े कठोर॥
मेरे आसा चितवनि तुमरी
और न दूजी दोर॥
तुम से हमकूँ एक हो जी
हमसी लाख करोर॥
ऊभी ठाड़ी अरज करत हूँ
अरज करत भयो भोर॥
मीराँ के प्रभु हरि अविनासी
देस्यूँ प्राण अकोर॥

1 tanak hari chitvau ji mori or.
2 hum chitvat tum chitvat naahi
  dil ke barre kathor.
3 mere aasa chitvani tumri
  aur na dooji dor.
4 tum se hamkoon ek ho ji
  hamsi laakh karor.
5 oobhi thaarri araj karat hoon
  araj karat bhayo bhor.
6 meeraan ke prabhu hari avinaasi
  desyoon praan akor.[16]

तुम पलक उघाड़ो दीनानाथ,
हूँ हाजिर नाजिर कबकी खड़ी॥टेक॥
साऊ थे दुसमण होइ लागे,
सब ने लगूँ कड़ी।
तुम बिन साऊ कोउ नहीं है,
डिगी नाव मेरी समँद अड़ी॥

1 tum palak ughaarro deenaa-naath,
  hoon haajir naajir kabki kharri. tek.
2 saa'u the dusman hoi laage,
  sab ne lagoon karri;
3 tum bin saa'u ko'u nahi hai,
  digi naav meri samand arri.

My mind no longer strays 3
   but is bound by chains of love.
My dear Beloved alone knows my pain; 4
   no one else can understand it.
My eyes shed a constant stream of tears; 5
   I am helpless, O Friend – what can I do?
Says Mira: O Lord, without meeting you, 6
   I am unable to calm my anxious heart.

Cast your glance at me for a moment, O Lord! 1
I adore you, but you do not even look at me – 2
   oh, how hard-hearted you are!
I hope only for a glance from you; 3
   I have no other desire.
For me, there is no one like you, O Lord; 4
   for you, there are countless ones like me.
Unmoving, I stand imploring, 5
   and absorbed in this way, dawn approaches.
To you, Mira's eternal Lord, 6
   I offer my life for that one glance.

Open your eyes, O benefactor of the meek – 1
   I have been standing in your presence for a long time.
Those who were once my protectors 2
   have now become my enemies;
   to them I appear like bitter poison.
My boat is precariously adrift at sea; 3
   besides you, I have no other protector.

दिन नहिं चैन रात नहिं निदरा,
सूखूँ खड़ी खड़ी।
बान बिरह के लगे हिये में,
भूलूँ न एक घड़ी॥
पत्थर की तो अहिल्या तारी,
बन के बीच पड़ी।
कहा बोझ मीरा में कहिये,
सौ ऊपर एक धड़ी॥
गुरु रैदास मिले मोहिं पुरे,
धुर से कलम भिड़ी।
सतगुरु सैन दई जब आ के,
जोत में जोत रली॥

4   *din nahin chain raat nahin nidra,*
     sookhoon kharri kharri;

5   *baan birah ke lage hiye mein,*
     bhooloon na ek gharri.

6   *patthar ki to ahilya taari,*
     ban ke beech parri;

7   *kaha bojh meera mein kahiye,*
     sau oopar ek gharri.

8   *guru raidaas mile mohen pure,*
     dhur se kalam bhirri.

9   *satguru sain dayi jab aa ke,*
     jot mein jot rali.[17]

तुम सुनो दयाल म्हाँरी अरजी॥ टेक॥
भौसागर में बही जात हूँ,
काढ़ो तो थाँरी मरजी॥
यो संसार सगो नहिं कोई,
साचा सगा रघुबर जी॥
मात पिता और कुटँब कबीलो,
सब मतलब के गरजी॥
मीरा की प्रभु अरजी सुन लो,
चरन लगाओ थाँरी मरजी॥

1   *tum suno dayaal mhaanri arji. tek.*

2   *bhausaagar mein bahi jaat hoon,*
     kaarrho to thaanri marji.

3   *yo sansaar sago nahin koi,*
     saacha saga raghubar ji.

4   *maat pita aur kutamb kabeelo,*
     sab matlab ke garji.

5   *Mira ki prabhu arji sun lo,*
     charan lagaa'o thaanri marji.[18]

Restless during the day and sleepless at night,   *4*
   I am wasting away waiting for you.

Arrows of intense longing pierce my heart;   *5*
   I cannot forget you even for a moment.

You liberated even Ahilya,   *6*
   who lay in the woods, turned into stone.*

What is Mira's weight compared to hers –   *7*
   a mere pound to a ton!

When Ravidas, my perfect Master, met me,   *8*
   the twig that was severed from the tree in the beginning
   was attached to it again.

When my Satguru came and showed me the way,   *9*
   my light merged back into the eternal Light.

Listen to my supplication, O merciful Lord!   *1*

I am drifting in the ocean of existence;   *2*
   if it be your will, pull me out.

In this world no one belongs to me;   *3*
   only you, dear Lord, are truly mine.

Mother, father, family and clan –   *4*
   all of them stay around for selfish ends.

Listen to Mira's plea, O Lord;   *5*
   if it be your will, grant me refuge at your feet!

---

* **Ahilya** was turned into stone by a curse, but as recounted in the Ramayana, was released from the curse when she was touched by Ram's feet.

बानी सूरदास जी

अबकी राखि लेहु भगवान।
हम अनाथ बैठी द्रुम डरियाँ,
पारधि साध्यो बान॥

ता के डर निकसन चाहत हौं,
ऊपर रह्यो सचान।

दोऊ भाँति दुख भयो कृपानिधि,
कौन उबारै प्रान॥

सुमिरत ही अहि डस्यो पारधी,
लाग्यो तीर सचान।

सूरदास गुन कहँ लग बरनौं,
जै जै कृपानिधान॥

दीनानाथ अब बार तुम्हारी।
पतित-उधारन बिरद जानि के,
बिगरी लेहु सँवारी॥

बालापन खेलत ही खोयो,
जुबा बिषय रस माते।

बृद्ध भये सुधि प्रगटी मो को,
दुखित पुकारत ता तें॥

सुतन तज्यो त्रिय भ्रात तज्यो सब,
तन तें तुचा भइ न्यारी।

श्रवन न सुनत चरन गति थाकी,
नैन बहे जल धारी॥

पलित केस कफ कण्ठ अब रूँध्यो,
कल न परै दिन राती।

माया मोह न छाड़ै तृस्ना,
यह दोऊ दुखदाती॥

Bani Surdas Ji

1 abki raakh leho bhagvaan,

2 ham anaath, baithi drum dariyaan,
paardhi saadhyo baan.

3 ta ke dar niksan chaahat haun,
oopar rahyo sachaan;

4 do'u bhaanti dukh bhayo kripaa-nidhi,
kaun ubaarai praan.

5 sumirat hi ahi dasyo paardhi,
laagyo teer sachaan;

6 Surdas gun kahan lag barnaun,
jai jai kripaa-nidhaan.[1]

1 deenaa-naath ab baar tumhaari,

2 patit-udhaaran birad jaani ke,
bigri leho sanvaari.

3 baalaapan khelat hi khoyo,
juba bishai ras maate;

4 briddh bhaye, sudhi pragati mo ko,
dukhit pukaarat ta tein.

5 sutan tajyo triy bhraat tajyo sab,
tan tein tucha bhayi nyaari;

6 sravan na sunat charan gati thaaki,
nain bahe jal dhaari.

7 palit kes kaph kanth ab roondhyo,
kal na parai din raati;

8 maaya moh na chhaarrai trisna,
yah do'u dukhdaati.

Surdas Ji

O Lord, protect me now! 1

Like a helpless bird, I am sitting on the branch of a tree 2
and a hunter has his arrow aimed at me.

Terrified of him, I am anxious to escape, 3
but a deathly hawk hovers above me.

O treasure of mercy, I fear them both – 4
who can save my life?

No sooner than I remembered you, 5
a snake bit the hunter and his arrow hit the hawk.

Says Surdas, how can I describe your virtues – 6
praise to you, O fountainhead of compassion!

O Lord, benefactor of the meek, now it is your turn! 1

Upholding your intrinsic nature as the redeemer of the fallen, 2
please rectify my mistakes.

I squandered my childhood in play, 3
my youth, in sensual pleasures.

With the onset of old age, I have come to my senses, 4
and in distress I implore you.

My sons, wife, brothers and all my kin have forsaken me. 5

My skin has become wrinkled, 6
my ears cannot hear, my gait has slowed
and my eyes water continuously.

My hair has greyed and phlegm clogs my throat; 7
I remain restless day and night.

I can give up neither my desires 8
nor my attachment to this illusory world –
both cause me distress.

अब यह ब्यथा दूर करिबे को,
और न समरथ कोई।

सूरदास प्रभु करुना-सागर,
तुम तें होय सो होई॥

9 ab yah byatha door karibe ko,
aur na samrath koi;

10 Surdas prabhu karuna-saagar,
tum tein hoye so hoi.[2]

मो सम कौन कुटिल खल कामी।
जिन तनु दियो ताहि बिसरायो,
ऐसो निमक-हरामी॥
भरि भरि उदर बिषय को धावों,
जैसे सूकर ग्रामी।
हरि-जन छाड़ हरी-बिमुखन की,
निसि दिन करत गुलामी॥
पापी कौन बड़ो है मो तें,
सब पतितन में नामी।
सूर पतित को ठौर कहाँ है,
सुनिये श्रीपति स्वामी॥

1 mo sam kaun kutil khal kaami,
2 jin tanu diyo taahe bisraayo,
aiso nimak-haraami.
3 bhari bhari udar, bishai ko dhaavon,
jaise sookar graami;
4 hari-jan chhaarr hari-bimukhan ki,
nisi din karat gulaami.
5 paapi kaun barro hai mo tein,
sab patitan mein naami;
6 soor patit ko thaur kahaan hai,
suniye shreepati swaami.[3]

नाथ मोहिं अबकी बेर उबारो॥टेक॥
तुम नाथन के नाथ सुवामी,
दाता नाम तिहारो।
करमहीन जनम को अंधो,
मो तें कौन नकारो॥
तीन लोक के तुम प्रति-पालक,
मैं तो दास तिहारो।
तारी जाति कुजाति प्रभू जी,
मो पर किरपा धारो॥

1 naath mohen abki ber ubaaro. tek.
2 tum naathan ke naath suwaami,
daata naam tihaaro;
karam-heen janam ko andho,
mo tein kaun nakaaro.
3 teen lok ke tum prati-paalak,
main to daas tihaaro;
taari jaati kujaati prabhu ji,
mo par kirpa dhaaro.

Eliminate this suffering now –   *9*
   no one else can do it.
Implores Surdas: you are the ocean of mercy, O Lord;   *10*
   whatever you will – only that comes to pass.

*I*s there anyone as devious, cruel and immoral as me?   *1*
I have even forsaken the one   *2*
   who blessed me with this human form –
   such an ungrateful wretch am I.
Like a village pig, I only fill my stomach   *3*
   and run after sensual pleasures.
Forsaking the devotees of the Lord,   *4*
   I am ever a slave to those who renounce the Lord.
There is no greater sinner than me –   *5*
   among them all I am the most infamous.
O Lord, listen to me –   *6*
   who else would grant refuge to this wretched Surdas?

O Lord, please liberate me this time!   *1*
You are the supreme Lord of all,   *2*
   renowned as the sole benefactor.
I am a wretched sinner, blind since birth –
   who could be more worthless than me?
You are the sustainer of the three realms;*   *3*
   I am but your slave.
You have redeemed all, O Lord, whether lowly or high-born –
   now shower your grace on me.

---

*The **three realms** are the physical, astral and causal worlds below the region of pure spirit.

पतितन में इक नायक कहिये,
नीचन में सरदारो ।
कोटि पापी इक पासँग मेरे,
अजामिल कौन बिचारो ॥
नाठो धरम नाम सुनि मेरो,
नरक कियो हठ तारो ।
मो को ठौर नहीं अब कोऊ,
अपनो बिरद सम्हारो ॥
छुद्र पतित तुम तारे रमापति,
अब न करो जिय गारो ।
सूरदास साचो तब माने,
जो है मम निस्तारो ॥

4   *patitan mein ik naayak kahiye,*
neechan mein sardaaro;
koti paapi ik paasang mere,
ajaamil kaun bichaaro.

5   *naatho dharam naam suni mero,*
narak kiyo hath taaro;
mo ko thaur nahi ab ko'u,
apno birad samhaaro.

6   *chhudr patit tum taare ramaapati,*
ab na karo jiy gaaro;
Surdas saacho tab maane,
jo hvai mam nistaaro.[4]

प्रभु जी मेरे औगुन चित न धरो ।
सम-दरसी है नाम तिहारो,
अब मोहिं पार करो ॥
इक नदिया इक नार कहावत,
मैलो नीर भरो ।
जब दोनों मिलि एक बरन भये,
सुरसरि नाम परो ॥
इक लोहा पूजा में राखत,
इक घर बधिक परो ।
पारस गुन अवगुन नहिं चितवै,
कंचन करत खरो ॥
यह माया भ्रम जाल निवारो,
सूरदास सगरो ।
अबकी बेर मोहिं पार उतारो,
नहिं प्रन जात टरो ॥

1   *prabhu ji mere augun chit na dharo,*
sam-darsi hai naam tihaaro,
ab mohen paar karo.

2   *ik nadiya, ik naar kahaavat,*
mailo neer bharo,
jab dono mili ek baran bhaye,
sursari naam paro.

3   *ik loha pooja mein raakhat,*
ik ghar badhik paro,
paaras gun avgun nahin chitvai,
kanchan karat kharo.

4   *yah maaya bhram jaal nivaaro,*
Surdas sagaro,
abki ber mohen paar utaaro,
nahin pran jaat taro.[5]

---

* **Ajamil** was a brahmin who sinned his whole life but was saved in the end by calling out his son's name, Narayan, which is also a name of the Lord.

Chief among the fallen am I, the leader of wretched sinners;   *4*
   millions of sinners are as nothing compared to me –
   Ajamil pales in comparison.*
At the very mention of my name, goodness flees;   *5*
   even hell adamantly refuses to accept me.
Left with no refuge, I beseech you
   to uphold your intrinsic nature.
O Lord, you have liberated the lowliest and the fallen –   *6*
   do not ruin your reputation now.
Surdas will truly believe in your greatness
   only if you take him across the ocean of existence.

*P*ay no heed to my failings, O Lord,   *1*
   you who are known to be impartial to all;
   ferry me across the ocean of existence this time.
When sewage drains into the river   *2*
   they merge and become one colour
   and are called the River Ganges.
If one piece of iron is placed on an altar of worship   *3*
   and another in a butcher's house,
   the philosopher's stone transforms both into pure gold,†
   not considering their good or bad attributes.
Pleads Surdas: liberate me from this web of delusion;   *4*
   this time ferry me across,
   lest your promise remain unfulfilled.

---

† The mythical **philosopher's stone** was much sought after by alchemists, who believed
it had the power to turn base metals into gold and to grant eternal youth.

प्रभु, मैं पीछौ लियौ तुम्हारौ।
तुम तौ दीनदयाल कहावत,
सकल आपदा टारौ॥
महा कुबुद्धि, कुटिल, अपराधी,
औगुन भरि लियौ भारौ।
सूर कूर की याही बिनती,
लै चरननि मैं डारौ॥

1 prabhu, main peechhau liyau tumhaarau,
tum tau deen-dayaal kahaavat,
sakal aapda taarau.
2 maha kubuddhi, kutil, apraadhi,
augun bhari liyau bhaarau;
soor koor ki yaahi binati,
lai charnani main daarau.[6]

तुम मेरी राखो लाज हरी।
तुम जानत सब अन्तरजामी,
करनी कछु न करी॥
औगुन मोसे बिसरत नाहीं,
पल छिन घरी घरी।
सब प्रपंच की पोट बाँध करि,
अपने सीस धरी॥
दारा सुत धन मोह लिये हौं,
सुधि बुधि सब बिसरी।
सूर पतित को बेग उधारो,
अब मेरी नाव भरी॥

1 tum meri raakho laaj hari,
tum jaanat sab antarjaami,
karni kachhu na kari.
2 augun mose bisrat naahi,
pal chhin ghari ghari;
sab prapanch ki pot baandh kar,
apne sees dhari.
3 daara sut dhan moh liye haun,
sudhi budhi sab bisri;
soor patit ko beg udhaaro,
ab meri naav bhari.[7]

I will follow you, O Lord –   1
    you are known as the benefactor of the meek
    and you prevent all adversities.
I am horribly depraved, devious and sinful,   2
    and am filled with vices.
The deceitful Surdas entreats you, O Lord:
    grant me refuge at your holy feet.

*P*lease uphold my honour, O Lord!   1
O knower of all hearts, you understand everything –
    I have not practised any devotion.
None of the vices can I relinquish;   2
    every moment I indulge in them.
I've gathered all my deceits and frauds –
    I carry the bundle on my head.
So strong are my attachments to wife, son and wealth   3
    they have rendered me completely indiscriminate.
Prays Surdas: now my boat is overloaded with misdeeds –
    O Lord! deliver this fallen one quickly.

बानी गोस्वामी तुलसीदास जी

आपनो कबहुँ करि जानिहौ।	1
राम गरीबनिवाज राजमनि,	2
बिरद-लाज उर आनिहौ॥	
सील-सिंधु, सुंदर, सब लायक,	3
समरथ, सदगुन-खानि हौ।	
पाल्यो है, पालत, पालहुगे प्रभु,	4
प्रनत-प्रेम पहिचानिहौ॥	
बेद-पुरान कहत, जग जानत,	5
दीनदयालु दिन-दानि हौ।	
कहि आवत, बलि जाउँ,	6
मनहुँ मेरी बार बिसारे बानि हौ॥	
आरत-दीन-अनाथनि के हित	7
मानत लौकिक कानि हौ।	
है परिनाम भलो तुलसीको	8
सरनागत-भय-भानि हौ॥	

Bani Goswami Tulsidas Ji

1 *aapno kabahun kari jaanihau,*

2 *raam gareeb-nivaaj raajmani,*
  birad-laaj ur aanihau.

3 *seel-sindhu, sundar, sab laayak,*
  samrath, sadgun-khaani hau;

4 *paalyo hai, paalat, paalhuge prabhu,*
  pranat-prem pahichaanihau.

5 *bed-puraan kahat, jag jaanat,*
  deen-dayaalu din-daani hau;

6 *kahi aavat, bali jaa'oon,*
  manahun meri baar bisaare baani hau.

7 *aarat-deen-anaathani ke hit*
  maanat laukik kaani hau;

8 *hai parinaam bhalo Tulsi ko*
  sarnaagat-bhay-bhaani hau.[1]

दीनबंधु, सुखसिंधु,	1
कृपाकर कारुनीक रघुराई।	
सुनहु नाथ! मन जरत त्रिबिध जुर,	2
करत फिरत बौराई॥	

1 *deen-bandhu, sukh-sindhu,*
  kripa kar kaaruneek raghuraa'i;

2 *sunahu naath! man jarat tribidh jur,*
  karat phirat bauraa'i.

Goswami Tulsidas Ji

When will you consider me to be your own?   1

You are the king of kings,   2
   the benefactor of the meek, O Lord –
   please be true to your reputation.

You are the ocean of compassion,   3
   handsome, supremely worthy, most able,
   the fountainhead of all virtues.

You have nurtured everyone, O Lord,   4
   are still doing so and will continue to do so –
   please recognize my humble love.

The Vedas and Puranas proclaim   5
   what the whole world knows:
   you are ever merciful to the meek
   and are their eternal benefactor.

I sacrifice myself unto you,   6
   but have you forgotten your inherent nature in my case?

O Lord, you are benevolent to the afflicted, meek and helpless –   7
   why would you go by what others say?

As you remove all the fears of your devotees,   8
   Tulsi is confident that the end result will be good.

O companion of the meek, ocean of bliss,   1–2
   O supremely benevolent, ever-merciful
   and sovereign Lord – hear me!

Under the burning influence of the three fevers, O Lord,*
   my wandering mind acts insanely.

---

* Hindu tradition describes **three fevers** or types of suffering arising from (1) conditions within the body or mind, (2) external natural phenomena and (3) supernatural sources.

कबहुँ जोगरत, भोग-निरत
सठ हठ बियोग-बस होई।
कबहुँ मोहबस द्रोह करत बहु,
कबहुँ दया अति सोई॥
कबहुँ दीन, मतिहीन, रंकतर,
कबहुँ भूप अभिमानी।
कबहुँ मूढ़, पंडित बिडंबरत,
कबहुँ धर्मरत ग्यानी॥
कबहुँ देव ! जग धनमय रिपुमय
कबहुँ नारिमय भासै।
संसृति-संनिपात दारुन दुख बिनु
हरि-कृपा न नासै॥
संजम, जप, तप, नेम, धरम,
ब्रत बहु भेषज-समुदाई।
तुलसिदास भव-रोग
रामपद-प्रेम-हीन नहिं जाई॥

3 kabahun jograt, bhog-nirat,
   sath hath, biyog-bas hoi;
4 kabahun moh-bas droh karat bahu,
   kabahun daya ati soi.
5 kabahun deen, matiheen, ranktar,
   kabahun bhoop abhimaani;
6 kabahun moorrh pandit bidambarat,
   kabahun dharmrat gyaani.
7 kabahun dev! jag dhanmay ripumay
   kabahun naarimay bhaasai;
8 sansriti-sanipaat daarun dukh binu
   hari-kripa na naasai.
9 sanjam, jap, tap, nem, dharam,
   brat bahu bheshaj-samudaa'i;
10 Tulsidas bhav-rog
   raampad-prem-heen nahin jaa'i.²

जाऊँ कहाँ तजि चरन तुम्हारे।
काको नाम पतित-पावन जग,
केहि अति दीन पियारे॥

1 jaa'oon kahaan taji charan tumhaare,
2 kaako naam patit-paavan jag,
   kehi ati deen pyaare.

Sometimes occupied with yoga 3
    or engrossed in sensual pleasures,
    sometimes stubbornly engaged in penance,
    my mind is at other times anguished by separation from you.
Sometimes extremely rebellious 4
    under the influence of attachments,
    it is at other times supremely compassionate.
At times forlorn, foolish and utterly wretched, 5
    it is at other times as arrogant as a king.
Sometimes my mind is like a foolish priest 6
    involved in hypocritical ceremonies;
    it is at other times as devout as a wise man
    intent upon righteousness.
O Lord, sometimes my mind dwells on the wealth of the world, 7
    sometimes it is filled with enmity
    and at other times it is involved in sensuality.
The dreadful suffering of births and deaths cannot be ended 8
    without the merciful grace of the Lord.
Self-control, repetition of mantras, penances, 9
    regulations, religious observances and fasts
    are numerous remedies.
But, says Tulsidas, the maladies of existence 10
    cannot be eradicated
    without love for the divine feet of the Lord.

If I left your lotus feet, where could I go? 1
In this world, who else is known 2
    as the redeemer of the fallen,
    and who else loves the meek and the poor?

कौने देव बराइ बिरद-हित,
हठि हठि अधम उधारे।
खग, मृग, ब्याध, पषान,
बिटप जड़, जवन-कवन सुर तारे॥
देव, दनुज, मुनि, नाग, मनुज सब,
माया-बिबस बिचारे।
तिनके हाथ दास तुलसी प्रभु,
कहा अपनपौ हारे॥

3   kaune dev baraa'i birad-hit,
     hathi hathi adham udhaare;
4   khag, mrig, byaadh, pashaan,
     bitap jarr, javan-kavan sur taare.
5   dev, danuj, muni, naag, manuj sab,
     maaya-bibas bichaare;
6   tin ke haath daas Tulsi prabhu,
     kaha apanpau haare.[3]

मैं हरि पतित-पावन सुने।
मैं पतित तुम पतित-पावन
दोउ बानक बने॥
ब्याध गनिका गज अजामिल
साखि निगमनि भने।
और अधम अनेक तारे
जात कापै गने॥
जानि नाम अजानि लीन्हें
नरक सुरपुर मने।
दासतुलसी सरन आयो,
राखिये आपने॥

1   main hari patit-paavan sune,
2   main patit tum patit-paavan
     do'u baanak bane.
3   byaadh ganika gaj ajaamil
     saakhi nigamani bhane.
4   aur adham anek taare
     jaat kaapai gane.
5   jaani naam ajaani leenhe
     narak surpur mane.
6   daas Tulsi saran aayo,
     raakhiye aapne.[4]

---

* In the Indian tradition, different stories tell how all of these were saved by the mercy of the Lord.

† The **hunter** may refer to Valmiki, the author of the Ramayana, who confessed that he had been a hunter and highway robber in his early life. **Ganika** was a prostitute who attained liberation through the practice of the Lord's Name. **Gajraj** was an elephant who cried out to the Lord and was saved from a crocodile's attack, and **Ajamil** a brahmin who sinned

Who else upholds his honourable reputation   3
   for redeeming even the most stubborn
   and hardened sinners?
What other god has saved the bird, the deer,   4
   the hunter, the stone, the inert tree
   and even the barbarian?*
Gods, demons, ascetics, celestial serpents and human beings –   5
   all are helpless under the influence of illusion.
O Lord, why should Tulsi, your slave, lose himself to them?   6

I have heard that the Lord liberates the fallen –   1–2
   I have sinned and you are the liberator of the sinners;
   both our roles are well-matched.
The scriptures give testimony that the hunter, Ganika,   3–4
   Gajraj, Ajamil and many other ignoble ones†
   were liberated by you – who can count them all?
Those who practised devotion to Nam –   5
   attentively or with scattered mind –
   were refused entry in both the heavens and the hells.‡
Your slave Tulsi has come to you for refuge, O Lord;   6
   please grant him your protection.

---

his whole life and was saved in the end by calling out his son's name, Narayan, which is also a name of the Lord.

‡ Goswami Tulsidas is trying to explain that for those who take the Lord's Nam, the doors to the heavens and the hells are closed because they are released from the cycle of transmigration and the only door open to them is the door to liberation.

मोहि मूढ़ मन बहुत बिगोयो।
याकें लिये सुनहु करुनामय,
मैं जग जनमि-जनमि दुख रोयो॥

1 mohe moorrh man bahut bigoyo.
yaake liye sunahu karunaamay,
main jag janam-janam dukh royo.

सीतल मधुर पियूष सहज सुख
निकटहि रहत दूरि जनु खोयो।
बहु भाँतिन स्रम करत मोहबस,
बृथहि मंदमति बारि बिलोयो॥

2 seetal madhur piyoosh sahaj sukh
nikatahi rahat doori janu khoyo;
bahu bhaantin sram karat mohbas,
brithahi mand-mati baari biloyo.

करम-कीच जिय जानि, सानि चित,
चाहत कुटिल मलहि मल धोयो।
तृषावंत सुरसरि बिहाय सठ
फिरि-फिरि बिकल अकास निचोयो॥

3 karam-keech jiy jaani, saani chit,
chaahat kutil malahi mal dhoyo;
trishaavant sursari bihaaye sath
phiri-phiri bikal akaas nichoyo.

तुलसिदास प्रभु! कृपा करहु अब,
मैं निज दोष कछू नहिं गोयो।
डासत ही गइ बीति निसा सब,
कबहुँ न नाथ! नींद भरि सोयो॥

4 Tulsidas prabhu! kripa karahu ab,
main nij dosh kachhu nahin goyo;
daasat hi gayi beeti nisa sab,
kabahun na naath! neend bhari soyo.[5]

राम कबहुँ प्रिय लागिहौ
जैसे नीर मीनको?
सुख जीवन ज्यों जीवको,
मनि ज्यों फनिको हित,
ज्यौं धन लोभ-लीनको॥

1 raam kabahun priy laagihau
jaisai neer meen ko?

2 sukh jeevan jyon jeev ko,
mani jyon phaniko hit,
jyaun dhan lobh-leen ko.

---

* A metaphor for longing for liberation (being thirsty) but refusing to engage in the spiritual practice that would result in liberation (drinking the water of the Ganges).

This foolish mind has thoroughly deluded me –   *1*
    please listen to me, O merciful Lord.
I have been born again and again in this world
    and have suffered untold miseries.
Although the tranquil sweet nectar of eternal bliss   *2*
    was ever so near, I lost opportunity after opportunity
    assuming that the bliss was far, far away.
Under the sway of attachments,
    I toiled hard in futile endeavours,
    my foolish mind churning water in vain.
Although I knew in my heart that karmas were filth   *3*
    and my devious mind was dirtied by them,
    I still tried washing filth with filth.
I was thirsty, yet ignoring the holy water of the river Ganges,*
    I have wandered about in despair;
    like a fool, I have tried to wring water from air.
Have mercy on me now, O Lord, says Tulsidas –   *4*
    I have not hidden any of my faults from you
    and have passed the entire night lying in bed
    without catching a moment's sleep.

O Lord, when will you become   *1*
    as dear to me as water is to fish?
Just as a happy life is dear to all creatures,   *2–3*
    treasure is dear to the snake,†
    and wealth is dear to the one obsessed with greed,

---

† Poisonous snakes were used to guard treasure. It was believed that they had been greedy when in human form and thus were placed amidst wealth in the body of a snake to satisfy that longing for wealth.

ज्यों सुभाय प्रिय लगति नागरी
नागर नवीनको।
त्यों मेरे मन लालसा
करिये करुनाकर!
पावन प्रेम पीनको॥
मनसाको दाता कहैं
श्रुति प्रभु प्रबीनको।
तुलसिदासको भावतो,
बलि जाउँ दयानिधि!
दीजै दान दीनको॥

3 jyon subhaaye priy lagti naagri
naagar naveen ko,
tyon mere man laalsa
kariye karunaakar!
paavan prem peen ko.

4 mansa ko daata kahain
shruti prabhu prabeen ko,
Tulsidas ko bhaavto,
bali jaa'un dayaa-nidhi!
deejai daan deen ko.[6]

तू दयालु, दीन हौं,
तू दानि, हौं भिखारी।
हौं प्रसिद्ध पातकी,
तू पाप-पुंज-हारी॥
नाथ तू अनाथको,
अनाथ कौन मोसो।
मो समान आरत नहिं
आरतिहर तोसो॥
ब्रह्म तू, हौं जीव,
तू है ठाकुर, हौं चेरो।
तात–मात, गुरु-सखा तू
सब बिधि हितु मेरो॥
तोहिं मोहिं नाते अनेक,
मानियै जौ भावै।
ज्यों त्यों तुलसी कृपालु!
चरन–सरन पावै॥

1 tu dayaalu, deen haun,
tu daani, haun bhikhaari;

2 haun prasiddh paatki,
tu paap-punj-haari.

3 naath tu anaath ko,
anaath kaun moso;

4 mo samaan aarat nahin
aaratihar toso.

5 brahm tu, haun jeev,
tu hai thaakur, haun chero;

6 taat-maat, guru-sakha tu
sab bidhi hitu mero.

7 tohen mohen naate anek,
maaniyai jau bhaavai;

8 jyon tyon Tulsi kripaalu!
charan-saran paavai.[7]

and just as an intelligent young woman is naturally loved
by an intelligent young man,
similarly, O compassionate Lord,
please create an intense desire in my mind for the love divine.
Almighty Lord, the Vedas call you the bestower   4
of the heart's desires.
O ocean of mercy, I sacrifice myself to you –
you are so dear to Tulsidas,
please grant your slave his heart's desire.

You are merciful and I am destitute, O Lord;   1
you are the generous giver and I am a beggar.
I am the most infamous sinner   2
and you are the destroyer of all sins.
You are the guardian of orphans   3
and there is no orphan like me.
There is no one more miserable than me   4
and there is no better destroyer of misery than you.
You are the Lord and I am the soul,   5
you are the Master and I am your disciple.
You are my father, mother, teacher and friend –   6
you are my only benefactor in every way.
You and I are related in many ways –   7–8
accept the relationship that pleases you,
so that by any means, O Compassionate One,
Tulsi may gain the shelter of your lotus feet.

तुम सम दीनबंधु,
न दीन कोउ मो सम,
सुनहु नृपति रघुराई।
मोसम कुटिल-मौलिमनि नहिं जग,
तुम सम हरि! न हरन कुटिलाई॥
हौं मन-वचन-कर्म पातक-रत,
तुम कृपालु पतितन-गतिदाई।
हौं अनाथ, प्रभु! तुम अनाथ-हित,
चित यहि सुरति कबहुँ नहिं जाई॥
हौं आरत, आरति-नासक तुम,
कीरति निगम पुराननि गाई।
हौं सभीत तुम हरन सकल भय,
कारन कवन कृपा बिसराई॥
तुम सुखधाम राम श्रम-भंजन,
हौं अति दुखित त्रिबिध श्रम पाई।
यह जिय जानि दास तुलसी कहँ
राखहु सरन समुझि प्रभुताई॥

1   *tum sam deen-bandhu,*
    na deen ko'u mo sam,
    sunahu nripati raghuraa'i;
2   *mosam kutil-maulimani nahin jag,*
    tum sam hari! na haran kutilaa'i.
3   *haun man-vachan-karm paatak-rat,*
    tum kripaalu patitan-gatidaa'i;
4   *haun anaath, prabhu! tum anaath-hit,*
    chit yahi surati kabahun nahin jaa'i.
5   *haun aarat, aarati-naasak tum,*
    keerati nigam puraanani gaa'i;
6   *haun sabheet tum haran sakal bhay,*
    kaaran kavan kripa bisraa'i.
7   *tum sukh-dhaam raam shram-bhanjan,*
    haun ati dukhit tribidh shram paa'i;
8   *yah jiy jaani daas Tulsi kahan*
    raakho saran samujhi prabhutaa'i.[8]

तुम तजि हौं कासों कहौं,
और को हितु मेरे?
दीनबंधु! सेवक, सखा, आरत,
अनाथपर सहज छोह केहि केरे॥
बहुत पतित भवनिधि तरे
बिनु तरि, बिनु बेरे।

1   *tum taji haun kaason kahaun,*
    aur ko hitu mere?
2   *deen bandhu! sevak, sakha, aarat,*
    anaathpar sahaj chhoh kehi kere.
3   *bahut patit bhavnidhi tare*
    binu tari, binu bere;

There is no other friend of the lowly like you –   1
   hear me, O sovereign Lord!

There is no one more lowly, deceitful and wicked than me,   2
   and there is no one like you, who can eliminate all deceit.

In thought, word and deed, I am immersed in sin,   3
   while you, O merciful Lord, grant salvation to sinners.

I am an orphan, O Lord, and the thought   4
   that you are the benefactor of all orphans
   never leaves my mind.

I am miserable and you eradicate all misery;   5
   the Vedas and Puranas have also sung your glory.

I am fearful and you eliminate all fears, O Lord –   6
   why have you forgotten to shower your mercy on me?

I am tormented by the three sufferings[*]   7
   and you are the fountainhead of bliss,
   the destroyer of all hardships.

Understanding this in my heart, your slave Tulsi pleads: 8
   O Lord, uphold your glory and keep me under your shelter.

You alone are my benefactor –   1
   except you, to whom shall I tell all?

O companion of the poor, who else is affectionate   2
   to devotees and friends, to orphans and the downtrodden?

Even without a boat or a raft,   3
   you have ferried many fallen souls
   across the ocean of existence.

---

[*] Hindu tradition describes three types of suffering arising from (1) conditions within the body or mind, (2) external natural phenomena and (3) supernatural sources.

कृपा-कोप-सतिभायहू,
धोखेहु-तिरछेहू,
राम! तिहारेहि हेरे ॥

जो चितवनि सौंधी लगै,
चितइये सबेरे ।

तुलसिदास अपनाइये, कीजै न ढील,
अब जिवन-अवधिअति नेरे॥

4 kripa-kop-sati-bhaayahu,
dhokhehu-tirchhehu,
raam! tihaarehi here.

5 jo chitvani saundhi lagai,
chita'iye sabere;

6 Tulsidas apnaa'iye, keejai na dheel,
ab jivan-avadhi ati nere.[9]

यह बिनती रघुबीर गुसाई।
और आस-बिस्वास-भरोसो,
हरो जीव-जड़ताई॥

चहौं न सुगति,
सुमति, संपति कछु,
रिधि-सिधि बिपुल बड़ाई।

हेतु-रहित अनुराग राम-पद
बढ़ै अनुदिन अधिकाई॥

कुटिल करम लै जाहिं मोहि
जहँ जहँ अपनी बरिआई ।

तहँ तहँ जनि
छिन छोह छाँड़ियो,
कमठ-अंडकी नाई ॥

या जगमें जहँ लगि या तनु की
प्रीति प्रतीति सगाई।

ते सब तुलसिदास प्रभु ही सों
होहिं सिमिटि इक ठाई॥

1 yah binati raghubeer gusaa'een,
aur aas-bisvaas-bharoso,
haro jeev-jarrtaa'i.

2 chahaun na sugati,
sumati, sampati kachhu,
ridhi-sidhi bipul barraa'i;

3 hetu-rahit anuraag raam-pad
barrhai anudin adhikaa'i.

4 kutil karam lai jaahen mohe
jahan jahan apni bariyaa'i;

5 tahan tahan jani
chhin chhoh chhaanrriyo,
kamath-andaki naa'een.

6 ya jag mein jahan lagi ya tanu ki
preet prateet sagaa'i.

7 te sab Tulsidas prabhu hi son
hohin simiti ik thaa'een.[10]

You can bestow salvation with just a merciful,   4
    angry, amiable or even oblique glance, O Lord!
Please hurry and bestow on me the look that pleases you.   5–6
Accept Tulsidas as your very own
    and do not delay, as the end of my life is drawing near.

This is my supplication to you, O compassionate Lord: 1
    banish the foolishness of this soul
    who places hope, belief and trust in others.
I have no desire for a heavenly state,   2
    nor for wisdom, wealth, widespread fame
    or supernatural powers and attainments.
I only wish that my selfless love for the Lord's holy feet   3
    may greatly increase day by day.
Wherever my evil karmas may forcibly drag me,   4–5
    from there also do not withdraw your love for me,
    even for a moment,
    just as a turtle never takes its attention from its eggs.
Tulsidas prays that as long as this body   6–7
    has attachments of love and faith in this world,
    may all of them be centred only in you, O Lord.

बानी सन्त दादू दयाल जी

Bani Sant Dadu Dayal Ji

अजहुँ न निकसै प्राण कठोर॥ टेक॥ 1   *ajahun na niksai praan kathor. tek.*

दरसन बिना बहुत दिन बीते, 2   *darsan bina bahut din beete,*
सुन्दर प्रीतम मोर॥   *sundar preetam mor.*

चारि पहर चारौं जुग बीते, 3   *chaari pahar chaaraun jug beete,*
रैन गँवाई भोर॥   *rain ganvaa'i bhor.*

अवधि गई अजहूँ नहिं आये, 4   *avadhi gayi ajahoon nahin aaye,*
कतहुँ रहे चित चोर॥   *katahun rahe chit chor.*

कबहूँ नैन निरखि नहिं देखे, 5   *kabahoon nain nirakhi nahin dekhe,*
मारग चितवत तोर॥   *maarag chitvat tor.*

दादू ऐसे आतुर बिरहणि, 6   *Dadu aise aatur birhani,*
जैसे चंद चकोर॥   *jaise chand chakor.*[1]

दरबार तुम्हारे दरदवंद, 1   *darbaar tumhaare daradvand,*
पिव पीव पुकारै।   *piv peev pukaarai;*

दीदार दरूनै दीजिये, 2   *deedaar daroonai deejiye,*
सुनि खसम हमारे॥ टेक॥   *suni khasam hamaare. tek.*

तनहा केतनि पीर है, 3   *tanha ketani peer hai,*
सुनि तुँहीं निवारै।   *suni toonhi nivaaarai;*

करम करीमा कीजिये, 4   *karam kareema keejiye,*
मिलि पीव पियारे॥   *mili peev pyaare.*

सूल सुलाकौं सौ सहूँ, 5   *sool sulaakaun sau sahoon,*
तेग तन मारै।   *teg tan maarai.*

मिलि साई सुख दीजिये, 6   *mili saa'een sukh deejiye,*
तूँहीं तुँ सँभारै॥   *toonhi tun sambhaarai.*

---

[*] The night was divided into **four watches** because a city guard could not stand watch all night.

Sant Dadu Dayal Ji

This cruel breath still has not ceased!   *1*

My glorious Beloved,   *2*
   many days have passed without your darshan.

The four watches of the night*   *3*
   have passed like the four yugas;
   thus was the night spent until dawn.

The promised time has passed and yet you have not come;   *4*
   you have stolen my heart – where are you now?

My eyes have not caught a glimpse of you   *5*
   for such a long time, yet I keep gazing your way.

Says Dadu: this lovelorn devotee pines for you in separation   *6*
   just as a moonbird yearns for the moon.†

I stand in your court with pain in my heart,   *1–2*
   loudly imploring you, my Beloved:
   listen to me, my Lord – reveal yourself within me.

I am lonely without you and filled with agony;   *3*
   hear me – only you can alleviate my suffering.

O merciful Lord, shower your compassion on me;   *4*
   my beloved Lord, meet me.

I have been stricken by the sword of separation;   *5*
   hundreds of wounds do I endure in agony.

Please meet me, O Lord, and bestow happiness –   *6*
   you alone can take care of me.

---

† The **moonbird** is a legendary bird that is in love with the moon. It watches the moon with such absorption that as the moon moves across the sky the moonbird keeps bending its head backwards until it touches its tail.

मैं सुहदा तन सोखता,
बिरहा दुख जारै।
जिव तरसै दीदार कूँ,
दादू न बिसारै॥

7 *main suhda tan sokhta,*
birha dukh jaarai;

8 *jiv tarsai deedaar koon,*
Dadu na bisaarai.[2]

हमारे तुमहीं हौ रखपाल।
तुम बिन और नहीं कोइ मेरे,
भौ दुख मेटणहार॥ टेक॥

1 *hamaare tumhi hau rakhpaal,*
tum bin aur nahi koi mere,
bhau dukh metanhaar. tek.

बैरी पंच निमख नहिं न्यारे,
रोकि रहे जम काल।

2 *bairi panch, nimash nahin nyaare,*
roki rahe jam kaal;

हा जगदीस दास दुख पावै,
स्वामी करो सँभाल॥

3 *ha jagdees daas dukh paavai,*
swaami karo sambhaal.

तुम बिन राम दहैं ये दुंदर,
दसौं दिसा सब साल।

4 *tum bin raam dahain ye dundar,*
dasaun disa sab saal;

देखत दीन दुखी क्यों कीजे,
तुम हौ दीनदयाल॥

5 *dekhat deen dukhi kyon keeje,*
tum hau deen-dayaal.

निर्भय नाँव हेत हरि दीजे,
दरसन परसन लाल।

6 *nirbhay naanv het hari deeje,*
darsan parsan laal.

दादू दीन लीन करि लीजै,
मेटहु सबै जँजाल॥

7 *Dadu deen leen kari leejai,*
metoh sabai janjaal.[3]

क्यों बिसरै मेरा पीव पियारा,
जीव की जीवन प्राण हमारा॥ टेक॥

1 *kyaun bisrai mera peev pyaara,*
jeev ki jeevan praan hamaara. tek.

क्यौंकर जीवै मीन जल बिछुरें,
तुम बिन प्राण सनेही।

2 *kyaun-kar jeevai meen jal bichhuren,*
tum bin praan sanehi;

च्यंतामणि जब कर थें छूटै,
तब दुख पावै देही॥

3 *chyantaamani jab kar thein chhootai,*
tab dukh paavai dehi.

I am a hermit; my body is worn out   7
   and scorched by the fire of separation from my Beloved.
Pleads Dadu: my heart pines for a glimpse of you –   8
   O Lord, do not forsake me.

You alone are my protector, O Lord!   1
Except you, I have no one else
   who can eliminate my suffering in this illusory world.
There is no respite, even for a moment, from the five enemies,   2
   and the lord of death has trapped me.
O Lord of the universe, your slave is gravely tormented –   3
   take me under your care, O Lord.
Without you, O Lord, these tormentors have set me ablaze,   4
   and misery surrounds me from all directions.
You are compassionate to the meek, O Lord –   5
   seeing me in agony, how can you let me suffer?
O Lord, give me your love and your Nam;   6
   by the practice of Nam I shall become fearless
   and attain your blissful darshan.
Merge poor Dadu with yourself, O Lord,   7
   and sever all entanglements.

My beloved Lord is the vital breath of my life,   1
   my very being – why has he forgotten me?
I cannot live without you, O beloved of my heart –   2
   how can a fish live out of water?
If a priceless gem slips out of one's hand,   3
   one is bound to be distressed.

माता बालक दूध न देवै,
सो कैसें करि पीवै।
निर्धन का धन अनत भुलाना,
सो कैसें करि जीवै॥
बरखहु राम सदा सुख अमृत,
नीझर निर्मल धारा।
प्रेम पियाला भरि भरि दीजै,
दादू दास तुम्हारा॥

4 maata baalak doodh na devai,
so kaisein kari peevai;
5 nirdhan ka dhan anat bhulaana,
so kaisein kari jeevai.
6 barkho raam sada sukh amrit,
neejhar nirmal dhaara;
7 prem piyaala bhar bhar deejai,
Dadu daas tumhaara. [4]

मेरे गृह आवहो गुर मेरा,
मैं बालिक सेवग तेरा॥ टेक॥
मात पिता तूं अम्हंचा स्वांमी,
देव हमारै अंतरजांमी॥
अम्हां सजण अम्हंचा बंधू,
प्राण हमारै अम्हंचा ज्यंदू॥
अम्हंचा प्रीतम अम्हंचा मेला,
अम्हंची जीविन आप अकेला॥
अम्हंचा साथी संग सनेही,
राम बिना दुख दादू देही॥

1 mere grih aavho gur mera,
main baalik sevag tera. tek.
2 maat pita toon amhancha swaami,
dev hamaarai antarjaami.
3 amhaan sajan amhancha bandhu,
praan hamaarai amhancha jyandu.
4 amhancha preetam amhancha mela,
amhanchi jeevin aap akela.
5 amhancha saathi sang sanehi,
raam bina dukh Dadu dehi. [5]

पार नहिं पाइये रे राम बिना
को निरबाहणहार॥ टेक॥
तुम बिन तारण को नहीं,
दूभर यहु संसार।
पैरत थाके केसवा,
सूझै वार न पार॥
बिषम भयानक भौजला,
तुम बिन भारी होइ।

1 paar nahin paa'iye re raam bina
ko nirbaahan-haar. tek.
2 tum bin taaran ko nahi,
doobhar yahu sansaar;
3 pairat thaake kesava,
soojhai vaar na paar.
4 bisham bhayaanak bhaujala,
tum bin bhaari hoi;

If a mother does not nurse her child,   4
  how can he drink her milk?
If a pauper's money is lost somewhere,   5
  how can he survive?
O Lord, shower me with the divine nectar of eternal bliss,   6
  which is like a constant flow of pure spring water.
Give me the cup brimming with your love,   7
  begs Dadu, your slave.

O Master, reveal yourself within my heart;   1
  I am a child and remain your devoted servant.
O Master, you are my mother and father;   2
  you are all-knowing, O Lord.
You are my friend and my brother;   3
  you are my life-breath, the bestower of my life.
You are my beloved and my companion;   4
  you alone exist in my life.
You are my confidant and my near and dear one;   5
  without you, O Lord, Dadu is in agony.

One cannot attain liberation without the Lord;   1
  there is no other benefactor besides him.
Except you, there is no liberator;   2
  formidable is this ocean of existence.
O Lord, swimming in this ocean has exhausted me   3
  and there is no shore in sight, on this side or the other.
Rough and dreadful indeed is this ocean of existence;   4
  crossing it is impossible without you.

तूँ हरि तारण केसवा,
दूजा नाहीं कोइ॥
तुम बिन खेवट को नहीं,
अतिर तिर्यो नहिं जाइ।
औघट भेरा डूबि है,
नाहीं आन उपाइ॥
यहु घट औघट बिषम है,
डूबत माहिं सरीर।
दादू काइर राम बिन,
मन नहिं बाँधै धीर॥

5   toon hari taaran kesava,
     dooja naahi koi.
6   tum bin khevat ko nahi,
     atir tiryo nahin jaa'i;
7   aughat bhera doobi hai,
     naahi aan upaa'i.
8   yahu ghat aughat bisham hai,
     doobat maahen sareer;
9   Dadu kaayar raam bin,
     man nahin baandhai dheer.[6]

राम कृपा करि होहु दयाला।
दरसन देहु करो प्रतिपाला॥
बालक दूध न देई माता।
तौ वै क्यूँ करि जिवै बिधाता॥
गुण औगुण हरि कुछ न बिचारै।
अंतरि हेत प्रीति करि पालै॥
अपनौ जानि करै प्रतिपाला।
नैन निकटि उर धरै गोपाला॥
दादू कहै नहीं बस मेरा।
तूँ माता मैं बालक तेरा॥

1   raam kripa kari hohu dayaala,
     darsan dehu karo pratipaala.
2   baalak doodh na deyi maata,
     tau vai kyoon kari jivai bidhaata.
3   gun augun hari kuchh na bichaarai,
     antari het preet kari paalai.
4   apnau jaani karai pratipaala,
     nain nikati ur dharai gopaala.
5   Dadu kahai nahi bas mera,
     toon maata main baalak tera.[7]

You, O Lord, are our saviour;   5
   except you, there is no one else.
There is no boatman besides you –   6–7
   I do not know how to swim,
   my boat is sinking and there is no other remedy.
This ocean of existence is overflowing with difficulties   8
   and I am drowning in it.
Dadu is afraid without the Lord   9
   because the mind does not stay steadfast.

Be merciful, O Lord, and bestow your grace;   1
   grant me your darshan; give me my sustenance!
If a mother does not give milk to her child,   2
   then, almighty Creator, how can he survive?
The Lord does not judge our merits and faults;   3
   he nurtures us from within through his affection and love.
Considering me to be his own,   4
   the Lord protects and sustains me
   and keeps me within his sight and in his heart.
Says Dadu: nothing is under my control;   5
   you are my mother and I am your child.

दोहे

तिल तिल का अपराधी तेरा,
रती रती का चोर।
पल पल का मैं गुनही तेरा,
बकसौ औगुण मोर॥

गुनहगार अपराधी तेरा,
भाजि कहाँ हम जाहिं।
दादू देख्या सोधि सब,
तुम बिन कहिं न समाहिं॥

आदि अंत लौं आइ करि,
सुकिरत कछू न कीन्ह।
माया मोह मद मंछरा,
स्वाद सबै चित दीन्ह॥

दादू बन्दीवान है,
तू बन्दीछोड़ दिवान।
अब जिनि राखौ बन्दि में,
मीराँ मेहरबान॥

राखणहारा राख तूँ,
यहु मन मेरा राखि।
तुम बिन दूजा को नहीं,
साधू बोलैं साखि॥

माया बिषय बिकार थैं,
मेरा मन भागै।
सोई कीजै साइयाँ,
तूँ मीठा लागै॥

Dohe

1 til til ka apraadhi tera,
rati rati ka chor;
2 pal pal ka main gunhi tera,
baksau augun mor.

1 gunah-gaar apraadhi tera,
bhaaji kahaan ham jaahen;
2 Dadu dekhya sodhi sab,
tum bin kahin na samaahen.

1 aadi ant laun aaye kari,
sukirat kachhu na keenh;
2 maaya moh mad manchhara,
svaad sabai chit deenh.

1 Dadu bandeevaan hai,
tu bandee-chhorr divaan;
2 ab jini raakhau bandi mein,
meeraan meharbaan.

1 raakhan-haara raakh toon,
yahu man mera raakhi;
2 tum bin dooja ko nahi,
saadhu bolain saakhi.

1 maaya bishai bikaar thain,
mera man bhaagai;
2 soi keejai saa'iyaan,
toon meetha laagai.

Dohas

I am a sinner to the core of my being;   *1*
  every pore of my body is your culprit.
Each and every moment I continue to sin against you –   *2*
  O Lord, please forgive my sins.

I am your transgressor and your sinner –   *1*
  where can I escape?
Dadu has searched everywhere;   *2*
  except you, O Lord, there is no other refuge.

From the very beginning to the end,   *1*
  I have not performed any virtuous deed.
Maya, attachment, ego, pride   *2*
  and sense pleasures have ensnared my mind.

Dadu is a prisoner   *1*
  and you are the warden who can liberate him.
O compassionate Lord,   *2*
  do not keep him imprisoned!

O Protector, take me under your shelter;   *1*
  please safeguard my mind.
Except you there is no other refuge;   *2*
  the Saints affirm this truth.

May my mind turn away   *1*
  from illusory attachments, passions and vices.
Execute your will in such a way, O Lord,   *2*
  that I may desire only you.

ज्यौं आपै देखै आप कौं,
सो नैना दे मुझ।
मीराँ मेरा मेहर करि,
दादू देखै तुझ॥

1 jyaun aapai dekhai aap kaun,
so naina de mujh;
2 meeraan mera mehar kari,
Dadu dekhai tujh.

(दादू कहै)
दिन दिन नौतम भगति दे,
दिन दिन नौतम नाँव।
दिन दिन नौतम नेह दे,
मैं बलिहारी जाँव॥

1 (Dadu kahai)
din din nautam bhagti de,
din din nautam naanv;
2 din din nautam neh de,
main balihaari jaanv.

साईं सत संतोष दे,
भाव भगति बेसास।
सिदक सबूरी साच दे,
माँगै दादूदास॥

1 saa'een sat santosh de,
bhaav bhagti besaas;
2 sidak saboori saach de,
maangai dadu-daas.

(दादू) पलक माहिं प्रगटै सही,
जे जन करै पुकार।
दीन दुखी तब देखि करि,
अति आतुर तिहिं बार॥

1 (dadu) palak maahen pragtai sahi,
je jan karai pukaar;
2 deen dukhi tab dekhi kari,
ati aatur tihin baar.

आगै पीछै सँगि रहै,
आप उठाये भार।
साध दुखी तब हरि दुखी,
ऐसा सिरजनहार॥

1 aagai peechhai sangi rahai,
aap uthaaye bhaar;
2 saadh dukhi tab hari dukhi,
aisa sirjan-haar.

Grant me the eyes   *1–2*
　　that are capable of beholding your vision,
　　and shower such grace on me, my Lord,
　　that Dadu may see you within.

Says Dadu: bless me every day with renewed devotion,   *1–2*
　　every day with renewed love for Nam
　　and every day with renewed love for all;
　　O Lord, I sacrifice myself unto you.

O Master, your slave Dadu begs   *1–2*
　　for true contentment, love, devotion and faith,
　　as well as steadfast fortitude,
　　unwavering patience and truth.

When a devotee cries for the Lord, says Dadu,   *1*
　　he reveals himself in an instant.
When he sees his humble devotee in anguish,   *2*
　　he too becomes distressed.

He is always with me,   *1*
　　sometimes ahead of me and sometimes behind me,
　　and he himself carries my burden.
So compassionate is the Creator   *2*
　　that when the devotee is unhappy
　　the Lord is also distressed.

समरथ सिरजनहार है,
जे कुछ करै सो होइ।
दादू सेवग राखि ले,
काल न लागै कोइ॥

1   *samrath sirjan-haar hai,*
    je kuchh karai so hoye;
2   *Dadu sevag raakhi le,*
    kaal na laagai koye.

साईं साचा नाँव दे,
काल झाल मिटि जाइ।
दादू निरभै है रहै,
कबहूँ काल न खाइ॥

1   *saa'een saacha naanv de,*
    kaal jhaal miti jaaye;
2   *Dadu nirbhai hvai rahai,*
    kabahoon kaal na khaaye.

जिन की रख्या तूँ करै,
ते उबरे करतार।
जे तैं छाडे हाथ थैं,
ते डूबे संसार॥

1   *jin ki rakhya toon karai,*
    te ubare kartaar;
2   *je tain chhaade haath thain,*
    te doobe sansaar.

राखणहारा एक तूँ,
मारणहार अनेक।
दादू के दूजा नहीं,
तूँ आपै ही देख॥

1   *raakhan-haara ek toon,*
    maaran-haar anek;
2   *Dadu ke dooja nahi,*
    toon aapai hi dekh.

जहँ तहँ बिषै बिकार थैं,
तुम ही राखणहार।
तन मन तुम कौं सौंपिया,
साचा सिरजनहार॥

1   *jahan tahan bishai bikaar thain,*
    tum hi raakhan-haar;
2   *tan man tum kaun saunpiya,*
    saacha sirjan-haar.

All-powerful is the Creator;   *1*
    whatever he wills, only that comes to pass.
Says Dadu: the Lord keeps the devotee under his protection;   *2*
    near the devotee the lord of death cannot venture.[*]

O Lord, grant me the true Nam,   *1*
    so that all the fires of Kal may be extinguished.
Then Dadu will become fearless   *2*
    and Kal can never devour him.

O Lord, only the ones you protect   *1*
    are ferried across.
If you let go of their hand,   *2*
    they will drown in the ocean of existence.

You alone are the saviour, O Lord,   *1*
    while many are the tormentors.
Except you, Dadu has no one else –   *2*
    you yourself take care of him.

Wherever vices and passions prevailed,   *1*
    there you were the only saviour.
You are the true creator;   *2*
    I surrender my body and mind to you.

---

[*] Dadu is not saying that the devotee will not die, but rather that he will not be accountable to the lord of death as he is now under the protection of the merciful Lord.

अंतरजामी एक तूँ,
आतम के आधार।
जे तुम छाडहु हाथ थैं,
तौ कौण सँबाहणहार॥

1   *antarjaami ek toon,*
      aatam ke aadhaar;
2   *je tum chhaadoh haath thain,*
      tau kaun sambaahan-haar.

तुम्ह हौ तैसी कीजिये,
तौ छूटैंगे जीव।
हम हैं ऐसी जिनि करौ,
मैं सदिकै जाऊँ पीव॥

1   *tumh hau taisi keejiye,*
      tau chhootainge jeev;
2   *ham hain aisi jini karau,*
      main sadikai jaa'oon peev.

अनाथौं का आसिरा,
निरधाराँ आधार।
निर्धन का धन राम है,
दादू सिरजनहार॥

1   *anaathaun ka aasira,*
      nirdhaaraan aadhaar;
2   *nirdhan ka dhan raam hai,*
      Dadu sirjan-haar.

साहिब दर दादू खड़ा,
निसि दिन करै पुकार।
मीराँ मेरा मिहर करि,
साहिब दे दीदार॥

1   *saahib dar Dadu kharra,*
      nisi din karai pukaar;
2   *meeraan mera mehar kari,*
      saahib de deedaar.

तुम हीं थैं तुम्ह कूँ मिलै,
एक पलक में आइ।
हम थैं कबहुँ न होइगा,
कोटि कलप जे जाहिं॥

1   *tum heen thain tumh koon milai,*
      ek palak mein aaye;
2   *ham thain kabahun na hoyga,*
      koti kalap je jaahen.

साहिब सूँ मिलि खेलते,
होता प्रेम सनेह।
दादू प्रेम सनेह बिन,
खरी दुहेली देह॥

1   *saahib soon mili khelte,*
      hota prem saneh;
2   *Dadu prem saneh bin,*
      khari duheli deh.

You know the secrets of all hearts   *1*
  and are the support of my soul.
If you let go of my hand,   *2*
  who will take care of me?

Only if you act in accordance with what you are   *1*
  can souls be liberated.
Do not judge me by my actions, O Beloved –   *2*
  I sacrifice my life unto you.

The Lord himself is the refuge of orphans   *1*
  and support of the helpless.
O Dadu, the all-pervading Creator himself   *2*
  is the wealth of the poor.

Dadu stands at the Lord's door,   *1*
  imploring him day and night.
O Beloved, have mercy on me;   *2*
  grant me your darshan, O Lord.

Only by your grace shall I be able to meet you;   *1*
  if you so will, it shall be within an instant.
This could never be accomplished by me alone,   *2*
  even in millions of aeons.

If only I had love and devotion,   *1*
  I would meet the Lord and revel in his presence.
Lack of love and devotion for him, says Dadu,   *2*
  causes immense suffering.

साहिब सूँ मिलि खेलते,
होता प्रेम सनेह।
परगट दरसन देखते,
दादू सुखिया देह॥

तुम कूँ भावै और कुछ,
हम कुछ कीया और।
मिहर करो तौ छूटिये,
नहीं त नाहीं ठौर॥

मुझ भावै सो मैं किया,
तुझ भावै सो नाहिं।
दादू गुनहगार है,
मैं देख्या मन माहिं॥

खुसी तुम्हारी त्यूँ करौ,
हम तौ मानी हारि।
भावै बंदा बकसिये,
भावै गहि करि मारि॥

1 saahib soon mili khelte,
   hota prem saneh;
2 pargat darsan dekhte,
   Dadu sukhiya deh.

1 tum koon bhaavai aur kuchh,
   ham kuchh keeya aur;
2 mehar karo tau chhootiye,
   nahi ta naahi thaur.

1 mujh bhaavai so main kiya,
   tujh bhaavai so naahen;
2 Dadu gunahgaar hai,
   main dekhya man maahen.

1 khusi tumhaari tyoon karau,
   ham tau maani haar;
2 bhaavai banda baksiye,
   bhaavai gahi kari maar.[8]

If only I had nurtured love and devotion for the Lord,　　　*1*
　　I would have met him and revelled in his presence.
I would have had his true vision, says Dadu,　　　*2*
　　and enjoyed the bliss of meeting him.

You are pleased with something,　　　*1*
　　but my actions have been totally contrary to your liking.
I shall attain liberation only if you shower your grace;　　　*2*
　　otherwise, I have no refuge.

I did whatever I pleased　　　*1*
　　rather than what would please you.
When I looked within, says Dadu,　　　*2*
　　I realized that I was the culprit.

Do whatever pleases you, O Lord –　　　*1*
　　I have accepted defeat.
Forgive me if it so pleases you,　　　*2*
　　or else catch hold of me and use the stick.

बानी जगजीवन साहिब जी

आरति अरज लेहु सुनि मोरी।
चरनन लागि रहै दृढ़ डोरी॥

कबहुँ निकट तें टारहु नाहीं।
राखहु मोहिं चरन की छाहीं॥

दीजै केतिक बास यहाँ कीजै।
अघ कर्म मेटि सरन करि लीजै॥

दासन दास है कहौं पुकारी।
गुन मोहिं नहिं तुम लेहु सँवारी॥

जगजीवन काँ आस तुम्हारी।
तुम्हरी छबि मूरति पर वारी॥

अब तुम होहु दयाल
तुम्हारी पैयाँ परौं॥ टेक॥

सूझत नहिं
मैं भ्रमत फिरत हौं,
पर्यो मोह के जाल॥

नाम तुम्हार सुमिरि नहिं आवै,
जग संगति जंजाल॥

आवत जब सुधि वहै समय की,
ब्याकुल होहुँ बेहाल॥

हाथ पाँव मेरे बल नाहीं है,
तुमहिं करहु प्रतिपाल॥

जगजीवन काँ दरसन दीजै,
अब मोहिं करहु निहाल॥

Bani Jagjivan Sahib Ji

1 *aarati araj lehu suni mori,*
charnan laagi rahai drirrh dori.

2 *kabahun nikat tein taarahu naahi,*
raakoh mohen charan ki chhaaheen.

3 *deejai ketik baas yahan keejai,*
agh karm meti saran kari leejai.

4 *daasan daas hvai kahaun pukaari,*
gun mohen nahin tum lehu sanvaari.

5 *Jagjivan kaan aas tumhaari,*
tumhri chhabi moorati par vaari.[1]

1 *ab tum hohu dayaal*
tumhaari paiyaan paraun. tek.

2 *soojhat nahin*
main bhramat phirat haun,
paryo moh ke jaal.

3 *naam tumhaar sumiri nahin aavai,*
jag sangati janjaal.

4 *aavat jab sudhi vahai samay ki,*
byaakul hohun behaal.

5 *haath paanv mere bal naahi hai,*
tumhin karahu pratipaal.

6 *Jagjivan kaan darsan deejai,*
ab mohen karahu nihaal.[2]

Jagjivan Sahib Ji

Listen to my prayer and supplication, O Master;　　　*1*
　let me be attached firmly to your lotus feet.
Never send me away from your presence;　　　*2*
　keep me under the shelter of your divine feet.
Let me stay in your refuge by any means;　　　*3*
　erase my countless sins and keep me under your protection.
This slave of slaves implores you:　　　*4*
　I have no merits, O Lord – adorn me with virtues.
Says Jagjivan: you are my only hope;　　　*5*
　I sacrifice everything to your resplendent form.

I bow at your feet – be merciful to me now.　　　*1*
I am caught in the web of attachments –　　　*2*
　as I wander about in delusion, I cannot think clearly.
Trapped in worldly associations,　　　*3*
　I forget to do simran of your Nam.
When realization of the time lost dawns on me,　　　*4*
　I become distressed and miserable.
There is no strength in my hands and feet –　　　*5*
　take me under your protection, O Lord!
Bestow your darshan on Jagjivan　　　*6*
　and grant me eternal bliss.

बालक बुद्धि हीन मति मोरी।
भरमत फिरौं नाहिं दृढ़ डोरी॥

सूरति राखौ चरनन मोरी।
लागि रहै कबहूँ नहिं तोरी॥

निरखत रहौं जाउँ बलिहारी।
दास जानि कै नाहिं बिसारी॥

तुमहिं सिखाय पढ़ायो ज्ञाना।
तब मैं धर्यौं
चरन का ध्याना॥

साई समरथ तुम हौ मोरे।
बिनती करौं ठाढ़ कर जोरे॥

अब दयाल ह्वे दाया कीजै।
अपने जन कहँ दरसन दीजै॥

नाम तुम्हार मोहिं है प्यारा।
सोई भजे घट भा उजियारा॥

जगजीवन चरनन दियो माथ।
साहब समरथ करहु सनाथ॥

1 baalak buddhi heen mati mori,
bharmat phiraun naahin drirrh dori.

2 soorati raakhau charnan mori,
laagi rahai kabahoon nahin tori.

3 nirkhat rahaun jaa'un balihaari,
daas jaani kai naahin bisaari.

4 tumhin sikhaaye parrhaayo gyaana,
tab main dharyaun
charan ka dhyaana.

5 saa'een samrath tum hau more,
binati karaun thaarrh kar jore.

6 ab dayaal hve daaya keejai,
apne jan kahan darsan deejai.

7 naam tumhaar mohen hai pyaara,
soi bhaje ghat bha ujiyaara.

8 Jagjivan charnan diyo maath,
saahab samrath karahu sanaath. [3]

हम तें चूक परत बहुतेरी।
मैं तौ दास अहौं चरनन का,
हम हूँ तन हरि हेरी॥

बाल-ज्ञान प्रभु अहै हमारा,
झूठ साँच बहुतेरी।
सो औगुन गुन का कहौं तुम तें,
भौसागर तें निबेरी॥

1 hum tein chook parat bahuteri,

2 main tau daas ahaun charnan ka,
hum hoon tan hari heri.

3 baal-gyaan prabhu ahai hamaara,
jhooth saanch bahuteri;

4 so augun gun ka kahaun tum tein,
bhausaagar tein niberi.

I have an immature mind and my thoughts are base; 1
 I wander about in delusion
 since my attachment to you is not strong, O Master.
Keep my attention focused on your feet, 2
 keep it always firm and never wavering.
Let my gaze remain fixed on you – 3
 I would sacrifice myself for you.
Consider me as your slave, O Master,
 and do not ever forget me.
It was you who taught me and guided me 4
 to the attainment of true knowledge;
 thus I contemplate on your lotus feet.
O most able Master, you are mine; 5
 I stand before you pleading with folded hands.
O Merciful One, show compassion now; 6
 bless your devotee with your darshan.
Your Nam is dear to me; 7
 when I meditate on it, my heart is filled with radiance.
Jagjivan has placed his head at your feet, O Master; 8
 now keep me under your care.

O Lord, I have committed countless misdeeds! 1
I am but a slave at your lotus feet – 2
 bless me with your merciful glance.
I have an immature sense of judgment, 3
 predisposed towards lies and deceit.
I have innumerable vices and no virtues – 4–5
 what can I say to you about myself?

भव तें भागि आयौं तुव सरनै,
कहत अहौं अस टेरी।
जगजीवन की बिनती सुनिये,
राखौ पत जन केरी॥

5 bhav tein bhaagi aayaun tuv sarnai,
   kahat ahaun as teri;
6 Jagjivan ki binati suniye,
   raakhau pat jan keri.[4]

केतिक बूझ का आरति करऊँ।
जैसे रखिहहिं तैसे रहऊँ॥
नाहीं कछु बसि आहै मोरी।
हाथ तुम्हारे आहै डोरी॥
जस चाहौ तस नाच नचावहु।
ज्ञान बास करि ध्यान लगावहु॥
तुमहिं जपत तुमहिं बिसरावत।
तुमहिं चेताइ सरन लै आवत॥
दूसर कवन एक हौ सोई।
जेहिं काँ चाहौ भक्त सो होई॥
जगजीवन करि बिनय सुनावै।
साहेब समरथ नहिं बिसरावै॥

1 ketik boojh ka aarati kara'oon,
   jaise rakhahin taise raha'oon.
2 naahi kachhu bas aahai mori,
   haath tamhaare aahai dori.
3 jas chaahau tas naach nachaavahu,
   gyaan baas kari dhyaan lagaavahu.
4 tumhin japat tumhin bisraavat,
   tumhin chetaa'e saran lai aavat.
5 doosar kavan ek hau soi,
   jehin kaan chaahau bhakt so hoi.
6 Jagjivan kari binay sunaavai,
   saaheb samrath nahin bisraavai.[5]

मेरे गुनाह
माफ करिये अब साईं॥ टेक॥
जैसे मातु सुतहिं पालत
छीर दै पियाई।
लिये गोद रहै निसु दिन
कबहुँ ना घिनाई॥
रहै सुखित दुक्ख नाहिं
कर ते ले उठाई।

1 mere gunaah
   maaf kariye ab saa'een. tek.
2 jaise maatu sutahin paalat
   chheer dai piyaa'i,
   liye god rahai nisu din
   kabahun na ghinaa'i.
3 rahai sukhit dukkh naahin
   kar te le uthaa'i,

O Lord, liberate me from this ocean of existence –
   fleeing from this world, I have come to you for refuge.
I implore you, listen to Jagjivan's plea: 6
   uphold the honour of your devotee.

I shall remain however you keep me, O Lord,   *1*
   but my understanding is limited –
   how can I worship you?
Nothing is under my control;   2
   the strings of my destiny are in your hands.
Make me dance however you please;   3
   you impart the wisdom that inspires me to meditate.
You are the one who motivates me to remember you   4
   and you are the one who makes me forget you.
It is you alone who makes me aware of you
   and brings me back to your refuge.
Besides you there is no other;   5
   whoever you are pleased with becomes your devotee.
Jagjivan beseeches you with utmost humility: 6
   never let me forget you, almighty Lord.

O Master, forgive my sins now!   *1*
See how a mother nurtures her child –   *2–3*
   she gives him milk, keeps him content
   in her lap day and night and never neglects the child;
   she picks him up at the first sign of distress,
   embraces him, kisses his face, cheers him and makes him laugh.

कंठ लावै मुक्ख चूमै
हुलसि के हँसाई॥

सुतहिं दुक्ख दुखित मातु
कछु ना सुहाई।

इहै मोर बिनती जानु
राखु ऐसी नाई॥

पतित अनेक तारि लीन्हे
गनत ना सिराई।

मेटि औगुन छिनक माहिं
लयो है अपनाई॥

सुने ते बिस्वास आवत
बेद सब्द गाई।

सूझि सत मत परा जबहीं
दियो तबहिं लखाई॥

बुद्धि केतनि अहै मोहिं माँ
करौं का कबिताई।

जगजीवन का करहु आपन
चरनन में लिपटाई॥

kanth laavai mukkh choomai
hulasi ke hansaa'i;
4 sutahin dukkh dukhit maatu
kachhu na suhaa'i,
ihai mor binati jaanu
raakhu aisi naa'een.
5 patit anek taari leenhe
ganat na siraa'i,
meti augun chhinak maahen
layo hai apnaa'i.
6 sune te bisvaas aavat
bed sabd gaa'i,
soojhi sat mat para jabaheen
diyo tabahin lakhaa'i.
7 buddhi ketani ahai mohen maan
karaun ka kabitaa'i,
Jagjivan ka karahu aapan
charnan mein liptaa'i.[6]

मेरी बिनय सुनिये राम।
भरमत हौं दिन रात छिन छिन,
कैसे सुमिरौं नाम॥

महा अहै अपार माया,
मोह सुख परि काम।

छूटि गे सत टूटि डोरी,
लागि हित धन धाम॥

मेटु सर्ब गुनाह मेरे,
पाप कर्म हराम।

जगजीवन काँ जानु आपन,
चरन केर गुलाम॥

1 meri binay suniye raam,
bharmat haun din raat chhin chhin,
kaise sumiraun naam.
2 maha ahai apaar maaya,
moh sukh pari kaam;
chhooti ge sat tooti dori,
laagi hit dhan dhaam.
3 metu sarb gunaah mere,
paap karm haraam;
Jagjivan kaan jaanu aapan,
charan ker gulaam.[7]

If the child is unhappy, so is the mother,   4
   and nothing pleases her.
Cherish me in the same manner, O Lord: that is my plea.
You have redeemed countless fallen ones,   5
   erasing their sins in an instant –
   you have accepted them as your own.
Even the Vedas extol the glory of Shabd;   6
   on hearing it, my mind gained faith.
Only when you revealed Shabd
  did true comprehension dawn on me.
What intellect do I possess,   7
   what poetry can I write in your praise?
Considering Jagjivan as your very own,
   grant him refuge at your feet, O Master!

Listen to my supplication, O Lord!   1
Deluded as I am every moment of the day and night,
   how can I do your simran?
Enormous and endless is the web of illusion,   2
   causing attachment to worldly pleasures and desires.
As I became attached to wealth and possessions,
   Truth was forsaken and the bond was broken.
O Lord, erase all my vices   3
   and all my sinful and disgraceful deeds.
Considering Jagjivan as your own,
   grant him refuge at your feet as a slave.

मेरी हाथ तुम्हारै डोरी॥टेक॥

है केतनि मति बुद्धि हीन है।
नहिं कछु अहै बूझ मति मोरी॥

मन कठोर आभाव भाव नहिं।
करौं कपट भ्रमि भटकौं चोरी॥

निसु बासर छिन छिन बिसरत है।
नहिं निरखि जात छबि तोरी॥

राखहु पास बिस्वास देहु बर,
बिनय कहौं कर जोरी।

जगजीवन चित चरनन दीन्हे,
रहै सीस कर जोरी॥

1 meri haath tumhaarai dori. tek.
2 hai ketani mati buddhi heen hai,
nahin kachhu ahai boojh mati mori.
3 man kathor aabhaav bhaav nahin,
karaun kapat bhram bhatkaun chori.
4 nisu baasar chhin chhin bisrat hai,
nahin nirakhi jaat chhabi tori.
5 raakhahu paas bisvaas dehu bar,
binay kahaun kar jori;
6 Jagjivan chit charnan deenhe,
rahai sees kar jori.[8]

प्रभु जी बक्सहु चूकि हमारी।
जो पुरबुज अपने कर्मन ते,
डार्यो सर्ब मिटा री॥

राखहु पास सदा चरनन के,
निकट ते नहीं टारी।

जानत रहहु सदाँ हित आपन,
कबहूँ नाहिं बिसारी॥

पाँच पचीस बड़े परपंची,
यइ डारत संसारी।

येई पल छिन छिनहिं भ्रमावत,
नाहीं लागु हमारी॥

अब मन लागि पागि रह तुम ते,
सूरति रहै न न्यारी।

जगजीवन को भक्ति बर दीजै,
जुग जुग आस तुम्हारी॥

1 prabhu ji baksoh chooki hamaari,
2 jo purbuj apne karman te,
daaryo sarb mita ri.
3 raakhahu paas sada charnan ke,
nikat te nahi taari;
4 jaanat rahahu sada hit aapan,
kabahoon naahi bisaari.
5 paanch pachees barre parpanchi,
ya'i daarat sansaari;
6 ye'i pal chhin chhin-hi bhramaavat,
naahi laagu hamaari.
7 ab man laagi paagi rah tum te,
soorati rahai na nyaari;
8 Jagjivan ko bhakti bar deejai,
jug jug aas tumhaari.[9]

The string of my destiny is in your hands, O Lord!   1

Of what use is my intellect when I lack wisdom   2
    and my mind has no sense of discernment?

My mind wanders about in delusion –   3
    callous, deceitful, culpable,
    devoid of feelings and without empathy.

Every moment, day and night, it continues to forget you   4
    and does not contemplate upon your form.

With folded hands I entreat you, O Lord: 5
    keep me near you and grant me the boon of faith.

Jagjivan has entrusted his heart to your lotus feet   6
    and with folded hands he bows before you.

O Lord, forgive all my omissions   1–2
    and erase all the karmas of my past births.

Keep me near your lotus feet forever   3
    and do not distance yourself from me.

Always consider me as your loved one   4
    and do not ever forget me.

The five vices and twenty-five tendencies*   5
    are extremely devious and lure me towards the world.

Every moment they delude me;   6
    I cannot control them.

May this mind remain absorbed   7
    in devotion to your lotus feet
    and may your divine form never part from me.

For ages you have been my only hope, O Lord –   8
    grant the boon of your devotion to Jagjivan.

---

* In Hindu metaphysics, interactions among the **five vices** or passions – lust, anger, greed, attachment and pride or ego – produce **twenty-five tendencies** in the human being.

प्रभु जी तुम जानत गति मेरी।

तुम ते छिपा नहीं आहै कछु,

कहा कहौं मैं टेरी॥

जहँ जहँ गाढ़ परयो

भक्तन कां,

तहँ तहँ कीन्ह्यो फेरी।

गाढ़ मिटाय तुरन्तहि डारयो,

दीन्ह्यो सुक्ख घनेरी॥

जुग जुग होत ऐसै चलि आवा,

सो अब साँझ सबेरी।

दियो जनाय सोई तस जानै,

बास मनहिं तेहि केरी॥

कर औ सीस दियो चरनन महँ,

नहिं अब पाछे हेरी।

जगजीवन के सतगुरु साहब,

आदि अंत तेहि केरी॥

प्रभु तुम सों मन लागा मोरा।

नेग जन्म के कर्म काटो,

माँगौं दरसन तोरा॥

मोहि ते तौ कछु कहि नहिं आवै,

मैं पापी हौं चोरा।

निसु दिन तुम कहँ सुमिरत राहौं,

इतना मानु निहोरा॥

यह अरदास मानि ले साई

तनिक देखिये कोरा।

जगजीवन काँ जानु आपना,

तोरु प्रीत नहिं डोरा॥

1 *prabhu ji tum jaanat gati meri,*

2 *tum te chhipa nahi aahai kachhu,*
  kaha kahaun main teri.

3 *jahan jahan gaarrh paryo*
  bhaktan kaan,
  tahan tahan keenhyo pheri;

4 *gaarrh mitaaye turant-hi daaryo,*
  deenhyo sukkh ghaneri.

5 *jug jug hot aisai chali aava,*
  so ab saanjh saberi;

6 *diyo janaaye soi tas jaanai,*
  baas manhin tehi keri.

7 *kar au sees diyo charnan mahan,*
  nahin ab paachhe heri;

8 *Jagjivan ke satguru saahab,*
  aadi ant tehi keri.[10]

1 *prabhu tum son man laaga mora,*

2 *neg janam ke karm kaato,*
  maangaun darsan tora.

3 *mohen te tau kachhu kahi nahin aavai,*
  main paapi haun chora;

4 *nisu din tum kahan sumirat raahaun,*
  itna maanu nihora.

5 *yah ardaas maani le saa'een,*
  tanik dekhiye kora;

6 *Jagjivan ka jaanu aapna,*
  toru preet nahin dora.[11]

O Lord, you know my condition!   *1*

Nothing is hidden from you – what can I tell you?   *2*

Wherever your devotees faced any adversity,   *3*
   you made your appearance there.

You immediately removed their suffering,   *4*
   bestowing untold happiness upon them.

This has continued for time without end;   *5*
   this time also turn my dusk into dawn.

Only the ones you bless with awareness   *6*
   realize that you reside in their hearts.

I have completely surrendered myself at your feet   *7*
   and now there is no turning back.

O Jagjivan's Satguru, from the beginning until the very end   *8*
   I remain only yours.

Lord, my mind is in love with you!   *1*

Cut the karmic bonds of my countless births –   *2*
   I beg for your darshan.

I know not what to say to you;   *3*
   a sinner and a culprit am I.

I beseech you to accept my plea   *4*
   that I may remain absorbed in your simran day and night.

O Lord, accept this ignorant one's plea;   *5*
   bless me with your merciful glance.

Considering Jagjivan as your own,   *6*
   do not break this bond of love.

साई मैं अजान अज्ञाना।
जानों नहीं बूझि नहिं आवै
भरमत फिरौं भुलाना॥
हौ समरत्थ सिद्धि के दाता
मोहिं सिखावहु ज्ञाना।
करौं सों जानि जनाय देव जब
धरौं चरन कै ध्याना॥
दीन लीन सुभ सुमन सुमारग
यह बर दीजै दाना।
आवै दृष्टि दिप्त देखत रहौं
परगट करौं बयाना॥
काहूँ रहौं सरन नहिं छूटै
तुम तजि भजौं न आना।
जगजीवन कर जोरि कहैं
यह निरखत रहौं निरबाना॥

1 saa'een main ajaan agyaana,
2 jaano nahi boojhi nahin aavai
  bharmat phiraun bhulaana.
3 hau samratth siddhi ke daata
  mohen sikhaavahu gyaana,
4 karaun son jaani janaaye dev jab
  dharaun charan kai dhyaana.
5 deen leen subh suman sumaarag
  yah bar deejai daana,
6 aavai drishti dipt dekhat rahaun
  pargat karaun bayaana.
7 kaahoon rahaun saran nahin chhootai
  tum taji bhajaun na aana,
8 Jagjivan kar jori kahain
  yah nirkhat rahaun nirbaana.[12]

साँई मोहि भरोस तुम्हारा।
मोरे बस नहिं अहै एकौ,
तुमहिं करो निस्तारा॥
मैं अज्ञान बुद्धि है नाहीं,
का करि सकौं बिचारा।
जब तुम लेत पढ़ाय सिखावत,
तब मैं प्रगट पुकारा॥
बहुतक भवसागर महँ बूड़त,
तेहि उबारि कै तारा।
बहु तन का जब कष्ट भयो है,
तिन कै कष्ट निवारा॥
अब तौ चरन कि सरनहिं आयों,
गह्यों मैं पच्छ तुम्हारा।
जगजीवन के साँई समरथ,
मोहि बल अहै तुम्हारा॥

1 saa'een mohe bharos tumhaara,
2 more bas nahin ahai ekau,
  tumahin karo nistaara.
3 main agyaan buddhi hai naahi,
  ka kari sakaun bichaara;
4 jab tum let parrhaaye sikhaavat,
  tab main pragat pukaara.
5 bahutak bhavsaagar mahan boorrat,
  tehi ubaari kai taara.
6 bahu tan ka jab kasht bhayo hai,
  tin kai kasht nivaara.
7 ab tau charan ki saran-hin aayon,
  gahyon main pacchh tumhaara;
8 Jagjivan ke saa'een samrath,
  mohe bal ahai tumhaara.[13]

O Lord, I am foolish and ignorant! 1

Knowing nothing, understanding nothing, 2
   I wander about lost in delusion.

You, O Lord, are truly able; you bestow all powers – 3
   reveal the true knowledge to me.

Only when you so will it shall I obtain understanding 4
   and be able to contemplate on your lotus feet.

Grant me the boon that this humble disciple 5
   may remain absorbed in this divine, blissful and true path.

May I attain your blessed darshan 6
   and, gazing at your Radiant Form, sing your glory.

Wherever I may be, may I never leave your refuge 7
   or devote myself to anyone but you.

O Master, with folded hands Jagjivan implores you: 8
   may he always behold your Radiant Form –
   the vision that grants salvation.

*L*ord, I have faith in you! 1

Nothing is under my control; 2
   only you can liberate me.

I am ignorant, bereft of intellect – 3
   how can I think at all?

Only when you taught me and guided me 4
   was I able to meditate on you.

You have saved and liberated many 5–6
   who were drowning in the ocean of existence
   and have eradicated the suffering of
   many others afflicted with pain.

Now I have taken refuge at your feet; 7
   I will abide only by your side.

O Lord of Jagjivan, you are truly almighty; 8
   you are my only strength!

तेरा नाम सुमिरि ना जाय।

नहीं बस कछु मोर आहै,

करहुँ कौन उपाय॥

जबहिं चाहत हितू करि कै,

लेत चरनन लाय।

बिसरि जब मन जात आहै,

देत सब बिसराय॥

अजब ख्याल अपार लीला,

अंत काहु न पाय।

जीव जंत पतंग जग महँ,

काहु ना बिलगाय॥

करौं बिनती जोरि दुउ कर,

कहत अहौं सुनाय।

जगजीवन गुरु चरन सरनं,

है तुम्हार कहाय॥

1   *tera naam sumiri na jaaye,*

nahi bas kachhu mor aahai,

karahun kaun upaaye.

2   *jabahin chaahat hitu kari kai,*

let charnan laaye;

bisari jab man jaat aahai,

det sab bisaraaye.

3   *ajab khyaal apaar leela,*

ant kaahu na paaye;

jeev jant patang jag mahan,

kaahu na bilgaaye.

4   *karaun binati jori do'u kar,*

kahat ahaun sunaaye;

Jagjivan guru charan sarnan,

hvai tumhaar kahaaye.[14]

तुम सों यह मन लागा मोरा।

करौं अरदास इतनी सुनि लीजै,

तको तनक मोहिं कोरा॥

कहँ लगि औगुन कहौं आपना,

कामी कुटिल औ लोभी चोरा।

तब के अब के बहु गुनाह भे,

नाहिं अंत कछु छोरा॥

साँईं अब गुनाह सब मेटहु,

चितै आपनी ओरा।

जगजीवन कै इतनी बिनती,

टूटै प्रीति न डोरा॥

1   *tum son yah man laaga mora,*

2   *karaun ardaas itni suni leejai,*

tako tanak mohen kora.

3   *kahan lagi augun kahaun aapna,*

kaami kutil au lobhi chora;

4   *tab ke ab ke bahu gunaah bhe,*

naahin ant kachhu chhora.

5   *saa'een ab gunaah sab metahu,*

chitai aapni ora;

6   *Jagjivan kai itni binati,*

tootai preet na dora.[15]

I am unable to do the simran of your Nam 1
   and nothing is under my control – what can I do?
Whenever you shower your grace on someone, 2
   you draw him to your feet, and when anyone forgets you,
   it is you who makes him do so.
Amazing is your will and boundless your creation; 3
   this no one can fathom, since none in this world –
   human, animal or insect – is free from illusion.
Hear my plea, O Master – I pray with folded hands; 4
   Jagjivan has taken refuge at your feet;
   he is known now to be yours alone.

This mind of mine has become devoted to you! 1
I beseech you, please hear my plea: 2
   favour this ignorant being with just one merciful glance.
I cannot begin to enumerate my faults; 3
   I am lustful, devious, greedy and thieving.
Over time I have committed countless sins; 4
   there is no end to them.
O Lord, erase all my sins now 5
   and turn my attention towards you.
Says Jagjivan: this is my only plea – 6
   do not ever break this bond of love.

बानी पलटू साहिब जी

Bani Paltu Sahib Ji

आरति राम गरीब-निवाजा,
तीनि लोक सब के सिरताजा॥ टेक॥

तुम्हरो पतित-पावनो बाना,
मैं तो पतित आपु सो जाना॥

नाम तुम्हारो अधम उधारा,
सब अधमन को मैं सिरदारा॥

नाम तुम्हारो दीन दयाला,
इहै जानि मैं लीन्हा माला॥

सुनेउ अनाथन के तुम नाथा,
यह सुनि आइ पसारेउ हाथा॥

नाँव तुम्हारो अंतरजामी,
पलटुदास क्या कहै अपानी॥

1   *aarati raam gareeb-nivaaja,*
    teeni lok sab ke sirtaaja. tek.

2   *tumhro patit paavno baana,*
    main to patit aapu so jaana.

3   *naam tumhaaro adham udhaara,*
    sab adhman ko main sirdaara.

4   *naam tumhaaro deen dayaala,*
    ihai jaani main leenha maala.

5   *sune'u anaathan ke tum naatha,*
    yah suni aaye pasaareo haatha.

6   *naanv tumhaaro antarjaami,*
    Paltudaas kya kahai apaani.[1]

पतितपावन बाना धर्यो
तुमहिं परी है लाज॥

तुमहिं परी है लाज
बात यह हम ने बूझी।

जब तुम बाना धर्यो
नाहिं तब तुम कहँ सूझी॥

अब तो तारे बनै
नहीं तो बाना उतारौ।

फिर काहे को बड़ा बाच
जो कहिकै हारौ॥

आगहिं तुम गये चूक
दोष नहिं दीजै मेरो।

तुम यह जानत नाहिं
पतित होइहैं बहुतेरो॥

1   *patit-paavan baana dharyo*
    tumahin pari hai laaj.

2   *tumahin pari hai laaj*
    baat yah ham ne boojhi,

3   *jab tum baana dharyo*
    naahin tab tum kahan soojhi.

4   *ab to taare banai*
    nahi to baana utaarau,

5   *phir kaahe ko barra baach*
    jo kahikai haarau.

6   *aagahin tum gaye chook*
    dosh nahin deejai mero,

7   *tum yah jaanat naahin*
    patit hoi-hain bahutero.

Paltu Sahib Ji

I worship you, O Lord, the saviour of the meek; 1
  you are the sovereign ruler of the three worlds.*

Your intrinsic nature is to redeem sinners, 2
  and you know that I am a sinner.

You are called redeemer of the fallen, 3
  and I am the lowest among them.

You are portrayed as merciful to the meek; 4
  knowing this, I have taken up the rosary of Nam.

Hearing that you are the protector of the destitute, 5
  I have come to you, begging with outstretched hands.

You are all-knowing, O Lord – 6
  what could slave Paltu possibly tell you about himself?

You have taken on the garb of redeemer of the fallen, 1
  and now your honour lies in fulfilling this responsibility.

I have realized that you have no choice 2–3
  but to uphold your honour –
  did this not occur to you
  when you accepted this responsibility?

You have no choice: liberate me now 4
  or forsake your claim of being a redeemer!

Why do you offer these grand promises 5
  if you do not intend to fulfil them?

You have already made the mistake; now do not blame me – 6–7
  did you not know I have countless sins in my account?

---

* The **three worlds** are the physical, astral and causal worlds below the region of pure spirit.

पलटू मैं तो पतित हौं
किये असुभ सब काज।
पतितपावन बाना धर्यो
तुमहिं परी है लाज॥

8 Paltu main to patit haun
kiye asubh sab kaaj,

9 patit-paavan baana dharyo
tumahin pari hai laaj.²

साहिब मेरा सब कुछ तेरा,
अब नाहीं कुछ मेरा है॥
यहि हमता ममता के कारन,
चौरासी किहा फेरा है॥
मृग-जल निरखि के तृषा बुझै नहिं,
सूखे अटका बेरा है॥
यह संसार रैन का सुपना,
रूपा भ्रम सीपी केरा है॥
पलटुदास सब अरपन कीन्हा,
तन मन धन औ देरा है॥

1 saahib mera sab kuchh tera,
ab naahi kuchh mera hai.

2 yahi hamta mamta ke kaaran,
chauraasi kiha phera hai.

3 mrig-jal nirakhi ke trisha bujhai nahin,
sookhe atka bera hai.

4 yah sansaar rain ka supna,
roopa bhram seepi kera hai.

5 Paltudaas sab arpan keenha,
tan man dhan au dera hai.³

तुम तजि दीना-नाथ जी,
करै कौन की आस।
पलटू जो दूसर करै,
तो होइ दास की हाँस॥
ना मैं किया न करि सकौं,
साहिब करता मोर।
करत करावत आपु है,
पलटू पलटू सोर॥
पलटू तेरी साहिबी,
जीव न पावै दुक्ख।
अदल होय बैकुंठ में,
सब कोइ पावै सुक्ख॥

1 tum taji deena-naath ji,
karai kaun ki aas;

2 Paltu jo doosar karai,
to hoi daas ki haans.

3 na main keeya na kari sakaun,
saahib karta mor;

4 karat karaavat aapu hai,
Paltu Paltu sor.

5 Paltu teri saahibi,
jeev na paavai dukkh;

6 adal hoye baikunth mein,
sab koi paavai sukkh.⁴

Says Paltu: I am an abject sinner 8
  and all my actions have been despicable.
You have taken on the garb of redeemer of the fallen; 9
  now your honour lies in saving me.

O Lord, whatever was mine is yours; 1
  there is nothing at all that is mine now.
It is because of ego and attachments 2
  that the wheel of eighty-four continues to spin.*
Thirst cannot be quenched by merely looking at a mirage; 3
  my boat has run aground and is stranded.
This world is like a dream in the night, 4
  and wealth, just like worthless seashells, is only an illusion.
Paltu Das has surrendered his all – 5
  body, mind, wealth and property – to you, O Lord!

If I were to forsake you, O benefactor of the meek, 1
  who else could I turn to?
If Paltu, your slave, turns to others, he would be ridiculed! 2
I have not accomplished anything, 3
  nor am I capable of doing so;
  my Lord alone accomplishes all.
He is the doer and he himself gets everything done, 4
  yet Paltu is the one who receives all the praise!
Says Paltu: under your patronage one suffers no pain; 5–6
  the rule of justice in your court
  is such that everyone attains peace.

---

* The **wheel of eighty-four** is the cycle of 8,400,000 life forms into which souls keep reincarnating.

बानी दरिया साहिब जी (बिहारवाले)

Bani Dariya Sahib Ji (Bihaar waale)

साहब मैं गुलाम हौं तेरा।	1 saahab main gulaam haun tera,
लिखि लीजे एह कागज कोरे	2 likhi leeje eh kaagaj kore
जनम जनम का चेरा॥	janam janam ka chera.
जैसे पूत कपूत जो होवै	3 jaise poot kapoot jo hovai
पिता करै प्रतिपाला।	pita karai pratipaala,
बहुत प्रेम मोद मन भरि के	4 bahut prem mod man bhari ke
नजरन्हि कीन्ह निहाला ॥...	najaranhi keenh nihaala.
जिवके गुन ऐगुन जनि खोजियै	5 jivke gun aigun jani khojiyai
ऐसी रहनि न आई।	aisi rahani na aa'i.
ऊठत बैठत नाम तुम्हारा	6 oothat baithat naam tumhaara
सरन सरन गोहराई॥	saran saran gohraa'i.
एही अरज सुनो सरवन में	7 ehi araj suno sarvan mein
हंस बिगोइ न जाई।	hans bigoi na jaa'i.
कहें दरिया ले नाम तुम्हारा	8 kahen Dariya le naam tumhaara
मुक्ति सदा फल पाई॥	mukti sada phal paa'i.[1]

तुम मेरो साईं मैं तेरो दास,	1 tum mero saa'een main tero daas,
चरन कँवल चित मेरो बास॥	charan kanval chit mero baas.
पल पल सुमिरौं नाम सुबास,	2 pal pal sumiraun naam subaas,
जीवन जग में देखो दास॥	jeevan jag mein dekho daas.
जल में कुमुदिनि चन्द अकास,	3 jal mein kumudini chand akaas,
छाइ रहा छबि पुहुप बिलास॥	chhaa'i raha chhabi puhup bilaas.
उनमुनि गगन भया परगास,	4 unmuni gagan bhaya pargaas,
कह दरिया मेटा जम त्रास॥	kah Dariya meta jam traas.[2]

Dariya Sahib Ji of Bihar

I am your slave, O Master!   *1*
Write on a blank piece of paper   *2*
  that I will be your slave for countless births.
Just as a father protects and nurtures even his wayward son   *3–5*
  and, with a heart filled with love and delight,
  watches out for his happiness,
  so also, look not to my virtues and vices –
  my conduct is not worthy of you.
Sitting or standing, I always remember your Nam   *6*
  and humbly plead and beg for your refuge.
Kindly lend an ear to this humble request: *7*
  please do not let my soul miss this opportunity.
Says Dariya: he on whom your Nam is bestowed   *8*
  always reaps the fruit of salvation.

You are my Master and I am your slave;   *1*
  your lotus feet are enshrined in my heart.
Every moment I repeat your blissful Nam –   *2*
  throughout my life in this world
  may I always be known as your slave.
Just as the lotus in the water blooms   *3–4*
  while enveloped by the moon's radiance,
  so also, says Dariya,
  is the inner sky illumined during deep meditation
  and the fear of death dispelled.

बानी सन्त चरनदास जी

Bani Sant Charandas Ji

अब जग फंद छुटावो जी
हौं तो चरण कमल को चेरो।
परो रहूँ दरबार तिहारे
संतन माहिं बसेरो॥

1 ab jag phand chhutaavo ji
haun to charan kamal ko chero,
paro rahoon darbaar tihaare
santan maahin basero.

बिना कामना करूँ चाकरी
आठों पहरे नेरो।
मनसब-भक्ति कृपा करि दीजै
मोहि यही बहुतेरो॥

2 bina kaamna karoon chaakri
aathon pahre nero,
mansab-bhakti kripa kari deejai
mohe yahi bahutero.

खानेजाद कदीमी कहियो
तुही आसरो मेरो।
झिड़क बिड़ारो तऊ न छाँड़ौं
सेवा सुमिरण तेरो॥

3 khaane-jaad kadeemi kahiyo
tuhi aasro mero,
jhirrak birraaro ta'u na chhaarraun
seva sumiran tero.

काहू और आन देवन सों
रह्यो नहीं उरझेरो।
जैसे राखो त्योंहीं रहहूँ
कर लीजो सुरझेरो॥

4 kaahu aur aan devan son
rahyo nahi urjhero,
jaise raakho tyonheen rahahoon
kar leejo surjhero.

तेरे घर बिन कहूँ न मेरो
ठौर ठिकानो डेरो।
मोसे पतित दीन को हरि जी
तुमही करो निबेरो॥

5 tere ghar bin kahoon na mero
thaur thikaano dero,
mose patit deen ko hari ji
tumhi karo nibero.

गुरु शुकदेव दया करि मोकूँ
ओर तिहारी फेरो।
चरणदास को शरणैं राखो
यही इनाम घनेरो॥

6 guru shukdev daya kari mokoon
or tihaari phero,
Charandas ko sharnai raakho
yahi inaam ghanero.[1]

अँखियाँ गुरु दरसन की प्यासी।
इकटक लागी पंथ निहारूँ
तन सूँ भई उदासी॥

1 ankhiyaan guru darsan ki pyaasi,
iktak laagi panth nihaaroon
tan soon bhayi udaasi.

Sant Charandas Ji

*R*elease me now from this worldly snare, O Lord –   1
   I am but a slave of your lotus feet.
Let me remain at your court
   and dwell with the Saints.
May I always remain in your presence   2
   and serve you without desire.
Bless me with the boon of steadfast devotion –
   just this much would suffice.
This eternal slave submits   3
   that you alone are his support.
Never will I give up your service or remembrance
   even if you rebuke me or turn me away.
I do not involve myself with any deity;   4
   I shall be happy however you keep me –
   please rescue me from here.
Besides your abode,   5
   I have no place of my own nor any other shelter.
Beloved Lord, only you can liberate
   a hopeless wretch like me.
Guru Sukdev showered his grace on me   6
   and turned me towards you.
Please keep Charandas under your shelter –
   this is his greatest reward.

*M*y eyes thirst for a glimpse of my Master;   1
   I have fixed my gaze your way
   and become oblivious of my body.

रैन दिना मोहिं चैन नहीं है
चिन्ता अधिक सतावै।
तलफत रहूँ कल्पना भारी
निश्चल बुधि नहिं आवै॥
तन गयो सूख हूक अति लागी
हिरदै पावक बाढ़ी।
खिन में लेटी खिन में बैठी
घर अंगना खिन ठाढ़ी॥
भीतर बाहर संग सहेली
बातन ही समझावैं।
चरनदास सुकदेव पियारे
नैनन ना दरसावैं॥

2 *rain dina mohen chain nahi hai*
chinta adhik sataavai,
talphat rahoon kalpana bhaari
nischal budhi nahin aavai.

3 *tan gayo sookh hook ati laagi*
hirdai paavak baarrhi,
khin mein leti khin mein baithi
ghar angana khin thaarrhi.

4 *bheetar baahar sang saheli*
baatan hi samjhaavain,
Charandas sukdev pyaare
nainan na darsaavain.[2]

गुरुदेव हमारे आवो जी।
बहुत दिनों से लगो उमाहो।
आनंद मंगल लावो जी॥
पलकन पंथ बुहारूँ तेरो।
नैन परे पग धारो जी।
बाट तिहारी निस दिन देखूँ।
हमरी ओर निहारो जी॥
करूँ उछाह बहुत मन सेती।
आंगन चौक पुराऊँ जी।
करूँ आरती तन मन वारूँ।
बार बार बलि जाऊँ जी॥
दै पैकरमा सीस नवाऊँ।
सुनि सुनि बचन अघाऊँ जी।
गुरु सुकदेव चरन हूँ दासा।
दरसन माहिं समाऊँ जी॥

1 *gurudev hamaare aavo ji,*

2 *bahut dino se lago umaaho,*
aanand mangal laavo ji.

3 *palkan panth buhaaroon tero,*
nain pare pag dhaaro ji;

4 *baat tihaari nis din dekhoon,*
hamri or nihaaro ji.

5 *karoon uchhaah bahut man seti,*
aangan chauk puraa'oon ji;

6 *karoon aarti tan man vaaroon,*
baar baar bali jaa'oon ji.

7 *dai paikarma sees navaa'oon,*
suni suni bachan aghaa'oon ji;

8 *guru sukdev charan hoon daasa,*
darsan maahin samaa'oon ji.[3]

Day and night, I find no respite   *2*
   and my anxiety causes me great distress.
Anguished and constantly buffeted by thoughts,
   my mind does not become still.
My body is worn out, I am in intense agony   *3*
   and my heart is afire with the pangs of separation.
Restless, I lie down for a moment
   only to sit up an instant later
   and in another second I rush to the courtyard.
Both inside and out, my friends and companions   *4*
   try to console me with empty talk,
   but, says Charandas, Sukdev, my Beloved,
   does not bless me with his darshan.

Come, my beloved Master, please come!   *1*
Many days have passed in eager anticipation –   *2*
   please bring forth bliss and blessings.
With my eyelashes I want to sweep the path you walk on;   *3*
   my eyes eagerly wait for you –
   please set your feet on the path.
Night and day I await your arrival –   *4*
   please turn your gaze towards me.
With heartfelt zeal I decorate my courtyard,   *5–6*
   trying to imagine how I would worship you –
   I sacrifice my body and mind to you.
I want to circle around you and bow my head at your feet –   *7*
   I would be content to simply listen to your words.
I am just a slave at your feet, O Master Sukdev!   *8*
I want to be completely absorbed in your darshan.

हमारो नैना दरस पियासा हो।
तन गयो सूखि हाय हिये बाढ़ी,
जीवत हूँ वोहि आसा हो॥
बिछुरन थारो मरन हमारो,
मुख में चलै न ग्रासा हो।
नींद न आवै रैनि बिहावै,
तारे गिनत अकासा हो॥
भये कठोर दरद नहिं जाने,
तुम कूँ नेक न साँसा हो।
हमरी गति दिन दिन औरे ही,
बिरह बियोग उदासा हो॥
सुकदेव प्यारे मत रहु न्यारे,
आनि करो उर बासा हो।
रनजीता अपनो करि जानी,
निज करि चरनन दासा हो॥

1 hamaaro naina daras piyaasa ho,
2 tan gayo sookhi haaye hiye baarrhi,
  jeevat hoon vohi aasa ho.
3 bichhuran thaaro maran hamaaro,
  mukh mein chalai na graasa ho,
4 neend na aavai rain bihaavai,
  taare ginat akaasa ho.
5 bhaye kathor daras nahin jaane,
  tum koon nek na saansa ho,
6 hamri gati din din aure hi,
  birah biyog udaasa ho.
7 sukdev pyaare mat rahu nyaare,
  aani karo ur baasa ho,
8 ranjeeta apno kari jaani,
  nij kari charnan daasa ho. [4]

मो कूँ कछु न चहिये राम।
तुम बिन सबहीं फीके लागैं,
नाना सुख धन धाम॥
आठ सिद्धि नौ निद्धि आपनी,
और जनन को दीजै।
मैं तौ चेरो जन्म जन्म को,
निज करि अपनो कीजै॥
स्वर्ग फलन की मोहिं न आसा,
ना बैकुंठ न मोच्छहिं चाहूँ।
चरन कमल के राखौ पासा,
यहि उर माहिं उमाहूँ॥

1 mo koon kachhu na chahiye raam,
  tum bin sabaheen pheeke laagain,
  naana sukh dhan dhaam.
2 aath siddhi nau niddhi aapni,
  aur janan ko deejai,
  main tau chero janam janam ko,
  nij kari apno keejai.
3 svarg phalan ki mohen na aasa,
  na baikunth na mocchh-hin chaahoon,
  charan kamal ke raakhau paasa,
  yahi ur maahen umaahoon.

---

* **Ranjita** was the name Sant Charandas's parents gave him at birth.
† The **eight supernatural powers** (*siddhis*) include the ability to shrink and expand one's size, to reduce and increase one's weight, to have access to all places, to realize

My eyes thirst for your darshan, O Master!　　　　　　　　*1*

My body has withered away　　　　　　　　　　　　　　*2*

　　and my anguished heart overflows with grief;

　　I live only in the hope of your darshan.

Separation from you is like a living death for me –　　　　*3–4*

　　I cannot swallow even a morsel of food;

　　sleep eludes me and I pass the night

　　counting the stars in the sky.

Heartless have you become – do you not know my pain　　*5*

　　or feel even a little concern about me?

My condition worsens with each passing day,　　　　　　*6*

　　tormented as I am by the agony of separation.

O beloved Sukdev, do not stay away from me.　　　　　*7–8*

Please come and dwell in my heart,

　　accept Ranjita as your very own*

　　and make him the slave of your lotus feet.

I do not desire anything, O Lord;　　　　　　　　　　*1*

　　all pleasure, wealth and possessions

　　are insipid without you.

Grant to others your eight supernatural powers　　　　　*2*

　　and nine treasures;†

I have been your devotee for countless births –

　　now make me your own.

I desire not the fruits of heaven, paradise or salvation;　　*3*

　　the sole desire of my heart is

　　that you keep me at your lotus feet.

---

one's desires, to control nature and to control others. The **nine treasures** refer to material
wealth, possessions and skills of all kinds.

भक्ति न छोड़ूँ
मुक्ति न माँगूँ,
सुन सुकदेव मुरारी।
चरनदास की यही टेक है,
तजूँ न गैल तुम्हारी॥

4 bhakti na chhodoon
mukti na maangoon,
sun sukdev muraari,
Charandas ki yahi tek hai,
tajoon na gail tumhaari.[5]

पतित उधारन बिरद तुम्हारो।
जो यह बात साँच है हरि जू,
तौ तुम हम कूँ पार उतारो॥
बालपने औ तरुन अवस्था,
और बुढ़ापे माहीं।
हम से भई सभी तुम जानो,
तुम से नेक छिपानी नाहीं॥
अनगिन पाप भये मन माने,
नखसिख औगुन धारी।
हिरि फिरि कै तुम सरनै आयौ,
अब तुम को है लाज हमारी॥
सुभ करमन को मारग छूटो,
आलस निद्रा घेरो।
एकहिं बात भली बन आई,
जग में कहायो तेरो चेरो॥
दीनदयाल कृपाल बिसंभर,
श्री सुकदेव गोसाई
जैसे और पतित घन तारे,
चरनदास की गहियो बाँहीं॥

1 patit udhaaran birad tumhaaro,
jo yah baat saanch hai hari ju,
tau tum ham koon paar utaaro.
2 baalpane au tarun avastha,
aur burrhaape maaheen;
ham se bhayi sabhi tum jaano,
tum se nek chhipaani naahi.
3 an-gin paap bhaye man maane,
nakhsikh augun dhaari;
4 hiri phiri kai tum sarnai aayau,
ab tum ko hai laaj hamaari.
5 subh karman ko maarag chhooto,
aalas nidra ghero;
ek-hin baat bhali ban aa'i,
jag mein kahaayo tero chero.
6 deen-dayaal kripaal bisambhar,
shri sukdev gosaa'een;
jaise aur patit ghan taare,
Charandas ki gahiyo baaheen.[6]

Beloved Sukdev, hear the plea of Charandas: 4
 may I never give up your devotion
 nor ask for salvation;
 may I never forsake your path.

You are renowned as the saviour of the fallen;   1
 O Lord, if this is true, then you must ferry me
 across the ocean of existence.
You know everything – all that I have done   2
 in my childhood, youth and old age –
 nothing can be hidden from your sight.
Under the sway of the mind I have committed countless sins   3
 and am filled with vice from head to toe.
After wandering from door to door   4
 I have taken refuge in you;
 now my honour lies in your hands.
I abandoned the path of virtue   5
 and laziness and sleep have overcome me;
 the only good thing is that I am now known as your disciple!
O Sukdev, my Master,   6
 merciful and compassionate sustainer of the universe,
 just as you have liberated many other sinners,
 so also take hold of Charandas's hand and liberate him.

प्रभु जू सरन तिहारी आयो।

जो कोइ सरन तिहारी नाहीं
भरम भरम दुख पायो॥

औरन के मन देवी देवा
मेरे मन तुहि भायो।

जब सों सुरति सम्हारी जग में
और न सीस नवायो॥

नरपति सुरपति आस तुम्हारी
यह सुनि कै मैं धायो।

तीरथ बरत सकल फल त्याग्यो
चरन कमल चित लायो॥

नारद मुनि अरु सिव ब्रह्मादिक
तेरो ध्यान लगायो।

आदि अनादि जुगादि तेरो जस
बेद पुरानन गायो॥

अब क्यो न बाँह गहो हरि मेरी
तुम काहे बिसरायो।

चरनदास कहैं करता तूही
गुरु सुकदेव बतायो॥

1 prabhu ju saran tihaari aayo,

2 jo koi saran tihaari naahi
bharam bharam dukh paayo.

3 auran ke man devi deva
mere man tuhi bhaayo,

4 jab son surati samhaari jag mein
aur na sees navaayo.

5 narpati surpati aas tumhaari
yah suni kai main dhaayo,

6 teerath barat sakal phal tyaagyo
charan kamal chit laayo.

7 naarad muni ar siv brahmaadik
tero dhyaan lagaayo,

8 aadi anaadi jugaadi tero jas
bed puraanan gaayo.

9 ab kyon na baanh gaho hari meri
tum kaahe bisraayo,

10 Charandas kahain karta toohi
guru sukdev bataayo.[7]

राखो जी लाज गरीब निवाज।
तुम बिन हमरे कौन सँवारै
सबहीं बिगरै काज॥

भक्तबछल हरि नाम कहावो
पतित उधारनहार।
करो मनोरथ पूरन जन को
सीतल दृष्टि निहार॥

1 raakho ji laaj gareeb nivaaj,
tum bin hamre kaun sanvaarai
sabaheen bigrain kaaj.

2 bhakt-bachhal hari naam kahaavo
patit udhaaran-haar,
karo manorath pooran jan ko
seetal drishti nihaar.

---

*The three gods in the Hindu triad are **Brahma** the creator, Vishnu the sustainer and **Shiva** the destroyer. **Narad** was a sage celebrated for his devotion who travelled through

Dear Lord, I have taken refuge in you.   1

Those who do not come under your shelter   2
  are lost in delusion and wander in misery.

Others believe in gods and goddesses,   3
  but your devotion alone delights my heart.

Ever since I gained understanding in this world   4
  I have not bowed my head to anyone else.

When I heard that even kings and the lord of all gods   5
  place their hope in you, I came running to you.

I renounced the fruits of all pilgrimages and penances   6
  and now my mind is focused solely at your lotus feet.

Even the sage Narad and the gods Shiva, Brahma and the rest*   7
  all contemplate upon you.

True from the Beginning, O Lord, you are eternal;   8
  throughout the ages, the Vedas and the Puranas
  have sung your glory.

O Lord, why do you not take hold of my hand now –   9
  why have you forgotten me?

You are the Creator, says Charandas;   10
  this is what Sukdev, my Guru, has taught me.

O benefactor of the destitute, uphold my honour –   1
  except you, who can correct all my ruinous mistakes?

O Lord, you are the lover of your devotees   2
  and redeemer of the fallen.

Fulfil my heart's desire –
  turn your soothing gaze upon me.

---

the worldly and higher realms playing the veena, singing God's Name and giving advice
to gods and human beings.

तुम जहाज मैं काग तिहारो   3   *tum jahaaj main kaag tihaaro*
तुम तजि अनत न जाऊँ।   *tum taji anat na jaa'oon,*
जो तुम हरि जू मारि निकासो   *jo tum hari ju maari nikaaso*
और ठौर नहिं पाऊँ॥   *aur thaur nahin paa'oon.*
चरनदास प्रभु सरन तिहारी   4   *Charandas prabhu saran tihaari*
जानत सब संसार।   *jaanat sab sansaar,*
मेरी हँसी सो हँसी तुम्हारी   *meri hansi so hansi tumhaari*
तुम हूँ देखु बिचार॥   *tum hoon dekh bichaar.*[8]

तुम साहब करतार हो   1   *tum saahab kartaar ho*
हम बंदे तेरे।   *ham bande tere,*
रोम रोम गुनेगार हैं   *rom rom gunegaar hain*
बखसो हरि मेरे॥   *bakhso hari mere.*
दसौ दुवारे मैल है   2   *dasau duvaare mail hai*
सब गंदम गंदा।   *sab gandam ganda,*
उत्तम तेरो नाम है   *uttam tero naam hai*
बिसरै सो अंधा॥   *bisrai so andha.*
गुन तजिकै औगुन कियो   3   *gun tajikai augun kiyo*
तुम सब पहिचानो।   *tum sab pahichaano,*
तुम सूँ कहा छिपाइये   *tum soon kaha chhipaa'iye*
हरि घट की जानो॥   *hari ghat ki jaano.*
रहम करो रहमान सूँ   4   *raham karo rahmaan soon*
यह दास तिहारो।   *yah daas tihaaro,*
भक्ति पदारथ दीजिये   *bhakti padaarath deejiye*
आवा गवन निवारो॥   *aava gavan nivaaro.*
गुरु सुकदेव उबारि लो   5   *guru sukdev ubaari lo*
अब मेहर करीजै।   *ab mehar kareejai,*
चरनहिं दास गरीब कूँ   *Charan-hin daas gareeb koon*
अपनो करि लीजै॥   *apno kari leejai.*[9]

---

[*] Crows detest flying over open water. If a ship is nearby, they will take refuge on it.

You are my ship and I am your crow;
   leaving you, I can go nowhere.*   3
If you were to banish me, O Lord,
   I would not find refuge anywhere else.
O Lord, the whole world knows   4
   that Charandas has taken refuge with you.
Think about it – my ridicule will mean your ridicule too.

O Master, you are the Creator and we are your souls.   1
I am a sinner even to the tiniest pore of my being –
   please forgive me, O Lord!
While the ten doors of the body are full of dirt,†   2
   and everything is soiled and filthy,
   supremely exalted is your Nam – blind is he who forgets it.
As you are fully aware,   3
   abandoning virtues, I indulged in vice;
   you are the knower of all hearts –
   what can anyone hide from you, O Lord?
O Merciful One, shower your mercy on this slave;   4
   bestow the boon of devotion on me
   and save me from the cycle of birth and death.
O Sukdev, my Guru, accept Charandas,   5
   the lowly slave of your feet, as your very own;
   shower your grace and liberate me now!

---

† The body has **ten doors**; nine (eyes, ears, nostrils, mouth, lower openings) lead outward
into the world and the tenth at the eye centre leads to the inner regions.

बानी सहजोबाई जी

अब तुम अपनी ओर निहारो।
हमरे औगुन पै नहिं जाओ,
तुमहीं अपना बिरद सम्हारो॥
जुग जुग साख तुम्हारी ऐसी,
वेद पुरानन गाई।
पतित-उधारन नाम तुम्हारो,
यह सुनके मन दृढ़ता आई॥
मैं अजान तुम सब कछु जानो,
घट घट अंतरजामी।
मैं तो चरन तुम्हारे लागी,
हो किरपाल दयालहि स्वामी॥
हाथ जोरि के अरज करत हौं,
अपनाओ गहि बाहीं।
द्वार तिहारे आय परी हौं,
पौरुष गुन मो में कछु नाहीं॥
चरनदास सहजिया तेरी,
दरसन की निधि पाऊँ।
लगन लगी अरु प्रान अड़े हैं,
तुमको छोड़ कहौ कित जाऊँ॥

Bani Sahjobai Ji

1 ab tum apni or nihaaro,

2 hamre augun pai nahin jaa'o,
   tumhi apna birad samhaaro.

3 jug jug saakh tumhaari aisi,
   ved puraanan gaa'i,

4 patit-udhaaran naam tumhaaro,
   yah sunke man drirrhta aa'i.

5 main ajaan tum sab kachhu jaano,
   ghat ghat antarjaami,

6 main to charan tumhaare laagi,
   ho kirpaal dayaalhi swaami.

7 haath jori ke araj karat haun,
   apnaa'o gahi baaheen,

8 dvaar tihaare aaye pari haun,
   paurush gun mo mein kacchu naahi.

9 charandas Sahajiya teri,
   darsan ki nidhi paa'oon,

10 lagan lagi aru praan arre hain,
   tumko chhorr kahau kit jaa'oon. [1]

Sahjobai Ji

Think of your own nature now, O Lord;   *1–2*
   pay no heed to my vices
   and be true to your intrinsic disposition.
Age after age your greatness has prevailed;   *3–4*
   the Vedas and the Puranas have sung your glory,
   calling you the redeemer of the fallen –
   hearing this, my mind has become steadfast.
I am ignorant and you are all-knowing;   *5*
   you know the innermost secrets of all hearts.
I have taken refuge at your lotus feet;   *6*
   bestow your grace, O merciful Master!
With folded hands, I plead before you –   *7*
   hold my hand and accept me as your own.
I have fallen at your door;   *8*
   without virtue and bereft of devotion am I.
Your devotee Sahjia intensely longs, O Master Charandas,   *9*
   for the immeasurable treasure of your darshan.
I have fallen in love   *10*
   and am hanging between life and death –
   tell me, without you where would I go?

नमो नमो गुरु तुम सरना।

तुम्हरे ध्यान भरम भय भागैं,

जीते पाँचौ मरना॥

दुख दारिद्र मिटैं तुम नाऊँ,

कर्म कटैं जो होहिं घना।

लोक परलोक सकल बिधि सुधरैं,

पग लागैं आय ज्ञान गुना॥

चरन छुए सब गति मति पलटैं,

पारस जैसे लोह सुना।

सीप परसि स्वाँती भयो मोती,

सोहत है सिर राज रना॥

ब्रह्म होय जीव बुधि नासै,

जब कैसो होना मरना।

अमर होय अमरापद पावै,

यह गुर कहियै गुरु बचना॥

चरनदास गुरु पूरे पाये,

जग का दुख सुख क्यों सहना।

सहजो बाई ब्याध छुटा कर,

आनँद मंगल में रहना॥

1 namo namo guru tum sarna,

2 tumhre dhyaan bharam bhay bhaagain,
jeete paanchau marna.

3 dukh daaridr mitain tum naa'oon,
karm katain jo hohin ghana;

4 lok parlok sakal bidhi sudhrain,
pag laagain aaye gyaan guna.

5 charan chhu'e sab gati mati paltain,
paaras jaise loh suna;

6 seep parasi svaanti bhayo moti,
sohat hai sir raaj rana.

7 brahm hoye jeev budhi naasai,
jab kaiso hona marna;

8 amar hoye amaraapad paavai,
yah gur kahiyai guru bachna.

9 charandas guru poore paaye,
jag ka dukh sukh kyon sahna;

10 Sahjo baa'i byaadh chhuta kar,
aanand mangal mein rahna.[2]

---

*The mythical **philosopher's stone** was much sought after by alchemists, who believed it had the power to turn base metals into gold and to grant eternal youth.

Over and over I bow at your feet, O Master,   1
  in gratitude for your having granted me refuge.

By contemplating on you, all doubts and fears are dispelled   2
  and victory is achieved over the five passions and death.

All sorrows and miseries are wiped out with your Nam   3
  and the heavy load of karma is cancelled.

Wisdom and virtues are obtained by taking refuge at your feet,   4
  and for me both this world and the next
  are improved in every way.

One is completely transformed by touching your feet   5–6
  just as iron turns to gold
  when touched by the philosopher's stone,*
  and a raindrop falling into an oyster shell
  turns into a pearl that adorns the crown of kings
  during the time of the Swati Constellation.†

When the mind is obliterated after enlightenment,   7
  how can the cycle of birth and death continue?

The Master explains that by following his instructions,   8
  one attains salvation and reaches the supreme stage.

Why should I endure the joys and sorrows of this world   9
  when I have found Guru Charandas, the perfect Master?

Says Sahjobai: delivered from all trials and tribulations,   10
  I now remain in a state of perpetual bliss.

---

† According to legend, when the moon passes through the **Swati Constellation**, very special raindrops fall.

तुम गुनवंत मैं औगुन भारी।

तुम्हरी ओट खोट बहु कीन्हे,

पतित उधारन लाल बिहारी ॥

खान पान बोलत अरु डोलत,

पाप करत है देह हमारी।

कर्म बिचारौं तौ नहिं छूटौं,

जो छूटौं तौ दया तुम्हारी ॥

मैं अधीन माया बस हो करि,

तुव सुधीन माया सूँ न्यारे।

मैं अनाथ तुम नाथ गुसाई

सब जीवन के प्रान पियारे ॥

भौसागर में डर लागत मोहिं,

तारौ बेगहि पार उतारी।

चरनदास गुर किरपा सेती,

सहजो पाई सरन तिहारी ॥

1 *tum gunvant main augun bhaari,*

2 *tumhri ot khot bahu keenhe,*
   patit udhaaran laal bihaari.

3 *khaan paan bolat ar dolat,*
   paap karat hai deh hamaari,

4 *karm bichaarau tau nahin chhootaun,*
   jo chhootaun tau daya tumhaari.

5 *main adheen maaya bas ho kari,*
   tuv sudheen maaya soon nyaare,

6 *main anaath tum naath gusaa'een,*
   sab jeevan ke praan pyaare.

7 *bhausaagar mein dar laagat mohen,*
   taarau begahi paar utaari,

8 *charandas gur kirpa seti,*
   Sahjo paa'i saran tihaari.[3]

You are the fountainhead of virtue 1
    and I am the embodiment of vice.
O beloved Lord, redeemer of the fallen, 2
    while under your shelter I have committed many sins.
Eating, drinking, talking or walking – 3
    at all times I commit bad deeds.
Only your mercy can liberate me; 4
    if you were to judge my actions, I could never be pardoned.
I am controlled and enslaved by maya, O Lord, 5
    but you are free and beyond illusion.
You are the sovereign Lord of all, 6
    dearer than life itself for all beings,
    while I am a mere orphan.
Liberate me and ferry me across without delay, O Lord – 7
    terrified am I in the ocean of existence.
It is only by the grace of my Master, Charandas, 8
    that Sahjo has found refuge in you.

बानी मलूकदास जी

दीन-बंधु दीना-नाथ
मेरी तन हेरिये ॥ टेक ॥
भाई नाहिं बन्धु नाहिं
कुटुम परिवार नाहिं,
ऐसा कोई मित्र नाहिं
जाके ढिग जाइये ॥
सोने की सलैया नाहिं
रूपे का रुपैया नाहिं,
कौड़ी पैसा गाँठ नहीं
जासे कछु लीजिये ॥
खेती नाहिं बारी नाहिं
बनिज ब्यौपार नाहिं,
ऐसा कोई साहु नाहिं
जासों कछु माँगिये ॥
कहत मलूकदास
छोड़दे पराई आस,
राम धनी पाय के अब
का की सरन जाइये ॥

Bani Malukdas Ji

1   *deen-bandhu deena-naath*
  meri tan heriye. tek.
2   *bhaa'i naahin bandhu naahin*
  kutum parivaar naahin,
  aisa koi mitr naahin
  jaake dhig jaa'iye.
3   *sone ki salaiya naahin*
  roope ka rupaiya naahin,
4   *kaurri paisa gaanth nahi*
  jaase kachhu leejiye.
5   *kheti naahin baari naahin*
  banij byaupaar naahin,
6   *aisa koi saahu naahin*
  jaason kachhu maangiye.
7   *kahat Malukdas*
  chhorrde paraa'i aas,
8   *raam dhani paaye ke ab*
  ka ki saran jaa'iye.[1]

Malukdas Ji

O companion of the poor, benefactor of the meek,   1
   turn your gaze towards me.
I have no brother or companion, no family or clan,   2
   and no close friend I can go to.
I have not even a sliver of gold   3–4
   or silver coin in my possession;
   not even a cowrie shell
   or paisa is in my pouch to buy anything.*
I own no farmland or garden   5–6
   and do not have any merchandise to trade;
   there is no moneylender from whom I can borrow.
Says Malukdas: give up all expectations of others –   7–8
   after realizing the bountiful Lord,
   why seek refuge with anyone else?

---

* Formerly used as currency in India, a **cowrie shell** symbolizes something almost worthless. Similarly, a **paisa** is 1/100th of a rupee, so it has little value.

नाम तुम्हारा निरमला,
निरमोलक हीरा।
तू साहेब समरत्थ,
हम मल मुत्र कै कीरा॥

पाप न राखै देंह में,
जब सुमिरन करिये।
एक अच्छर के कहत ही,
भौसागर तरिये॥

अधम-उधारन सब कहैं,
प्रभु बिरद तुम्हारा।
सुनि सरनागत आइया,
तब पार उतारा॥

तुझ सा गरुवा औ धनी,
जा में बड़ई समाई।
जरत उबारे पांडवा,
ताती बाव न लाई॥

कोटिक औगुन जन करै,
प्रभु मनहि न आनै।
कहत मलूकादास को,
अपना करि जानै॥

1   *naam tumhaara nirmala,*

     nirmolak heera;

     tu saaheb samratth,

     ham mal mutr kai keera.

2   *paap na raakhai deh mein,*

     jab sumiran kariye;

     ek acchhar ke kahat hi,

     bhausaagar tariye.

3   *adham-udhaaran sab kahain,*

     prabhu birad tumhaara;

     sun sarnaagat aa'iya,

     tab paar utaara.

4   *tujh sa garuva au dhani,*

     ja mein barrayi samaa'i;

     jarat ubaare paandava,

     taati baav na laa'i.

5   *kotik augun jan karai,*

     prabhu manahi na aanai;

     kahat Malukadas ko,

     apna kari jaanai.[2]

---

*The Pandavas are the five sons of King Pandu, who fought their jealous cousins in the great war of the Mahabharata to regain their kingdom. In the incident referred to here, the cousins had invited the Pandavas to a palace that was made of materials containing

Your Nam is pure, O Lord, a priceless gem; *1*
    you are the almighty Lord; I, a mere insect of the dirt.

When someone does simran, his body is purged of all evils; *2*
    by repeating Nam, he is ferried across the ocean of existence.

Everyone says that you are the redeemer of the fallen – *3*
    that is your intrinsic nature, O Lord.

Hearing this, I have taken shelter at your feet,
    that you may ferry me across.

No one can match your grandeur, abundance and greatness; *4*
    you saved the Pandavas from burning
    and did not let even the hot air harm them.*

Countless misdeeds are committed by your devotee, *5*
    but you, O Lord, do not take them to heart.

Pleads Malukdas: please accept me as your very own.

---

flammable sealing wax so they could set it on fire while the Pandavas were staying there.
The plot was discovered by their uncle, who secretly arranged for a tunnel to be built so
they could escape.

बानी धरनीदास जी

Bani Dharnidas Ji

अजहूँ मिलो मेरे प्रान-पियारे।	1	ajahoon milo mere praan-pyaare,
दीनदयाल कृपाल कृपानिधि,	2	deen-dayaal kripaal kripaa-nidhi,
करहु छिमा अपराध हमारे॥		karahu chhima apraadh hamaare.
कल न परत अति बिकल सकल तन,	3	kal na parat ati bikal sakal tan,
नैन सकल जनु बहत पनारे;		nain sakal janu bahat panaare;
माँस पचो अरु रक्त भे,	4	maans pacho aru rakt bhe,
हाड़ दिनहुँ जिन होत उघारे॥		haarr dinhun jin hot ughaare.
नासा नैन श्रवन रसना रस,	5	naasa nain sravan rasna ras,
इन्द्री स्वाद जुआ जनु हारे।		indri svaad jua janu haare;
दिवस दसो दिसि पंथ निहारति,	6	divas daso disi panth nihaarati,
राति बिहात गनत जस तारे॥		raati bihaat ganat jas taare.
जो दुख सहत कहत न बनत मुख,	7	jo dukh sahat kahat na banat mukh,
अंतरगत के हौ जाननहारे।		antargat ke hau jaanan-haare;
धरनी जिव झलमलित दीप ज्यों,	8	Dharni jiv jhalmalit deep jyon,
होत अंधार करो उँजियारे॥		hot andhaar karo unjiyaare.[1]

मैं निरगुनियाँ गुन नहिं जाना।	1	main nirguniyaan gun nahin jaana,
एक धनी के हाथ बिकाना॥		ek dhani ke haath bikaana.
सोइ प्रभु पक्का मैं अति कच्चा।	2	soi prabhu pakka main ati kaccha,
मैं झूँठा मेरा साहब सच्चा॥		main jhoontha mera saahab saccha.
मैं ओछा मेरा साहब पूरा।	3	main ochha mera saahab poora,
मैं कायर मेरा साहब सूरा॥		main kaayar mera saahab soora.
मैं मूरख मेरा प्रभु ज्ञाता।	4	main moorakh mera prabhu gyaata,
मैं किरपिन मेरा साहब दाता॥		main kirpin mera saahab daata.
धरनी मन मानो इक ठाउँ।	5	Dharni man maano ik thaa'un,
सो प्रभु जीवो मैं मरिजाउँ॥		so prabhu jeevo main mari-jaa'oon.[2]

Dharnidas Ji

O Beloved, dearer than life, meet me now!   *1*

O compassionate benefactor of the meek   *2*
    and gracious ocean of mercy – please forgive my sins.

I am restless, my entire body is in intense anguish   *3*
    and tears stream from my eyes.

My skin has withered and my body wastes away;   *4*
    with each passing day my bones protrude even more.

My senses of smell, sight, hearing and taste have lost their power,   *5*
    I am like a gambler who has squandered everything.

Every day I intensely look for you in all the ten directions,*   *6*
    and I pass every night counting the stars.

The suffering that I endure I cannot describe in words;   *7*
    you know my inner condition, O knower of all hearts!

Like a shimmering lamp, O Lord, manifest your radiance   *8*
    and dispel the darkness within me, prays Dharni.

I am without any merit and have no virtues,   *1*
    but I have been sold off to a benefactor.

The Lord alone is unshakeable   *2*
    while I am completely vulnerable;
    I am false and my Lord is true.

I am lowly and my Lord is supremely exalted;   *3*
    I am a coward and my Lord is fearless.

I am ignorant and my Lord is all-knowing;   *4*
    I am a miser and my Lord is the generous giver.

Says Dharni: my mind is fully convinced;   *5*
    the Lord is eternal and I am transient.

---

*The **ten directions** are north, south, east, west, northeast, northwest, southeast, south-
west, above and below, conveying the sense of everywhere.

मेरे प्रभु तुमहिं अवर नहिं कोइ।
बहु बिधि कहत सुनत नर लोइ॥
तुव बिस्वास दास मन मान।
जुग जुग भगत-बछल जा की बान॥
अवरन्ह तें मेरो होत अकाज।
छोड़ि कुल कानि बिसरि जग लाज॥
धरनी जनम हारि भावे जीति।
अब मन बच क्रम हृदै प्रतीति॥

1 mere prabhu tumhin avar nahin koi,
bahu bidhi kahat sunat nar loi.

2 tuv bisvaas daas man maan,
jug jug bhagat-bachhal ja ki baan.

3 avaranh tein mero hot akaaj,
chhorri kul kaani bisari jag laaj.

4 Dharni janam haari bhaave jeeti,
ab man bach kram hridai prateeti.[3]

मो सों प्रभु नाहिं दुखित,
तुम सों सुखदाई॥ टेक॥
दीनबन्धु बान तेरो,
आइ करु सहाई।
मो सों नहिं दीन और,
निरखो नर लोई॥
पतित-पावन निगम कहत,
रहत हौ कित गोई।
मो सों नहिं पतित और,
देखो जग टोई॥
अधम को उधारन तुम,
चारो जुग ओई।
मो तें अब अधम आहि,
कवन धौं बड़ोई॥
धरनी मन मनिया,
एक ताग में परोई।
आपन करि जानि लेहु,
कर्म फंद छोई॥

1 mo son prabhu naahin dukhit,
tum so sukhdaa'i. tek.

2 deen-bandhu baan tero,
aaye karu sahaa'i;
mo son nahin deen aur,
nirkho nar loi.

3 patit-paavan nigam kahat,
rahat hau kit goi;
mo son nahin patit aur,
dekho jag toi.

4 adham ko udhaaran tum,
chaaro jug o'i;
mo tein ab adham aahe,
kavan dhaun barroi.

5 Dharni man maniya,
ek taag mein paroi;
aapan kari jaani lehu,
karm phand chhoi.[4]

My Lord, there is no one else but you for me;　　　　　　1
　　people sing and hear your praises in a multitude of ways.
Your slave has faith only in you,　　　　　　　　　　2
　　for it is your essential nature
　　to be a lover of your devotees in all the ages.
Since attachment to others diverts me from my goal,　　3
　　I have forsaken pride of lineage and fear of public opinion.
In thought, word and deed, my heart accepts your will;　　4
　　says Dharni: now it matters not
　　whether I win or lose the game of life.

There is no one as distressed as me　　　　　　　　1
　　and no bestower of bliss like you, O Lord.
Protecting the lowly is inherent in your nature –　　2
　　please come and give me your support.
If you compare me with other people in the world,
　　you will find there is no one worse than me.
The Vedas say that you are redeemer of the fallen –　　3
　　where do you hide yourself?
You may search the whole world;
　　there is no one more sinful than me.
In all the four ages you liberate the lowly;　　　　　4
　　I do not know anyone more despicable than me.
Says Dharni: now my mind is at peace　　　　　　5
　　and I have threaded its scattered beads on a single string.
O Lord, consider me to be your own
　　and free me from the snare of karmas.

तुहि अवलंब हमारे हो।

भावै पगु नाँगे करो,

भावै तुरय सवारे हो॥

जनम अनेकन बादि गौ,

निजु नाम बिसारे हो।

अब सरनागत रावरी,

जन करत पुकारे हो॥

भवसागर बेरा परो,

जल माँझ मँझारे हो।

संतत दीनदयाल हो,

कर पार निकारे हो॥

धरनी मन बच कर्मना,

तन मन धन वारे हो।

अपनो बिरद निबाहिये,

नहिं बनत बिचारे हो॥

1 tuhi avalamb hamaare ho,

bhaavai pagu naange karo,

bhaavai turay savaare ho.

2 janam anekan baadi gau,

niju naam bisaare ho;

ab sarnaagat raavri,

jan karat pukaare ho.

3 bhavsaagar bera paro,

jal maanjh manjhaare ho;

santat deen-dayaal ho,

kar paar nikaare ho.

4 Dharni man bach karmana,

tan man dhan vaare ho;

apno birad nibaahiye,

nahin banat bichaare ho.[5]

O Lord, you alone are my support;   1
   it matters not whether you keep me barefoot or on horseback.
Countless lifetimes have passed in vain   2
   because I forgot your true Nam;
   now I have taken refuge in you –
   your servant begs you, O Lord!
My ship is caught in the ocean of existence   3
   and you are the captain who can take it across;
   you are eternally benevolent to the destitute –
   please ferry me across.
In thought, word and deed, says Dharni,   4
   I dedicate my body, mind and wealth to you, O Lord –
   uphold the honour of your glory,
   because your reputation is at stake.

दोहे

धरनी जन की बीनती,
करु करुनामय कान।
दीजै दरसन आपनो,
माँगों कछु नहिं आन॥

धरनी बिलखि बिनती करै,
सुनिये प्रभू हमार।
सब अपराध छिमा करो,
मैं हौं सरन तिहार॥

काहू के बहु बिभव भइ,
काहू बहु परिवार।
धरनी कहत हमहिं बल,
ए हो राम तुम्हार॥

धरनी नहिं बैराग बल,
नाहिं जोग सन्यास।
मनसा बाचा कर्मना,
बिस्वंभर बिस्वास॥

बिनती लीजे मानि करि,
जानि दास को दास।
धरनी सरनी राखिये,
अवर न दूसर आस॥

Dohe

1 Dharni jan ki beenati,
   karu karunaamay kaan;
2 deejai darsan aapno,
   maangon kachhu nahin aan.

1 Dharni bilakhi binati karai,
   suniye prabhu hamaar;
2 sab apraadh chhima karo,
   main haun saran tihaar.

1 kaahu ke bahu bibhav bhayi,
   kaahu bahu parivaar;
2 Dharni kahat hamhin bal,
   e ho raam tumhaar.

1 Dharni nahin bairaag bal,
   naahin jog sanyaas;
2 mansa baacha karmana,
   bisvambhar bisvaas.

1 binati leeje maani kari,
   jaani daas ko daas;
2 Dharni sarni raakhiye,
   avar na doosar aas.[6]

Dohas

O Compassionate One,   1–2
  listen to the humble request of your devotee Dharni:
  grant me your darshan –
I do not ask for anything else.

Dharni cries for you and pleads: 1–2
  hear me, my Lord,
  please forgive all my transgressions –
I have taken refuge with you.

Some have abundant wealth   1–2
  and some a large family, says Dharni,
  but you, O Lord,
  are my only source of strength.

Says Dharni: strength lies not in renunciation   1–2
  or in leaving home and becoming a yogi or sanyasi;*
  in thought, word and deed,
  I have complete reliance on the Creator alone.

Consider me a slave of your devotees   1–2
  and accept this plea, O Lord:
  keep Dharni under your shelter – he desires nothing else.

---

* A **sanyasi** is a Hindu ascetic who has renounced the world. He puts on ochre-coloured robes and lives without any worldly possessions for the achievement of liberation.

बानी गरीबदास जी

दीन के दयाल,
भक्ति बिर्द दीजिये।
खानाजाद गुलाम,
अपन कर लीजिये॥

खानाजाद गुलाम,
तुम्हारा है सही।
मिहरबान महबूब,
जुगन जुग पत रही॥

बाँदी–जाद गुलाम,
गुलाम गुलाम है।
खड़ा रहै दरबार,
सु आठो जाम है॥

सेवक तलबदार,
तुम्हरे दर कूकहीं।
औगुन अनंत अपार,
परा मोहिं चूक हीं॥

मैं घर का बन्दाजादा,
अरज मेरी मानिये।
कहता दास गरीब,
अपन कर जानिये॥

Bani Garibdas Ji

1 deen ke dayaal,
bhakti bird deejiye;
khaanaa-jaad gulaam,
apan kar leejiye.

2 khaanaa-jaad gulaam,
tumhaara hai sahi,
meharbaan mahboob,
jugan jug pat rahi.

3 baandi-jaad gulaam,
gulaam gulaam hai,
kharra rahai darbaar,
su aatho jaam hai.

4 sevak talabdaar,
tumhre dar kookaheen.
augun anant apaar,
para mohen chook heen.

5 main ghar ka bandaa-jaada,
araj meri maaniye.
kahta daas Garib,
apan kar jaaniye.[1]

Garibdas Ji

O Lord, compassionate to the meek,   *1*
   grant me the boon of your devotion;
   I am your eternal slave – please make me your own.
This eternal slave belongs undeniably to you,   *2*
   my benevolent Beloved –
   for ages my honour has been in your hands.
This slave born of slaves is your slave forever,   *3*
   and day and night stands at attention in your court.
This servant, always at your beck and call,   *4*
   cries for help only at your door.
Countless and beyond limit are my faults
   and my failures weigh me down.
I am your eternal slave – please accept my supplication;   *5*
   says Garib, your slave: now accept me as your own.

बानी शेख फ़रीद जी

Bani Sheikh Farid Ji

सलोक सेख फरीद के

Slok Sheikh Farid ke

देख फरीदा जे थीआ
1 dekh fareeda je theeya

सकर होई विस ॥
sakkar hoi vis.

सांई बाझहो आपणे
2 saa'een baajho aapane

वेदण कहीऐ किस॥ १० ॥
vedan kaheeyai kis.

जोबन जांदे ना डरां
1 joban jaande na daraan

जे सह प्रीत न जाए॥
je sah preet na jaaye.

फरीदा कितीं जोबन प्रीत बिन
2 fareeda kiteen joban preet bin

सुक गए कुमलाए॥ ३४॥
suk gaye kumalaaye.

फरीदा चिंत खटोला वाण दुख
1 fareeda chint khatola vaan dukh

बिरह विछावण लेफ॥
birah vichhaavan lef.

एह हमारा जीवणा
2 eh hamaara jeevna

तू साहिब सचे वेख॥ ३५॥
tu saahib sache vekh.

फरीदा बार पराइऐ बैसणा
1 fareeda baar paraa'eeyai baisna

सांई मुझै न देह॥
saa'een mujhai na deh.

जे तू एवै रखसी
2 je tu evai rakhasi

जीउ सरीरहो लेह॥ ४२॥
jee'o sareerho leh.

फरीदा जे दिह नाला कपिआ
1 fareeda je deh naala kappiya

जे गल कपह चुख॥
je gal kappah chukh.

पवन न इती मामले
2 pavan na iti maamale

सहां न इती दुख॥ ७६ ॥
sahaan na itti dukh.

---

*This means that pleasures which once tasted sweet in the end afflict the body with disease and loss of vitality.

Sheikh Farid Ji

Sloks, Sheikh Farid

See what has transpired, O Farid –   1
   sugar has turned into poison.*
Who is there except my Lord   2
   to whom I can tell my tale of woe? [10]

I am not afraid of losing my youth –   1
   if only my Lord would not deprive me of his love.
It is for want of love, O Farid,   2
   that many a youth has withered away. [34]

Worry is my bed, O Farid, pain is my bed-string†   1
   and pangs of separation my bedcover and blanket.
This is my life –   2
   I beg for your merciful glance, O true Lord! [35]

Prays Farid: O Lord, do not make me   1
   linger at another's doorstep.
Should you wish to keep me in that way,   2
   please take the life out of my body. [42]

O Farid, if on the day my umbilical cord was cut   1–2
   my throat had been slit instead,
   then I would not have faced so many problems,
   nor suffered so much pain. [76]

---

† **bed-string:** Refers to the twine used in making woven Indian beds.

फरीदा तन सुका पिंजर थीआ
तलीआं खूंदह काग॥
अजै सो रब न बाहुड़िओ
देख बंदे के भाग॥९०॥

1 fareeda tan suka pinjar theeya
  taleeyaan khoondah kaag.
2 ajai so rab na baahurrio
  dekh bande ke bhaag.

कागा करंग ढंढोलिआ
सगला खाइआ मास॥
ए दुए नैना मत छुहउ
पिर देखन की आस॥९१॥

1 kaaga karang dhandholiya
  sagla khaaya maas.
2 e duye naina mat chhuho
  pir dekhan ki aas.

कागा चूंड न पिंजरा
बसै त उडर जाहे॥
जित पिंजरै मेरा सहु वसै
मास न तिदू खाहे॥९२॥

1 kaaga choond na pinjra
  basai ta udar jaahe.
2 jit pinjrai mera sahu vasai
  maas na tidu khaahe.

तन तपै तनूर जिउ
बालण हड बलंन्ह॥
पैरी थकां सिर जुलां
जे मूं पिरी मिलंन्ह॥११९॥

1 tan tapai tanoor jio
  baalan hadd balanh.
2 pairi thakaan sir julaan
  je moon piri milanh.

सरवर पंखी हेकड़ो
फाहीवाल पचास॥
इह तन लहरी गड थीआ
सचे तेरी आस॥१२५॥

1 sarvar pankhi hekarro
  phaaheevaal pachaas.
2 eh tan lahri gadd thiya
  sache teri aas.[1]

My body has shrunk to a skeleton, O Farid,   1
   and ravens are pecking at the soles of my feet.
Even now God has not revealed himself –   2
   look how pitiful is the human plight! [90]

Ravens have pecked through my skeleton   1
   and devoured all my flesh.
Please spare my two eyes, O ravens,   2
   for in these eyes there still lingers the hope
   of seeing my Beloved. [91]

Fly away, O raven,   1
   and do not peck at the emaciated frame
   on which you have settled.
Do not eat flesh from the body   2
   in which my Lord abides. [92]

My body burns like an oven,   1
   with my bones serving as firewood.
If my feet get tired of walking,   2
   I shall walk on my head –
   if only I could meet my Beloved! [119]

Fifty hunters lie in wait   1
   for the solitary fowl floating on the lake.*
This body is trapped in the waves of passion;   2
   you are my only hope, O true Lord! [125]

---

*Like the solitary fowl in the lake, we are surrounded by numerous deadly passions that are like hunters, trapping us in the cycle of transmigration.

कलाम साई बुल्लेशाह

Kalaam Saa'een Bulleh Shah

आ मिल यार सार लै मेरी,
जान दुक्खां ने घेरी।

1 aa mil yaar saar lai meri,
jaan dukkhaan ne gheri.

अंदर खवाब विछोड़ा होया,
ख़बर न पैंदी तेरी।

2 andar khwaab vichhorra hoya,
khabar na paindi teri.

सुंझी बन विच लुट्टी साईं,
चोर शंग ने घेरी।

3 sunji ban vich lutti saa'een,
chor shang ne gheri.

मुल्लां काज़ी राह बतावण,
देण धर्म दे फेरे।

4 mullaan qaazi raah bataavan,
den dharm de phere.

इह तां ठग ने जग दे झीवर,
लावण जाल चुफेरे।

5 eh taan thag ne jag de jheevar,
laavan jaal chufere.

करम शरआ दे धरम बतावण,
संगल पावण पैरीं।

6 karam shar'a de dharam bataavan,
sangal paavan paireen.

जात मज़हब एह इश्क न पुछदा,
इश्क शरआ दा वैरी।

7 jaat mazhab eh ishq na puchhda,
ishq shar'a da vairi.

नदियों पार मुलक सज्जन दा,
लोभ लहर ने घेरी।

8 nadeeyon paar mulak sajjan da,
lobh lahar ne gheri.

सतगुर बेड़ी फड़ी खलोते,
तैं क्यों लाई ए देरी।

9 satgur berri pharri khalote,
tain kyon laa'i e deri.

बुल्ला शाह शौह तैनूं मिलसी,
दिल नूं देह दलेरी।

10 Bullah shah shauh tainu milsi,
dil nu deh daleri.

प्रीतम पास ते टोलना किसनूं,
भुलयों सिखर दुपहरी।

11 preetam paas te tolana kisnu,
bhullyon sikhar dupahri.

आ मिल यार सार लै मेरी,
जान दुक्खां ने घेरी।

12 aa mil yaar saar lai meri,
jaan dukkhaan ne gheri.[1]

---

*A **mullah** is a Muslim religious leader or teacher and a **qazi** is an administrator of Islamic religious law.

Sain Bulleh Shah

Come, Friend, come to my help –
  my life is steeped in troubles!   *1*

In a dream, I became separated from you;
  on waking, I could not find you.   *2*

Alone in a jungle, I have been robbed, O Lord,
  and thieves and dacoits surround me.   *3*

Mullahs and qazis lead me astray*
  through a maze of religious rituals.   *4*

They are like bird hunters and thugs
  who have laid their nets everywhere.   *5*

They preach the so-called ways of piety –
  chains around my feet.   *6*

Love cares not for caste or creed;
  it is the opposite of orthodox religion.   *7*

The land of the Beloved lies across the river,
  yet waves of avarice have engulfed me.   *8*

The Master is holding the boat –
  why do you tarry, why this delay?   *9*

O Bullah, you will surely realize the Lord;†
  give your heart encouragement.   *10*

The Beloved is right within you –
  whom do you search for outside?   *11*
Why are you deluded in broad daylight?

Come, Friend, come to my help –
  my life is steeped in troubles.   *12*

---

† When Bulleh Shah speaks of himself, he calls himself **Bullah**.

आपणे संग रलाई प्यारे,
आपणे संग रलाई।

पहलों नेहों लगाया सी तैं,
आपे चाई चाई।

मैं लाया ए कि तुध लाया,
आपणी ओड़ निभाई।

राह पवां तां धाड़े बेले,
जंगल लक्ख बलाई।

भौंकण चीते ते चितमचित्ते,
भौंकण करन अदाई।

पार तेरे जगातर चढ़या,
कंधे लक्ख बलाई।

हौल दिले दा थर थर कंबदा,
बेड़ा पार लंघाई।

कर लई बंदगी रब्ब सचे दी,
पवण कबूल दुआई।

बुल्ले शाह ते शाहां दा मुखड़ा,
घुंगट खोल विखाई।

आपणे संग रलाई प्यारे,
आपणे संग रलाई।

1	aapne sang ralaayeen pyaare, aapne sang ralaayeen.
2	pehlon nehon lagaaya si tain, aape chaayeen chaayeen.
3	main laaya e ki tudh laaya, aapni orr nibhaayeen.
4	raah pavaan taan dhaarre bele, jangal lakkh balaayeen.
5	bhaunkan cheete te chit-machitte, bhaunkan karan adaayeen.
6	paar tere jagaatar charrhiya, kandhe lakkh balaayeen.
7	haul dile da thar thar kambda, berra paar langhaayeen.
8	kar layeen bandagi rabb sache di, pavan kabool duaayeen.
9	Bulleh Shah te shaahaan da mukhrra, ghungat khol vikhaayeen.
10	aapne sang ralaayeen pyaare, aapne sang ralaayeen.[2]

अब क्यों साजन चिर लायो रे। टेक।
ऐसी मन में आई का,
दुख सुख सभ वंजायो रे।

हार शिंगार को आग लगाऊं,
घट पर ढांड मचायो रे।

सुण के ज्ञान की ऐसी बातां,
नाम निशान सभी अणघातां।

कोयल वांगूं कूकां आतां,
तैं अजे वी तरस ना आयो रे।

1	ab kyon saajan chir laayo re. tek.
2	aisi man mein aa'i ka, dukh sukh sabh vanjaayo re.
3	haar shingaar ko aag lagaa'oon, ghat par dhaand machaayo re.
4	sun ke gyaan ki aisi baataan, naam nishaan sabhi an'ghaataan.
5	koyal vaangoon kookaan aataan, tain aje vi taras na aayo re.

Merge me in you, O my Beloved, 1
  merge me in you!
At first you fervently provoked love in me; 2–3
  pray, keep this love going forever,
  regardless of whether I loved you or you loved me.
My path is beset with fearsome robbers 4
  and evil spirits hound me in terrifying jungles.
Cheetahs, leopards and wolves roam in my path, 5–6
  the customs officer demands payment
  and countless demons stalk the riverbank.
My heart trembles with fear; 7
  pray, take my boat to safety.
I implore the true Lord to accept my prayers – 8–9
  unveil your kingly face to Bullah, O Lord.
Merge me in you, O my Beloved, merge me in you! 10

Why have you taken so long, my Friend? 1
I know not what came into my mind, 2
  that I forgot all joys and sorrows.
I flung my jewellery into the fire, 3
  you kindled such a blaze in my heart.
When I heard your words of wisdom, 4
  the shaft of Nam dealt me a mortal blow.
I call like a cuckoo, night after night; 5
  still you feel no compassion for me!

मुल्लां इश्क ने बांग दिवाई,
उठ दौड़न गल्ल वाजब आई।

6 mullaan ishq ne baang divaa'i,
uth daurran gall vaajab aa'i.

कर कर सजदे घर वल धाई,
मत्थे महराब टिकायो रे।

7 kar kar sajde ghar val dhaa'i,
matthe mahraab tikaayo re.

प्रेम नगर दे उलटे चाले,
ख़ूनी नैन होए खुशहाले।

8 prem nagar de ulte chaale,
khooni nain hoye khush-haale

आपे आप फसे विच जाले,
फस फस आप कुहायो रे।

9 aape aap phase vich jaale,
phas phas aap kuhaayo re.

बुल्ला शौह संग प्रीत लगाई,
सोहणी बण तण सभ कोई आई।

10 Bullah shauh sang preet lagaa'i,
sohni ban tan sabh koi aa'i.

वेख के शाह इनाइत साईं,
जीअ मेरा भरमाइयो रे।

11 vekh ke shaah inaayat saa'een,
jee'a mera bharmaayo re.[3]

अब लगन लग्गी किह करीए?
न जी सकीए ते न मरीए।

1 ab lagan laggi kih kareeye?
na ji sakeeye te na mareeye.

तुम सुनो हमारे बैना,
मोहे रात दिने नहीं चैना।

2 tum suno hamaare baina,
mohe raat dine nahi chaina.

हुण पी बिन पलक न सरीए।

3 hun pee'y bin palak na sareeye.

अब लगन...।

4 ab lagan...

एह अगन बिरहों दी जारी,
कोई हमरी प्रीत निवारी।

5 eh agan birhon di jaari,
koi hamri preet nivaari.

बिन दर्शन कैसे तरीए।

6 bin darshan kaise tareeye.

अब लगन...।

7 ab lagan...

बुल्ले पई मुसीबत भारी,
कोई करो हमारी कारी।

8 bulleh payi museebat bhaari,
koi karo hamaari kaari.

---

* The **muezzin** calls Muslims to prayer from the minaret of the mosque. The **muezzin of love** refers to Bulleh Shah's Master.

The muezzin of love has given his call* 6
  and I must listen to it.

Turning homeward, I bow again and again 7
  at the prayer niche that adorns my forehead.†

Strange are the ways of the city of love, 8
  where bloodshot eyes become cups of pleasure.

I have become entangled in the snare – 9
  willingly have I got myself slaughtered.

Bullah has fallen in love with the Beloved; 10
  each bride comes adorned and embellished.

On beholding Shah Inayat, my Master, 11
  my heart is ever charmed and beguiled.

I have been pierced by the arrow of love – 1
  what shall I do? I can neither live, nor can I die.

Listen to my ceaseless outpourings: 2–3
  night and day, I have no peace;
  I cannot live without my Beloved even for a moment.

I have been pierced by the arrow of love – 4
  what shall I do? I can neither live, nor can I die.

The fire of separation is unceasing – 5
  let someone take care of my love.

How can I be saved without my Beloved's darshan? 6

I have been pierced by the arrow of love – 7
  what shall I do? I can neither live, nor can I die.

O Bullah, I am in deep trouble – 8
  let someone come and help me.

---

† Muslims bow in the direction of Mecca when they pray. The direction to face is indicated by a **prayer niche** (*mihrab*) in the mosque, which here symbolizes the eye centre leading to the inner regions.

एह अजेहे दुख कैसे जरीए।   9   *eh ajehe dukh kaise jareeye.*

अब लगन...।   10   *ab lagan...*[4]

ऐब नमाणी दे कज्ज ओ यार।   1   *aib namaani de kajj o yaar.*

घुंघट खोल मुख वेख़ न मेरा,   2   *ghunghat khol mukh vekh na mera,*

ऐब नमाणी दे कज्ज ओ यार।   *aib namaani de kajj o yaar.*

मैं अणजाणी तेरा नेहों किह जाणा,   3   *main anjaani tera nehon kih jaana,*

लावण दा नहीं चज्ज ओ यार।   *laavan da nahi chajj o yaar.*

हाजी लोक मक्के नूँ जाँदे,   4   *haaji lok makke nu jaande,*

साडा हैं तूँ हज्ज ओ यार।   *saada hain toon hajj o yaar.*

डूंघी नदी ते तुलाह पुराणाँ,   5   *doonghi nadi te tulaah puraana,*

मिलसाँ केहड़े पज्ज ओ यार।   *milsaan kehrre pajj o yaar.*

बुल्ला शौह मैं ज़ाहर डिट्ठा,   6   *Bullah shauh main zaahar dittha,*

लाह मुँह तों लज्ज ओ यार।   *laah munh ton lajj o yaar.*[5]

बस कर जी हुण बस कर जी,   1   *bas kar ji hun bas kar ji,*

इक बात असां नाल   *ik baat asaan naal*

हस्स कर जी।टेक।   *hass kar ji. tek.*

तुसीं दिल मेरे विच वसदे हो,   2   *tuseen dil mere vich vasde ho,*

ऐवें साथों   *aiven saathon*

दूर क्यों नसदे हो।   *door kyon nasde ho.*

नाले घत्त जादू दिल खसदे हो,   3   *naale ghatt jaadu dil khasde ho,*

हुण कित वल जासो नस्स कर जी।   *hun kit val jaaso nass kar ji.*

तुसीं मोयां नूँ मार ना मुकदे सी,   4   *tuseen moyaan nu maar na mukde si,*

खिद्दो वांग खूंडीं नित कुट्टदे सी।   *khiddo vaang khoondeen nit kuttde si.*

गल्ल करदयां दा गल घुट्टदे सी,   5   *gall kardayaan da gal ghuttde si,*

हुण तीर लगाओ कस्स कर जी।   *hun teer lagaa'o kass kar ji.*

How will I endure such torture? 9

I have been pierced by the arrow of love – 10
    what shall I do? I can neither live, nor can I die.

*H*ide the flaws of this lowly one, O Friend! 1

Do not lift the veil and look at my face; 2
    hide the flaws of this lowly one, O Friend!

I am ignorant, O Friend, and know not how to love you – 3
    what do I know of your love?

The hajji pilgrims travel to Mecca; 4
    you are my hajj, O Friend.*

Deep is the river and old my raft – 5
    what excuse should I use to meet you, O Friend?

Says Bullah: I have seen the Beloved's manifest form; 6
    now shed this coyness, O Friend.

*N*o more of this! Now no more of this – 1
    speak a few words to me happily, O dear one.

You dwell right within my heart – 2
    why then do you run away from me?

Casting your spell, you stole my heart – 3
    pray, where will you run to now?

You did not stop slaying the already-slain, 4–5
    but treated me like a ball and beat me with a stick.

You gagged me if I uttered a word
    and now you shoot me with an arrow!

---

* A Muslim who has successfully completed the **hajj**, the pilgrimage to Mecca, a city sacred to Muslims, is called a **hajji**.

तुसीं छपदे हो असां पकड़े हो,
असां नाल ज़ुलफ़ दे जकड़े हो।

6 tuseen chhapde ho asaan pakrre ho,
asaan naal zulaf de jakrre ho.

तुसीं अजे छपण नूं तकड़े हो,
हुण जाण न मिलदा नस्स कर जी।

7 tuseen aje chhapan nu takrre ho,
hun jaan na milda nass kar ji.

बुल्ला शौह मैं तेरी बरदी हां,
तेरा मुख वेखण नूं मरदी हां।

8 Bullah shauh main teri bardi haan,
tera mukh vekhan nu mardi haan.

नित्त सौ सौ मिंनतां करदी हां,
हुण बैठ पिंजर विच धस्स कर जी।

9 nitt sau sau minntaan kardi haan,
hun baith pinjar vich dhass kar ji.[6]

भावें जाण न जाण वे,
वेहड़े आ वड़ मेरे।

1 bhaaven jaan na jaan ve,
vehrre aa varr mere.

मैं तेरे कुरबान वे,
वेहड़े आ वड़ मेरे।

2 main tere qurbaan ve,
vehrre aa varr mere.

तेरे जेहा मैनूं होर न कोई,
ढूंडां जंगल बेला रोही।

3 tere jeha mainu hor na koi,
dhoondaan jangal bela rohi.

ढूंडां तां सारा जहान वे,
वेहड़े आ वड़ मेरे।

4 dhoondaan taan saara jahaan ve,
vehrre aa varr mere.

लोकां दे भाणे चाक महीं दा,
रांझा तां लोकां विच कहीदा।

5 lokaan de bhaane chaak maheen da,
raanjha taan lokaan vich kaheeda.

साडा तां दीन ईमान वे,
वेहड़े आ वड़ मेरे।

6 saada taan deen eemaan ve,
vehrre aa varr mere.

मापे छोड़ लग्गी लड़ तेरे,
शाह इनायत साईं मेरे।

7 maape chhorr laggi larr tere,
shaah inaayat saa'een mere.

लाइयां दी लज्ज पाल वे,
वेहड़े आ वड़ मेरे।

8 laa'eeyaan di lajj paal ve,
vehrre aa varr mere.[7]

You hide yourself, but I search you out 6
   and catch you tightly in my tresses.
You are adept at hiding yourself, 7
   but there is nowhere you can run from me now.
O Lord of Bullah, I am your slave, 8
   pining for a glimpse of your face.
I make countless pleas; 9
   now establish yourself in the cage of my body.

Whether you acknowledge me or not, 1
   pray, walk into my courtyard!
I am a sacrifice unto you – 2
   pray, walk into my courtyard!
There is no one else for me like you; 3
   I have searched forests, jungles and deserts.
Indeed, I have searched the whole world – 4
   pray, walk into my courtyard!
For other people you are a herdsman; 5
   I call you Ranjha in the presence of others.*
But you are my very faith and honour – 6
   pray, walk into my courtyard!
O my beloved King Inayat, I left my parents 7
   to take your shelter.
Now honour this bond of our love – 8
   pray, walk into my courtyard!

---

* In Punjabi folklore, the herdsman **Ranjha** is tormented by intense love for the beautiful, unavailable Heer, who was married against her will to another. Here Bulleh Shah compares himself to Heer pining for her lost Ranjha.

दिल लोचे माही यार नूं।

इक हस हस गल्लां करदियां,
इक रोंदियां
धोंदियां मरदियां।

कहो फुल्ली बसंत बहार नूं,
दिल लोचे माही यार नूं।

मैं न्हाती धोती रह गई,
इक गंध माही दिल बह गई।

भाह लाईए हार शिंगार नूं,
दिल लोचे माही यार नूं।

मैं कमली कीती दूतियां,
दुख घेर चुफ़ेरों लीतियां।

घर आ माही दीदार नूं,
दिल लोचे माही यार नूं।

बुल्ला शौह मेरे घर आया,
मैं घुट रांझण गल लाया।

दुख गए समुंदर पार नूं,
दिल लोचे माही यार नूं।

इक रांझा मैंनूं लोड़ीदा।

कुन फयकूनों
अग्गे दीआं लगिआं,
नेहों न लगड़ा चोरी दा।

आप छिड़ जांदा नाल मज्झीं दे,
सानूं क्यों बेलयों मोड़ीदा।
इक रांझा मैंनूं लोड़ीदा।

रांझे जेहा मैंनूं होर न कोई,
मिनतां कर कर मोड़ीदा।

माण वालियां दे नैन सलोने,
सूहा दुपट्टा गोरी दा।

इक रांझा मैंनूं लोड़ीदा।

1	*dil loche maahi yaar nu.*
2	*ik has has gallaan kardeeyaan,*
	ikrondeeyaan
	dhondeeyaan mardeeyaan.
3	*kaho phulli basant bahaar nu,*
	dil loche maahi yaar nu.
4	*main nhaati dhoti rah gayi,*
	ik gandh maahi dil bah gayi.
5	*bhaah laa'eeye haar shingaar nu,*
	dil loche maahi yaar nu.
6	*main kamli keeti dooteeyaan,*
	dukh gher chuferon leeteeyaan.
7	*ghar aa maahi deedaar nu,*
	dil loche maahi yaar nu.
8	*Bullah shauh mere ghar aaya,*
	main ghut raanjhan gal laaya.
9	*dukh gaye samundar paar nu,*
	dil loche maahi yaar nu.[8]

1	*ik raanjha mainu lorreeda.*
2	*kun faykoono*
	agge deeyaan lageeyaan,
	nehon na lagrra chori da.
3	*aap chhirr jaanda naal majjheen de,*
	saanu kyon belyon morreeda.
	ik raanjha mainu lorreeda.
4	*raanjhe jeha mainu hor na koi,*
	minntaan kar kar morreeda.
5	*maan vaaleeyaan de nain salone,*
	sooha dupatta gori da.
	ik raanjha mainu lorreeda.

My heart pines for my beloved Friend! 1

Some laugh and chat and rejoice 2
 while others weep and wail and grieve.

Go and proclaim to the spring in bloom – 3
 my heart pines for my beloved Friend!

My washing and bathing have all gone to waste; 4
 a knot has settled in my Beloved's heart.

Oh, set fire to this jewellery and adornment – 5
 my heart pines for my beloved Friend!

Enemies have driven me mad* 6
 and I am completely engulfed in anguish.

Beloved, come home that I may have a glimpse of you – 7
 my heart pines for my beloved Friend!

O Bullah, my Beloved has come home; 8
 I have clasped Ranjha close to my heart.

My grief has vanished beyond the seas – 9
 my heart pines for my beloved Friend!

The only one I long for is Ranjha! 1

My love for him is older than creation, 2
 and our love was not hidden from others.

He himself goes to graze the buffaloes – 3
 why does he not take me along to the pasture?

The only one I long for is Ranjha!

There is no one like Ranjha for me; 4
 I call him back with repeated prayers.

Charming are the eyes of one who is proud of her Beloved, 5
 and crimson is her scarf.

The only one I long for is Ranjha!

---

*The **enemies** are not external, but the passions of the mind.

अहद अहमद विच
फरक न बुल्लया,
इक रत्ती भेत मरोड़ी दा।
इक रांझा मैनूं लोड़ीदा।

6 ahad ahmad vich
pharak na bulliya,
ik ratti bhet marorri da.
ik raanjha mainu lorreeda.[9]

केहे लारे देना एं सानूं,
दो घड़ियां मिल जाई। टेक।
नेड़े वस्सें थां न दस्सें,
ढूंडां कित वल जाहीं।
आपे झाती पाई अहमद,
वेखां तां मुड़ नाहीं।
आख गयों मुड़ आयों नाहीं,
सीने दे विच भड़कण भाहीं।
इकसे घर विच वसदयां रसदयां,
कित वल कूक सुणाई।
पांधी जा मेरा देह सुनेहा,
दिल दे ओह्ले लुकदा केहा।
नाम अल्ला दे न हो वैरी,
मुख वेखन नूं न तरसाई।
बुल्ला शौह की लाया मैनूं,
रात अद्धी है तेरी मैहमा।
औझड़ बेले सभ कोई डरदा,
शौह ढूंडां
मैं चाई चाई।
केहे लारे देना एं सानूं,
दो घड़ियां मिल जाई।

1 kehe laare dena en saanu,
do gharriyaan mil jaa'een. tek.
2 nerre vassen thaan na dassen,
dhoondaan kit val jaaheen.
3 aape jhaati paa'i ahmad,
vekhaan taan murr naahi.
4 aakh gayon murr aayon naahi,
seene de vich bharrkan bhaaheen.
5 ikse ghar vich vasdiyaan rasdiyaan,
kit val kook sunaa'een.
6 paandhi ja mera deh suneha,
dil de ohle lukda keha.
7 naam alla de na ho vairi,
mukh vekhan nu na tarsaa'een.
8 Bullah shauh ki laaya mainu,
raat addhi hai teri maihma.
9 aujharr bele sabh koi darda,
shauh dhoondaan
main chaa'een chaa'een.
10 kehe laare dena en saanu,
do gharriyaan mil jaa'een.[10]

---

* Only a small **turn of the pen** is needed to make the letter em in the Urdu script, which turns the word Ahad (the One) into Ahmad (the Prophet Muhammad). This indicates that there is no significant difference between the Master and God.

There is no difference between Ahad and Ahmad, O Bullah;   6
    it is only a little turn of the pen.*
The only one I long for is Ranjha!

My Beloved, why torment me with false promises?   1
Please come and meet me, even if only for a moment or two.
Your abode is near, yet you do not tell me where –   2
    which way shall I go to search for you?
O Master, you showed me a glimpse,   3
    but when I turned around, you were not there.
In spite of your promise, you did not return,   4
    and now the fire of longing blazes in my heart.
You and I dwell in the same house† –   5
    to whom but you should I cry out my sorrow?
O wayfarer, go and deliver my message to him –   6
    why does he hide behind the door of my heart?
I beseech you in the name of the Lord: be not my enemy;   7
    do not make me yearn to see your face.
From midnight on, I sing his glory –   8
    O Bullah, what kind of love has the Lord obsessed me with?
Everyone is afraid of trackless jungles,   9
    yet it is there that I look for my Beloved with great fervour!
My Beloved, why torment me with false promises?   10
Please come and meet me, even if only for a moment or two.

---

† At initiation, the Master places his inner form within the disciple at the eye centre, where the disciple may access it by meditating and going within to the higher planes. Thus Bulleh Shah says that he and the Master dwell in the same house.

मैं क्योंकर जावां काअबे नूं,
दिल लोचे तखत हज़ारे नूं। टेक।

लोकी सजदा काअबे नूं करदे,
साडा सजदा यार प्यारे नूं।

औगण वेख न भुल मीआं रांझा,
याद करीं उस कारे नूं।

मैं अनतारू तरन न जाणां,
शरम पई तुध तारे नूं।

तेरा सानी कोई नहीं मिलया,
ढूंढ लिआ जग सारे नूं।

बुल्ला शौह दी प्रीत अनोखी
तारे औगुणहारे नूं।

1 main kyon kar jaavaan qaabe nu,
dil loche takhat hazaare nu. tek.

2 loki sajda qaabe nu karde,
saada sajda yaar pyaare nu.

3 augun vekh na bhul meeyaan raanjha,
yaad kareen us kaare nu.

4 main antaaru taran na jaana,
sharam payi tudh taare nu.

5 tera saani koi nahi miliya,
dhoondh liya jag saare nu.

6 Bullah shauh di preet anokhi
taare augun-haare nu.[11]

मैं उडीकां कर रही,
कदी आ कर फेरा। टेक।

मैं जो तैनूं आखया,
कोई घल सुनेहड़ा।

चशमां सेज विछाईआं
दिल कीता डेरा।

लटक चलंदा आंवदा
शाह इनायत मेरा।

ओह अजेहा कौण है
जा आखे जेहड़ा।

मैं विच की तकसीर है
मैं बरदा तेरा।

तैं बाझों मेरा कौण है
दिल ढाह न मेरा।

1 main udeekaan kar rahi,
kadi aa kar phera. tek.

2 main jo tainu aakhya,
koi ghal sunehrra.

3 chashmaan sej vichhaa'eeyaan
dil keeta dera.

4 latak chalanda aanvada
shaah inaayat mera.

5 oh ajeha kaun hai
ja aakhe jehrra.

6 main vich ki takseer hai
main barda tera.

7 tain baajhon mera kaun hai
dil dhaah na mera.

---

*The **Ka'ba** is the shrine in Mecca, Saudi Arabia, that Muslims consider to be the most sacred place on earth.

Why should I go to the Ka'ba*   1
 when my heart pines for Takht Hazara?†
People prostrate themselves before Ka'ba –   2
 my prostrations are to my Beloved.
Do not forsake me for my sins, O Ranjha –   3
 recall to mind that covenant!
I am a novice and know not how to swim: 4
 my drowning will be your shame!
I have searched the whole world   5
 but have not found anyone like you.
O Bullah, unique is my Lord's love;   6
 he redeems all sinners like me.

I am eagerly awaiting you –   1
 pray, come sometime soon!
I plead with you to send me a message –   2–3
 come, rest in my eyes
 and dwell in my heart.
Come with your swaying gait, my King Inayat –   4–5
 who can give you this message?
I am your slave –   6
 what fault is there in me?
Do not break my heart –   7
 who is mine but you?

---

† **Takht Hazara** is the place where Ranjha was born; here it signifies the abode of the Lord.

ढूंढ शहर सभ भालया	8	*dhoondh shahar sabh bhaalya*
कासद घल्लां केहड़ा।		*kaasad ghallaan kehrra.*
चढ़ियां डोली प्रेम दी	9	*charrhiyaan doli prem di*
दिल धड़के मेरा।		*dil dharrke mera.*
आओ इनायत कादरी	10	*aa'o inaayat kaadari*
जी चाहे मेरा।		*ji chaahe mera.*
पहली पौड़ी प्रेम दी	11	*pahli paurri prem di*
पुलसराते डेरा।		*pulsaraate dera.*
हाजी मक्के हज करन,	12	*haaji makke haj karan,*
मैं मुख वेखां तेरा।		*main mukh vekhaan tera.*
आ इनायत कादरी	13	*aa inaayat kaadari*
हत्थ पकड़ीं मेरा।		*hatth pakrreen mera.*
जल बल आहीं मारिआं	14	*jal bal aaheen maareeyaan*
दिल पत्थर तेरा।		*dil patthar tera.*
पा के कुंडी प्रेम दी	15	*pa ke kundi prem di*
दिल खिचयो मेरा।		*dil khichyo mera.*
मैं विच कोई न आ पीआ	16	*main vich koi na aa peeya*
विच परदा तेरा।		*vich parda tera.*
दसत कंगण बाहीं चूड़ियां	17	*dasat kangan baaheen choorreeyaan*
गल नौरंग चोला।		*gal naurang chola.*
रांझण मैनूं कर गया	18	*raanjhan mainu kar gaya*
कोई रावल–रौला।		*koi raaval-raula.*
आण नवें दु:ख पै गए	19	*aan naven dukh pai gaye*
कोई सूलां दा घेरा।		*koi soolaan da ghera.*
मैं जाता दुख मैनूं आहा	20	*main jaata dukh mainu aaha*
दुख पए घर सइयां।		*dukh paye ghar sa'eeyaan.*

---

*Inayat Shah was a Master in the Sufi Qadiri lineage, so he is sometimes called **Inayat Qadiri**.

†In Muslim tradition, the **Sirat Bridge**, a way across the infernal fire, is described as finer than a hair and sharper than a sword. The righteous pass over it swiftly, but the wicked lose their footing.

I have searched the whole city –   8
    whom should I send as my messenger?
Riding in the palanquin of love,   9–10
    my heart beats faster;
    come, Inayat Qadiri –
    my heart yearns for you!*
The first rung of love is like the Sirat Bridge;†   11–12
    the hajjis go on pilgrimages to Mecca,‡
    but it is your face that I seek.
Come, Inayat Qadiri, come and hold my hand,   13
    come and hold my hand!
I heave sighs, consumed in your love,   14
    but you have a heart of stone.
Casting your hook of love, you pulled my heart,   15–16
    you pulled my heart.
There is nothing but your own veil
    that comes between us.
Adorning my arms with bracelets   17–18
    and my wrists with bangles,
    I put on a brand-new dress,
    but I have been tricked by Ranjha
    and am left forsaken.§
New sorrows have besieged me   19
    like a garland of thorns.
I thought only I was in trouble,   20
    but my friends were affected as well.

---

‡ A Muslim who has successfully completed the hajj, the pilgrimage to Mecca, a city sacred to Muslims, is called a **hajji**.
§ In Punjabi folklore, the herdsman **Ranjha** is tormented by intense love for the beautiful, unavailable Heer, who was married against her will to another.

सिर सिर भांबड़ भड़क्या
सभ तपदिआं गइयां।

हुण आण बणी सिर आपणे
सभ चुक गया झेड़ा।

जेहड़िआं साहवरे मंनिआं
सोई पेके होवण।

शौह जिन्हां ते मायल ए
चढ़ सेजे सोवण।

जिस घर कौंत न बोलया
सोई खाली वेहड़ा।

बुल्ला शौह दे वासते
दिल भड़कन भाहीं।

औखा पैंडा प्रेम दा
सो घटदा नाहीं।

दिल विच धक्के झेड़दे
सिर धाई बेड़ा।

मैं उडीकां कर रही
कदी आ कर फेरा।

21 sir sir bhaambarr bharrkya
sabh tapdeeyaan gayeeaan.

22 hun aan bani sir aapne
sabh chuk gaya jherra.

23 jehrreeyaan saahvare manneeyaan
soi peke hovan.

24 shauh jinhaan te maayal e
charrh seje sovan.

25 jis ghar kaunt na bolya
soi khaali verrha.

26 Bullah shauh de vaaste
dil bharrkan bhaaheen.

27 aukha painda prem da
so ghatda naahi.

28 dil vich dhakke jherrde
sir dhaayeen berra.

29 main udeekaan kar rahi,
kadi aa kar phera.[12]

मैनूं छड गए आप लद गए,
मैं विच की तकसीर।

रातीं नींद न दिन सुख सुत्ती,
अक्खीं पलटया नीर।

छविआं ते तलवारां कोलों,
इश्क दे तिक्खे तीर।

इश्क जेड न ज़ालम कोई,
एह ज़हमत बेपीर।

1 mainu chhadd gaye aap ladd gaye,
main vich ki takseer.

2 raateen neend na din sukh sutti,
akkheen paltiya neer.

3 chhaveeyaan te talvaaraan kolon,
ishq de tikkhe teer.

4 ishq jed na zaalam koi,
eh zahmat bepeer.

Every head was ablaze   21
   and everyone left, consumed in fire.
Now that misfortunes have befallen me,   22
   my quarrels with others are over.
Those who are honoured at their husbands' house   23
   are accepted at their parents' house too.*
The one whom the bridegroom favours   24
   sleeps blissfully in his bed.
Empty is that courtyard   25
   where the husband does not speak.
O Bullah, in longing for my Beloved,   26
   fires blaze in my heart.
Difficult is the path of love;   27
   it does not end.
My heart throbs;   28
   my boat is tossed in a storm.
I am eagerly awaiting you –   29
   pray, come sometime soon!

*H*e left me, he departed –   1
   what did I do wrong?
I do not sleep in peace, not at night nor in the day,   2
   tears flowing constantly from my eyes.
Sharper than swords and spears   3
   are the arrows of love.
There is no one as cruel as my love –   4
   beyond cure is my affliction.

---

* When a couple marries, traditionally they live at the house of the groom's parents. If his parents accept the bride, her parents will feel she has honoured the family.

इक पल साइत आराम न आवे,
बुरी बिरहों दी पीर।
बुल्ला शौह जे करे इनायत,
दुख होवण तग़ईर।
मैनूं छड गए आप लद गए,
मैं विच की तकसीर।

5   *ik pal saayat aaraam na aave,*
    buri birhon di peer.
6   *Bullah shauh je kare inaayat,*
    dukh hovan taga'eer.
7   *mainu chhadd gaye aap ladd gaye,*
    main vich ki takseer.[13]

मेरे माही क्यों चिर लाया ए।
कह बुल्ला हुण प्रेम कहाणी,
जिस तन लग्गे सो तन जाणे।
अंदर झिड़कां बाहर ताहने,
नेहों ला एह सुख पाया ए।
नैनां कार रोवन दी पकड़ी,
इक मरना दो जग दी फकड़ी।
बिरहों जिंद अवल्ली जकड़ी,
नी मैं रो रो हाल वंजाया ए।
इश्क मुल्लां ने बांग दिवाई,
शौह आवण दी गल्ल सुणाई।
कर नियत सजदे दे वल्ल आई,
नी मैं मुँह महराब लगाया ए।
बुल्ला शौह घर लपट लगाई,
रसते मूं सभ बण तण आई।
मैं वेखाँ आ इनायत साईं
जिस मैनूं शौह मिलाया ए।

1   *mere maahi kyon chir laaya e.*
2   *kah Bullah hun prem kahaani,*
    jis tan lagge so tan jaane.
3   *andar jhirrkaan baahar taahne,*
    nehon la eh sukh paaya e.
4   *naina kaar rovan di pakarri,*
    ik marna do jag di phakarri.
5   *birhon jind avalli jakarri,*
    ni main ro ro haal vanjaaya e.
6   *ishq mullan ne baang divaa'i,*
    shauh aavan di gall sunaai.
7   *kar niyat sajde de vall aayi.*
    ni main munh mahraab lagaaya e.
8   *bullah shauh ghar lapat lagaa'i,*
    raste moon sabh ban tan aa'een.
9   *main vekhaan aa inaayat saa'een,*
    jis mainu shauh milaaya e.[14]

---

* The **muezzin** calls Muslims to prayer from the minaret of the mosque.

I experience no peace, not even for a moment, 5
    so acute is the pain of separation.
O Bullah, if the Lord were to shower his grace, 6
    my sorrows would be ended!
He left me, he departed – 7
    what did I do wrong?

O my Beloved, why do you take so long? 1
Narrate now, O Bullah, your love story; 2
    only he who has loved knows love.
Rebukes within and taunts without: 3
    such is the pleasure I have found in love!
My eyes have taken to weeping – 4
    first, this separation feels like death;
    second, the world's ridicule pains me.
Helplessly caught in the grip of yearning, 5
    I have cried my heart out in anguish.
The muezzin of love has given his call,* 6
    announcing the news of the Beloved's arrival.
Possessed by the desire to bow before him, 7
    I turned my face towards the prayer niche.†
O Bullah, cherish the fragrance of the Lord; 8
    embellish yourself when you come to him.
Come, let me behold you, my Master Inayat – 9
    you who have made me one with my Lord.

---

† The **prayer niche** (*mihrab*) refers to the third eye or tenth gate, the eye centre, at which one enters the inner regions.

साडे वल्ल मुखड़ा मोड़ वे प्यारया,	1	saade vall mukhrra morr ve pyaaria,
साडे वल्ल मुखड़ा मोड़। टेक।		saade vall mukhrra morr. tek.
आपे पाईआं कुंडीयां तैं,	2	aape paayee'aan kundeeyaan tain,
ते आपे खिचना एँ डोर।		te aape khichna en dor.
साडे वल्ल मुखड़ा मोड़ वे प्यारया,	3	saade vall mukhrra morr ve pyaaria,
साडे वल्ल मुखड़ा मोड़।		saade vall mukhrra morr.
अरश कुरसी ते बांगां मिलियां,	4	arash kurasi te baangaan mileeyaan,
मक्के पै गया शोर।		makke pai gaya shor.
साडे वल्ल मुखड़ा मोड़ वे प्यारया,	5	saade vall mukhrra morr ve pyaaria,
साडे वल्ल मुखड़ा मोड़।		saade vall mukhrra morr.
बुल्ला शौह असां मरना नाहीं,	6	Bullah shauh asaan marna naahi,
मर जावे कोई होर।		mar jaave koi hor.
साडे वल्ल मुखड़ा मोड़ वे प्यारया,	7	saade vall mukhrra morr ve pyaaria,
साडे वल्ल मुखड़ा मोड़।		saade vall mukhrra morr.[15]

तेरे इश्क़ नचाइआं	1	tere ishq nachaa'eeyaan
कर थइआ थइआ। टेक।		kar thayya thayya. tek.
तेरे इश्क़ ने डेरा	2	tere ishq ne dera
मेरे अंदर कीता।		mere andar keeta.
भर के ज़हर प्याला		bhar ke zahar pyaala
मैं तां आपे पीता।		main taan aape peeta.
झबदे बहुड़ीं वे तबीबा	3	jhabade bahurreen ve tabeeba
नहीं ते मैं मर गइआं।		nahi te main mar ga'eeyaan.
तेरे इश्क़ नचाइआं	4	tere ishq nachaa'eeyaan
कर थइआ थइआ।		kar thayya thayya.
छुप गया वे सूरज	5	chhup gaya ve sooraj
बाहर रह गई आ लाली।		baahar rah gayi aa laali.

---

*Mecca, the birthplace of the Prophet Muhammad, is a sacred site and place of pilgrimage for Muslims.

†Bulleh Shah is saying that he has become immortal in his Master's love while his mind's control over his soul has died.

Turn your face towards me, my Beloved,   *1*
   turn your face towards me!
It was you who caught me with your hook,   *2*
   and now you yourself pull the line.
Turn your face towards me, my Beloved,   *3*
   turn your face towards me!
From your heavenly seat you gave out the call,   *4*
   and a tumult arose in Mecca.*
Turn your face towards me, my Beloved,   *5*
   turn your face towards me!
O Lord of Bullah, I will not die;   *6*
   it is someone else who has died.†
Turn your face towards me, my Beloved,   *7*
   turn your face towards me!

Your love has made me dance   *1*
   to its own rhythm!‡
Your love has made my heart its home;   *2*
   I willingly drank this cup full of poison.
Come quickly, O physician,   *3–4*
    otherwise I shall die –
   your love has made me dance
   to its own rhythm!
The sun has set,   *5*
   yet the reddish tinge of dusk still lingers;
   I shall sacrifice myself unto you
   if you show me your face again.

---

‡ When Bulleh Shah displeased his Master, Inayat Shah, he was banned from his presence and lived in agony. Finally, dressed in the clothes of a dancing girl, he danced for his Master, who accepted him back.

वे मैं सदके होवां
देवें मुड़ जे वखाली।

6 पीरा मैं भुल गइआं
तेरे नाल न गइआं।

7 तेरे इश्क़ नचाइआं
कर थइआ थइआ।

8 ऐस इश्क़े दे कोलों
मैंनूं हटक न माए।

लाहू जांदड़े बेड़े
केहड़ा मोड़ लिआवे।

9 मेरी अकल जो भुल्ली
नाल मुहाणयां दे गइआं।

10 तेरे इश्क़ नचाइआं
कर थइआ थइआ।

11 ऐस इश्क़ दी झंगी विच मोर बुलेंदा।
सानूं किबला ते काअबा
सोहणा यार दखेंदा।

12 सानूं घायल करके
फिर ख़बर न लइआ।

13 तेरे इश्क़ नचाइआं
कर थइआ थइआ।

14 बुल्ला शौह ने आंदा
मैंनूं इनाइत दे बूहे।
जिस ने मैंनूं पवाए
चोले सावे ते सूहे।

15 जां मैं मारी है अड्डी
मिल पया है वहीआ।

16 तेरे इश्क़ नचाइआं
कर थइआ थइआ।

ve main sadke hovaan
deven murr je vakhaali.

6 peera main bhull ga'eeaan
tere naal na ga'eeyaan.

7 tere ishq nachaa'eeyaan
kar thayya thayya.

8 es ishqe de kolon
mainu hatak na maaye.

laahu jaandarre berre
kehrra morr lyaave.

9 meri akal jo bhulli
naal muhaaniyaan de ga'eeyaan.

10 tere ishq nachaa'eeyaan
kar thayya thayya.

11 es ishq di jhangi vich mor bulenda.
saanu kibla te qaaba
sohna yaar dakhenda.

12 saanu ghaayal karke
phir khabar na la'eeya.

13 tere ishq nachaa'eeyaan
kar thayya thayya.

14 Bullah shauh ne aanda
mainu inaayat de boohe.
jis ne mainu pavaaye
chole saave te soohe.

15 jaan main maari hai addi
mil paya hai vaheeya.

16 tere ishq nachaa'eeyaan
kar thayya thayya.[16]

---

* The **Ka'ba** is a sacred building in Mecca, the focal point of the Islamic world, and **qibla** is the direction of the Ka'ba, which Muslims face while praying.

I made a grave mistake, O Master,   *6–7*
   when I did not go with you –
   your love has made me dance
   to its own rhythm!
Do not keep me from this love, O mother –   *8*
   who will bring back the boat adrift in stormy waters?
My sense has left me; it has gone with the ferryman –   *9–10*
   your love has made me dance
   to its own rhythm!
In this forest of love the peacock gives its call;   *11*
   for me my Beloved is both qibla and Ka'ba.*
After inflicting the grievous wound,   *12–13*
   you did not enquire after me –
   your love has made me dance
   to its own rhythm!
O Bullah, the Lord has brought me to the door of Inayat,   *14*
   who has made me wear garments of green and red.†
When I danced a step, I found Him the same as ever –   *15–16*
   your love has made me dance
   to its own rhythm!

---

† **garments of green and red**: Clothes worn at weddings or other celebrations.

कलाम हज़रत सुलतान बाहू

Kalaam Hazrat Sultan Bahu

चढ़ चंना ते कर रुशनाई,
ज़िकर करेंदे तारे हू।
गलियां दे विच फिरन निमाणे,
लालां दे वणजारे हू।
शाला कोई न थिवे मुसाफ़र,
कक्ख जिन्हां तों भारे हू।
ताड़ी मार उडा न सानूं,
आपे उड्डणहारे हू।

1 *charrh channa te kar rushnaa'i,*
 zikar karende taare hu.
2 *galeeyaan de vich phiran nimaane,*
 laalaan de vanjaare hu.
3 *shaala koi na theeve musaafar,*
 kakkh jinhaan ton bhaare hu.
4 *taarri maar uda na saanu,*
 aape uddan-haare hu.[1]

चढ़ चंना ते कर रुशनाई,
ज़िकर करेंदे तेरा हू।
तेरे जहे चंन कई सै चढ़दे,
सजणां बाझ हनेरा हू।
जित्थे चंन असाडा चढ़दा,
क़दर नहीं कुझ तेरा हू।
जिस दे कारन जनम गवाया,
यार मिले इक फेरा हू।

1 *charrh channa te kar rushnaa'i,*
 zikar karende tera hu.
2 *tere jahe chann kayi sai charrhde,*
 sajna baajh hanera hu.
3 *jitthe chann asaada charrhda,*
 qadar nahi kujh tera hu.
4 *jis de kaaran janam gavaaya,*
 yaar mile ik phera hu.[2]

एह तन मेरा चश्मां होवे,
मुर्शिद वेख न रज्जां हू।
लूं लूं दे मुढ
लक्ख लक्ख चश्मां,
हिक्क खोलां हिक्क कज्जां हू।

1 *eh tan mera chashma hove,*
 murshid vekh na rajjaan hu.
2 *loon loon de mudh*
 lakkh lakkh chashma,
 hikk kholaan hikk kajjaan hu.

Hazrat Sultan Bahu*

Rise, O moon, spread your light across the heavens;   *1*
    the stars remember you in silent prayer.
Those who were once merchants of rubies in their homeland   *2*
    now roam the alleyways of earthly life like beggars.
Never let it happen, O Lord,   *3*
    that anyone should have to leave his own home,
    for no one is worth even a piece of straw in an alien land.
Clap not your hands, O Bahu,   *4*
    to startle us into flying out of this world.
Already predisposed are we
    to fly back to our long-lost home.

Rise, O moon, and spread your light –   *1*
    everyone is talking fondly of you.
Even if thousands of moons like you were to rise,   *2*
    without my Beloved, I would still be in utter darkness.
Where my true moon rises,   *3*
    your light pales to nothing.
May my beloved Friend, for whom I would sacrifice my life,   *4*
    reveal himself to me just once!

If my whole body were adorned with eyes,   *1*
    I would gaze at my Master with untiring zeal.
If only each pore of my body had a million eyes,   *2*
    then even if some eyes blinked
    others would remain open to see.

---

* **Hazrat** is an honorific, a term of veneration used for Muslim religious leaders and other respected people.

इतनयां डिठयां सबर न आवे,
होर किते वल भज्जां हू।
मुर्शिद दा दीदार है बाहू,
लक्ख करोड़ां हज्जां हू।

3 itnyaan dithyaan sabar na aave,
hor kite val bhajjaan hu.
4 murshid da deedaar hai Bahu,
lakkh karorraan hajjaan hu.[3]

इश्क़ माही दे लाइयां अग्गीं,
लग्गी कौन बुझावे हू।
मैं की जाणा ज़ात इश्क़,
जो दर दर चा झुकावे हू।
न सौवें न सौवण देवे,
सुतयां आण जगावे हू।
मैं क़ुरबान हां उसदे जेहड़ा,
विछड़े यार मिलावे हू।

1 ishq maahi de laa'eeyaan aggeen,
laggi kaun bujhaave hu.
2 main ki jaana zaat ishq,
jo dar dar cha jhukaave hu.
3 na sauven na sauvan deve,
sutyaan aan jagaave hu.
4 main qurbaan haan usde jehrra,
vichharre yaar milaave hu.[4]

मैं कोझी मेरा दिलबर सोहणा,
क्यों कर उस नूं भावां हू।
विहड़े साडे वड़दा नाहीं,
लक्ख वसीले पावां हू।
न सोहणी न दौलत पल्ले,
क्यों कर यार मनावां हू।
दुख हमेशा इह रहसी बाहू,
रोंदी ही मर जावां हू।

1 main kojhi mera dilbar sohna,
kyon kar us nu bhaavaan hu.
2 vehrre saade varrda naahi,
lakkh vaseele paavaan hu.
3 na sohni na daulat palle,
kyon kar yaar manaavaan hu.
4 dukh hamesha eh rahsi Bahu,
rondi hi mar jaavaan hu.[5]

Even so, my thirst to see my Master   *3*
  would remain unquenched –
  who else can I run to?
A glimpse of the Master, says Bahu,   *4*
  is better than millions of pilgrimages.

*M*y heart is ablaze with the love of my Beloved –   *1*
  who could extinguish the flame?
How could I have known the nature of this love,   *2*
  which has made me bow my head at every doorstep?
It neither sleeps nor allows me to sleep –   *3*
  if I fall asleep, it wakes me up.
O Bahu, I would sacrifice my life for the one   *4*
  who would unite me with my long-lost Beloved.

*B*eautiful is my Beloved and ugly am I –   *1*
  how can I ever win his heart?
Despite my countless efforts   *2*
  he has not entered the courtyard of my heart.
I have neither beauty nor wealth –   *3*
  how am I to please him?
Says Bahu: I am always tormented by the thought   *4*
  that I might die crying in anguish for my Beloved.

न मैं सेर न पाअ छटाकी,
न पूरी सरसाही हू।

1   na main ser na pa chhataaki,
     na poori sarsaahi hu.

न मैं तोला, न मैं मासा,
गल्ल रत्तियां ते आई हू।

2   na main tola, na main maasa,
     gall ratteeyaan te aa'i hu.

रत्ती होवां रत्तियां तुल्लां,
ओह वी पूरी नाही हू।

3   ratti hovaan ratteeyaan tullaan,
     oh vi poori naahi hu.

वज़न तोल पूरा तद होसी,
जद होसी फ़ज़ल इलाही हू।

4   vazan tol poora tad hosi,
     jad hosi fazal ilaahi hu.[6]

सुण फ़रयाद पीरां दिया पीरा,
अरज़ सुणी कंन धर के हू।

1   sun faryaad peeraan diya peera,
     araz sun i kann dhar ke hu.

बेड़ा अड़या विच कपरां दे,
जिथ मच्छ न बैह्न्दे डर के हू।

2   berra arrya vich kaparaan de,
     jith machh na baihnde dar ke hu.

शाह जिलानी महबूब सुबहानी,
ख़बर लयो झट कर के हू।

3   shaah jilaani mahboob subahaani,
     khabar layo jhat kar ke hu.

पीर जिन्हां दा मीरां बाहू,
कद्धी लगदे तर के हू।

4   peer jinhaan da meeraan Bahu,
     kaddhi lagde tar ke hu.[7]

सुण फ़रयाद पीरां दिया पीरा,
आख सुणावां कैनूं हू।

1   sun faryaad peeraan diya peera,
     aakh sunaavaan kainu hu.

तैं जेहा मैनूं होर न कोई,
मैं जेहियां लक्ख तैनूं हू।

2   tain jeha mainu hor na koi,
     main jeheeyaan lakkh tainu hu.

फोल न काग़ज़ बदियां वाले,
दर तों धक्क न मैनूं हू।

3   phol na kaagaz badeeyaan vaale,
     dar ton dhakk na mainu hu.

मैं विच ऐड गुनाह न हुंदे,
तूं बख़शेंदों कैनूं हू।

4   main vich aid gunaah na hunde,
     toon bakhshendon kainu hu.[8]

---

[*] A *seer* is a weight measure slightly less than a kilogram. Bahu takes *seer* as the standard representing a spiritually mature person. He mentions other weight measures (given in italics) in their descending order – right down to **ratti**, a very small measure. This verse indicates Sultan Bahu's humility.

I am neither a *seer* nor a *paav*,   1–3
   not a *chhatak* or a *sarsahi*
   or even a *tola* or a *masha*.
Even a *ratti* is greater than me!*
I will assume my true worth   4
   only when the Lord showers his grace on me!

*H*ear my plea, O Master of Masters –   1
   listen intently to my supplication.
My ship is caught in perilous seas   2
   where even mighty whales dare not venture.
O Shah Jilani, beloved of God,†   3
   make haste and come to my rescue!
Those who have Meeran as their Master and saviour, O Bahu,‡   4
   will safely swim across the ocean of existence.

*T*ake heed of my lament, O Master of Masters –   1
   to whom should I relate my tale of woe?
For me, there is no one like you,   2
   but there are millions like me for you.
Do not read the scroll of my evil deeds;   3
   pray, do not push me away from your door.
Says Bahu: had I not been such a blatant sinner,   4
   whom would you have forgiven, O Master?

---

† **Shah Jilani**, the first Master of the Sufi Qadiri lineage, was Sultan Bahu's Master.
‡ **Meeran** (the Exalted) is a term of endearment and reverence Sultan Bahu uses out of love for his Master.

बानी गुरु नानक देव जी

Bani Guru Nanak Dev Ji

राग सूही असटपदीआ
महला १ घरु १

Raag Soohi Astpadee'a
Mahala Pahila Ghar Pahila

सभ अवगण मै गुण नही कोई॥	1	sabh avgan mai gun nahi koi.
किउ कर कंत मिलावा होई॥१॥		kio kar kant milaava hoi.
ना मै रूप न बंके नैणा॥	2	na mai roop na banke naina.
ना कुल ढंग		na kul dhang
न मीठे बैणा॥१॥ रहाउ॥		na meethe baina. rahaa'o.
सहज सीगार कामण कर आवै॥	3	sahaj seegaar kaaman kar aavai.
ता सोहागण जा कंतै भावै॥२॥		ta sohaagan ja kantai bhaavai.
ना तिस रूप न रेखिआ काई॥	4	na tis roop na rekhya kaa'i.
अंत न साहिब सिमरिआ जाई॥३॥		ant na saahib simarya jaa'i.
सुरत मत नाही चतुराई॥	5	surat mat naahi chaturaa'i.
कर किरपा प्रभ लावहो पाई॥४॥		kar kirpa prabh laavho paa'i.
खरी सिआणी कंत न भाणी॥	6	khari syaani kant na bhaani.
माइआ लागी भरम भुलाणी॥५॥		maaya laagi bharam bhulaani.
हउमै जाई ता कंत समाई॥	7	haumai jaa'i ta kant samaa'i.
तउ कामण पिआरे		tau kaaman pyaare
नव निध पाई॥६॥		nav nidh paa'i.
अनिक जनम बिछुरत दुख पाइआ॥	8	anik janam bichhurat dukh paaya.
कर गह लेहो प्रीतम		kar gah leho preetam
प्रभ राइआ॥७॥		prabh raaya.
भणत नानक सहु है भी होसी॥	9	bhanat Nanak sauh hai bhi hosi.
जै भावै पिआरा तै रावेसी॥८॥		jai bhaavai pyaara tai raavesi.[1]

---

[*]The hymns from the Adi Granth composed by the Gurus in the line of Guru Nanak include a header line giving the name of the raga (the musical measure of the hymn) and the Guru who composed the hymn, listed by order of succession. Guru Nanak is the first Guru, Guru Amar Das the third Guru, Guru Ram Das the fourth, Guru Arjun Dev the fifth and Guru Tegh Bahadur the ninth Guru. The header sometimes also includes the name of the verse form of the hymn, for example, astpadi or slok. See the Glossary for descriptions of the various verse forms.

Guru Nanak Dev Ji

Raga Soohi, Astpadi, First Guru*

Full of vices and without any virtue,   1
   how can I unite with my Husband?

I have neither beauty nor bewitching eyes,   2
   no noble family tradition or sweet voice.

The bride may adorn herself with calm and bliss,   3
   but only when she becomes pleasing to her Husband
   does she become a happy wife.

The Lord has neither form nor features   4
   and cannot be remembered at the last moment.

I have no understanding, wisdom or intelligence –   5
   have mercy, O Lord, and attach me to your feet.

With all my cleverness I have not won my Lord over;   6
   attached to maya, I have strayed into delusion.

When her ego departs and the bride is absorbed in the Lord,   7
   then alone does she receive the nine treasures of his love.†

In separation from you, birth after birth,   8
   I have suffered much pain –
   hold my hand now, O my beloved sovereign Lord.

Says Nanak: the Lord is and shall ever be;   9
   he enjoys union with the bride with whom he is pleased.

---

† Ancient Indian scriptures enumerate **nine treasures** having to do with material wealth and possessions of all kinds as well as worldly skills. In the teachings of the Saints, the nine treasures symbolize the wealth of Nam, through which one attains the spiritual treasure God has placed within all.

वार सूही की महला ३
सलोक महला १

सतगुर भीखिआ देह मै
तूं समग्रथ दातार॥

हउमै गरब निवारीऐ काम क्रोध
अहंकार॥

लब लोभ परजालीऐ
नाम मिलै आधार॥

अहिनिस नवतन निरमला
मैला कबहूं न होए॥

नानक इह बिध छुटीऐ
नदर तेरी सुख होए॥१॥

Vaar Soohi Ki Mahala Teeja
Slok Mahala Pahila

1 satgur bheekhya deh mai
toon samrath daataar.

2 haumai garab nivaareeyai
kaam krodh ahankaar.

3 lab lobh parjaaleeyai
naam milai aadhaar.

4 ahinis navtan nirmala
maila kabahoon na hoye.

5 Nanak eh bidh chhuteeyai
nadar teri sukh hoye.²

राग सिरीराग महला १
घर ४

तू दरीआउ दाना बीना
मै मछुली कैसे अंत लहा॥

जह जह देखा तह तह तू है
तुझ ते निकसी फूट मरा॥१॥

न जाणा मेउ न जाणा जाली॥
जा दुख लागै
ता तुझै समाली॥१॥ रहाउ॥

तू भरपूर जानिआ मै दूर॥
जो कछु करी सो तेरै हदूर॥

तू देखह हउ मुकर पाउ॥
तेरै कंम न तेरै नाए॥२॥

Raag Sireeraag Mahala Pahila
Ghar Chautha

1 tu dareeyaa'o daana beena
mai machhuli kaise ant laha.

2 jah jah dekha tah tah tu hai
tujh te nikasi phoot mara.

3 na jaana meyo na jaana jaali.
ja dukh laagai
ta tujhai samaali. rahaa'o.

4 tu bharpoor jaanya mai door.
jo kachhu kari so terai hadoor.

5 tu dekhah hau mukar paa'u.
terai kamm na terai naaye.

Var Soohi, Third Guru

Slok, First Guru

Bless me with the alms of your grace, O Satguru –   *1*
    you are the almighty giver.

Eradicate my ego, pride,   *2*
    lust, anger and self-conceit.

Burn away my greed and give me the support of Nam   *3–4*
    so that day and night I may remain
    pure, immaculate and unsoiled by sin.

O Nanak, this is the way to liberation,   *5*
    and it is your grace, O Lord, that it also leads to bliss.

Raga Srirag, First Guru

You are the ocean, all-knowing and all-seeing –   *1*
    how can I, a mere fish, find your limit?

Wherever I look, I find you;   *2*
    cast out I die in the torment of separation.

I am aware neither of the fisherman nor of his net;   *3*
    only in distress do I remember you.

You are all-pervading;   *4*
    although I consider you to be far away,
    everything I do is done in your presence.

You watch all my actions and yet I deny doing them;   *5*
    I neither serve you nor meditate on your Nam.

जेता देह तेता हउ खाउ॥
बिआ दर नाही कै दर जाउ॥
नानक एक कहै अरदास॥
जीउ पिंड सभ तेरै पास॥ ३॥
आपे नेड़ै दूर आपे ही
आपे मंझ मिआनो॥
आपे वेखै सुणे आपे ही
कुदरत करे जहानो॥
जो तिस भावै नानका
हुकम सोई परवानो॥ ४॥

6   jeta deh teta hau khaa'u.
    bya dar naahi kai dar jaa'u.
7   Nanak ek kahai ardaas.
    jee'o pind sabh terai paas.
8   aape nerrai door aape hi
    aape manjh myaano.
9   aape vekhai sune aape hi
    kudrat kare jahaano.
10 jo tis bhaavai naanaka
    hukam soi parvaano.[3]

I eat whatever you provide for me –   6
   when there is no other door open to me,
   where else shall I go?
Nanak makes only one supplication, O Lord: 7
   may my body and soul remain at your disposal.
The Lord himself dwells nearby, far away   8
   and all places in between.
He himself sees all and hears all,   9
   and with his own power he creates the universe.
Whatever pleases him, O Nanak,   10
   is his command, which alone merits acceptance.

बानी गुरु अमरदास जी

Bani Guru Amar Das Ji

वार मलार की महला १
सलोक महला ३

Vaar Malaar Ki Mahala Pahila
Slok Mahala Teeja

बाबीहा बेनती करे
कर किरपा देहो जीअ दान ॥

1 baabeeha benati kare
kar kirpa deho jee'a daan.

जल बिन पिआस न ऊतरै
छुटक जांहे मेरे प्रान ॥

2 jal bin pyaas na ootrai
chhutak jaanhe mere praan.

तू सुखदाता बेअंत है
गुणदाता नेधान ॥

3 tu sukh-daata be'ant hai
gun-daata nedhaan.

नानक गुरमुख बखस लए
अंत बेली होए भगवान ॥ २ ॥

4 Nanak gurmukh bakhas laye
ant beli hoye bhagvaan.[1]

राग धनासिरी महला ३
घर ४

Raag Dhanaasiri Mahala Teeja
Ghar Chautha

हम भीखक भेखारी तेरे
तू निज पत है दाता ॥

1 ham bheekhak bhekhaari tere
tu nij pat hai daata.

होह दैआल नाम देहो
मंगत जन कंउ
सदा रहउ रंग राता ॥ १ ॥

2 hoh dayaal naam deho
mangat jan kau
sada rahau rang raata.

हंउ बलिहारै जाउ
साचे तेरे नाम विटहो ॥

3 haun balihaarai jaa'au
saache tere naam vitho.

करण कारण सभना का एको
अवर न दूजा कोई ॥ १ ॥ रहाउ ॥

4 karan kaaran sabhna ka eko
avar na dooja koi. rahaa'o.

बहुते फेर पए किरपन कउ
अब किछ किरपा कीजै ॥

5 bahute pher paye kirpan kau
ab kichh kirpa keejai.

---

[*] A *chaatrik* is a legendary bird that keeps flying with its beak open to the heavens, constantly crying for the pure raindrops that fall during the period of the Swati Constellation, and never descending to drink impure water from rivers and ponds.

Guru Amar Das Ji

Var Malar, First Guru
Slok, Third Guru

Prays the *chaatrik:*[*]   1
  grant me the boon of life, O Lord.
Without the water of life my thirst is not quenched   2
  and my life is ebbing away.
You are the eternal Lord –   3
  the bestower of peace and the treasure of virtues.
It is through the Guru, O Nanak,[†]   4
  that the Lord grants pardon
  and in the end becomes one's friend.

Raga Dhanasari, Third Guru

We are beggars at your door, O Lord;   1
  you are your own Master and the provider of all.
Be merciful and bless this beggar with your Nam   2
  so that I may always remain absorbed in your love.
I sacrifice myself to your Nam, O true Lord!   3
The Lord is the Cause of all causes;   4
  there is no one else.
This wretched creature has drifted   5
  through numerous cycles of birth and death –
  O Lord, show me some compassion now.

[†] As a symbolic gesture of their merging of identities, Guru Nanak's successors referred
to themselves in their hymns not by their own names, as is customary, but as **Nanak**.

होह दइआल दरसन देहो अपना
ऐसी बखस करीजै॥ २॥
भनत नानक भरम पट खूल्हे
गुर परसादी जानिआ॥
साची लिव लागी है भीतर
सतगुर सिउ मन मानिआ॥ ३॥

6 hoh dayaal darsan deho apna
aisi bakhas kareejai.

7 bhanat Nanak bharam pat khoole
gur parsaadi jaaniya.

8 saachi liv laagi hai bheetar
satgur sio man maaniya.[2]

राग बिलावल की वार
महला ४ सलोक महला ३

जगत जलंदा रख लै
आपणी किरपा धार॥
जित दुआरै उबरै
तितै लैह उबार॥
सतगुर सुख वेखालिआ
सचा सबद बीचार॥
नानक अवर न सुझई
हर बिन बखसणहार॥ १॥

Raag Bilaaval Ki Vaar
Mahala Chautha Slok Mahala Teeja

1 jagat jalanda rakh lai
aapani kirpa dhaar.

2 jit duaarai ubrai
titai laih ubaar.

3 satgur sukh vekhaalya
sacha sabad beechaar.

4 Nanak avar na sujhayi
har bin bakhsan-haar.[3]

राग प्रभाती महला ३
चउपदे

जो तेरी सरणाई हर जीउ
तिन तू राखन जोग॥
तुध जेवड मै अवर न सूझै
ना को होआ न होग॥ १॥
हर जीउ सदा तेरी सरणाई॥
जिउ भावै तिउ राखहो मेरे सुआमी
एह तेरी वडिआई॥ १॥ रहाउ॥

Raag Prabhaati Mahala Teeja
Chaupade

1 jo teri sarnaa'i har jee'o
tin tu raakhan jog.

2 tudh jevad mai avar na soojhai
na ko ho'a na hog.

3 har jee'o sada teri sarnaa'i.

4 jio bhaavai tio raakho mere suaami
eh teri vadiaa'i. rahaa'o.

Be merciful and bless me with your darshan;   6
    O Lord, grant me such a boon.
Says Nanak: it was by the Guru's grace   7
    that the door of illusion was thrown open
    and I realized the Lord.
True love has blossomed within me   8
    and my mind has put faith in the Satguru.

Raga Bilawal ki Var, Fourth Guru
Slok, Third Guru
The world is in flames, O Lord –   1–2
    show your grace and save it
    in whatever way it can be saved.
Through meditation on the true Nam   3
    the Satguru has shown the way to peace.
Other than the Lord, O Nanak,   4
    I see no one who can grant forgiveness.

Raga Prabhati, Third Guru
O Lord, you are the protector of those   1
    who seek refuge in you.
O Lord, I see no one as great as you –   2
    no one has ever been, no one shall ever be.
Let me always remain   3
    under your protection, O Lord!
Keep me the way you will, my Master –   4
    in that lies your greatness.

जो तेरी सरणाई हर जीउ
तिन की करह प्रतिपाल॥
आप क्रिपा कर राखहो हर जीउ
पोह न सकै जमकाल॥ २॥
तेरी सरणाई सची हर जीउ
ना ओह घटै न जाए॥
जो हर छोड दूजै भाए लागै
ओह जंमै तै मर जाए॥ ३॥
जो तेरी सरणाई हर जीउ
तिना दूख भूख किछ नाहे॥
नानक नाम सलाहे सदा तू
सचै सबद समाहे॥ ४॥

5   *jo teri sarnaa'i har jee'o*
     tin ki karah pratipaal.

6   *aap kripa kar raakho har jee'o*
     poh na sakai jamkaal.

7   *teri sarnaa'i sachi har jee'o*
     na oh ghatai na jaaye.

8   *jo har chhod doojai bhaaye laagai*
     oh jammai tai mar jaaye.

9   *jo teri sarnaa'i har jee'o*
     tina dookh bhookh kichh naahe.

10   *Nanak naam salaahe sada tu*
     sachai sabad samaahe.[4]

राग गउड़ी पूरबी छंत
महला ३

मिल मेरे प्रीतमा जीउ
तुध बिन खरी निमाणी॥
मै नैणी नींद न आवै जीउ
भावै अंन न पाणी॥
पाणी अंन न भावै
मरीऐ हावै
बिन पिर किउ सुख पाईऐ॥
गुर आगै करउ बिनंती
जे गुर भावै
जिउ मिलै तिवै मिलाईऐ॥
आपे मेल लए सुखदाता
आप मिलिआ घर आए॥
नानक कामण सदा सुहागण
ना पिर मरै न जाए॥ ४॥

**Raag Gaurri Poorbi Chhant
Mahala Teeja**

1   *mil mere preetama jee'o*
     tudh bin khari nimaani.

2   *mai naini need na aavai jee'o*
     bhaavai ann na paani.

3   *paani ann na bhaavai*
     mareeyai haavai
     bin pir kio sukh paayee'ai.

4   *gur aagai karau binanti*
     je gur bhaavai
     jio milai tivai milaayee'ai.

5   *aape mel laye sukh-daata*
     aap milya ghar aaye.

6   *Nanak kaaman sada suhaagan*
     na pir marai na jaaye.[5]

You nurture all those 5
  who seek your shelter, O Lord.
In your grace, O Lord, you save them, 6
  and the messenger of death can do them no harm.
True is your refuge, O Lord – 7
  neither diminishing nor fading away.
One who turns away from you 8
  and attaches himself to duality, O Lord,
  continues to die and be reborn.
O Lord, those under your protection 9
  suffer neither pain nor hunger.
Always contemplate on God's Nam, O Nanak, 10
  so that through devotion to the true Shabd,
  you may merge into the Lord.

Raga Gauri Poorbi, Chhant, Third Guru

Meet me, O my Beloved; 1
  without you I am utterly without honour.
My eyes are without sleep 2
  and I have no taste for food or water.
Having no taste for food or water 3
  I will die sighing with grief,
  for in separation from the Beloved
  how can one find peace?
I pray to the Guru to unite me with the Lord 4
  in whatever way he can, if it be his will.
May the Lord, the bestower of bliss, come to my home 5
  and unite me with himself.
Such a bride always enjoys marital bliss, O Nanak, 6
  for her Husband neither dies nor abandons her.

राग रामकली महला ३

अनंद

साची लिवै बिन देह निमाणी॥

देह निमाणी लिवै बाझहो

किआ करे वेचारीआ॥

तुध बाझ समरथ कोए नाही

क्रिपा कर बनवारीआ॥

एस नउ होर थाउ नाही

सबद लाग सवारीआ॥

कहै नानक लिवै बाझहो

किआ करे वेचारीआ॥ ६॥

Raag Raamkali Mahala Teeja

Anand

1 saachi livai bin deh nimaani.

2 deh nimaani livai baajhoh
kya kare vechaareeya.

3 tudh baajh samrath koe naahi
kripa kar banvaareeya.

4 es nau hor thaa'o naahi
sabad laag savaareeya.

5 kahai Nanak livai baajhho
kya kare vechaareeya.[6]

Raga Ramkali, Third Guru, Anand

Without true devotion 1
    the body is without honour.
Bereft of devotion and without honour, 2
    what can the poor helpless body do?
Show mercy to me, O Lord; 3
    no one but you has the power.
This body has no other refuge – 4
    it is through Shabd that it is adorned.
Says Nanak: without true devotion, 5
    what can the poor helpless body do?

बानी गुरु रामदास जी

राग देवगंधारी
महला ४ घर १

अब हम चली ठाकुर पह हार॥

जब हम सरण प्रभू की आई
राख प्रभू भावै मार॥१॥ रहाउ॥

लोकन की चतुराई उपमा
ते बैसंतर जार॥

कोई भला कहउ भावै बुरा कहउ
हम तन दीओ है ढार॥१॥

जो आवत सरण ठाकुर प्रभ तुमरी
तिस राखहो किरपा धार॥

जन नानक सरण तुमारी हर जीउ
राखहो लाज मुरार॥२॥

राग धनासरी महला ४
घर १ चउपदे

हम अंधुले अंध बिखै बिख राते
किउ चालह गुर चाली॥

सतगुर दइआ करे सुखदाता
हम लावै आपन पाली॥१॥

गुरसिख मीत चलहो गुर चाली॥

जो गुर कहै सोई भल मानहो
हर हर कथा निराली॥१॥ रहाउ॥

हर के संत सुणहो जन भाई
गुर सेविहो बेग बेगाली॥

Bani Guru Ram Das Ji

Raag Devgandhaari
Mahala Chautha Ghar Pahila

1   *ab ham chali thaakur pah haar.*

2   *jab ham saran prabhu ki aa'i*
    raakh prabhu bhaavai maar. rahaa'o.

3   *lokan ki chaturaa'i upma*
    te baisantar jaar.

4   *koi bhala kahau bhaavai bura kahau*
    ham tan dee'o hai dhaar.

5   *jo aavat saran thaakur prabh tumri*
    tis raakho kirpa dhaar.

6   *jan Nanak saran tumaari har jee'o*
    raakho laaj muraar.[1]

Raag Dhanaasari Mahala Chautha
Ghar Pahila Chaupade

1   *ham andhule andh bikhai bikh raate*
    kio chaalah gur chaali.

2   *satgur daya kare sukh-daata*
    ham laavai aapan paali.

3   *gursikh meet chalho gur chaali.*
    jo gur kahai soi bhal maanho
    har har katha niraali. rahaa'o.

4   *har ke sant sunho jan bhaa'i*
    gur seviho beg begaali.

Guru Ram Das Ji

Raga Devagandhari, Fourth Guru

Exhausted, I have come   1
  seeking refuge with the Lord.
Now that I seek your protection, O Lord,   2
  keep me or destroy me as is your will.
I have burnt to ashes people's artful praise –   3
  whether someone calls me good or bad,
  I have surrendered myself to you, O Lord.
O Lord, you in your grace protect anyone   4–5
  who comes to you seeking your protection.
O Lord, protect the honour of your slave, Nanak,   6
  who has come to your shelter.

Raga Dhanasari, Fourth Guru, Chaupadas

I am blind and thoroughly engrossed   1
  in the poison of sensual pleasures –
  how can I follow in my Guru's footsteps?
It is through his grace that the Satguru,   2
  the fountainhead of bliss, attaches us to himself.
Follow the Guru's teaching,   3
  O Guru's disciples – my friends –
  and accept as good what the Guru advises,
  for unique is his discourse on God.
Listen, O God's Saints – my brothers –   4
  be prompt in serving the Guru.

सतगुर सेव खरच हर बाधहो
मत जाणहो आज कि काल्ही॥ २॥

हर के संत जपहो हर जपणा
हर संत चलै हर नाली॥

जिन हर जपिआ से हर होए
हर मिलिआ केल केलाली॥ ३॥

हर हर जपन जप लोच लोचानी
हर किरपा कर बनवाली॥

जन नानक संगत साध हर मेलहो
हम साध जना पग राली॥ ४॥

5 satgur sev kharach har baadho
   matt jaanho aaj ke kaalhi.

6 har ke sant japho har japna
   har sant chalai har naali.

7 jin har japiya se har hoye
   har miliya kel kelaali.

8 har har japan jap loch lochaani
   har kirpa kar banvaali.

9 jan Nanak sangat saadh har melho
   ham saadh jana pag raali.[2]

राग आसा महला ४ छंत
घर ४

हम किआ गुण तेरे विथरह सुआमी
तूं अपर अपारो राम राजे॥

हर नाम सालाहह दिन रात
एहा आस आधारो॥

हम मूरख किछूअ न जाणहा
किव पावह पारो॥

जन नानक हर का दास है
हर दास पनिहारो॥ ३॥

जिउ भावै तिउ राख लै
हम सरण प्रभ आए राम राजे॥

हम भूल विगाड़ह दिनस रात
हर लाज रखाए॥

Raag Aasa Mahala Chautha
Chhant Ghar Chautha

1 ham kya gun tere vitharah suaami
   toon apar apaaro raam raaje.

2 har naam salaahahe din raat
   eha aas aadhaaro.

3 ham moorakh kichhu na jaanha
   kiv paavah paaro.

4 jan Nanak har ka daas hai
   har daas panihaaro.

5 jio bhaavai tio raakh lai
   ham saran prabh aaye raam raaje.

6 ham bhool vigaarrah dinas raat
   har laaj rakhaaye.

By serving the Satguru 5
    gather the provisions for your journey to God
    without putting it off until tomorrow.
God's devotees remember God's Nam 6
    and go with him after their death.
The wondrous and playful Lord meets those 7
    who become one with him
    through remembrance of his Nam.
I earnestly yearn to remember your Nam – 8
    be merciful to me, O Lord!
Lead your slave Nanak 9
    to the company of Saints, O Lord,
    and make him the dust of their feet.

Raga Asa, Fourth Guru, Chhant

How can I describe your merits, O divine King, 1
    when you are eternal and limitless?
My only hope and support 2
    lies in praising the Lord's Nam day and night.
Foolish and without any understanding, 3
    how can I reach the far shore?
Nanak is the Lord's slave 4
    and the menial servant of his devotees.
Keep me as you will, O Lord – 5
    I have come seeking refuge in you, O divine King.
Day and night I go astray and bring discredit to myself, 6
    but the Lord saves my honour.

हम बारिक तूं गुर पिता है
दे मत समझाए॥

जन नानक दास हर कांढिआ
हर पैज रखाए॥४॥

7 ham baarik toon gur pita hai
de mat samjhaaye.

8 jan Nanak daas har kaandhiya
har paij rakhaaye.[3]

राग बिलावल महला ४
घर ३

Raag Bilaaval Mahala Chautha
Ghar Teeja

हम मूरख मुगध अगिआन मती
सरणागत पुरख अजनमा॥

1 ham moorakh mugadh agyaan mati
sarnaagat purakh ajanma.

कर किरपा रख लेवहो मेरे ठाकुर
हम पाथर हीन अकरमा॥१॥

2 kar kirpa rakh levho mere thaakur
ham paathar heen akarma.

मेरे मन भज राम नामै रामा॥

गुरमत हर रस पाईऐ
होर तिआगहो
निहफल कामा॥१॥रहाउ॥

3 mere man bhaj raam naamai raama.
gurmat har ras paa'eeyai
hor tyaagho
nihphal kaama. rahaa'o.

हर जन सेवक से हर तारे
हम निरगुन राख उपमा॥

4 har jan sevak se har taare
ham nirgun raakh upma.

तुझ बिन अवर न कोई मेरे ठाकुर
हर जपीऐ वडे करंमा॥२॥

5 tujh bin avar na koi mere thaakur
har japeeyai vade karamma.

नामहीन ध्रिग जीवते
तिन वड दूख सहंमा॥

6 naam-heen dhrig jeevte
tin vad dookh sahamma.

ओए फिर फिर जोन भवाईअह
मंदभागी मूड़ अकरमा॥३॥

7 oye phir phir jon bhavaa'ee'ah
mand-bhaagi moorr akarma.

हर जन नाम अधार है
धुर पूरब लिखे वड करमा॥

8 har jan naam adhaar hai
dhur poorab likhe vad karma.

गुर सतगुर नाम द्रिड़ाइआ
जन नानक सफल जनंमा॥४॥

9 gur satgur naam drirraaya
jan Nanak saphal janamma.[4]

I am your child, O my Guru, my father –   7
    instruct me in your wisdom.
Nanak is known as the Lord's slave –   8
    may the Lord protect his honour.

Raga Bilawal, Fourth Guru

Foolish, ignorant and without understanding,   1
    I have come seeking refuge with the eternal Lord.
Take pity on me and save me, my Lord;   2
    I am like a stone – ill-fated and worthless.
Devote yourself to God's all-pervading Nam, O my mind;   3
    receive God's nectar through the Guru's instruction
    and discard other deeds, which are fruitless.
The Lord redeems his servants and devotees;   4
    in saving a meritless one like me lies his glory.
My Lord, other than you there is no one for me –   5
    remembrance of God's Nam
    comes as a result of great good fortune.
Cursed is the life of those without Nam;   6
    they will suffer much pain.
Lacking divine grace, they are ill-fated and foolish   7
    and will keep revolving in the cycle of birth and death.
Nam is the support of God's devotees;   8
    good fortune is inscribed in their primal destiny.
The Satguru has enshrined Nam within them;   9
    O Nanak, the purpose of their lives is fulfilled.

राग बिलावल महला ४

घर ३

हमरा चित लुभत मोह बिखिआ	1
बहु दुरमत मैल भरा॥	
तुम्हरी सेवा कर न सकह प्रभ	2
हम किउ कर मुगध तरा॥१॥	

Raag Bilaaval Mahala Chautha

Ghar Teeja

1 *hamra chitt lubhat moh bikhya*
bahu durmat mail bhara.

2 *tumhri seva kar na sakah prabh*
ham kio kar mugadh tara.

मेरे मन जप नरहर नाम नरहरा॥
जन ऊपर किरपा प्रभ धारी
मिल सतगुर पार परा॥१॥रहाउ॥

3 *mere man jap narhar naam narhara.*
jan oopar kirpa prabh dhaari
mil satgur paar para. rahaa'o.

हमरे पिता ठाकुर प्रभ सुआमी
हर देहो मती जस करा॥
तुम्हरै संग लगे से उधरे
जिउ संग कासट लोह तरा॥२॥

4 *hamre pita thaakur prabh suaami*
har deho mati jas kara.

5 *tumhrai sang lage se udhre*
jio sang kaasat loh tara.

साकत नर होछी मत मधिम
जिन्ह हर हर सेव न करा॥
ते नर भागहीन दुहचारी
ओए जनम मुए फिर मरा॥३॥

6 *saakat nar hochhi mat maddhim*
jin har har sev na kara.

7 *te nar bhaag-heen duh-chaari*
oye janam muye phir mara.

जिन कउ तुम्ह हर मेलहो सुआमी
ते न्हाए संतोख गुर सरा॥
दुरमत मैल गई हर भजिआ
जन नानक पार परा॥४॥

8 *jin kau tum har melho suaami*
te nhaaye santokh gur sara.

9 *durmat mail gayi har bhajya*
jan Nanak paar para.[5]

राग गोंड चउपदे

महला ४ घर १

हर दरसन कउ मेरा मन बहु तपतै
जिउ त्रिखावंत बिन नीर॥१॥
मेरै मन प्रेम लगो हर तीर॥
हमरी बेदन हर प्रभ जानै
मेरे मन अंतर की पीर॥१॥रहाउ॥

Raag Gond Chaupade

Mahala Chautha Ghar Pahila

1 *har darsan kau mera man bahu taptai*
jio trikhaavant bin neer.

2 *merai man prem lago har teer.*
hamri bedan har prabh jaanai
mere man antar ki peer. rahaa'o.

Raga Bilawal, Fourth Guru

Filled with the dirt of evil thinking   1
   my mind is lured by the love of maya.

Unable to devote myself to you, O Lord,   2
   how can I, ignorant as I am,
   swim across the ocean of existence?

Repeat the mighty Lord's Nam, O my mind;   3
   the Lord showed mercy to his slave,
   who then met with the Satguru
   and was ferried across.

O Lord, my father and divine Master,   4
   grant me the wisdom to sing your praises.

O Lord, those attached to you swim across the ocean   5
   like iron in the company of wood.

Worldly people who do not devote themselves to God   6
   are shallow and dense.

They are unfortunate sinful people,   7
   born to die again and again.

Those whom you attach to yourself, O Lord,   8
   bathe in the Guru's pool of nectar and are content.

Through devotion to the Lord   9
   the dirt of foul thinking vanishes
   and God's slave, Nanak, crosses the ocean of existence.

Raga Gond, Fourth Guru, Chaupadas

Like a thirsty person without water,   1
   my mind yearns deeply for the Lord's darshan.

The arrow of divine love has struck my heart;   2
   the Lord alone knows my suffering,
   the pain that has penetrated my heart.

मेरे हर प्रीतम की कोई बात सुनावै

सो भाई सो मेरा बीर ॥ २ ॥

मिल मिल सखी

गुण कहो मेरे प्रभ के

ले सतगुर की मत धीर ॥ ३ ॥

जन नानक की हर आस पुजावहो

हर दरसन सांत सरीर ॥ ४ ॥

3 *mere har preetam ki koi baat sunaavai*

so bhaa'i so mera beer.

4 *mil mil sakhi*

gun kaho mere prabh ke

le satgur ki mat dheer.

5 *jan Nanak ki har aas pujaavho*

har darsan saant sareer.[6]

राग गउड़ी पूरबी

महला ४ चउपदे

Raag Gaurri Poorbi

Mahala Chautha Chaupade

हर हर अरथ सरीर हम बेचिआ

पूरे गुर कै आगे ॥

सतगुर दातै नाम दिड़ाइआ

मुख मसतक भाग सभागे ॥ १ ॥

राम गुरमत हर लिव लागे ॥ १ ॥ रहाउ ॥

घट घट रमईआ रमत राम राए

गुर सबद गुरू लिव लागे ॥

हउ मन तन देवउ काट गुरू कउ

मेरा भ्रम भउ गुर बचनी भागे ॥ २ ॥

अंधिआरै दीपक आन जलाए

गुर गिआन गुरू लिव लागे ॥

अगिआन अंधेरा बिनस बिनासिओ

घर वसत लही मन जागे ॥ ३ ॥

1 *har har arath sareer ham bechya*

poore gur kai aage.

2 *satgur daatai naam dirraaya*

mukh mastak bhaag sabhaage.

3 *ram gurmat har liv laage. rahaa'o.*

4 *ghat ghat rama'eeya ramat raam raaye*

gur sabad guru liv laage.

5 *hau man tan devau kaat guru kau*

mera bhram bhau gur bachni bhaage.

6 *andhyaarai deepak aan jalaaye*

gur gyaan guru liv laage.

7 *agyaan andhera binas binaasio*

ghar vasat lahi man jaage.

---

*When Guru Ram Das says he has **sold** his body to the Guru, it means that he has surrendered to him.

One who talks with me about my Beloved   3
  is my brother and true friend.
Let us join together, O sisters,   4
  and sing the praises of my Lord
  in keeping with the Satguru's sublime wisdom.
Fulfil the yearning of your slave Nanak, O Lord,   5
  and let your darshan bring peace into his body.

Raga Gauri Poorbi, Fourth Guru
In order to attain the Lord   1
  I have sold my body to the perfect Guru.*
The generous Satguru instilled his Nam within me   2
  and thus inscribed an auspicious destiny on my forehead.
We become attached to you, O Lord,   3
  by following the Guru's teaching.
The Lord pervades all hearts,   4
  and through the Guru's Shabd we are devoted to him.
I shall cut my mind and body into pieces   5
  and surrender them to my Guru,†
  as it is through my Guru's words
  that my fears and doubts have vanished.
The Guru comes and lights his lamp in the darkness; 6
  through the enlightenment he grants
  I become attached to him.
The darkness of ignorance is shattered –   7
  my mind awakens and finds the treasure within its home.

---

† This is a way of saying that one is ready to sacrifice all to the Guru.

साकत बधिक माइआधारी	8	*saakat badhik maayaa-dhaari*
तिन जम जोहन लागे॥		*tin jam johan laage.*
उन सतगुर आगै सीस न बेचिआ	9	*un satgur aagai sees na bechya*
ओए आवहे जाहे अभागे॥ ४॥		*oye aavhe jaahe abhaage.*
हमरा बिनउ सुनहो प्रभ ठाकुर	10	*hamra binau sunho prabh thaakur*
हम सरण प्रभू हर मागे॥		*ham saran prabhu har maage.*
जन नानक की लज पात गुरू है	11	*jan Nanak ki laj paat guru hai*
सिर बेचिओ सतगुर आगे॥ ५॥		*sir bechio satgur aage.*[7]

सो दर राग गूजरी
महला ४

So Dar Raag Goojri
Mahala Chautha

हर के जन सतगुर सतपुरखा	1	*har ke jan satgur sat-purkha*
बिनउ करउ गुर पास॥		*binau karau gur paas.*
हम कीरे किरम सतगुर सरणाई	2	*ham keere kiram satgur sarnaa'i*
कर दइआ नाम परगास॥ १॥		*kar daya naam pargaas.*
मेरे मीत गुरदेव	3	*mere meet gurdev*
मो कउ राम नाम परगास॥		*mo kau raam naam pargaas.*
गुरमत नाम मेरा प्रान सखाई	4	*gurmat naam mera praan sakhaa'i*
हर कीरत हमरी रहरास॥ १॥ रहाउ॥		*har keerat hamri rahraas. rahaa'o.*
हर जन के वड भाग वडेरे	5	*har jan ke vad bhaag vadere*
जिन हर हर सरधा हर पिआस॥		*jin har har sardha har pyaas.*
हर हर नाम मिलै त्रिपतासह	6	*har har naam milai triptaasah*
मिल संगत गुण परगास॥ २॥		*mil sangat gun pargaas.*
जिन हर हर हर रस नाम न पाइआ	7	*jin har har har ras naam na paaya*
ते भागहीण जम पास॥		*te bhaag-heen jam paas.*
जो सतगुर सरण संगत नही आए	8	*jo satgur saran sangat nahi aaye*
धिग जीवे धिग जीवास॥ ३॥		*dhrig jeeve dhrig jeevaas.*

The angel of death stalks worldly people,   8
  killers and materialists.
They have not surrendered their heads to the true Guru;   9
  these unfortunate ones will keep coming and going.
Listen to my supplication, O Lord, my Master –   10
  I beg for your protection.
The Guru is the honour and inspiration of Nanak,   11
  and to the true Guru he has sold his head.

Raga Goojari, Fourth Guru

I beseech you, O my true Guru,   1
  the chosen one of God and the true being.
I, a lowly worm, a fallen creature,   2
  seek shelter with you, O Satguru –
  shower your grace and illumine me with Nam.
Bless me with the light of God's Nam,   3
  O my Guru, my friend.
The Nam that flows from the Guru's teaching   4
  is my life support,
  and God's praise is my daily prayer.
Greatly fortunate are the devotees   5
  who have faith in God and thirst for him.
Having received God's Nam they are fulfilled,   6
  and in the company of Saints their virtues shine forth.
Those who have not received the elixir of God's Nam   7
  are the unfortunate ones caught in Yama's snare.
Cursed is and ever will be the life of those   8
  who do not seek the company
  and protection of the Satguru.

जिन हर जन सतगुर संगत पाई
तिन धुर मसतक लिखिआ लिखास॥
धन धंन सतसंगत
जित हर रस पाइआ
मिल जन नानक नाम परगास॥४॥

9 jin har jan satgur sangat paa'i
tin dhur mastak likhya likhaas.
10 dhan dhann sat-sangat
jit har ras paaya
mil jan Nanak naam pargaas.[8]

राग सूही असटपदीआ
महला ४ घर २

Raag Soohi Astpadee'a
Mahala Chautha Ghar Dooja

कोई आण मिलावै मेरा प्रीतम पिआरा
हउ तिस पह आप वेचाई॥१॥
दरसन हर देखण कै ताई॥
क्रिपा करह ता सतगुर मेलह
हर हर नाम धिआई॥१॥रहाउ॥
जे सुखु देह त तुझह अराधी
दुख भी तुझै धिआई॥२॥
जे भुख देह त इत ही राजा
दुख विच सूख मनाई॥३॥
तन मन काट काट सभ अरपी
विच अगनी आप जलाई॥४॥
पखा फेरी पाणी ढोवा
जो देवह सो खाई॥५॥
नानक गरीब ढह पइआ दुआरै
हर मेल लैहो वडिआई॥६॥

1 koi aan milaavai mera preetam pyaara
hau tis pah aap vechaa'i.
2 darsan har dekhan kai taa'i.
kripa karah ta satgur melah
har har naam dhiaa'i. rahaa'o.
3 je sukh deh ta tujhah araadhi
dukh bhi tujhah dhiaa'i.
4 je bhukh deh ta it hi raaja
dukh vich sookh manaa'i.
5 tan man kaat kaat sabh arpi
vich agni aap jalaa'i.
6 pakha pheri paani dhova
jo devah so khaa'i.
7 Nanak gareeb dhah paya duaarai
har mel laiho vadiaa'i.

God's devotees who are blessed 9
   with the company of the Satguru
   are those in whose primal destiny it is so inscribed.
Blessed, blessed is the company of Saints, 10
   where the elixir of God is found, O Nanak –
   by meeting them one's heart is illumined with Nam.

Raga Soohi, Astpadi, Fourth Guru

Oh, how I wish someone would come 1
   and unite me with my Beloved –
   I would sell myself to him.
To let me have his darshan the Lord will, in his grace, 2
   bring me in touch with the Satguru
   so that I may meditate on the Lord's Nam.
If you bring me happiness, I shall worship you, O Lord; 3
   even in pain I shall meditate on you.
If you give me hunger, I shall feel satisfied; 4
   I will perceive pain as pleasure.
I shall cut my body and mind into pieces 5
   to make an offering to you
   and burn myself in a sacrificial fire.
I shall wave the fan over you, draw water for you 6
   and eat what you give.
Humble Nanak has fallen at your doorstep, O Lord, 7
   so that you will, in your greatness,
   unite him with yourself.

अखी काढ धरी चरणा तल
सभ धरती फिर मत पाई॥ ७॥

जे पास बहालह ता तुझह अराधी
जे मार कढह भी धिआई॥ ८॥

जे लोक सलाहे ता तेरी उपमा
जे निंदै त छोड न जाई॥ ९॥

जे तुध वल रहै ता कोई किहु आखउ
तुध विसरिऐ मर जाई॥ १०॥

वार वार जाई गुर ऊपर
पै पैरी संत मनाई॥ ११॥

नानक विचारा भइआ दिवाना
हर तउ दरसन कै ताई॥ १२॥

झखड़ झागी मीह वरसै
भी गुर देखण जाई॥ १३॥

समुंद सागर होवै बहु खारा
गुरसिख लंघ गुर पह जाई॥ १४॥

जिउ प्राणी जल बिन है मरता
तिउ सिख गुर बिन मर जाई॥ १५॥

जिउ धरती सोभ करे जल बरसै
तिउ सिख गुर मिल बिगसाई॥ १६॥

सेवक का होए सेवक वरता
कर कर बिनउ बुलाई॥ १७॥

नानक की बेनंती हर पह
गुर मिल गुर सुख पाई॥ १८॥

8 *akhi kaadh dhari charna tal*
   sabh dharti phir mat paa'i.

9 *je paas bahaalah ta tujhah araadhi*
   je maar kadhah bhi dhiaa'i.

10 *je lok salaahe ta teri upma*
   je nindai ta chhod na jaa'i.

11 *je tudh val rahai ta koi kihu aakhau*
   tudh visariyai mar jaa'i.

12 *vaar vaar jaa'i gur oopar*
   pai pairee sant manaa'i.

13 *Nanak vichaara bhaya divaana*
   har tau darsan kai taa'i.

14 *jhakharr jhaagi meeh varsai*
   bhi gur dekhan jaa'i.

15 *samund saagar hovai bahu khaara*
   gursikh langh gur pah jaa'i.

16 *jio praani jal bin hai marta*
   tio sikh gur bin mar jaa'i.

17 *jio dharti sobh kare jal barsai*
   tio sikh gur mil bigsaa'i.

18 *sevak ka hoye sevak varta*
   kar kar binau bulaa'i.

19 *Nanak ki benanti har pah*
   gur mil gur sukh paa'i.[9]

Having roamed the whole earth
  I have gained the wisdom to remove my eyes
  and place them under your feet, O Lord.*   8

If you seat me close to you, I shall worship you,
  and if you drive me away
  I shall still remain devoted to you.   9

If people praise me, it is owing to your glory;
  if they slander me, I shall not walk away from you.   10

If you are on my side, let people say what they will,
  but if I turn my back on you, it will cause my death.   11

Again and again I sacrifice myself to my Guru;
  falling at his feet, I shall please the Saint.   12

O Lord, poor Nanak has gone mad in his longing
  for a glimpse of your darshan.   13

Even in a fierce storm and torrential downpour
  the disciple goes for the Guru's darshan.   14

The Guru's disciple crosses the vast salty oceans
  to meet his Guru.   15

Just as a creature dies without water,
  so does a disciple die without the Guru.   16

Just as the earth turns beautiful after a rainfall,
  so does a disciple's heart bloom on meeting his Guru.   17

I am the slave of your slaves, O Lord;
  I unceasingly call upon you in my humble prayers.   18

Nanak prays to the Lord to unite him with the Guru
  so that he can attain the bliss
  that comes from the Guru alone.   19

---

*Placing one's eyes under the Guru's feet means that in his eagerness to meet his Guru
the disciple focuses his sight on the path by which the Guru is coming to meet him.

राग कलिआन महला ४

प्रभ कीजै क्रिपा निधान
हम हर गुन गावहगे॥
हउ तुमरी करउ नित आस
प्रभ मोहे
कब गल लावहिगे॥१॥ रहाउ॥
हम बारक मुगध इआन
पिता समझावहिगे॥
सुत खिन खिन भूल बिगार
जगत पित भावहिगे॥१॥
जो हर सुआमी तुम देहो
सोई हम पावहगे॥
मोहे दूजी नाही ठउर
जिस पह हम जावहगे॥२॥
जो हर भावह भगत
तिना हर भावहिगे॥
जोती जोत मिलाए
जोत रल जावहगे॥३॥
हर आपे होए क्रिपाल
आप लिव लावहिगे॥
जन नानक सरन दुआर
हर लाज रखावहिगे॥४॥

Raag Kaliaan Mahala Chautha

1   prabh keejai kripa nidhaan
    ham har gun gaavahnge.
2   hau tumri karau nit aas
    prabh mohe
    kab gal laavahnge. rahaa'o.
3   ham baarik mugadh iyaan
    pita samjhaavahnge.
4   sut khin khin bhool bigaar
    jagat pit bhaavahnge.
5   jo har suaami tum deho
    soi ham paavahnge.
6   mohe dooji naahi thaur
    jis pah ham jaavahnge.
7   jo har bhaavah bhagat
    tina har bhaavahnge.
8   joti jot milaaye
    jot ral jaavahnge.
9   har aape hoye kripaal
    aap liv laavahnge.
10 jan Nanak saran duaar
    har laaj rakhaavahnge.[10]

राग गउड़ी की वार
महला ४

सा धरती भई हरीआवली
जिथै मेरा सतगुर बैठा आए॥
से जंत भए हरीआवले
जिनी मेरा सतगुर देखिआ जाए॥

Raag Gaurri Ki Vaar
Mahala Chautha

1   sa dharti bhayi hareeyaavali
    jitthai mera satgur baitha aaye.
2   se jant bhaye hareeyaavale
    jini mera satgur dekhya jaaye.

Raga Kalyan, Fourth Guru

You are the fountainhead of grace, O Lord; 1
  show your mercy so I may sing your praises.
I always rest my hopes in you, O Lord – 2
  when will you hold me in your arms?
I am your foolish and ignorant child; 3
  I look to you, my father, to teach me.
The child makes mistakes again and again, 4
  and yet he is pleasing to the father of the universe.
I receive what you provide me, O Lord; 5–6
  there is no other place I can go.
Devotees who have the Lord's approval 7
  are the only ones who love the Lord.
Their light blends with God's light 8
  and into that light they are finally merged.
When the Lord becomes merciful, 9
  he himself inspires love in the devotee.
The Lord's slave Nanak seeks refuge at his doorstep 10
  in the hope that the Lord will save his honour.

Raga Gauri ki Var, Fourth Guru

That place becomes blessed 1
  where my Satguru comes to take his abode.
The creatures who go to see my Satguru 2
  also become blessed.

धन धंन पिता धन धंन कुल
धन धन सो जननी
जिन गुरू जणिआ माए॥

धन धंन गुरू
जिन नाम अराधिआ
आपि तरिआ
जिनी डिठा तिना लए छडाए॥

हर सतगुर मेलहो दइआ कर
जन नानक धोवै पाए॥ २ ॥

3 *dhan dhann pita dhan dhann kul*
dhan dhan so janani
jin guru janya maaye.

4 *dhan dhann guru*
jin naam araadhya
aap tarya jini dittha
tina laye chhadaaye.

5 *har satgur melho daya kar*
jan Nanak dhovai paaye.[11]

राग देवगंधारी
महला ४ घर १

Raag Devgandhaari
Mahala Chautha Ghar Pahila

सेवक जन बने ठाकुर लिव लागे॥
जो तुमरा जस कहते गुरमत
तिन मुख भाग सभागे॥१॥रहाउ॥

1 *sevak jan bane thaakur liv laage.*
2 *jo tumra jas kahte gurmat*
tin mukh bhaag sabhaage. rahaa'o.

टूटे माइआ के बंधन फाहे
हर राम नाम लिव लागे॥

3 *toote maaya ke bandhan phaahe*
har raam naam liv laage.

हमरा मन मोहिओ गुर मोहन
हम बिसम भई मुख लागे॥१॥

4 *hamra man mohio gur mohan*
ham bisam bhayi mukh laage.

सगली रैण सोई अंधिआरी
गुर किंचत किरपा जागे॥

5 *sagli rain soi andhiaari*
gur kinchat kirpa jaage.

जन नानक के प्रभ सुंदर सुआमी
मोहे तुम सर अवर न लागे॥२॥

6 *jan Nanak ke prabh sundar suaami*
mohe tum sar avar na laage.[12]

Blessed be the father, blessed be the family 3
    and blessed be the mother who gave birth to the Guru.
Blessed, blessed be the Guru who, 4
    having meditated on Nam, has liberated himself
    and all those who have met him.
Have mercy and help me meet the Satguru, O Lord, 5
    so that your slave Nanak may wash his feet.

Raga Devagandhari, Fourth Guru

Those imbued with God's love become his devotees. 1
O Lord, good fortune is inscribed 2
    on the faces of those who sing your praises
    under the Guru's instruction.
For them the bonds and snares of maya are broken, 3
    for they have devoted themselves to the Lord's Nam.
The Guru, the charmer, has captivated my heart – 4
    on seeing him I am wonderstruck.
In darkness I slept away the whole night of my life, 5
    but was awakened by the smallest ray of the Guru's grace.
O beautiful Lord of Nanak, your slave, 6
    for me there is no one like you!

राग सूही महला ४

घर ७

तेरे कवन कवन गुण कह कह गावा

तू साहिब गुणी निधाना॥

तुमरी महिमा बरन न साकउ

तूं ठाकुर ऊच भगवाना॥१॥

मै हर हर नाम धर सोई॥

जिउ भावै तिउ राख मेरे साहिब

मै तुझ बिन अवर न कोई॥१॥ रहाउ॥

मै ताण दीबाण तूहै मेरे सुआमी

मै तुध आगै अरदास॥

मै होर थाउ नाही

जिस पह करउ बेनंती

मेरा दुख सुख तुझ ही पास॥ २॥

विचे धरती विचे पाणी

विच कासट अगन धरीजै॥

बकरी सिंघ इकतै थाए राखे

मन हर जप भ्रम भउ दूर कीजै॥ ३॥

हर की वडिआई देखहो संतहो

हर निमाणिआ माण देवाए॥

जिउ धरती चरण तले ते ऊपर आवै

तिउ नानक साध जना जगत आण

सभ पैरी पाए॥ ४॥

Raag Soohi Mahala Chautha

Ghar Sattvaan

1 tere kavan kavan gun kah kah gaava

  tu saahib guni nidhaana.

2 tumri mahima baran na saakau

  toon thaakur ooch bhagvaana.

3 mai har har naam dhar soi.

  jio bhaavai tio raakh mere saahib

  mai tujh bin avar na koi. rahaa'o.

4 mai taan deebaan toohai mere suaami

  mai tudh aagai ardaas.

5 mai hor thaa'o naahi

  jis pah karau benanti

  mera dukh sukh tujh hi paas.

6 vicche dharti vicche paani

  vich kaasat agan dhareejai.

7 bakri singh iktai thaaye raakhe

  man har jap bhram bhau door keejai.

8 har ki vadiaa'i dekho santoh

  har nimaaniya maan devaaye.

9 jio dharti charan tale te oopar aavai

  tio Nanak saadh jana jagat aan

  sabh pairi paaye.[13]

Raga Soohi, Fourth Guru

You are the treasure of virtues, O Lord – 1
   how can I sing your praises and describe all your qualities?

You are most exalted, O Lord; 2
   I am unable to describe your splendour.

The Lord's Nam is my sole mainstay – 3
   keep me however it pleases you, O Lord,
   for other than you there is no support for me.

You are my strength and my mainstay – 4
   O my Lord, I pray to you alone.

There is no other place 5
   where I could offer supplication,
   for my pleasure and pain lie in your hand.

Earth and water are made to coexist, 6
   and within wood is placed fire.

The lion and the lamb are held in one place – 7
   O my mind, shed your fears and doubts
   through remembrance of the Lord's Nam.

O Saints, see the glory of the Lord, 8
   who bestows honour on those
   who are without recognition.

As dust rises from underneath the feet, O Nanak, 9
   so does the whole world bow before the Saints.

राग गउड़ी पूरबी

महला ४ चउपदे

तुम दइआल सरब दुख भंजन

इक बिनउ सुनहो दे काने॥

जिस ते तुम हर जाने सुआमी

सो सतगुर मेल मेरा प्राने॥१॥

राम हम सतगुर

पारब्रहम कर माने॥

हम मूड़ मुगध असुध मत होते

गुर सतगुर कै बचन

हर हम जाने॥१॥रहाउ॥

जितने रस अन रस हम देखे

सभ तितने फीक फीकाने॥

हर का नाम अंम्रित रस चाखिआ

मिल सतगुर मीठ रस गाने॥२॥

जिन कउ गुर सतगुर नही भेटिआ

ते साकत मूड़ दिवाने॥

तिन के करमहीन धुर पाए

देख दीपक मोहे पचाने॥३॥

जिन कउ तुम दइआ कर मेलहो

ते हर हर सेव लगाने॥

जन नानक हर हर हर जप प्रगटे

मत गुरमत नाम समाने॥४॥

Raag Gaurri Poorbi

Mahala Chautha Chaupade

1 tum dayaal sarab dukh bhanjan

   ik binau sunho de kaane.

2 jis te tum har jaane suaami

   so satgur mel mera praane.

3 raam ham satgur

   paar-brahm kar maane.

   ham moorr mugadh asudh mat hote

   gur satgur kai bachan

   har ham jaane. rahaa'o.

4 jitne ras an ras ham dekhe

   sabh titne pheek pheekaane.

5 har ka naam amrit ras chaakhya

   mil satgur meeth ras gaane.

6 jin kau gur satgur nahi bhetya

   te saakat moorr divaane.

7 tin ke karamaheen dhur paaye

   dekh deepak mohe pachaane.

8 jin kau tum daya kar melho

   te har har sev lagaane.

9 jan Nanak har har har jap pragte

   mat gurmat naam samaane.[14]

Raga Gauri Poorbi, Fourth Guru, Chaupadas

You are the compassionate Lord, who eradicates all pain –   1
  please lend an ear to my supplication.

Unite me with the Satguru – my very life –   2
  through whom you are known, O Lord.

O Lord, I recognize the Satguru as the Supreme Being.   3
Being foolish, ignorant and of impure mind,
  I know the Lord only through the Satguru's words.

All the pleasures and tastes that I have experienced   4
  have turned sour.

On meeting the Satguru   5
  I have tasted the ambrosial nectar of God's Nam,
  sweet like sugarcane juice.

Those who have not met the Satguru   6
  are foolish and deluded, worshippers of maya.

From their primal destiny they are ill-fated –   7
  seeing the flame of worldly love,
  they burn themselves in it.

Those whom you in your grace unite with yourself, O Lord,   8
  devote themselves to your service.

Nanak, the Lord's slave, has become known   9
  through his repetition of God's Nam,
  and has merged in Nam through the Guru's instruction.

बानी गुरु अर्जुन देव जी

Bani Guru Arjun Dev Ji

राग बिलावल महला ५
दुपदे घर ८

Raag Bilaaval Mahala Panjvaan
Dupade Ghar Atthvaan

ऐसी दीखिआ जन सिउ मंगा॥ 1 *aisi deekhiya jan sio manga.*
तुम्हरो धिआन तुम्हारो रंगा॥ *tumhro dhyaan tumhaaro ranga.*
तुम्हरी सेवा तुम्हारे अंगा॥१॥रहाउ॥ *tumhri seva tumhaare anga. rahaa'o.*
जन की टहल संभाखन जन सिउ 2 *jan ki tahal sambhaakhan jan sio*
ऊठन बैठन जन कै संगा॥ *oothan baithan jan kai sanga.*
जन चर रज मुख माथै लागी 3 *jan char raj mukh maathai laagi*
आसा पूरन अनंत तरंगा॥१॥ *aasa pooran anant taranga.*
जन पारब्रहम जा की निरमल महिमा 4 *jan paar-brahm ja ki nirmal mahima*
जन के चरन तीरथ कोट गंगा॥ *jan ke charan teerath kot ganga.*
जन की धूर कीओ मजन नानक 5 *jan ki dhoor kee'o majan Nanak*
जनम जनम के हरे कलंगा॥२॥ *janam janam ke hare kalanga.* [1]

राग बिलावल महला ५
दुपदे घर ८

Raag Bilaaval Mahala Panjvaan
Dupade Ghar Atthvaan

ऐसी किरपा मोहे करहो॥ 1 *aisi kirpa mohe karho.*
संतह चरण हमारो माथा *santah charan hamaaro maatha*
नैन दरस तन धूर परहो॥१॥रहाउ॥ *nain daras tan dhoor parho. rahaa'o.*
गुर को सबद मेरै हीअरै बासै 2 *gur ko sabad merai heeyarai baasai*
हर नामा मन संग धरहो॥ *har naama man sang dharho.*
तसकर पंच निवारहो ठाकुर 3 *taskar panch nivaarho thaakur*
सगलो भरमा होम जरहो॥१॥ *saglo bharma hom jarho.*

---

* Saints refer to themselves as the Lord's **slaves**. Applying the dust of their feet to one's forehead is considered to be an act of deep reverence and an expression of humility and submission.

Guru Arjun Dev Ji

Raga Bilawal, Fifth Guru

O Lord, I ask your devotee for instruction 1
  so that I may meditate on you,
  be absorbed in your love,
  serve you and become one with you.
May I serve your slaves, talk with them, 2
  and forever abide in their company.
May the dust of the feet of his slaves 3
  touch my face and forehead*
  and fulfil the countless waves of my desire.
Pure is the glory of the supreme Lord's slaves; 4
  their feet are holier than a million pilgrimages
  to the holy Ganges.
Nanak has bathed in the dust of their feet 5
  and washed away the sins of myriad lives.

Raga Bilawal, Fifth Guru

Show me such mercy, O Lord, 1
  that I bow my forehead at the feet of the Saints,
  that my eyes have their darshan
  and my body is bathed in the dust of their feet.
May the Guru's Shabd abide in my heart 2
  and the Lord's Nam be enshrined in my mind.
Destroy the five robbers, O Lord,† 3
  and set fire to all my illusions.

---

† The **five robbers**—lust, anger, greed, attachment and pride—are five modes of destructive mental action which beset human beings and prevent the soul from uniting with the Lord.

जो तुम्ह करहो सोई भल मानै
भावन दुबिधा दूर टरहो॥
नानक के प्रभ तुम ही दाते
संतसंग ले मोहे उधरहो॥ २॥

4 jo tum karho soi bhal maanai
bhaavan dubidha door tarho.
5 Nanak ke prabh tum hi daate
sant-sang le mohe udharho.[2]

राग देवगंधारी
महला ५

Raag Devgandhaari
Mahala Panjvaan

अपुने सतगुर पह बिनउ कहिआ॥
भए क्रिपाल दइआल दुख भंजन
मेरा सगल अंदेसरा गइआ॥ रहाउ॥
हम पापी पाखंडी लोभी
हमरा गुन अवगुन सभ सहिआ॥
कर मसतक धार साज निवाजे
मुए दुसट जो खइआ॥ १॥
परउपकारी सरब सधारी
सफल दरसन सहजइआ॥
कहो नानक निरगुण कउ दाता
चरण कमल उर धरिआ॥ २॥

1 apne satgur pah binau kahia.
bhaye kripaal dayaal dukh bhanjan
mera sagal andesara ga'ia. rahaa'o.
2 ham paapi paakhandi lobhi
hamra gun avgun sabh sahia.
3 kar mastak dhaar saaj nivaaje
muye dust jo kha'ia.
4 paraupkaari sarab sadhaari
saphal darsan sahajia.
5 kaho Nanak nirgun kau daata
charan kamal ur dharia.[3]

राग बिलावल महला ५
दुपदे घर ८

Raag Bilaaval Mahala Panjvaan
Dupade Ghar Atthvaan

अपने सेवक कउ कबहु न बिसारहो॥
उर लागहो सुआमी प्रभ मेरे
पूरब प्रीत
गोबिंद बीचारहो॥ १॥ रहाउ॥
पतित पावन प्रभ बिरद तुम्हारो
हमरे दोख रिदै मत धारहो॥
जीवन प्रान हर धन सुख तुम ही
हउमै पटल क्रिपा कर जारहो॥ १॥

1 apne sevak kau kabahu na bisaarho.
ur laagoh suaami prabh mere
poorab preet
gobind beechaarho. rahaa'o.
2 patit paavan prabh birad tumhaaro
hamre dokh ridai mat dhaarho.
3 jeevan praan har dhan sukh tum hi
haumai patal kripa kar jaarho.

May I accept as good whatever you do, O Lord;   *4*
  help me overcome my wavering mind.
You are the sole benefactor of Nanak, O Lord –   *5*
  redeem me through the company of Saints.

Raga Devagandhari, Fifth Guru

I have related my prayer to my Satguru.   *1*
The compassionate Lord, the destroyer of suffering,
  has become merciful to me – all my anxieties are gone.
Sinful, hypocritical and greedy as I am,   *2*
  the Lord has put up with my virtues and vices.
Placing his hand on my forehead   *3*
  he has adorned and exalted me,
  and my adversaries have been destroyed.
The Guru is the benevolent support of all,   *4*
  the bestower of peace, whose darshan is fruitful.
Says Nanak: he is the benefactor of the meritless,   *5*
  and I have enshrined his lotus feet in my heart.

Raga Bilawal, Fifth Guru, Dupadas

In consideration of my primal love,   *1*
  hold me to your heart, O Lord, my Master,
  and never forget this slave.
To purify and redeem the fallen   *2*
  is your intrinsic nature, O Lord –
  do not hold my failings in your heart.
You are my life, my soul,   *3*
  my wealth and my peace, O Lord –
  kindly burn away my veil of ego.

जल बिहून मीन कत जीवन
दूध बिना रहन कत बारो ॥

जन नानक पिआस चरन कमलन्ह की
पेख दरस सुआमी सुख सारो ॥ २ ॥

4 jal bihoon meen kat jeevan
doodh bina rahan kat baaro.

5 jan Nanak pyaas charan kamalan ki
pekh daras suaami sukh saaro.[4]

राग आसा घर ७
महला ५

Raag Aasa Ghar Sattvaan
Mahala Panjvaan

चरन कमल की आस पिआरे ॥
जमकंकर नस गए विचारे ॥
तू चित आवह तेरी मइआ ॥
सिमरत नाम
सगल रोग खइआ ॥ १ ॥ रहाउ ॥
अनिक दुख देवह अवरा कउ ॥
पहुच न साकह जन तेरे कउ ॥ २ ॥
दरस तेरे की पिआस मन लागी ॥
सहज अनंद बसै बैरागी ॥ ३ ॥
नानक की अरदास सुणीजै ॥
केवल नाम रिदे मह दीजै ॥ ४ ॥

1 charan kamal ki aas pyaare.
jam kankar nas gaye vichaare.

2 tu chit aavah teri ma'ia.
simrat naam
sagal rog kha'ia. rahaa'o.

3 anik dookh devah avara kau.
pahunch na saakah jan tere kau.

4 daras tere ki pyaas man laagi.
sahaj anand basai bairaagi.

5 Nanak ki ardaas suneejai.
keval naam ride mah deejai.[5]

राग सूही महला ५
घर ३

Raag Soohi Mahala Panjvaan
Ghar Teeja

दरसन देख जीवा गुर तेरा ॥
पूरन करम होए प्रभ मेरा ॥ १ ॥
इह बेनंती सुण प्रभ मेरे ॥
देह नाम कर अपणे चेरे ॥ १ ॥ रहाउ ॥
अपणी सरण राख प्रभ दाते ॥
गुर प्रसाद किनै विरलै जाते ॥ २ ॥

1 darsan dekh jeeva gur tera.
pooran karam hoye prabh mera.

2 eh benanti sun prabh mere.
deh naam kar apne chere. rahaa'o.

3 apni saran raakh prabh daate.
gur prasaad kinai virlai jaate.

How can a fish survive without water   4
    or a child without milk?
Nanak thirsts for the Lord's lotus feet,   5
    for in his darshan lies the essence of bliss.

Raga Asa, Fifth Guru

As I have tied my hopes to your lotus feet, O Lord,   1
    the helpless messengers of death have run away.
It is by your grace, O Lord, that one remembers you,   2
    and through simran of your Nam
    all one's maladies are destroyed.
The messenger of death inflicts great pain on others,   3
    but your devotee is out of his reach.
As my mind grows thirsty for your darshan,   4
    it becomes absorbed in the bliss of sahaj*
    and is detached from the world.
Listen to Nanak's prayer, O Lord –   5
    instil your Nam alone in his heart.

Raga Soohi, Fifth Guru

O my Guru, let me live by having your darshan   1
    so that the purpose of my life is fulfilled.
Pay heed to my supplication, O my Lord;   2
    grant me your Nam and make me your slave.
Keep me under your shelter, O benevolent Lord,   3
    for only a rare one realizes you by the Guru's grace.

---

* sahaj: Easy, natural, spontaneous; the state of mental and spiritual equipoise attained through concentration in meditation. In the state of sahaj, the soul transcends mind and matter, realizes its intrinsic nature and spontaneously achieves a state of bliss.

सुनहो बिनउ प्रभ मेरे मीता॥   4   *sunho binau prabh mere meeta.*

चरण कमल वसह मेरै चीता॥ ३॥   *charan kamal vasah merai cheeta.*

नानक एक करै अरदास॥   5   *Nanak ek karai ardaas.*

विसर नाही पूरन गुणतास॥ ४॥   *visar naahi pooran guntaas.*[6]

राग जैतसरी महला ५   Raag Jaitsari Mahala Panjvaan

घर २ छंत   Ghar Dooja Chhant

दूसर नाही ठाउ   1   *doosar naahi thaa'o*

का पह जाईऐ॥   *ka pah jaa'eeyai.*

आठ पहर कर जोड़   2   *aath pahar kar jorr*

सो प्रभ धिआईऐ॥   *so prabh dhiaa'eeyai.*

धिआए सो प्रभ सदा अपुना   3   *dhiaaye so prabh sada apuna*

मनह चिंदिआ पाईऐ॥   *manah chindia paa'eeyai.*

तज मान मोह विकार दूजा   4   *taj maan moh vikaar dooja*

एक सिउ लिव लाईऐ॥   *ek sio liv laa'eeyai.*

अरप मन तन प्रभ आगै   5   *arap man tan prabh aagai*

आप सगल मिटाईऐ॥   *aap sagal mitaa'eeyai.*

बिनवंत नानक धार किरपा   6   *binvant Nanak dhaar kirpa*

साच नाम समाईऐ॥ २॥   *saach naam samaa'eeyai.*[7]

राग गउड़ी   Raag Gaurri

महला ५ मांझ   Mahala Panjvaan Maanjh

दुख भंजन तेरा नाम जी   1   *dukh bhanjan tera naam ji*

दुख भंजन तेरा नाम॥   *dukh bhanjan tera naam.*

आठ पहर आराधीऐ   2   *aath pahar aaraadheeyai*

पूरन सतगुर गिआन॥ १॥ रहाउ॥   *pooran satgur gyaan. rahaa'o.*

जित घट वसै पारब्रहम   3   *jit ghat vasai paarbrahm*

सोई सुहावा थाउ॥   *soi suhaava thaa'o.*

Listen to my prayer, O my Lord, my friend: 4
  may your lotus feet abide in my heart.

Nanak submits only one prayer, O Lord: 5
  may he never forget you,
  O perfect treasure of virtues.

Raga Jaitsri, Fifth Guru, Chhant

With hands joined in prayer   1
  you should meditate on God day and night.

There is no other shelter –   2
  where else can you go?

Through constant meditation on your Lord   3
  you attain your heart's desire.

Renouncing pride, attachment, sin and duality,   4
  attach yourself to the one Lord.

Submitting your body and mind to the Lord,   5
  fully eradicate your ego.

Nanak prays to you for your grace, O Lord,   6
  that he may remain absorbed in your true Nam.

Raga Gauri, Fifth Guru

Your Nam, O Lord, is the destroyer of pain.   1

Let us meditate on Nam day and night –   2
  this is the perfect teaching of the Satguru.

The heart in which the supreme Lord abides   3
  is the most beautiful of all places.

जम कंकर नेड़ न आवई
रसना हर गुण गाउ॥ १॥

सेवा सुरत न जाणीआ
ना जापै आराध॥

ओट तेरी जगजीवना
मेरे ठाकुर अगम अगाध॥ २॥

भए क्रिपाल गुसाईआ
नठे सोग संताप॥

तती वाउ न लगई
सतगुर रखे आप॥ ३॥

गुर नाराइण दयु गुर
गुर सचा सिरजणहार॥

गुर तुठै सभ किछ पाइआ
जन नानक सद बलिहार॥ ४॥

4 jam kankar nerr na aavayi
rasna har gun gaa'o.

5 seva surat na jaaneeya
na jaapai aaraadh.

6 ot teri jag-jeevna
mere thaakur agam agaadh.

7 bhaye kripaal gusaa'eeyaan
nathe sog santaap.

8 tatti vaa'o na lagayi
satgur rakhe aap.

9 gur naaraa'in dayi gur
gur sacha sirjan-haar.

10 gur tutthai sabh kichh paaya
jan Nanak sad balihaar.[8]

राग धनासरी महला ५

हा हा प्रभ राख लेहो॥
हम ते किछू न होए मेरे स्वामी
कर किरपा
अपुना नाम देहो॥ १॥ रहाउ॥

अगन कुटंब सागर संसार॥
भरम मोह अगिआन अंधार॥ १॥

ऊच नीच सूख दूख॥
ध्रापस नाही त्रिसना भूख॥ २॥

मन बासना रच बिखै बिआध॥
पंच दूत संग महा असाध॥ ३॥

जीअ जहान प्रान धन तेरा॥
नानक जान सदा हर नेरा॥ ४॥

Raag Dhanaasari Mahala Panjvaan

1 ha ha prabh raakh leho.
ham te kichhu na hoye mere swaami
kar kirpa
apuna naam deho. rahaa'o.

2 agan kutamb saagar sansaar.
bharam moh agyaan andhaar.

3 ooch neech sookh dookh.
dhraapas naahi trisna bhookh.

4 man baasna rach bikhai byaadh.
panch doot sang maha asaadh.

5 jee'a jahaan praan dhan tera.
Nanak jaan sada har nera.[9]

The messenger of death does not go near anyone 4
   who sings the praises of the Lord.
I was not aware of the way to serve the Lord 5
   or meditate on his Nam.
I seek your protection, O life of the universe – 6
   my inaccessible and unfathomable Lord.
When the Lord becomes merciful, 7
   sorrows and ailments run away.
The winds of adversity cannot touch the one 8
   who is protected by the Satguru himself.
The Guru is the all-pervading, merciful Lord; 9
   the Guru is the true Creator.
God's slave Nanak forever sacrifices himself to the Guru, 10
   through whose pleasure he receives all boons.

Raga Dhanasari, Fifth Guru

Save me, O save me, my Lord; 1
   on my own I can accomplish nothing –
   be merciful and bless me with your Nam.
Family and the world are like an ocean on fire, 2
   and through delusion and worldly love
   one is engulfed in the darkness of ignorance.
Tossed between the states 3
   of high and low, pleasure and pain,
   one's hunger and thirst are never satisfied.
Engrossed in passions and the malady of vice, 4
   the mind is exposed to five incurable demons.
My soul, the world, my life-breath and wealth 5
   all belong to you, O Lord;
   know, O Nanak, that he is close by.

राग सोरठ महला ५
घर २ चउपदे

हम मैले तुम ऊजल करते
हम निरगुन तू दाता॥

हम मूरख तुम चतुर सिआणे
तू सरब कला का गिआता॥१॥

माधो हम ऐसे तू ऐसा॥

हम पापी तुम पाप खंडन
नीको ठाकुर देसा॥ रहाउ॥

तुम सभ साजे साज निवाजे
जीउ पिंड दे प्राना॥

निरगुनीआरे गुन नही कोई
तुम दान देहो मिहरवाना॥ २॥

तुम करहो भला हम भलो न जानह
तुम सदा सदा दइआला॥

तुम सुखदाई पुरख बिधाते
तुम राखहो अपुने बाला॥ ३॥

तुम निधान अटल सुलितान
जीअ जंत सभ जाचै॥

कहो नानक हम इहै हवाला
राख संतन कै पाछै॥४॥

Raag Sorath Mahala Panjvaan
Ghar Dooja Chaupade

1 ham maile tum oojal karte
  ham nirgun tu daata.

2 ham moorakh tum chatur syaane
  tu sarab kala ka gyaata.

3 maadho ham aise tu aisa.
  ham paapi tum paap khandan
  neeko thaakur desa. rahaa'o.

4 tum sabh saaje saaj nivaaje
  jee'o pind de praana.

5 nirguneeyaare gun nahi koi
  tum daan deho meharvaana.

6 tum karho bhala ham bhalo na jaanah
  tum sada sada dayaala.

7 tum sukhdaa'i purakh bidhaate
  tum raakhho apune baala.

8 tum nidhaan atal sulitaan
  jee'a jant sabh jaachai.

9 kaho Nanak ham ehai havaala
  raakh santan kai paachhai.[10]

राग केदारा महला ५
घर ४

हर हर हर गुन गावहो॥

करहो क्रिपा गोपाल गोबिंदे
अपना नाम जपावहो॥ रहाउ॥

काढ लीए प्रभ आन बिखै ते
साधसंग मन लावहो॥

Raag Kedaara Mahala Panjvaan
Ghar Chautha

1 har har har gun gaavho.
  karho kripa gopaal gobinde
  apna naam japaavho. rahaa'o.

2 kaadh leeye prabh aan bikhai te
  saadh-sang man laavho.

Raga Sorath, Fifth Guru, Chaupadas

We are defiled, O Lord, and you purify us;   *1*
    we are meritless and you are the bestower of merit.

We are ignorant; you are wise and enlightened,   *2*
    a master of all skills.

We are what we are, O Lord,   *3*
    and you are what you are.

We are sinners and you are the destroyer of sin;
    O Lord, beautiful is your abode.

Having created all, you have blessed everyone   *4*
    with life, body and breath.

We are meritless and without any qualities –   *5*
    bless us with the boon of merits, O merciful Lord.

You do us good but we fail to recognize it,   *6*
    yet you are forever and ever merciful.

You are the bestower of peace, O Creator –   *7*
    please save us, your children.

You are the eternal king, our treasure,   *8*
    and all living beings beg you for your grace.

Says Nanak: such is our condition, O Lord –   *9*
    help us follow in the footsteps of Saints.

Raga Kedara, Fifth Guru

Keep singing the praises of God –   *1*
    O my Lord, my Master, show your grace
    and help me repeat your Nam.

Pull me out of the abyss of sin, O Lord,   *2*
    and attach my mind to the company of Saints.

भ्रम भउ मोह कटिओ गुर बचनी
अपना दरस दिखावहो॥१॥

3 bhram bhau moh katio gur bachni
apna daras dikhaavho.

सभ की रेन होए मन मेरा
अहंबुध तजावहो॥

4 sabh ki ren hoye man mera
aham-budh tajaavho.

अपनी भगति देह दइआला
वडभागी नानक हर पावहो॥२॥

5 apni bhagti deh dayaala
vad-bhaagi Nanak har paavho.[11]

राग सूही महला ५
असटपदीआ घर १० काफी

Raag Soohi Mahala Panjvaan
Astpadee'a Ghar Dasvaan Kaafi

जे भुली जे चुकी साई
भी तहिंजी काढीआ॥

1 je bhulli je chukki saa'een
bhi tahinji kaadheeya.

जिन्हा नेह दूजाणे लगा
झूर मरहो से वाढीआ॥

2 jinha neh doojaane lagga
jhoor marho se vaadheeya.

हउ ना छोडउ कंत पासरा॥

3 hau na chhodaun kant paasra.

सदा रंगीला लाल पिआरा
एह महिंजा आसरा॥१॥रहाउ॥

sada rangeela laal pyaara
eh mahinja aasra. rahaa'o.

सजण तूहै सैण तू
मै तुझ उपर बहु माणीआ॥

4 sajjan toohai sain tu
mai tujh upar bahu maaneeya.

जा तू अंदर ता सुखे
तूं निमाणी माणीआ॥२॥

5 ja tu andar ta sukhe
toon nimaani maaneeya.

जे तू तुठा क्रिपा निधान
ना दूजा वेखाल॥

6 je tu tuttha kripa nidhaan
na dooja vekhaal.

एहा पाई मू दातड़ी
नित हिरदै रखा समाल॥३॥

7 eha paa'i mu daatarri
nit hirdai rakha samaal.

पाव जुलाई पंध तउ
नैणी दरस दिखाल॥

8 paav julaa'i pandh tau
naini daras dikhaal.

स्रवणी सुणी कहाणीआ
जे गुर थीवै किरपाल॥४॥

9 sravani suni kahaaneeya
je gur theevai kirpaal.

किती लख करोड़ पिरिए
रोम न पुजन तेरिआ॥

10 kitti lakh karorr pireeye
rom na pujjan teriya.

Freeing us from doubt, fear and worldly love,   3
   you show your vision through the Guru's Word.
Help me rid myself of self-conceit   4
   so that my mind may become the dust of the feet of all.
Bless Nanak with your devotion, O merciful Lord,   5
   so that through his great good fortune he may attain you.

Raga Soohi, Fifth Guru, Astpadi, Kafi

Even as I have gone astray and faltered, O Lord,   1
   still I am known as your bride.
Those who entertain love of duality   2
   are the abandoned lot who die repentant.
I shall not leave my Husband's side;   3
   always charming and youthful,
   my Beloved is my sole support.
You are my friend and my true relation, O Lord,   4
   and in you I take immense pride.
When you manifest yourself within me I am at peace –   5
   you are the honour of this helpless one.
If you are pleased with me, O Lord,   6
   do not make me look to another.
Bless me with the boon   7
   that I may always cherish you in my heart.
Let my feet walk on your path, O Lord,   8
   and my eyes have your darshan.
O Lord, if the Guru showers his mercy,   9
   let my ears hear stories about you.
O beloved Lord, millions upon millions of the virtuous   10
   cannot equal a hair on your body.

तू साही हू साहु

हउ कह न सका गुण तेरिआ॥५॥

सहीआ तऊ असंख

मंझहो हभ वधाणीआ॥

हिक भोरी नदर निहाल

देह दरस रंग माणीआ॥६॥

जै डिठे मन धीरीऐ

किलविख वंञन्ह दूरे॥

सो किउ विसरै माउ मै

जो रहिआ भरपूरे॥७॥

होए निमाणी ढह पई

मिलिआ सहज सुभाए॥

पूरब लिखिआ पाइआ

नानक संत सहाए॥८॥

11   tu saahi hu saahu

      hau kah na saka gun teriya.

12   saheeya ta'u asankh

      manjoh habh vadhaaneeya.

13   hik bhori nadar nihaal

      deh daras rang maaneeya.

14   jai ditthe man dheereeyai

      kilvikh vanjan doore.

15   so kio visrai maa'o mai

      jo rahiya bharpoore.

16   hoye nimaani dhah payi

      miliya sahaj subhaaye.

17   poorab likhiya paaya

      Nanak sant sahaaye.[12]

राग सूही महला ५

घर ७

जिस के सिर ऊपर तूं सुआमी

सो दुख कैसा पावै॥

बोल न जाणै माइआ मद माता

मरणा चीत न आवै॥१॥

मेरे राम राए

तूं संता का संत तेरे॥

तेरे सेवक कउ भउ किछ नाही

जम नही आवै नेरे॥१॥रहाउ॥

जो तेरै रंग राते सुआमी

तिन्ह का जनम मरण दुख नासा॥

Raag Soohi Mahala Panjvaan

Ghar Sattvaan

1   jis ke sir oopar toon suaami

      so dukh kaisa paavai.

2   bol na jaanai maaya mad maata

      marna cheet na aavai.

3   mere raam raaye

      toon santaan ka sant tere.

4   tere sevak kau bhau kichh naahi

      jam nahi aavai nere. rahaa'o.

5   jo terai rang raate suaami tin ka

      janam maran dukh naasa.

You are the king of kings, O Lord,   *11*
  and your virtues I am unable to express.

Countless are your brides, O Lord – all better than me.   *12*

Bless me with a glimpse of your merciful glance;   *13*
  give me your darshan and let me enjoy your love.

O mother, why should I forget the Lord,   *14–15*
  who pervades all, whose sight brings peace to the mind
  and who drives away sins.

In utter humility I have fallen at the Lord's feet,   *16*
  and without any effort on my part
  he has revealed himself to me.

With the help of the Saints, Nanak has received   *17*
  what was recorded in his destiny.

Raga Soohi, Fifth Guru

O Lord, how can anyone   *1*
  who is under your protection suffer pain?

Those intoxicated with the wine of maya   *2*
  do not know how to remember God's Nam
  and do not think of their death.

You belong to the Saints, O my sovereign Lord,   *3*
  and the Saints belong to you.

Your devotee has nothing to fear,   *4*
  for the messenger of death cannot get near him.

The pain of birth and death flees from those, O Lord,   *5*
  who are dyed in your love.

तेरी बखस न मेटै कोई

सतगुर का दिलासा॥ २॥

नाम धिआइन सुख फल पाइन

आठ पहर आराधह॥

तेरी सरण तेरै भरवासै

पंच दुसट लै साधह॥ ३॥

गिआन धिआन किछ करम न जाणा

सार न जाणा तेरी॥

सभ ते वडा सतगुर

नानक जिन कल राखी मेरी॥ ४॥

6 teri bakhas na metai koi

   satgur ka dilaasa.

7 naam dhiaayin sukh phal paayin

   aath pahar aaraadhah.

8 teri saran terai bharvaasai

   panch dust lai saadhah.

9 gyaan dhyaan kichh karam na jaana

   saar na jaana teri.

10 sabh te vadda satgur

   Nanak jin kal raakhi meri.[13]

राग सूही छंत

महला ५ घर ३

कर किरपा मेरे प्रीतम सुआमी

नेत्र देखह दरस तेरा राम॥

लाख जिहवा देह मेरे पिआरे

मुख हर आराधे मेरा राम॥

हर आराधे जम पंथ साधे

दूख न विआपै कोई॥

जल थल महीअल पूरन सुआमी

जत देखा तत सोई॥

भरम मोह बिकार नाठे

प्रभ नेरहू ते नेरा॥

नानक कउ प्रभ किरपा कीजै

नेत्र देखह दरस तेरा॥ १॥

Raag Soohi Chhant

Mahala Panjvaan Ghar Teeja

1 kar kirpa mere preetam suaami

   netar dekhah daras tera raam.

2 laakh jihva deh mere pyaare

   mukh har aaraadhe mera raam.

3 har aaraadhe jam panth saadhe

   dookh na vyaapai koi.

4 jal thal maheeyal pooran suaami

   jat dekha tat soi.

5 bharam moh bikaar naathe

   prabh nerhu te nera.

6 Nanak kau prabh kirpa keejai

   netr dekhah daras tera.[14]

That no one can erase your blessings, O Lord,   6
  is the assurance that comes from the Satguru.
Those who meditate on your Nam   7
  receive the fruit of peace
  and contemplate on you day and night.
Under your protection and with faith in you,   8
  they overcome the five demons.
Lacking knowledge, contemplation and good deeds,   9
  O Lord, I do not realize your magnitude.
Supreme above all is the Satguru, O Nanak,   10
  who has upheld my honour in the divine court.

Raga Soohi, Chhant, Fifth Guru

Be merciful to me, O my beloved Lord,   1
  so that my eyes may have your darshan.
Grant me a million tongues, O Beloved,   2
  with which I may repeat your Nam.
Meditating on God, the path of death is conquered   3
  and one suffers no pain.
The Lord permeates water, land and sky –   4
  wherever I look, I see him pervading all.
My illusions, attachments and sins have vanished,   5
  and I see the Lord closer than the closest.
Be merciful to Nanak, O Lord,   6
  and grant him the vision to behold your darshan.

राग गउड़ी पूरबी
महला ५

कवन गुन प्रानपत
मिलउ मेरी माई॥ १॥ रहाउ॥
रूप हीन बुध बल हीनी
मोहे परदेसन दूर ते आई॥ १॥
नाहिन दरब न जोबन माती
मोहे अनाथ की करहो समाई॥ २॥
खोजत खोजत भई बैरागन
प्रभ दरसन कउ हउ फिरत तिसाई॥ ३॥
दीन दइआल क्रिपाल प्रभ नानक
साधसंग मेरी जलन बुझाई॥ ४॥

Raag Gaurri Poorbi
Mahala Panjvaan

1 *kavan gun praan-pat*
milau meri maa'i. rahaa'o.
2 *roop heen buddh bal heeni*
mohe pardesan door te aa'i.
3 *naahin darab na joban maati*
mohe anaath ki karoh samaa'i.
4 *khojat khojat bhayi bairaagan*
prabh darsan kau hau phirat tisaa'i.
5 *deen dayaal kripaal prabh Nanak*
saadh-sang meri jalan bujhaa'i.[15]

राग रामकली महला ५
घर १

किरपा करहो दीन के दाते
मेरा गुण अवगण न बीचारहो कोई॥
माटी का किआ धोपै सुआमी
माणस की गत एही॥ १॥
मेरे मन सतगुर सेव सुख होई॥
जो इछहो सोई फल पावहो
फिर दुख न विआपै कोई॥ १॥ रहाउ॥
काचे भांडे साज निवाजे
अंतर जोत समाई॥
जैसा लिखत लिखिआ धुर करतै
हम तैसी किरत कमाई॥ २॥
मन तन थाप कीआ सभ अपना
एहो आवण जाणा॥
जिन दीआ सो चित न आवै
मोह अंध लपटाणा॥ ३॥

Raag Raamkali Mahala Panjvaan
Ghar Pahila

1 *kirpa karho deen ke daate*
mera gun avgan na beechaarho koi.
2 *maati ka kya dhopai suaami*
maanas ki gat ehi.
3 *mere man satgur sev sukh hoi.*
jo ichhoh soi phal paavho
phir dookh na vyaapai koi. rahaa'o.
4 *kaache bhaande saaj nivaaje*
antar jot samaa'i.
5 *jaisa likhat likhiya dhur kartai*
ham taisi kirat kamaa'i.
6 *man tan thaap keeya sabh apna*
eho aavan jaana.
7 *jin deeya so chit na aavai*
moh andh laptaana.

Raga Gauri Poorbi, Fifth Guru

O mother, what qualities will help me meet my Lord?   *1*

I lack beauty, understanding and strength;   *2*
   I am a stranger from a far-off land.

I have neither wealth nor the pride of youth;   *3*
   I am destitute, O Lord – please unite me with yourself.

In my constant search I have renounced all   *4*
   and wander about thirsty for the Lord's darshan.

Merciful to the meek is Nanak's compassionate Lord,   *5*
   who has quenched my thirst through the company of Saints.

Raga Ramkali, Fifth Guru

O benefactor of the meek, be merciful to me   *1*
   and disregard my virtues and vices.

How can soil be washed clean of dirt, O Lord –   *2*
   this is the nature of human endeavour!

My mind, all bliss lies in devotion to the Satguru –   *3*
   all your desires will be fulfilled
   and you will no longer undergo suffering.

God has created vessels of clay, adorned them   *4*
   and infused his light into them.

As is the primal writ inscribed by the Creator,   *5*
   so are the actions we perform.

Our presumption that we own this body, mind and all else   *6*
   causes our coming and going in transmigration.

Not remembering the One who blessed him with these,   *7*
   the blind one is engrossed in his attachment to them.

जिन कीआ सोई प्रभ जाणै
हर का महल अपारा॥

8 jin keeya soi prabh jaanai
har ka mahal apaara.

भगति करी हर के गुण गावा
नानक दास तुमारा॥४॥

9 bhagti kari har ke gun gaava
Nanak daas tumaara.[16]

**राग जैतसरी महला ५
घर ४ दुपदे**

**Raag Jaitsari Mahala Panjvaan
Ghar Chautha Dupade**

कोई जन हर सिउ देवै जोर॥

1 koi jan har sio devai jor.

चरन गहउ बकउ सुभ रसना
दीजह प्रान अकोर॥१॥रहाउ॥

2 charan gahau bakau subh rasna
deejah praan akor. rahaa'o.

मन तन निरमल करत किआरो
हर सिंचै सुधा संजोर॥

3 man tan nirmal karat kyaaro
har sinchai sudha sanjor.

इआ रस मह मगन होत किरपा ते
महा बिखिआ ते तोर॥१॥

4 iya ras mah magan hot kirpa te
maha bikhya te tor.

आइओ सरण दीन दुख भंजन
चितवउ तुम्हरी ओर॥

5 aayo saran deen dukh bhanjan
chitvau tumhri or.

अभै पद दान सिमरन सुआमी को
प्रभ नानक बंधन छोर॥२॥

6 abhai pad daan simran suaami ko
prabh Nanak bandhan chhor.[17]

**राग कानड़ा महला ५
घर ३**

**Raag Kaanarra Mahala Panjvaan
Ghar Teeja**

कुचिल कठोर कपट कामी॥
जिउ जानह

1 kuchil kathor kapat kaami.
jio jaanah

तिउ तार सुआमी॥१॥रहाउ॥

tio taar suaami. rahaa'o.

तू समरथ सरन जोग
तू राखह अपनी कल धार॥१॥

2 tu samrath saran jog
tu raakhah apni kal dhaar.

The Lord alone knows the universe that he has created,   8
   and beyond all limits is his mansion.
Your slave Nanak renders devotion to you, O Lord,   9
   and sings your praises.

Raga Jaitsri, Fifth Guru, Dupadas

Oh, how I wish   1
   someone would unite me with God!
I shall submit myself at his feet, utter sweet words   2
   and dedicate my life to him.
Making clean flowerbeds of my mind and body,   3
   I irrigate them with divine nectar.
By God's grace one becomes absorbed in the divine elixir   4
   and the bonds of maya are severed.
With thoughts centred on you,   5
   O destroyer of the suffering of the meek,
   I have come seeking your protection.
You are the destroyer of bonds to the creation, O Lord;   6
   grant Nanak the state of fearlessness*
   and the simran of your Nam.

Raga Kanara, Fifth Guru

Defiled, stone-hearted, devious and lustful as I am,   1
   save me, O Lord, in whatever way it pleases you.
O Lord, you are all-powerful and capable of giving shelter –   2
   exercise your power and protect us.

---

* **Fearlessness** occurs when one takes refuge in and is therefore protected by the Guru.

जाप ताप नेम सुच संजम 3   *jaap taap nem such sanjam*
नाही इन बिधे छुटकार॥   *naahi in bidhe chhutkaar.*
गरत घोर अंध ते काढहो 4   *garat ghor andh te kaadhoh*
प्रभ नानक नदर निहार॥ २॥   *prabh Nanak nadar nihaar.*[18]

राग सूही महला ५   Raag Soohi Mahala Panjvaan
घर १   Ghar Pahila

किआ गुण तेरे सार सम्हाली 1   *kya gun tere saar samhaali*
मोहे निरगुन के दातारे॥   *mohe nirgun ke daata re.*
बै खरीद किआ करे चतुराई 2   *bai khareed kya kare chaturaa'i*
इह जीउ पिंड सभ थारे॥१॥   *eh jee'o pind sabh thaare.*
लाल रंगीले प्रीतम मनमोहन 3   *laal rangeele preetam manmohan*
तेरे दरसन कउ हम बारे॥१॥रहाउ॥ *tere darsan kau ham baare. rahaa'o.*
प्रभ दाता मोहे दीन भेखारी 4   *prabh daata mohe deen bhekhaari*
तुम्ह सदा सदा उपकारे॥   *tum sada sada upkaare.*
सो किछ नाही जे मै ते होवै 5   *so kichh naahi je mai te hovai*
मेरे ठाकुर अगम अपारे॥ २॥   *mere thaakur agam apaare.*
किआ सेव कमावउ 6   *kya sev kamaavau*
किआ कह रीझावउ   *kya kah reejhaavau*
बिध कित पावउ दरसारे॥   *bidh kit paavau darsaare.*
मित नही पाईऐ अंत न लहीऐ 7   *mit nahi paa'eeyai ant na laheeyai*
मन तरसै चरनारे॥ ३॥   *man tarsai charnaare.*
पावउ दान ढीठ होए मागउ 8   *paavau daan dheeth hoye maangau*
मुख लागै संत रेनारे॥   *mukh laagai sant renaare.*
जन नानक कउ गुर किरपा धारी 9   *jan Nanak kau gur kirpa dhaari*
प्रभ हाथ दे निसतारे॥ ४॥   *prabh haath dey nistaare.*[19]

---

*In the bhakti tradition, applying the **dust from the feet of the Saints** to one's forehead is considered to be an act of deep reverence and an expression of humility and submission. Esoterically, the dust of the Guru's feet does not refer to physical dust, but represents the

Liberation is not attained 3
   through recitation of holy texts, penances,
   religious vows, ritual purification and self-restraint.
Through your merciful glance, O Lord, 4
   pull Nanak out of the deep and dark abyss.

Raga Soohi, Fifth Guru

How many of your qualities may I recount, 1
   O benevolent Lord of this worthless creature?
What cleverness can I, your bought slave, show 2
   when my body and soul belong to you?
I sacrifice myself to your darshan, 3
   O my bewitching Beloved, charmer of my heart.
You are the generous giver and I a humble beggar; 4
   you are forever and ever the beneficent one.
There is nothing that I can accomplish on my own, 5
   O my unfathomable and boundless Lord.
What service can I render unto you, O Lord, 6
   what can I say to please you
   and by what means can I have your darshan?
Although your limit cannot be ascertained 7
   nor your end found,
   yet my mind yearns for your darshan.
With stubborn persistence I ask you 8
   for the gift of the dust from the feet of the Saints,
   which I would apply to my forehead.*
The Guru has shown grace to God's slave Nanak; 9
   extending his hand, God has saved him.

---

misty radiance emanating from the feet of his radiant form within, also called the lotus
feet, which the devotee experiences on an inner plane and which brings light to inner
darkness.

राग टोडी महला ५
घर २ दुपदे

राग आसा घर ८ काफी
महला ५

Raag Todi Mahala Panjvaan
Ghar Dooja Dupade

1 maagau daan thaakur naam.
avar kachhu merai sang na chaalai
milai kripa gun gaam. rahaa'o.

2 raaj maal anek bhog ras
sagal tarvar ki chhaam.

3 dhaaye dhaaye bahu bidh kau dhaavai
sagal niraarath kaam.

4 bin govind avar je chaahau
deesai sagal baat hai khaam.

5 kaho Nanak sant ren maagau
mero man paavai bisraam. [20]

Raag Aasa Ghar Atthvaan Kaafi
Mahala Panjvaan

1 mai banda bai khareed
sach saahib mera.

2 jee'o pind sabh tis da
sabh kichh hai tera.

3 maan nimaane toon dhani
tera bharvaasa.

4 bin saache an tek hai
so jaanho kaacha. rahaa'o.

5 tera hukam apaar hai
koi ant na paaye.

6 jis gur poora bhetsi
so challai rajaaye.

मागउ दान ठाकुर नाम॥
अवर कछू मेरै संग न चालै
मिलै क्रिपा गुण गाम॥१॥रहाउ॥
राज माल अनेक भोग रस
सगल तरवर की छाम॥
धाए धाए बहु बिध कउ धावै
सगल निरारथ काम॥१॥
बिन गोविंद अवर जे चाहउ
दीसै सगल बात है खाम॥
कहो नानक संत रेन मागउ
मेरो मन पावै बिश्राम॥२॥

मै बंदा बै खरीद
सच साहिब मेरा॥
जीउ पिंड सभ तिस दा
सभ किछ है तेरा॥१॥
माण निमाणे तूं धणी
तेरा भरवासा॥
बिन साचे अन टेक है
सो जाणहो काचा॥१॥रहाउ॥
तेरा हुकम अपार है
कोई अंत न पाए॥
जिस गुर पूरा भेटसी
सो चलै रजाए॥२॥

Raga Todi, Fifth Guru, Dupadas

I beg for the alms of your Nam, O Lord;   1
   nothing else will accompany me hereafter –
   be merciful and grant me
   the gift of singing your praises.

Authority, wealth and the various sensual enjoyments   2
   are all like the shadow of a tree.

One constantly rushes about in worldly pursuits,   3
   but all this is worthless endeavour.

Other than God, whatever I desire is of no value.   4

Says Nanak: I seek the dust of the feet of the Saints   5
   so that my mind may attain peace.

Raga Asa, Kafi, Fifth Guru

I am your bought slave, and you are my true Master.   1

This body, soul and all else that is mine   2
   belong to you, O Lord.

You are the honour of the meek,   3
   and in you, O Master, I have put my faith.

Consider the one who seeks   4
   the support of anyone other than God to be false.

Beyond all limits is your will, O Lord –   5
   no one can fathom its extent.

Those alone who have met the perfect Guru   6
   walk in your will.

चतुराई सिआणपा
कितै काम न आईऐ॥

7 chaturaa'i siaanpa
kitai kaam na aa'eeyai.

तुठा साहिब जो देवै
सोई सुख पाईऐ॥३॥

8 tuttha saahib jo devai
soi sukh paa'eeyai.

जे लख करम कमाईअह
किछ पवै न बंधा॥

9 je lakh karam kamaayee'ah
kichh pavai na bandha.

जन नानक कीता नाम धर
होर छोडिआ धंधा॥४॥

10 jan Nanak keeta naam dhar
hor chhodya dhandha.[21]

राग बिलावल महला ५
घर २

Raag Bilaaval Mahala Panjvaan
Ghar Dooja

मै मन तेरी टेक मेरे पिआरे
मै मन तेरी टेक॥

1 mai man teri tek mere pyaare
mai man teri tek.

अवर सिआणपा बिरथीआ पिआरे
राखन कउ तुम एक॥१॥रहाउ॥

2 avar syaanpa birtheeya pyaare
raakhan kau tum ek. rahaa'o.

सतगुर पूरा जे मिलै पिआरे
सो जन होत निहाला॥

3 satgur poora je milai pyaare
so jan hot nihaala.

गुर की सेवा सो करे पिआरे
जिस नो होए दइआला॥

4 gur ki seva so kare pyaare
jis no hoye dayaala.

सफल मूरत गुरदेउ सुआमी
सरब कला भरपूरे॥

5 saphal moorat gurde'o suaami
sarab kala bharpoore.

नानक गुर पारब्रहम परमेसर
सदा सदा हजूरे॥१॥

6 Nanak gur paarbrahm parmesar
sada sada hajoore.[22]

राग तिलंग महला ५
घर ३

Raag Tilang Mahala Panjvaan
Ghar Teeja

मिहरवान साहिब मिहरवान॥
साहिब मेरा मिहरवान॥
जीअ सगल कउ दे दान॥रहाउ॥

1 meharvaan saahib meharvaan.
saahib mera meharvaan.
jee'a sagal kau de daan. rahaa'o.

तू काहे डोलह प्राणीआ
तुध राखैगा सिरजणहार॥

2 tu kaahe dolah praaneeya
tudh raakhaiga sirjan-haar.

Cleverness and worldly wisdom are of no avail;   7–8
   only that which the Lord is pleased to bestow brings peace.
A million ritual actions do not put an end to desire.   9
Abandoning all other pursuits   10
   Nanak has made Nam his mainstay.

Raga Bilawal, Fifth Guru

*M*y mind finds support in you, O Beloved;   1
   in you my mind finds its support.
Other clever devices are futile, O Beloved –   2
   you alone are my saviour.
Those who meet the perfect Guru, O Beloved, are blessed.   3
Only the one on whom the Lord showers his mercy   4
   devotes himself to the Guru's service.
Fruitful is the form of the divine Guru,   5
   in whom all powers abound.
O Nanak, the Guru forever and ever abides   6
   in the presence of the supreme Lord.

Raga Tilang, Fifth Guru

*M*erciful, merciful is the Lord;   1
   merciful is my Lord, who showers all with his blessings!
Why do you waver in your purpose, O mortal,   2
   when the Creator is there to protect you?

जिन पैदाइस तू कीआ	3 jin paidaa'is tu keeya
सोई दे आधार ॥१॥	soi de aadhaar.
जिन उपाई मेदनी	4 jin upaa'i medni
सोई करदा सार ॥	soi karda saar.
घट घट मालक दिला का	5 ghat ghat maalak dila ka
सचा परवदगार ॥२॥	sacha parvadgaar.
कुदरत कीम न जाणीऐ	6 kudrat keem na jaaneeyai
वडा वेपरवाह ॥	vada veparvaah.
कर बंदे तू बंदगी	7 kar bande tu bandagi
जिचर घट मह साह ॥३॥	jichar ghat mah saah.
तू समरथ अकथ अगोचर	8 tu samrath akath agochar
जीउ पिंड तेरी रास ॥	jee'o pind teri raas.
रहम तेरी सुख पाइआ	9 raham teri sukh paaya
सदा नानक की अरदास ॥४॥	sada Nanak ki ardaas.[23]

राग माझ महला ५	**Raag Maajh Mahala Panjvaan**
चउपदे घर १	**Chaupade Ghar Pahila**
मेरा मन लोचै गुर दरसन ताई ॥	1 mera man lochai gur darsan taa'een.
बिलप करे चात्रिक की निआई ॥	bilap kare chaatrik ki nyaa'een.
त्रिखा न उतरै सांत न आवै	2 trikha na utrai saant na aavai
बिन दरसन संत पिआरे जीउ ॥१॥	bin darsan sant pyaare jee'o.
हउ घोली जीउ घोल घुमाई	3 hau gholi jee'o ghol ghumaa'i
गुर दरसन संत	gur darsan sant
पिआरे जीउ ॥१॥ रहाउ ॥	pyaare jee'o. rahaa'o.
तेरा मुख सुहावा जीउ	4 tera mukh suhaava jee'o
सहज धुन बाणी ॥	sahaj dhun baani.
चिर होआ देखे सारिंगपाणी ॥	chir ho'a dekhe saaring-paani.

The One who has created you 3
   will himself lend you his support.
The One who has created the earth 4
   will himself care for it.
He is the true nourisher 5
   and the Master of all hearts.
He is the great carefree Lord, 6
   whose power is beyond estimation.
Devote yourself to him, O friend, 7
   as long as the breath in your body endures.
O Lord, you are almighty, indescribable and unknowable – 8
   my soul and body are your property.
Your servant Nanak prays, O Lord, 9
   that in your mercy he finds peace.

Raga Majh, Fifth Guru, Chaupadas
My heart cries out like a *chaatrik** 1
   yearning for a glimpse of my Guru.
Without seeing the beloved Saint 2
   my thirst is not quenched, nor is peace attained.
Time and again I sacrifice myself 3
   to the vision of the beloved Saint, my Guru.
Beautiful is your face, and your voice resounds 4
   with a spontaneous melody of peace.
Ages have passed
   since I last had your darshan, O my Lord.

---

*A *chaatrik* is a legendary bird that keeps flying with its beak open to the heavens, constantly crying for the pure raindrops that fall during the period of the Swati Constellation and never coming down to drink from rivers and ponds.

धंन सो देस जहा तूं वसिआ
मेरे सजण मीत मुरारे जीउ॥ २॥

हउ घोली हउ घोल घुमाई
गुर सजण मीत
मुरारे जीउ॥ १॥ रहाउ॥

इक घड़ी न मिलते
ता कलिजुग होता॥
हुण कद मिलीऐ
प्रिअ तुध भगवंता॥

मोहे रैण न विहावै नीद न आवै
बिन देखे गुर दरबारे जीउ॥ ३॥

हउ घोली जीउ घोल घुमाई
तिस सचे गुर दरबारे जीउ॥ १॥ रहाउ॥

भाग होआ गुर संत मिलाइआ॥
प्रभ अबिनासी घर मह पाइआ॥

सेव करी पल चसा न विछुड़ा
जन नानक दास तुमारे जीउ॥ ४॥

हउ घोली जीउ घोल घुमाई
जन नानक
दास तुमारे जीउ॥ रहाउ॥ १॥

5 dhann so des jaha toon vasiya
   mere sajan meet muraare jee'o.

6 hau gholi hau ghol ghumaa'i
   gur sajan meet
   muraare jee'o. rahaa'o.

7 ik gharri na milte
   ta kaljug hota.
   hun kad mileeyai
   priy tudh bhagvanta.

8 mohe rain na vihaavai need na aavai
   bin dekhe gur darbaare jee'o.

9 hau gholi jee'o ghol ghumaa'i
   tis sache gur darbaare jee'o. rahaa'o.

10 bhaag ho'a gur sant milaaya.
   prabh abinaasi ghar mah paaya.

11 sev kari pal chasa na vichhurra
   jan Nanak daas tumaare jee'o.

12 hau gholi jee'o ghol ghumaa'i
   jan Nanak
   daas tumaare jee'o. rahaa'o.[24]

राग धनासरी महला ५
घर १ चउपदे

पानी पखा पीसउ संत आगै
गुण गोविंद जस गाई॥
सास सास मन नाम सम्हारै
इह बिस्राम निध पाई॥ १॥
तुम्ह करहो दइआ मेरे साई॥
ऐसी मत दीजै मेरे ठाकुर
सदा सदा तुध धिआई॥ १॥ रहाउ॥

Raag Dhanaasari Mahala

Panjvaan Ghar Pahila Chaupade

1 paani pakkha peesau sant aagai
   gun govind jas gaa'i.

2 saas saas man naam samhaarai
   eho bisraam nidh paa'i.

3 tum karoh daya mere saa'een.
   aisi mat deejai mere thaakur
   sada sada tudh dhiaa'i. rahaa'o.

Blessed is the land where you live,   5
   my Lord and beloved friend, my divine companion!
Time and again do I sacrifice myself   6
   to my Lord and beloved Guru, my divine companion.
When I was separated from you just for a moment,   7
   it was as if a dark age had descended upon me –
   when am I going to see you now, O my beloved Lord?
Without seeing my Guru's court   8
   I cannot pass my sleepless nights.
Time and again do I sacrifice myself   9
   at the Satguru's court.
My good fortune has united me with my Guru,   10
   by whose grace I have found the eternal Lord
   within my own self.
I am your slave, O Master – may I serve you   11
   and not ever be separated from you.
Time and again I sacrifice myself to you, O Lord;   12
   forever at your service is your slave Nanak.

Raga Dhanasari, Fifth Guru, Chaupadas
I shall fan the Saints, fetch water   1
   and grind corn for them;
   I sing songs in praise of God's virtues.
Through remembrance of Nam with every breath   2
   my mind finds the treasure of peace.
Show your compassion, O my Lord,   3
   and grant me the wisdom always to meditate on you.

तुम्हरी क्रिपा ते मोह मान छूटै
बिनस जाए भरमाई॥

4 tumhri kripa te moh maan chhootai
binas jaaye bharmaa'i.

अनद रूप रविओ सभ मधे
जत कत पेखउ जाई॥ २ ॥

5 anad roop ravio sabh madhe
jat kat pekhau jaa'i.

तुम्ह दइआल किरपाल क्रिपा निध
पतित पावन गोसाई॥

6 tum dayaal kirpaal kripa nidh
patit paavan gosaa'een.

कोट सूख आनंद राज पाए
मुख ते निमख बुलाई॥ ३ ॥

7 kot sookh aanand raaj paaye
mukh te nimakh bulaa'i.

जाप ताप भगति सा पूरी
जो प्रभ कै मन भाई॥

8 jaap taap bhagti sa poori
jo prabh kai man bhaa'i.

नाम जपत त्रिसना सभ बुझी है
नानक त्रिपत अघाई ॥ ४ ॥

9 naam japat trisna sabh bujhi hai
Nanak tripat aghaa'i.[25]

राग सूही महला ५
घर ७

Raag Soohi Mahala Panjvaan
Ghar Sattvaan

पारब्रहम परमेसर सतगुर
आपे करणैहारा॥

1 paarbrahm parmesar satgur
aape karnai-haara.

चरण धूड़ तेरी सेवक मागै
तेरे दरसन कउ बलिहारा॥ १ ॥

2 charan dhoorr teri sevak maagai
tere darsan kau balihaara.

मेरे राम राए
जिउ राखह तिउ रहीऐ॥

3 mere raam raaye
jio raakhah tio rahee'ai.

तुध भावै ता नाम जपावह
सुख तेरा दिता लहीऐ॥ १ ॥ रहाउ

tudh bhaavai ta naam japaavah
sukh tera ditta lahee'ai. rahaa'o.

मुकत भुगत जुगत तेरी सेवा
जिस तूं आप कराए॥

4 mukat bhugat jugat teri seva
jis toon aap karaaye.

तहा बैकुंठ जह कीरतन तेरा
तूं आपे सरधा लाए॥ २ ॥

5 taha baikunth jah keertan tera
toon aape sardha laaye.

---

* Esoterically, the **dust of the Guru's feet** does not refer to physical dust, but represents the misty radiance emanating from his inner feet, also called the lotus feet, which the devotee experiences on a spiritual plane within and which brings light to inner darkness.

By your grace, worldly love and pride are eliminated 4
and all delusion is shattered.

God, the embodiment of bliss, pervades all, 5
so wherever I go I see him.

You, O Lord, are merciful and compassionate, 6
a treasure of grace and purifier of sinners.

Remembrance of your Nam, even for a moment, 7
brings millions of comforts, joys and kingdoms.

Only the repetition, penance or devotion 8
that is pleasing to the Lord is perfect.

Through repetition of Nam all thirst is quenched 9
and Nanak is contented and fulfilled.

Raga Soohi, Fifth Guru

The Satguru is the Supreme Being and the primal Lord; 1
he himself is the Creator.

Your devotee begs for the dust of your feet* 2
and sacrifices himself to your darshan.†

I live the way you keep me, O my divine King; 3
we remember your Nam if it be your will
and attain peace if it is granted by you.

Salvation, all comforts of life 4
and all manner of devotion come to the devotee
whom you inspire to your service.

Heaven is where your praises are sung, 5
and you yourself inspire faith and devotion.

---

† The mystics generally use the term **darshan** for inner darshan of the radiant form of the Master. This darshan elevates the soul to spheres of higher consciousness and is attained through a process of deep inner contemplation.

सिमर सिमर सिमर नाम जीवा
तन मन होए निहाला॥

6 *simar simar simar naam jeeva*
tan man hoye nihaala.

चरण कमल तेरे धोए धोए पीवा
मेरे सतगुर दीन दइआला॥ ३॥

7 *charan kamal tere dhoye dhoye peeva*
mere satgur deen dayaala.

कुरबाण जाई उस वेला सुहावी
जित तुमरै दुआरै आइआ॥

8 *kurbaan jaa'i us vela suhaavi*
jit tumrai duaarai aaya.

नानक कउ प्रभ भए क्रिपाला
सतगुर पूरा पाइआ॥ ४॥

9 *Nanak kau prabh bhaye kripaala*
satgur poora paaya.[26]

राग सारग महला ५
दुपदे घर ४

Raag Saarag Mahala Panjvaan
Dupade Ghar Chautha

प्रभ जी मोहे कवन अनाथ बिचारा॥

1 *prabh ji mohe kavan anaath bichaara.*

कवन मूल ते मानुख करिआ
इह परताप तुहारा॥ १॥ रहाउ॥

2 *kavan mool te maanukh karya*
eho partaap tuhaara. rahaa'o.

जीअ प्राण सरब के दाते
गुण कहे न जाहे अपारा॥

3 *jee'a praan sarab ke daate*
gun kahe na jaahe apaara.

सभ के प्रीतम स्रब प्रतिपालक
सरब घटां आधारा॥ १॥

4 *sabh ke preetam srab pratipaalak*
sarab ghataan aadhaara.

कोए न जाणै तुमरी गत मित
आपह एक पसारा॥

5 *koye na jaanai tumri gat mit*
aapah ek pasaara.

साध नाव बैठावहो नानक
भव सागर पार उतारा॥ २॥

6 *saadh naav baithaavoh Nanak*
bhav saagar paar utaara.[27]

राग बिलावल महला ५
दुपदे घर ६

Raag Bilaaval Mahala Panjvaan
Dupade Ghar Chevaan

प्रभ जी तू मेरे प्रान अधारै॥
नमसकार डंडउत बंदना
अनिक बार जाउ बारै॥ १॥ रहाउ॥

1 *prabh ji tu mere praan adhaarai.*
namaskaar dandaut bandana
anik baar jaa'au baarai. rahaa'o.

ऊठत बैठत सोवत जागत
इह मन तुझह चितारै॥

2 *oothat baithat sovat jaagat*
eh man tujhah chitaarai.

In constant remembrance of your Nam   6
    I find life, and my body and mind are blessed.
In submission I drink the water used to wash your feet,   7
    O my Satguru, merciful to the meek.
I sacrifice myself to the blissful moment   8
    when I submitted myself at your door.
The Lord has become merciful to Nanak –   9
    he has found the Satguru.

Raga Sarang, Fifth Guru, Dupadas
What am I, O Lord, but a poor helpless creature!   1
It is your glory, O Lord,   2
    that from lowly origins you made me human.
You are the giver of life and breath to all beings;   3
    beyond description are your infinite virtues.
You are the beloved nourisher of all   4
    and the support of all beings.
No one can fathom your state and extent –   5
    you are the sole creator of this expanse.
Help Nanak board the ship of Saints, O Lord,   6
    that he may sail across the ocean of existence.

Raga Bilawal, Fifth Guru, Dupadas
You are the support of my life, O Lord –   1
    in humble obeisance I prostrate before you
    and time and again I sacrifice myself to you.
Whether I am standing or sitting, asleep or awake,   2
    my mind contemplates on you alone.

सूख दूख इस मन की बिरथा
तुझ ही आगै सारै॥१॥

3   *sookh dookh is man ki birtha*
tujh hi aagai saarai.

तू मेरी ओट बल बुध धन तुम ही
तुमहे मेरै परवारै॥

4   *tu meri ot bal budh dhan tum hi*
tumhe merai parvaarai.

जो तुम करहो सोई भल हमरै
पेख नानक सुख चरनारै॥२॥

5   *jo tum karho soi bhal hamrai*
pekh Nanak sukh charnaarai.[28]

राग टोडी महला ५
घर ५ दुपदे

Raag Todi Mahala Panjvaan
Ghar Panjvaan Dupade

प्रभ तेरे पग की धूर॥
दीन दइआल प्रीतम मनमोहन
कर किरपा मेरी लोचा पूर॥१॥रहाउ॥

1   *prabh tere pag ki dhoor.*
deen dayaal preetam manmohan
kar kirpa meri locha poor. rahaa'o.

दह दिस रव रहिआ जस तुमरा
अंतरजामी सदा हजूर॥

2   *dah dis rav rahya jas tumra*
antarjaami sada hajoor.

जो तुमरा जस गावह करते
से जन कबहु न मरते झूर॥१॥

3   *jo tumra jas gaavah karte*
se jan kabahu na marte jhoor.

धंध बंध बिनसे माइआ के
साधू संगत मिटे बिसूर॥

4   *dhandh bandh binse maaya ke*
saadhu sangat mite bisoor.

सुख संपत भोग इस जीअ के
बिन हर नानक जाने कूर॥२॥

5   *sukh sampat bhog is jee'a ke*
bin har Nanak jaane koor.[29]

राग बिलावल महला ५
घर ५ चउपदे

Raag Bilaaval Mahala Panjvaan
Ghar Panjvaan Chaupade

राखहो अपनी सरण प्रभ
मोहे किरपा धारे॥
सेवा कछू न जानऊ
नीच मूरखारे॥१॥

1   *raakhoh apni saran prabh*
mohe kirpa dhaare.
seva kachhu na jaana'u
neech moorkhaare.

I place before you my pleasures and pains 3
    and all the states of my mind.
You are my shelter and strength, 4
    my wisdom and wealth, O Lord,
    and you alone are my family.
Whatever you do is good for us – 5
    seeing your lotus feet, Nanak finds peace.

Raga Todi, Fifth Guru, Dupadas

I am the dust of your feet, O Lord. 1
O my Beloved, compassionate to the meek
    and enchanter of the heart, show your mercy
    and fulfil the yearning of my heart.
O omnipresent Lord, knower of inner secrets, 2
    your glory extends in all ten directions.*
Your devotees who sing your praises, O Creator, 3
    never die grieving.
In the company of Saints 4
    the entanglements of maya are eliminated
    and all suffering comes to an end.
Without devotion to God, Nanak considers 5
    the pleasures of wealth and enjoyments of life to be false.

Raga Bilawal, Fifth Guru, Chaupadas

Show your grace, O Lord, 1
    and keep me under your protection –
    I am low and ignorant and know not how to serve you.

---

* The **ten directions** are north, south, east, west, northeast, northwest, southeast, south-
west, above and below, conveying the sense of everywhere.

मान करउ तुध ऊपरे
मेरे प्रीतम पिआरे॥

2 *maan karau tudh oopare*
mere preetam pyaare.

हम अपराधी सद भूलते
तुम्ह बखसनहारे॥१॥रहाउ॥

3 *ham apraadhi sad bhoolte*
tum bakhsan-haare. rahaa'o.

हम अवगन करह असंख नीत
तुम्ह निरगुन दातारे॥

4 *ham avgan karah asankh neet*
tum nirgun daataare.

दासी संगत प्रभू तिआग
ए करम हमारे॥२॥

5 *daasi sangat prabhu tyaag*
e karam hamaare.

तुम्ह देवहो सभ किछ दइआ धार
हम अकिरतघनारे॥

6 *tum devho sabh kichh daya dhaar*
ham akirat-ghanaare.

लाग परे तेरे दान सिउ
नह चित खसमारे॥३॥

7 *laag pare tere daan sio*
nah chit khasamaare.

तुझ ते बाहर किछ नही
भव काटनहारे॥

8 *tujh te baahar kichh nahi*
bhav kaatan-haare.

कहो नानक सरण दइआल
गुर लेहो मुगध उधारे॥४॥

9 *kaho Nanak saran dayaal gur*
leho mugadh udhaare.[30]

राग गउड़ी पूरबी
महला ५

Raag Gaurri Poorbi
Mahala Panjvaan

राख पिता प्रभ मेरे।
मोहे निरगुन
सभ गुन तेरे॥१॥रहाउ॥

1 *raakh pita prabh mere.*
mohe nirgun
sabh gun tere. rahaa'o.

पंच बिखादी एक गरीबा
राखहो राखनहारे॥

2 *panch bikhaadi ek gareeba*
raakhoh raakhan-haare.

खेद करह अर बहुत संतावह
आइओ सरन तुहारे॥१॥

3 *khed karah ar bahut santaavah*
aayo saran tuhaare.

कर कर हारिओ अनिक बहु भाती
छोडह कतहूं नाही॥

4 *kar kar haaryo anik bahu bhaati*
chhodah katahoon naahi.

In you lies my confidence, O my beloved Lord;   *2–3*
    for we are sinners, always erring,
    and you are ever forgiving.
We go on committing innumerable sins   *4*
    yet you are benevolent to us meritless ones.
Forsaking God, we associate with his servant Maya –   *5*
    such are our actions.
In your compassion you grant us all boons,   *6*
    but we remain unappreciative.
We become attached to your gifts   *7*
    but forget the Master who bestows them.
Nothing exists outside of you,   *8*
    O terminator of the cycle of birth and death.
Says Nanak: I have come to your refuge, O merciful Guru –   *9*
    please redeem this ignorant one.

Raga Gauri Poorbi, Fifth Guru
Save me, O Lord, my Father –   *1*
    all virtues are yours, while I have none.
Five are the rowdy adversaries*   *2*
    arrayed against this poor solitary soul.
Protect me from them, O my saviour –   *3*
    they torment me and cause me great anguish
    and I have come seeking your shelter.
I am tired of using various techniques,   *4*
    but these enemies never relax their grip on me.

---

*The five **adversaries** – lust, anger, greed, attachment and pride – are five modes of destructive mental action which beset human beings and prevent the soul from uniting with the Lord.

एक बात सुन ताकी ओटा
साधसंग मिट जाही॥ २॥
कर किरपा संत मिले मोहे
तिन ते धीरज पाइआ॥
संती मंत दीओ मोहे निरभउ
गुर का सबद कमाइआ॥ ३॥
जीत लए ओए महा बिखादी
सहज सुहेली बाणी॥
कहो नानक मन भइआ परगासा
पाइआ पद निरबाणी॥ ४॥

5 ek baat sun taaki ota
saadh-sang mit jaahi.
6 kar kirpa sant mile mohe
tin te dheeraj paaya.
7 santi mant dee'o mohe nirbhau
gur ka sabad kamaaya.
8 jeet laye oye maha bikhaadi
sahaj suheli baani.
9 kaho Nanak man bhaya pargaasa
paaya pad nirbaani.[31]

राग माझ महला ५
चउपदे घर १

Raag Maajh Mahala Panjvaan
Chaupade Ghar Pahila

सगल संतन पह वसत इक मांगउ॥
करउ बिनंती मान तिआगउ॥
वार वार जाई लख वरीआ
देहो संतन की धूरा जीउ॥ १॥
तुम दाते तुम पुरख बिधाते॥
तुम समरथ सदा सुखदाते॥
सभ को तुम ही ते वरसावै
अउसर करहो हमारा पूरा जीउ॥ २॥
दरसन तेरै भवन पुनीता॥
आतम गड़ बिखम तिना ही जीता॥
तुम दाते तुम पुरख बिधाते
तुध जेवड अवर न सूरा जीउ॥ ३॥

1 sagal santan pah vast ik maangau.
karau binanti maan tyaagau.
2 vaar vaar jaa'i lakh vareeya
deho santan ki dhoora jee'o.
3 tum daate tum purakh bidhaate.
tum samrath sada sukhdaate.
4 sabh ko tum hi te varsaavai
ausar karho hamaara poora jee'o.
5 darsan terai bhavan puneeta.
aatam garr bikham tina hi jeeta.
6 tum daate tum purakh bidhaate
tudh jevad avar na soora jee'o.

I have heard of one way – 5
    that is to seek refuge with the Saints
    in whose company the adversaries are destroyed.
Mercifully, the Saints have met me 6
    and from them I have obtained contentment.
The Saints have blessed me 7
    with the mantra of the fearless Lord*
    and I have devoted myself to the Guru's Shabd.
With the help of the sublime Word 8
    I have overcome those great tormentors.
Says Nanak: my mind is illumined 9
    and I have attained the state of deliverance.

Raga Majh, Fifth Guru, Chaupadas

I beg the Saints to grant me a boon 1
    and pray to them that I shed my pride.
I sacrifice myself a million times over 2
    for the gift of the dust of a Saint's feet.
You are the almighty Lord, 3
    the giver and the maker of destiny,
    the source of eternal bliss.
All accomplish their tasks with your blessings – 4
    please fulfil the objective of my life.
One who purifies the temple of his body 5
    with your darshan
    conquers the formidable fort of his self.
You are the giver and the maker of destiny, O Lord; 6
    no one is as valiant as you.

---

* A **mantra** is a sacred word, phrase or sound repeated to aid concentration in meditation.

रेन संतन की मेरै मुख लागी ॥
दुरमत बिनसी कुबुध अभागी ॥
सच घर बैस रहे गुण गाए
नानक बिनसे कूरा जीउ ॥ ४ ॥

7 *ren santan ki merai mukh laagi.*
durmat binsi kubudh abhaagi.
8 *sach ghar bais rahe gun gaaye*
Nanak binse koora jee'o.[32]

राग टोडी महला ५
घर २ दुपदे

Raag Todi Mahala Panjvaan
Ghar Dooja Dupade

सतगुर आइओ सरण तुहारी ॥
मिलै सूख नाम हर सोभा
चिंता लाहे हमारी ॥ १ ॥ रहाउ ॥
अवर न सूझै दूजी ठाहर
हार परिओ तउ दुआरी ॥
लेखा छोड अलेखै छूटह
हम निरगुन लेहो उबारी ॥ १ ॥
सद बखसिंद सदा मिहरवाना
सभना दे अधारी ॥
नानक दास संत पाछै परिओ
राख लेहो इह बारी ॥ २ ॥

1 *satgur aayo saran tuhaari.*
2 *milai sookh naam har sobha*
chinta laahe hamaari. rahaa'o.
3 *avar na soojhai dooji thaahar*
haar paryo tau duaari.
4 *lekha chhod alekhai chhootah*
ham nirgun leho ubaari.
5 *sad bakhsind sada meharvaana*
sabhna de adhaari.
6 *Nanak daas sant paachhai paryo*
raakh leho eh baari.[33]

राग सूही महला ५
घर ६

Raag Soohi Mahala Panjvaan
Ghar Chevaan

सतगुर पास बेनंतीआ
मिलै नाम आधारा ॥
तुठा सचा पातसाह
ताप गइआ संसारा ॥ १ ॥
भगता की टेक तूं संता की ओट तूं
सचा सिरजनहारा ॥ १ ॥ रहाउ ॥

1 *satgur paas benanteeya*
milai naam aadhaara.
2 *tutha sacha paatsaah*
taap gaya sansaara.
3 *bhagta ki tek toon santa ki ot toon*
sacha sirjan-haara. rahaa'o.

As I applied to my forehead 7
    the dust of the Saints' feet, my negative thinking
    and base intellect vanished.
Singing God's praises, Nanak has settled in his true home 8
    and all falsehood is shattered.

Raga Todi, Fifth Guru, Dupadas

I have come seeking refuge in you, O my Satguru! 1
Grant me the peace and glory of Nam 2
    and take away my anxieties.
Exhausted and seeing no other place of rest, 3
    I have fallen prostrate at your door.
I am without merit, O Lord – 4
    pay no heed to the account of my deeds,
    for only if you close this account will I be saved.
Always forgiving, always merciful, 5
    O Lord, you lend your support to all.
Your slave Nanak follows the path of the Saints – 6
    O Lord, grant him liberation in this life.

Raga Soohi, Fifth Guru

I pray to my Satguru to lend me the support of his Nam; 1–2
    when the true King is pleased, worldly affliction will end.
O true creator, you are the support of your devotees 3
    and the shelter of your Saints.

सच तेरी सामगरी
सच तेरा दरबारा॥

4   *sach teri saamagri*
    sach tera darbaara.

सच तेरे खाजीनिआ
सच तेरा पासारा॥ २॥

5   *sach tere khaajeeniya*
    sach tera paasaara.

तेरा रूप अगंम है
अनूप तेरा दरसारा॥

6   *tera roop agamm hai*
    anoop tera darsaara.

हउ कुरबाणी तेरिआ सेवका
जिन्ह हर नाम पिआरा॥ ३॥

7   *hau kurbaani teriya sevaka*
    jin har naam pyaara.

सभे इछा पूरीआ
जा पाइआ अगम अपारा॥

8   *sabhe icchha pooreeya*
    ja paaya agam apaara.

गुर नानक मिलिआ पारब्रहम
तेरिआ चरणा कउ बलिहारा॥ ४॥

9   *gur Nanak miliya paarbrahm*
    teriya charna kau balihaara.[34]

राग बिलावल महला ५
चउपदे घर १

Raag Bilaaval Mahala Panjvaan
Chaupade Ghar Pahila

सुख निधान प्रीतम प्रभ मेरे॥
अगनत गुण ठाकुर प्रभ तेरे॥

1   *sukh nidhaan preetam prabh mere.*
    aganat gun thaakur prabh tere.

मोहे अनाथ तुमरी सरणाई॥
कर किरपा हर चरन धिआई॥ १॥

2   *mohe anaath tumri sarnaa'i.*
    kar kirpa har charan dhiaa'i.

दइआ करहो बसहो मन आए॥
मोहे निरगुन लीजै लड़ लाए॥ रहाउ॥

3   *daya karho basoh man aaye.*
    mohe nirgun leejai larr laaye. rahaa'o.

प्रभ चित आवै ता कैसी भीड़॥
हर सेवक नाही जम पीड़॥

4   *prabh chit aavai ta kaisi bheerr.*
    har sevak naahi jam peerr.

सरब दूख हर सिमरत नसे॥
जा कै संग सदा प्रभ बसै॥ २॥

5   *sarab dookh har simrat nase.*
    ja kai sang sada prabh basai.

प्रभ का नाम मन तन आधार॥
बिसरत नाम होवत तन छार॥

6   *prabh ka naam man tan aadhaar.*
    bisrat naam hovat tan chhaar.

प्रभ चित आए पूरन सभ काज॥
हर बिसरत सभ का मुहताज॥ ३॥

7   *prabh chitt aaye pooran sabh kaaj.*
    har bisrat sabh ka muhtaaj.

True are the constituents of your creation,   4-5
   true is your court, true are your treasures
   and true is your expanse.
Your form is inaccessible and your sight unique;   6–7
   I sacrifice myself to your devotees,
   who hold your Nam dear to their hearts.
When the inaccessible and infinite Lord is attained,   8
   all one's desires are fulfilled.
Nanak has met his Guru, the supreme Lord –   9
   he sacrifices himself at your feet, O Lord.

Raga Bilawal, Fifth Guru, Chaupadas
O beloved Lord, treasure of bliss,   1
   countless are your qualities.
I am helpless and seek your protection, O Lord –   2
   inspire me to contemplate on your feet.
Be merciful, O Lord, come and abide in my heart   3
   and attach this worthless devotee to yourself.
What hardship can befall one who remembers God –   4
   God's devotee is not subject to Yama's torments!
All suffering leaves the one   5
   who devotes himself to God's simran;
   with him the Lord abides forever.
God's Nam is the support of my mind and body;   6
   forgetting Nam, the body turns to ashes.
Remembrance of God brings all tasks to fruition;   7
   by forgetting God one becomes dependent on all.

चरन कमल संग लागी प्रीत॥
बिसर गई सभ दुरमत रीत॥
मन तन अंतर हर हर मंत॥
नानक भगतन कै घर
सदा अनंद॥४॥

8 *charan kamal sang laagi preet.*
bisar gayi sabh durmat reet.
9 *man tan antar har har mant.*
Nanak bhagtan kai ghar
sada anand.[35]

राग बिहागड़ा महला ५
छंत घर २

सुनहो बेनंतीआ सुआमी मेरे राम॥
कोट अप्राध भरे भी तेरे चेरे राम॥
दुख हरन किरपा करन मोहन
कल कलेसह भंजना॥
सरन तेरी रख लेहो मेरी
सरब मै निरंजना॥
सुनत पेखत संग सभ कै
प्रभ नेरहू ते नेरे॥
अरदास नानक सुन सुआमी
रख लेहो घर के चेरे॥१॥

Raag Bihaagarra Mahala Panjvaan
Chhant Ghar Dooja

1 *sunoh benanteeya suaami mere raam.*
kot apraadh bhare bhi tere chere raam.
2 *dukh haran kirpa karan mohan*
kal kalesah bhanjana.
3 *saran teri rakh leho meri*
sarab mai niranjana.
4 *sunat pekhat sang sabh kai*
prabh nerahu te nere.
5 *ardaas Nanak sun suaami*
rakh leho ghar ke chere.[36]

राग टोडी महला ५
घर २ दुपदे

स्वामी सरन परिओ दरबारे॥
कोट अपराध खंडन के दाते
तुझ बिन कउन उधारे॥१॥रहाउ॥
खोजत खोजत बहु परकारे
सरब अरथ बीचारे॥
साधसंग परम गत पाईऐ
माइआ रच बंध हारे॥१॥

Raag Todi Mahala Panjvaan
Ghar Dooja Dupade

1 *swaami saran paryo darbaare.*
kot apraadh khandan ke daate
tujh bin kaun udhaare. rahaa'o.
2 *khojat khojat bahu parkaare*
sarab arth beechaare.
3 *saadh-sang param gat paa'eeyai*
maaya rach bandh haare.

When I became attached to the Lord's lotus feet, 8
  I forgot all my evil ways of thinking.
In mind and body I repeat the mantra of God's Nam – 9
  in the homes of God's devotees, O Nanak,
  eternal bliss abides.

Raga Bihagara, Fifth Guru, Chhant

Listen to my supplication, O Lord, my Master – 1
  though filled with millions of sins,
  still I am your disciple.
O Lord, you are the dispeller of pain, bestower of grace 2–3
  and the one whose charms
  terminate all affliction and strife.
I have come seeking your protection –
  please save my honour,
  O immaculate, omnipresent Lord.
Listening to all, watching all and pervading all, 4
  the Lord is nearer than the nearest.
Listen to Nanak's prayer, O Master – 5
  protect the honour of your household slave.

Raga Todi, Fifth Guru, Dupadas

I seek the refuge of your court, O Lord. 1
O bountiful giver and destroyer of countless sins,
  who other than you can grant liberation?
After searching continuously in many ways 2–3
  I have reflected on all the meanings of life and concluded
  that we attain the supreme state in the company of Saints –
  obsession with maya only brings bondage and defeat.

चरन कमल संग प्रीत मन लागी
सुर जन मिले पिआरे॥
नानक अनद करे हर जप जप
सगले रोग निवारे॥२॥

4 charan kamal sang preet man laagi
sur jan mile pyaare.
5 Nanak anad kare har jap jap
sagle rog nivaare.[37]

राग बिलावल महला ५
घर ५ चउपदे

टहल करउ तेरे दास की
पग झारउ बाल॥
मसतक अपना भेट देउ
गुन सुनउ रसाल॥१॥
तुम्ह मिलते मेरा मन जीओ
तुम्ह मिलहो दइआल॥
निस बासुर मन अनद होत
चितवत किरपाल॥१॥ रहाउ॥
जगत उधारन साध प्रभ
तिन्ह लागहो पाल॥
मो कउ दीजै दान प्रभ
संतन पग राल॥२॥
उकत सिआनप कछु नही
नाही कछु घाल॥
भ्रम भै राखहो मोह ते
काटहो जम जाल॥३॥
बिनउ करउ करुणापते
पिता प्रतिपाल॥
गुण गावउ तेरे साधसंग
नानक सुख साल॥४॥

Raag Bilaaval Mahala Panjvaan
Ghar Panjvaan Chaupade

1 tahal karau tere daas ki
pag jhaarau baal.
2 mastak apna bhet deo
gun sunau rasaal.
3 tum milte mera man jee'o
tum milho dayaal.
4 nis baasur man anad hot
chitvat kirpaal. rahaa'o.
5 jagat udhaaran saadh prabh
tin laagho paal.
6 mo kau deejai daan prabh
santan pag raal.
7 ukat syaanap kachhu nahi
naahi kachhu ghaal.
8 bhram bhai raakhoh moh te
kaatho jam jaal.
9 binau karau karunaapate
pita pratipaal.
10 gun gaavau tere saadh-sang
Nanak sukh saal.[38]

On meeting the beloved divine Guru,   4
  my mind becomes attached to his lotus feet.
In constant remembrance of God, Nanak finds bliss   5
  and all his afflictions are cured.

Raga Bilawal, Fifth Guru, Chaupadas

May I serve your slave, O Lord,   1
  and dust his feet with my hair.
I shall offer him my head   2
  and hear about your inspiring qualities.
Meet me, O merciful Lord –   3
  on meeting you my soul is revived.
Remembering you, O merciful Lord,   4
  my mind abides in bliss day and night.
God's Saints are the emancipators of the world,   5–6
  so I attach myself to them – grant me, O Lord,
  the blessing of the dust of their feet.*
I have no skill or wisdom and no devotion to my credit.   7
Save me from doubt, fear and worldly attachments, O Lord,   8
  and cut me free from Yama's web.
Nanak prays to you, O merciful Lord,   9–10
  my father, my provider,
  that he may sing your praises
  in the company of Saints, the home of bliss.

---

* Esoterically, the **dust of the Saint's feet** does not refer to physical dust, but represents the misty radiance emanating from his inner feet, also called the lotus feet, which the devotee experiences on a spiritual plane within and which brings light to inner darkness.

राग रामकली महला ५

घर २

तेरी सरण पूरे गुरदेव॥

तुध बिन दूजा नाही कोए॥

तू समरथ पूरन पारब्रहम॥

सो धिआए पूरा जिस करम॥१॥

तरण तारण प्रभ तेरो नाउ॥

एका सरण गही मन मेरै

तुध बिन दूजा नाही ठाउ॥१॥रहाउ॥

जप जप जीवा तेरा नाउ॥

आगै दरगह पावउ ठाउ॥

दूख अंधेरा मन ते जाए॥

दुरमत बिनसै राचै हर नाए॥२॥

चरन कमल सिउ लागी प्रीत॥

गुर पूरे की निरमल रीत॥

भउ भागा निरभउ मन बसै॥

अंम्रित नाम रसना नित जपै॥३॥

कोट जनम के काटे फाहे॥

पाइआ लाभ सचा धन लाहे॥

तोट न आवै अखुट भंडार॥

नानक भगत सोहहे हर दुआर॥४॥

राग सारग महला ५ दुपदे

घर ४

ठाकुर तुम्ह सरणाई आइआ॥

उतर गइओ मेरे मन का संसा

जब ते दरसन पाइआ॥१॥रहाउ॥

अनबोलत मेरी बिरथा जानी

अपना नाम जपाइआ॥

Raag Raamkali Mahala Panjvaan
Ghar Dooja

1 *teri saran poore gurdev.*

tudh bin dooja naahi koye.

2 *tu samrath pooran paarbrahm.*

so dhiaaye poora jis karam.

3 *taran taaran prabh tero naa'o.*

4 *eka saran gahi man merai*

tudh bin dooja naahi thaa'o. rahaa'o.

5 *jap jap jeeva tera naa'o.*

aagai dargah paavau thaa'o.

6 *dookh andhera man te jaaye.*

durmat binsai raachai har naaye.

7 *charan kamal sio laagi preet.*

gur poore ki nirmal reet.

8 *bhau bhaaga nirbhau man basai.*

amrit naam rasna nit japai.

9 *kot janam ke kaate phaahe.*

paaya laabh sacha dhan laahe.

10 *tot na aavai akhut bhandaar.*

Nanak bhagat sohahe har duaar.[39]

Raag Saarag Mahala Panjvaan
Dupade Ghar Chautha

1 *thaakur tum sarnaa'i aaya.*

utar gayo mere man ka sansa

jab te darsan paaya. rahaa'o.

2 *anbolat meri birtha jaani*

apna naam japaaya.

Raga Ramkali, Fifth Guru

I seek refuge with you, O perfect divine Guru;   1
    for me there is no one other than you.

You are the all-powerful, perfect, supreme Lord;   2
    only someone with a perfect destiny meditates on you.

Your Nam, O Lord, is the ship that will take us across;   3–4
    my mind holds on to your refuge alone –
    there is no other shelter for me.

I live by constantly repeating your Nam,   5
    and hereafter I shall find a place in your court.

On becoming absorbed in the Lord's Nam   6
    pain and darkness depart from my mind
    and my evil thinking is shattered.

I have fallen in love with the Lord's lotus feet;   7
    pure is the way of the perfect Guru.

With the Fearless One abiding in my mind,   8
    my fears have fled and I constantly repeat
    the nectar-sweet Nam.

The noose of millions of lives has been cut loose,   9
    and I have gained the profit of the true wealth of Nam.

This is the inexhaustible treasure that never runs short.   10
In the divine court, O Nanak, the devotees shine in splendour.

Raga Sarang, Fifth Guru, Dupadas

I came seeking refuge with you, O Lord –   1
    on having your darshan my mind's anxieties have left me.

Without any explanation you knew my state   2
    and inspired me to repeat your Nam.

दुख नाठे सुख सहज समाए
अनद अनद गुण गाइआ॥१॥
बाह पकर कढ लीने अपुने
ग्रिह अंध कूप ते माइआ॥
कहो नानक गुर बंधन काटे
बिछुरत आन मिलाइआ॥ २॥

3 *dukh naathe sukh sahaj samaaye*
anad anad gun gaaya.
4 *baah pakar kaddh leene apane*
grih andh koop te maaya.
5 *kaho Nanak gur bandhan kaate*
bichhurat aan milaaya.[40]

राग सूही महला ५
घर ३
तूं जीवन तूं प्रान अधारा॥
तुझ ही पेख पेख मन साधारा॥१॥
तूं साजन तूं प्रीतम मेरा॥
चितह न बिसरह काहू बेरा॥१॥ रहाउ॥
बै खरीद हउ दासरो तेरा॥
तूं भारो ठाकुर गुणी गहेरा॥ २॥
कोट दास जा कै दरबारे॥
निमख निमख वसै तिन्ह नाले॥३॥
हउ किछ नाही सभ किछ तेरा॥
ओत पोत नानक संग बसेरा॥४॥

Raag Soohi Mahala Panjvaan
Ghar Teeja
1 *toon jeevan toon praan adhaara.*
tujh hi pekh pekh man saadhaara.
2 *toon saajan toon preetam mera.*
chitah na bisrah kaahu bera. rahaa'o.
3 *bai khareed hau daasro tera.*
toon bhaaro thaakur guni gahera.
4 *kot daas ja kai darbaare.*
nimakh nimakh vasai tin naale.
5 *hau kichh naahi sabh kichh tera.*
ot pot Nanak sang basera.[41]

राग माझ महला ५
चउपदे घर १
तूं मेरा पिता तूंहै मेरा माता॥
तूं मेरा बंधप तूं मेरा भ्राता॥
तूं मेरा राखा सभनी थाई॥
ता भउ केहा काड़ा जीउ॥१॥
तुमरी क्रिपा ते तुध पछाणा॥
तूं मेरी ओट तूंहै मेरा माणा॥

Maajh Mahala Panjvaan
Chaupade Ghar Pahila
1 *toon mera pita toon-hai mera maata.*
toon mera bandhap toon mera bhraata.
2 *toon mera raakha sabhni thaayeen*
ta bhau keha kaarra jee'o.
3 *tumri kripa te tudh pachhaana.*
toon meri ot toon-hai mera maana.

My anxieties have vanished,   *3*
   and absorbed in a state of calm serenity I sing your praises
   as I abide in supreme peace and bliss.

Holding my arm you have pulled me   *4*
   out of the dark hole of attachments and maya.

Says Nanak: the Guru has cut my bonds   *5*
   and united me with the Lord,
   from whom I had been separated.

Raga Soohi, Fifth Guru

You are my life, the sustenance of my life-breath,   *1*
   and your sight gives support to my mind.

You are my beloved friend   *2*
   and I never forget you even for a moment.

I am your bought slave,   *3*
   and you my great Master and treasure of virtue.

Millions of devotees serve in your court   *4*
   and every moment you abide with them.

I am nothing, O Lord – all belongs to you;   *5*
   you abide with Nanak, woven into the thread of his life.

Raga Majh, Fifth Guru, Chaupadas

You are my father, you are my mother,   *1*
   you are my friend and you are my brother.

With you as my protector in all places,   *2*
   what fears and worries can I have?

By your grace I have recognized you;   *3*
   you are my shelter, you are my honour.

तुझ बिन दूजा अवर न कोई
सभ तेरा खेल अखाड़ा जीउ॥ २॥
जीअ जंत सभ तुध उपाए॥
जित जित भाणा तित तित लाए॥
सभ किछ कीता तेरा होवै
नाही किछ असाड़ा जीउ॥ ३॥
नाम धिआए महा सुख पाइआ॥
हर गुण गाए मेरा मन सीतलाइआ॥
गुर पूरै वजी वाधाई
नानक जिता बिखाड़ा जीउ॥ ४॥

4   tujh bin dooja avar na koi
    sabh tera khel akhaarra jee'o.
5   jee'a jant sabh tudh upaaye.
    jit jit bhaana tit tit laaye.
6   sabh kichh keeta tera hovai
    naahi kichh asaarra jee'o.
7   naam dhiaaye maha sukh paaya.
    hargun gaaye mera man seetlaaya.
8   gur poorai vaji vaadhaa'i
    Nanak jita bikhaarra jee'o.[42]

राग गउड़ी गुआरेरी
महला ५ चउपदे

तूं समरथ तूं है मेरा सुआमी॥
सभ किछ तुम ते तूं अंतरजामी॥ १॥
पारब्रहम पूरन जन ओट॥
तेरी सरण
उधरह जन कोट॥ १॥ रहाउ॥
जेते जीअ तेते सभ तेरे॥
तुमरी क्रिपा ते सूख घनेरे॥ २॥
जो किछ वरतै सभ तेरा भाणा॥
हुकम बूझै सो सच समाणा॥ ३॥
कर किरपा दीजै प्रभ दान॥
नानक सिमरै नाम निधान॥ ४॥

Raag Gaurri Guaareri
Mahala Panjvaan Chaupade

1   toon samrath toon hai mera suaami.
    sabh kichh tum te toon antarjaami.
2   paar-brahm pooran jan ot.
    teri saran
    udhrah jan kot. rahaa'o.
3   jete jee'a tete sabh tere.
    tumri kripa te sookh ghanere.
4   jo kichh vartai sabh tera bhaana.
    hukam boojhai so sach samaana.
5   kar kirpa deejai prabh daan.
    Nanak simrai naam nidhaan.[43]

Other than you, no one exists – 4
    the whole creation is your theatre for the drama of life.
All living beings are created by you 5
    and tasks are assigned to them according to your will.
Everything happens as you will; 6
    nothing is in our power.
Through meditation on Nam I attained great bliss, 7
    and by singing the praises of God my mind was pacified.
By the perfect Guru's grace, celebrations are held 8
    as Nanak emerges victorious in the tough battlefield of life.

Raga Gauri Guareri, Fifth Guru, Chaupadas

You are the almighty Lord, my Master – 1
    everything emerges from you
    and you know all inner secrets.
You, O supreme Lord, are absolute perfection 2
    and the refuge of your devotees –
    millions who take shelter in you are saved.
All living beings belong to you, O Lord, 3
    and innumerable comforts arise from your grace.
All that happens results from your will, 4
    and whoever realizes your will merges into Truth.
Grant Nanak the boon, O Lord, that by your grace 5
    he may contemplate the treasure of Nam.

राग वडहंस महला ५
घर १

तू बेअंत को विरला जाणै॥
गुर प्रसाद को सबद पछाणै॥१॥
सेवक की अरदास पिआरे॥
जप जीवा
प्रभ चरण तुमारे॥१॥रहाउ॥
दइआल पुरख मेरे प्रभ दाते॥
जिसह जनावहो तिनह तुम जाते॥२॥
सदा सदा जाई बलिहारी॥
इत उत देखउ ओट तुमारी॥३॥
मोहे निरगुण गुण किछू न जाता॥
नानक साधू देख मन राता॥४॥

Raag Vadahans Mahala Panjvaan
Ghar Pahila

1 tu be'ant ko virla jaanai.
gur prasaad ko sabad pachhaanai.
2 sevak ki ardaas pyaare.
jap jeeva
prabh charan tumaare. rahaa'o.
3 dayaal purakh mere prabh daate.
jisah janaavoh tinah tum jaate.
4 sada sada jaa'i balihaari.
it ut dekhau ot tumaari.
5 mohe nirgun gun kichhu na jaata.
Nanak saadhu dekh man raata.[44]

राग भैरउ महला ५
चउपदे घर २

तू मेरा पिता तूहै मेरा माता॥
तू मेरे जीअ प्रान सुखदाता॥
तू मेरा ठाकुर हउ दास तेरा॥
तुझ बिन अवर नही को मेरा॥१॥
कर किरपा करहो प्रभ दात॥
तुम्हरी उसतत
करउ दिन रात॥१॥रहाउ॥
हम तेरे जंत तू बजावनहारा॥
हम तेरे भिखारी दान देह दातारा॥
तउ परसाद रंग रस माणे॥
घट घट अंतर तुमह समाणे॥२॥
तुम्हरी क्रिपा ते जपीऐ नाउ॥
साधसंग तुमरे गुण गाउ॥
तुम्हरी दइआ ते होए दरद बिनास॥

Raag Bhairau Mahala Panjvaan
Chaupade Ghar Dooja

1 tu mera pita toohai mera maata.
tu mere jee'a praan sukhdaata.
2 tu mera thaakur hau daas tera.
tujh bin avar nahi ko mera.
3 kar kirpa karho prabh daat.
tumri ustat
karau din raat. rahaa'o.
4 ham tere jant tu bajaavan-haara.
ham tere bhikhaari daan deh daataara.
5 tau parsaad rang ras maane.
ghat ghat antar tumah samaane.
6 tumhri kripa te japeeyai naa'o.
saadh-sang tumre gun gaa'o.
7 tumhri daya te hoye darad binaas.

Raga Wad-hans, Fifth Guru

You are infinite, O Lord – only that rare one knows you   *1*
   who, by the Guru's grace, devotes himself to Shabd.

It is this devotee's prayer, O beloved Lord,   *2*
   that he live by contemplating on your feet.

O my compassionate Lord, bestower of blessings,   *3*
   he alone realizes you to whom you grant realization.

Forever and ever I sacrifice myself to you;   *4*
   both here and hereafter I look to you for shelter.

Being without virtue myself,   *5*
   I was unable to recognize your virtues,
   but now that Nanak has met the Saint, O Lord,
   his heart is dyed in your love.

Raga Bhairon, Fifth Guru, Chaupadas

You are my father, O Lord, you are my mother,   *1*
   you are my life-breath and the bestower of peace.

You are my Master, I am your servant –   *2*
   other than you, no one belongs to me.

In your grace grant me the boon, O Lord,   *3*
   that I sing your praises day and night.

We are your instruments, you are the player;   *4*
   we are beggars seeking alms from the generous giver.

With your grace we enjoy the delights of life;   *5*
   you pervade all hearts.

By your grace we repeat your Nam, O Lord,   *6*
   and sing your praises in the company of Saints.

तुमरी मइआ ते कमल बिगास॥ ३॥

तुमरी माइआ ते कमल बिगास॥ ३॥   *tumri ma'ia te kamal bigaas.*

हउ बलिहार जाउ गुरदेव॥   8   *hau balihaar jaa'u gurdev.*

सफल दरसन जा की निरमल सेव॥   *saphal darsan ja ki nirmal sev.*

दइआ करहो ठाकुर प्रभ मेरे॥   9   *daya karho thaakur prabh mere.*

गुण गावै नानक नित तेरे॥ ४॥   *gun gaavai Nanak nit tere.*[45]

राग आसा घर ७   Raag Aasa Ghar Sattvaan

महला ५   Mahala Panjvaan

तू मेरा तरंग हम मीन तुमारे॥   1   *tu mera tarang ham meen tumaare.*

तू मेरा ठाकुर हम तेरै दुआरे॥ १॥   *tu mera thaakur ham terai duaare.*

तूं मेरा करता हउ सेवक तेरा॥   2   *toon mera karta hau sevak tera.*

सरण गही प्रभ गुनी गहेरा॥ १॥ रहाउ॥   *saran gahi prabh guni gahera. rahaa'o.*

तू मेरा जीवन तू आधार॥   3   *tu mera jeevan tu aadhaar.*

तुझह पेख बिगसै कउलार॥ २॥   *tujhah pekh bigsai kaulaar.*

तू मेरी गत पत तू परवान॥   4   *tu meri gat pat tu parvaan.*

तू समरथ मै तेरा ताण॥ ३॥   *tu samrath mai tera taan.*

अनदिन जपउ नाम गुणतास॥   5   *an-din japau naam guntaas.*

नानक की प्रभ पह अरदास॥ ४॥   *Nanak ki prabh pah ardaas.*[46]

राग बिहागड़ा महला ५   Raag Bihaagarra Mahala Panjvaan

घर २ छंत   Ghar Dooja Chhant

तू समरथ सदा   1   *tu samrath sada*

हम दीन भेखारी राम॥   *ham deen bhekhaari raam.*

माइआ मोह मगन   2   *maaya moh magan*

कढ लेहो मुरारी राम॥   *kadh leho muraari raam.*

---

*When a disciple has reached a high state of concentration, the **lotus of the heart blooms,** meaning that the spiritual heart – the eye centre or inner eye – opens and the

By your grace all pain is eradicated   7
   and the lotus of the heart blooms.*
I sacrifice myself to my divine Guru,   8
   whose darshan is fruitful and whose service is purifying.
Show your mercy, O my Master, my Lord,   9
   so that Nanak always sings your praises.

Raga Asa, Fifth Guru

You are my wave and I am your fish;   1
   you are my Lord and I am a beggar at your door.
You are my creator and I am your servant;   2
   I have taken refuge in you, O treasure of virtues!
O Lord, you are my life, you are my mainstay;   3
   the lotus of my heart blooms at your sight.
You are my salvation and my honour   4
   and the one who grants me approval;
   you are all-powerful and you are my strength.
It is Nanak's prayer, O treasure of virtues,   5
   that day and night he repeats your Nam.

Raga Bihagara, Fifth Guru, Chhant

You are the almighty, eternal Lord,   1
   and I am a humble beggar.
O Lord, save me from my attachment to maya,   2
   in which I am engrossed.

Guru's Shabd Form manifests there. This is the point of contact between the soul and Shabd and the beginning of the soul's journey into higher regions.

लोभ मोह बिकार बाधिओ
अनिक दोख कमावने॥

3 lobh moh bikaar baadhyo
anik dokh kamaavane.

अलिपत बंधन रहत करता
कीआ अपना पावने॥

4 alipat bandhan rahat karta
keeya apna paavane.

कर अनुग्रह पतित पावन
बहु जोन भ्रमते हारी॥

5 kar anugrah patit paavan
bahu jon bhramte haari.

बिनवंत नानक दास हर का
प्रभ जीअ प्रान अधारी॥ २॥

6 binvant Nanak daas har ka
prabh jee'a praan adhaari.

तू समरथ वडा
मेरी मत थोरी राम॥

7 tu samrath vadda
meri mat thori raam.

पालह अकिरतघना
पूरन द्रिसटि तेरी राम॥

8 paalah akirtaghana
pooran dristi teri raam.

अगाध बोध अपार करते
मोहे नीच कछू न जाना॥

9 agaadh bodh apaar karte
mohe neech kachhu na jaana.

रतन तिआग संग्रहन कउडी
पसू नीच इआना॥

10 ratan tyaag sangrahan kaudi
pasu neech iyaana.

तिआग चलती महा चंचल
दोख कर कर जोरी॥

11 tyaag chalti maha chanchal
dokh kar kar jori.

नानक सरन समरथ सुआमी
पैज राखहो मोरी॥ ३॥

12 Nanak saran samrath suaami
paij raakhoh mori.[47]

**राग गउड़ी सुखमनी
महला ५**

**Raag Gaurri Sukhmani
Mahala Panjvan**

तू ठाकुर तुम पह अरदास॥
जीउ पिंड सभ तेरी रास॥

1 tu thaakur tum pah ardaas.
jee'o pind sabh teri raas.

तुम मात पिता हम बारिक तेरे॥
तुमरी क्रिपा मह सूख घनेरे॥

2 tum maat pita ham baarik tere.
tumri kripa mah sookh ghanere.

Caught in greed, worldly love and evil deeds,   *3*
    I have committed many sins.

The Creator is detached and free from bondage,   *4*
    but we are bound by the outcome of our actions.

Show mercy to me, O purifier of the fallen –   *5*
    wandering through numerous births has worn me out.

Prays Nanak: I am the Lord's slave   *6*
    and he is the support of my life and breath.

You are the almighty Supreme Being, O Lord,   *7*
    and I am of limited understanding.

O Lord, perfect is your merciful glance,   *8*
    through which you care for even the ungrateful.

You are unfathomable and beyond comprehension,   *9*
    O Creator, while I am lowly and know nothing.

A low and ignorant beast,   *10*
    I discard the jewel for a cowrie shell.*

The wealth that is amassed through sin   *11*
    is of a highly volatile nature –
    it rejects the one who possesses it and moves on.

Nanak has taken refuge with the almighty Lord   *12*
    and prays to him to save his honour.

Raga Gauri, Sukhmani, Fifth Guru

You are the object of our devotion, O Lord,   *1*
    and we pray to you;
    our souls and bodies are your gifts to us.

You are our mother, you are our father;   *2*
    we are your children,
    and by your grace we enjoy profound bliss.

---

* Formerly used as currency in India, here a **cowrie shell** symbolizes something almost worthless.

कोए न जानै तुमरा अंत॥

ऊचे ते ऊचा भगवंत॥

सगल समग्री तुमरै सूत्र धारी॥

तुम ते होए सो आगिआकारी॥

तुमरी गत मित तुम ही जानी॥

नानक दास सदा कुरबानी॥८॥

3 koye na jaanai tumra ant.

ooche te oocha bhagvant.

4 sagal samagri tumrai sootar dhaari.

tum te hoye so aagyaa-kaari.

5 tumri gat mit tum hi jaani.

Nanak daas sada kurbaani.[48]

राग सूही महला ५

घर ७

Raag Soohi Mahala Panjvaan
Ghar Sattvaan

तुध चित आए महा अनंदा

जिस विसरह सो मर जाए॥

दइआल होवह जिस ऊपर करते

सो तुध सदा धिआए॥१॥

मेरे साहिब तूं मै माण निमाणी॥

अरदास करी प्रभ अपने आगै

सुण सुण जीवा तेरी बाणी॥१॥ रहाउ॥

चरण धूड़ तेरे जन की होवा

तेरे दरसन कउ बल जाई॥

अंम्रित बचन रिदै उर धारी

तउ किरपा ते संग पाई॥२॥

अंतर की गत तुध पह सारी

तुध जेवड अवर न कोई॥

जिस नो लाए लैह सो लागै

भगत तुहारा सोई॥३॥

दुए कर जोड़ मागउ इक दाना

साहिब तुतै पावा॥

सास सास नानक आराधे

आठ पहर गुण गावा॥४॥

1 tudh chitt aaye maha ananda

jis visarah so mar jaaye.

2 dayaal hovah jis oopar karte

so tudh sada dhiaaye.

3 mere saahib toon mai maan nimaani.

ardaas kari prabh apne aagai

sun sun jeeva teri baani. rahaa'o.

4 charan dhoorr tere jan ki hova

tere darsan kau bal jaa'i.

5 amrit bachan ridai ur dhaari

tau kirpa te sang paa'i.

6 antar ki gat tudh pah saari

tudh jevad avar na koi.

7 jis no laaye laih so laagai

bhagat tuhaara soi.

8 doye kar jorr maangau ik daana

saahib tutthai paava.

9 saas saas Nanak aaraadhe

aath pahar gun gaava.[49]

---

* 'No one can fathom your limit' means that the Lord is limitless.
† The expression 'your slaves' refers to realized souls. Esoterically, the dust of their feet does not refer to physical dust, but represents the misty radiance emanating from the

No one can fathom your limit, O Lord,* 3-4
    as you are the highest of the high –
    the entire creation is held together by your string.
Having emerged from you,
    your creation submits to your command.
You alone know your state and extent, 5
    and Nanak, your slave, sacrifices himself to you forever.

Raga Soohi, Fifth Guru

Supreme bliss lies in remembering you, O Lord, 1
    and one who forgets you is without life.
One to whom you show grace, O Lord, 2
    always contemplates on you.
O my Master, you are the honour of the meek; 3
    I pray to you, O my Lord, that I may live
    constantly listening to your Word.
May I become the dust of the feet of your slaves† 4
    and sacrifice myself to your darshan.
May I enshrine your ambrosial Word in my heart 5
    and with your grace attain union with you.
I place my inner state before you, O Lord – 6
    no one is as great as you.
He alone is attached to you, O Lord, 7
    whom you attach to yourself,
    and he alone becomes your devotee.
With hands joined in prayer I ask for a boon, 8-9
    which I can receive only through your pleasure –
    may Nanak meditate on you with every breath
    and sing your praises day and night.

---

feet of the radiant form within, also called the lotus feet, which the devotee experiences
on an inner plane and which brings light to inner darkness.

राग गउड़ी पूरबी

महला ५

तुझ बिन कवन हमारा॥

मेरे प्रीतम प्रान अधारा॥१॥ रहाउ॥

अंतर की बिध तुम ही जानी

तुम ही सजन सुहेले॥

सरब सुखा मै तुझ ते पाए

मेरे ठाकुर अगह अतोले॥१॥

बरन न साकउ तुमरे रंगा

गुण निधान सुखदाते॥

अगम अगोचर प्रभ अबिनासी

पूरे गुर ते जाते॥२॥

भ्रम भउ काट कीए निहकेवल

जब ते हउमै मारी॥

जनम मरण को चूको सहसा

साधसंगत दरसारी॥३॥

चरण पखार करउ गुर सेवा

बार जाउ लख बरीआ॥

जिह प्रसाद इह भउजल तरिआ

जन नानक प्रिअ संग मिरीआ॥४॥

Raag Gaurri Poorbi
Mahala Panjvaan

1 tujh bin kavan hamaara.

mere preetam praan adhaara. rahaa'o.

2 antar ki bidh tum hi jaani

tum hi sajan suhele.

3 sarab sukha mai tujh te paaye

mere thaakur agah atole.

4 baran na saakau tumre ranga

gun nidhaan sukhdaate.

5 agam agochar prabh abinaasi

poore gur te jaate.

6 bhram bhau kaat keeye nihkeval

jab te haumai maari.

7 janam maran ko chooko sahsa

saadh-sangat darsaari.

8 charan pakhaar karau gur seva

baar jaa'o lakh bareeya.

9 jeh prasaad eh bhaujal tarya

jan Nanak priy sang mireeya.[50]

राग धनासरी महला ५

घर १ चउपदे

तुम दाते ठाकुर प्रतिपालक

नाइक खसम हमारे॥

निमख निमख तुम ही प्रतिपालहो

हम बारिक तुमरे धारे॥१॥

Raag Dhanaasari Mahala Panjvaan
Ghar Pahila Chaupade

1 tum daate thaakur pratipaalak

naa'ik khasam hamaare.

2 nimakh nimakh tum hi pratipaalho

ham baarik tumre dhaare.

Raga Gauri Poorbi, Fifth Guru

Other than you, who is mine,   1
  O beloved sustainer of my life!

You alone know my inner state,   2
  as you alone are my friend and source of comfort.

All comforts I have received from you,   3
  O my unfathomable and immeasurable Lord.

I am unable to describe your manifestations,   4
  O treasure of virtues and bestower of peace.

By the perfect Guru's grace you are known,   5
  O inaccessible, unknowable and imperishable Lord.

Ever since my ego was eradicated,   6
  the Lord has eliminated my doubts and fears
  and made me pure.

When I had your darshan in the company of Saints, O Lord,   7
  my fear of birth and death disappeared.

I wash the Guru's feet, serve him   8
  and sacrifice myself to him a million times over.

It was through his grace   9
  that Nanak swam across the ocean of existence
  and united with the beloved Lord.

Raga Dhanasari, Fifth Guru, Chaupadas

You are the giver, the Master, the sustainer;   1
  you are our king and our beloved Lord.

Each moment you alone nurture us,   2
  and we, your children, rely solely on your support.

जिहवा एक कवन गुन कहीऐ॥
बेसुमार बेअंत सुआमी
तेरो अंत न
किन ही लहीऐ॥१॥रहाउ॥

3 jihva ek kavan gun kaheeyai.
besumaar be'ant suaami
tero ant na
kin hi laheeyai. rahaa'o.

कोट पराध हमारे खंडहो
अनिक बिधी समझावहो॥

4 kot paraadh hamaare khandho
anik bidhi samjhaavho.

हम अगिआन अलप मत थोरी
तुम आपन बिरद रखावहो॥२॥

5 ham agyaan alap mat thori
tum aapan birad rakhaavho.

तुमरी सरण तुमारी आसा
तुम ही सजन सुहेले॥

6 tumri saran tumaari aasa
tum hi sajan suhele.

राखहो राखनहार दइआला
नानक घर के गोले॥३॥

7 raakhoh raakhan-haar dayaala
Nanak ghar ke gole.[51]

राग वडहंस महला ५
घर १

Raag Vadahans Mahala Panjvaan
Ghar Pahila

विसर नाही प्रभ दीन दइआला॥
तेरी सरण
पूरन किरपाला॥१॥रहाउ॥

1 visar naahi prabh deen dayaala.
teri saran
pooran kirpaala. rahaa'o.

जह चित आवह सो थान सुहावा॥
जित वेला विसरह
ता लागैहावा॥१॥

2 jah chitt aavah so thaan suhaava.
jit vela visarah
ta laagai haava.

तेरे जीअ तू सद ही साथी॥
संसार सागर ते कढ दे हाथी॥२॥

3 tere jee'a tu sad hi saathi.
sansaar saagar te kadh de haathi.

आवण जाणा तुम ही कीआ॥
जिस तू राखह
तिस दूख न थीआ॥३॥

4 aavan jaana tum hi keeya.
jis tu raakhah
tis dookh na theeya.

तू एको साहिब अवर न होर॥
बिनउ करै नानक कर जोर॥४॥

5 tu eko saahib avar na hor.
binau karai Nanak kar jor.[52]

With but one tongue 3
   how many of your virtues may I narrate?
You are the infinite and boundless Lord,
   whose limit no one can fathom.
You destroy millions of our sins 4
   and instruct us in numerous ways.
We are ignorant and have little understanding, 5
   but you save us through your forgiving nature.
We seek your protection and put all our hopes in you, 6
   our benevolent friend.
Redeem Nanak, O compassionate Lord, 7
   for he is your household slave.

Raga Wad-hans, Fifth Guru

O Lord, merciful to the meek, 1
   do not turn your back on me –
   I seek your refuge, O perfect, gracious One.
Blessed is the place where you are remembered; 2
   the moment I forget you, I fall into deep remorse.
All creatures belong to you 3
   and you are their unfailing companion;
   extending your hand to them,
   you pull them out of the ocean of existence.
You have yourself brought about our coming and going, 4
   but the one whom you protect suffers no pain.
You are the only Master, without equal, 5
   and Nanak entreats you with hands joined in prayer.

बानी गुरु तेग़ बहादुर जी

Bani Guru Tegh Bahadur Ji

राग धनासरी महला ९

Raag Dhanaasari Mahala Nauvaan

अब मै कउन उपाउ करउ॥
जिह बिध मन को संसा चूकै
भउ निध पार परउ॥१॥रहाउ॥

1   *ab mai kaun upaa'o karau.*
jih bidh man ko sansa chookai
bhau nidh paar parau. rahaa'o.

जनम पाए कछु भलो न कीनो
ता ते अधिक डरउ॥

2   *janam paaye kachhu bhalo na keeno*
ta te adhik darau.

मन बच क्रम हर गुन नही गाए
यह जीअ सोच धरउ॥१॥

3   *man bach kram har gun nahi gaaye*
yah jee'a soch dharau.

गुरमत सुन कछु गिआन न उपजिओ
पसु जिउ उदर भरउ॥

4   *gurmat sun kachhu gyaan na upjio*
pasu jio udar bharau.

कहो नानक प्रभ बिरद पछानउ
तब हउ पतित तरउ॥२॥

5   *kaho Nanak prabh birad pachhaanau*
tab hau patit tarau.[1]

राग आसा महला ९

Raag Aasa Mahala Nauvaan

बिरथा कहउ कउन सिउ मन की॥
लोभ ग्रसिओ दस हू दिस धावत
आसा लागिओ धन की॥१॥रहाउ॥

1   *birtha kahau kaun sio man ki.*
lobh grasio das hu dis dhaavat
aasa laagyo dhan ki. rahaa'o.

सुख कै हेत बहुत दुख पावत
सेव करत जन जन की॥

2   *sukh kai het bahut dukh paavat*
sev karat jan jan ki.

दुआरह दुआर सुआन जिउ डोलत
नह सुध राम भजन की॥१॥

3   *duaarah duaar suaan jio dolat*
nah sudh raam bhajan ki.

मानस जनम अकारथ खोवत
लाज न लोक हसन की॥

4   *maanas janam akaarth khovat*
laaj na lok hasan ki.

नानक हर जस किउ नही गावत
कुमत बिनासै तन की॥२॥

5   *Nanak har jas kio nahi gaavat*
kumat binaasai tan ki.[2]

Guru Tegh Bahadur Ji

Raga Dhanasari, Ninth Guru

What means may I adopt now   *1*
   to eliminate doubt from my mind
   and sail across the ocean of existence?
I greatly fear that I have not put to good use   *2–3*
   the human birth that was granted to me,
   and I am consumed by deep remorse
   that I have not praised God in thought, word and deed.
Listening to the Guru's teaching   *4*
   has brought me no enlightenment –
   I only fill my belly like a beast.
Says Nanak: bring into play your forgiving nature, O Lord –   *5*
   only then will a sinner like me be saved.

Raga Asa, Ninth Guru

To whom shall I relate the miserable plight of my mind?   *1*
Overwhelmed by greed, it runs around in all ten directions*
   in the hope of gathering wealth.
In pursuit of happiness, one suffers much pain   *2*
   and fawns upon all and sundry.
Like a dog, he wanders from door to door   *3*
   without any notion of meditation on God's Nam.
He lets his human birth go to waste,   *4*
   feeling no remorse when people mock his ways.
Nanak wonders why he does not sing God's praises   *5*
   and drive all evil out of his body.

---

* The **ten directions** are north, south, east, west, northeast, northwest, southeast, south-west, above and below, conveying the sense of everywhere.

राग सारंग महला ९

हर बिन तेरो को न सहाई॥

कां की मात पिता सुत बनिता
को काहू को भाई॥१॥ रहाउ॥

धन धरन अर संपत सगरी
जो मानिओ अपनाई॥

तन छूटै कछु संग न चालै
कहा ताहे लपटाई॥१॥

दीन दइआल सदा दुख भंजन
ता सिउ रुचि न बढाई॥

नानक कहत जगत सभ मिथिआ
जिउ सुपना रैनाई॥२॥

राग जैतसरी महला ९

हर जू राख लेहो पत मेरी॥

जम को त्रास भइओ उर अंतर
सरन गही
किरपा निध तेरी॥१॥ रहाउ॥

महा पतित मुगध लोभी फुन
करत पाप अब हारा॥

भै मरबे को बिसरत नाहिन
तिह चिंता तन जारा॥१॥

कीए उपाव मुकत के कारन
दह दिस कउ उठ धाइआ॥

घट ही भीतर बसै निरंजन
ता को मरम न पाइआ॥२॥

नाहिन गुन नाहिन कछु जप तप
कउन करम अब कीजै॥

नानक हार परिओ सरनागत
अभै दान प्रभ दीजै॥३॥

Raag Saarang Mahala Nauvaan

1 har bin tero ko na sahaa'i.

ka ki maat pita sut banita
ko kaahu ko bhaa'i. rahaa'o.

2 dhan dharni ar sampat sagri
jo maanyo apnaa'i.

3 tan chhootai kachhu sang na chaalai
kaha taahe laptaa'i.

4 deen dayaal sada dukh bhanjan
ta sio ruchi na badhaa'i.

5 Nanak kahat jagat sabh mithia
jio supna rainaa'i. [3]

Raag Jaitsari Mahala Nauvaan

1 har ju raakh leho pat meri.

jam ko traas bhayo ur antar
saran gahi
kirpa nidh teri. rahaa'o.

2 maha patit mugadh lobhi phun
karat paap ab haara.

3 bhai marbe ko bisrat naahin
tih chinta tan jaara.

4 keeye upaav mukat ke kaaran
dah dis kau utth dhaaya.

5 ghat hi bheetar basai niranjan
ta ko maram na paaya.

6 naahin gun naahin kachhu jap tap
kaun karam ab keejai.

7 Nanak haar paryo sarnaagat
abhai daan prabh deejai. [4]

Raga Sarang, Ninth Guru

No one but the Lord is your help and support,   *1*
   for who is whose mother, father, son or wife,
   and who is whose brother?

Why do you cling to wealth, land and properties,   *2–3*
   believing them to be your own –
   none of them can go with you
   when you leave your body behind.

You did not enhance your love for the Lord,   *4*
   who is merciful to the meek and eradicates suffering.

Like a dream that ends when the night is over,   *5*
   the world, says Nanak, is just an illusion.

Raga Jaitsri, Ninth Guru

Save my honour, dear Lord!   *1*
The dread of Yama has gripped my heart,
   so I have taken refuge with you, O merciful Lord.

I am a great sinner, thoughtless and greedy,   *2*
   but I am now weary of my heinous deeds.

I am unable to get over the fear of death   *3*
   and that apprehension is consuming me.

Many means have I tried, venturing in all ten directions   *4*
   in pursuit of liberation.

Still I could not unravel the mystery   *5*
   of the immaculate Lord, who abides in my own heart.

I have not acquired any virtues,   *6*
   nor engaged in contemplation or austerities –
   I am at a loss to figure out what to do now!

Thus, exhausted and defeated, I have taken refuge in you.   *7*
Prays Nanak: O Lord, please grant me the gift of fearlessness.*

---

* **Fearlessness** occurs when one takes refuge in and is therefore protected by the Guru.

राग मारू महला ९

Raag Maaru Mahala Nauvaan

हर को नाम सदा सुखदाई॥
जा कउ सिमर अजामल उधरिओ
गनिका हू गत पाई॥ ९ ॥ रहाउ॥
पंचाली कउ राज सभा मह
राम नाम सुध आई॥
ता को दूख हरिओ करुणा मै
अपनी पैज बढाई॥ ९ ॥
जिह नर जस किरपा निध गाइओ
ता कउ भइओ सहाई॥
कहो नानक मै इही भरोसै
गही आन सरनाई॥ २ ॥

1 *har ko naam sada sukhdaa'i.*
   ja kau simar ajaamal udharyo
   ganika hu gat paa'i. rahaa'o.
2 *panchaali kau raaj sabha mah*
   raam naam sudh aa'i.
3 *ta ko dookh hario karuna mai*
   apni paij badhaa'i.
4 *jih nar jas kirpa nidh gaayo*
   ta kau bhayo sahaa'i.
5 *kaho Nanak mai ehi bharosai*
   gahi aan sarnaa'i.[5]

राग सोरठ महला ९

Raag Sorath Mahala Nauvaan

माई मै किह बिध लखउ गुसाई॥
महा मोह अगिआन तिमर
मो मन रहिओ उरझाई॥ ९ ॥ रहाउ॥
सगल जनम भरम ही भरम खोइओ
नह असथिर मत पाई॥
बिखिआसकत रहिओ निस बासुर
नह छूटी अधमाई॥ ९ ॥
साधसंग कबहू नही कीना
नह कीरत प्रभ गाई॥
जन नानक मै नाहे कोऊ गुन
राख लेहो सरनाई॥ २ ॥

1 *maa'i mai kih bidh lakhau gusaa'een.*
   maha moh agyaan timar
   mo man rahyo urjhaa'i. rahaa'o.
2 *sagal janam bharam hi bharam khoyo*
   nah asthir mat paa'i.
3 *bikhya-sakat rahyo nis baasur*
   nah chhooti adhmaa'i.
4 *saadh-sang kabahu nahi keena*
   nah keerat prabh gaa'i.
5 *jan Nanak mai naahe ko'u gun*
   raakh leho sarnaa'i.[6]

---

* **Ajamil** was a brahmin who sinned his whole life but was saved in the end by calling out his son's name, Narayan, which is also a name of the Lord. **Ganika** was a prostitute who attained liberation through the practice of the Lord's Name.

Raga Maru, Ninth Guru

God's Nam is the source of eternal bliss –   1
  through its remembrance Ajamil was saved
  and Ganika secured liberation.*
When in the king's court   2–3
  Draupadi remembered God's Name,†
  the merciful Lord ended her suffering
  and enhanced his own glory.
The compassionate Lord helps everyone   4
  who sings his praises.
Moved by this conviction, says Nanak,   5
  I have taken refuge in him.

Raga Sorath, Ninth Guru

By what means can I see the Lord, O mother,   1
  when my mind is entangled in gross attachments
  and lost in the darkness of ignorance?
All my life I have been lost in doubt and uncertainty,   2
  and I failed to acquire an unwavering mind.
Engrossed night and day in the poison of maya,   3
  I was unable to overcome the vile tendencies of my mind.
I never sought the company of Saints,   4
  nor did I sing the praises of the Lord.
Begs your servant Nanak: I am without merit, O Lord –   5
  keep me under your protection.

---

† In the Mahabharata, **Draupadi** is the daughter of King Drupada of Panchala and wife of the five Pandava brothers. The Lord saves her from humiliation at the hands of the Kauravas.

राग मारू महला ९

Raag Maaru Mahala Nauvaan

माई मै मन को मान न तिआगिओ॥

1 maa'i mai man ko maan na tyaagyo.

माइआ के मद जनम सिराइओ
राम भजन नही लागिओ॥१॥ रहाउ॥

maaya ke mad janam siraayo
raam bhajan nahi laago. rahaa'o.

जम को डंड परिओ सिर ऊपर
तब सोवत तै जागिओ॥

2 jam ko dand paryo sir oopar
tab sovat tai jaagio.

कहा होत अब कै पछुताए
छूटत नाहिन भागिओ॥१॥

3 kaha hot ab kai pachhutaaye
chhootat naahin bhaagio.

इह चिंता उपजी घट मह जब
गुर चरनन अनुरागिओ॥

4 eh chinta upji ghat mah jab
gur charnan anuraagio.

सुफल जनम नानक तब हूआ
जउ प्रभ जस मह पागिओ॥२॥

5 suphal janam Nanak tab hoo'a
jau prabh jas mah paagio.[7]

राग सोरठ महला ९

Raag Sorath Mahala Nauvaan

माई मन मेरो बस नाहे॥

1 maa'i man mero bas naahe.

निस बासुर बिखिअन कउ धावत
किह बिध रोकउ ताहे॥१॥ रहाउ॥

nis baasur bikhiyan kau dhaavat
kih bidh rokau taahe. rahaa'o.

बेद पुरान सिम्रिति के मत सुन
निमख न हीए बसावै॥

2 bed puraan simriti ke mat sun
nimakh na heeye basaavai.

पर धन पर दारा सिउ रचिओ
बिरथा जनम सिरावै॥१॥

3 par dhan par daara sio rachyo
birtha janam siraavai.

मद माइआ कै भइओ बावरो
सूझत नह कछु गिआना॥

4 mad maaya kai bhayo baavro
soojhat nah kachhu gyaana.

घट ही भीतर बसत निरंजन
ता को मरम न जाना॥२॥

5 ghat hi bheetar basat niranjan
ta ko maram na jaana.

जब ही सरन साध की आइओ
दुरमत सगल बिनासी॥

6 jab hi saran saadh ki aayo
durmat sagal binaasi.

तब नानक चेतिओ चिंतामन
काटी जम की फासी॥३॥

7 tab Nanak chetyo chintaman
kaati jam ki phaasi.[8]

Raga Maru, Ninth Guru

I have not shed the pride of my mind, O mother!   *1*
Intoxicated with maya, I have wasted my life,
  not applying myself to meditation on God.
You will awaken from your slumber   *2*
  only when Yama's club strikes you on the head.
How will this belated repentance help –   *3*
  you will not be able to flee from him.
This realization arose in my mind   *4*
  when love for the Guru's feet blossomed within.
Only when I absorbed myself in his devotion   *5*
  was the purpose of my life fulfilled.

Raga Sorath, Ninth Guru

I have no hold over my mind, O mother!   *1*
Night and day it runs after carnal pleasures
  and I do not know how to keep it in check.
Despite hearing the precepts of the Vedas and Puranas,   *2*
  my mind completely fails to absorb them.
Captivated by someone else's wealth and woman,   *3*
  it wastes away the human birth.
Inebriated with the wine of maya,   *4–5*
  the mind is totally unable to comprehend the divine wisdom
  and know the mystery of the Lord,
  who abides within its own self.
The moment the mind takes refuge in a Saint,   *6*
  all its evil thinking vanishes.
Then it meditates on the wish-fulfilling Lord   *7*
  and cuts itself free from death's noose.

राग रामकली महला ९
तिपदे

साधो कउन जुगत अब कीजै॥
जा ते दुरमत सगल बिनासै
राम भगति मन भीजै॥ ९॥ रहाउ॥
मन माइआ मह उरझ रहिओ है
बूझै नह कछु गिआना॥
कउन नाम जग जा कै सिमरै
पावै पद निरबाना॥ ९॥
भए दइआल क्रिपाल संत जन
तब इह बात बताई॥
सरब धरम मानो तिह कीए
जिह प्रभ कीरत गाई॥ २॥
राम नाम नर निस बासुर मह
निमख एक उर धारै॥
जम को त्रास मिटै नानक तिह
अपुनो जनम सवारै॥ ३॥

Raag Raamkali Mahala Nauvaan
Tipade

1 *saadho kaun jugat ab keejai.*
ja te durmat sagal binaasai
raam bhagti man bheejai. rahaa'o.
2 *man maaya mah urajh rahyo hai*
boojhai nah kachhu gyaana.
3 *kaun naam jag ja kai simrai*
paavai pad nirbaana.
4 *bhaye dayaal kripaal sant jan*
tab eh baat bataa'i.
5 *sarab dharam maano tih keeye*
jih prabh keerat gaa'i.
6 *raam naam nar nis baasur mah*
nimakh ek ur dhaarai.
7 *jam ko traas mitai Nanak tih*
apuno janam savaarai.[9]

Raga Ramkali, Ninth Guru

What means should I now adopt, O Saints,   1
   to destroy all my evil thoughts
   and absorb my mind in devotion to God?
My mind is entangled in maya   2
   and has not attained divine knowledge.
What kind of Nam should the world contemplate   3
   to attain emancipation?
When the Saints became kind and merciful,   4
   they revealed the secret.
Understand that when someone sings God's praises   5
   he has performed all acts of piety.
Anyone who remembers God's Nam   6–7
   even for a moment, day or night,
   will get over the fear of Yama, O Nanak,
   and fulfil the purpose of his life.

बानी गुरु गोबिन्द सिंह जी

Bani Guru Gobind Singh Ji

मित्र पिआरे नूं
हाल मुरीदां दा कहिणा।

तुध बिन रोग रजाइआँ दा ओढण
नाग निवासां दे रहिणा।

सूल सुराही खंजर पिआला
बिंग कसाइआँ दा सहिणा।

यारड़े दा सानूं सत्थर चंगा
भट्ठ खेड़िआँ दा रहिणा॥

1 mittar pyaare nu
haal mureedaan da kahina.

2 tudh bin rog rajaa'eeyaan da odhan
naag nivaasaan de rahina.

3 sool suraahi khanjar pyaala
bing kasaa'eeyaan da sahina.

4 yaararre da saanu satthar changa
bhatth kherryaan da rahina.[1]

Guru Gobind Singh Ji

Oh, would someone convey to my beloved Friend   *1*
   the sorrowful plight of this disciple?
Tell him: without you, having a soft bed   *2–4*
   and living in a palatial residence
   stings me like a snake bite.
The water pitcher is an impaling stake
   and the cup a dagger that hurts
   like the thrust of a butcher's knife.
A straw mat is a bed of luxury
   when you are with me, O Beloved; without you,
   the Khera mansions are like a burning oven.[*]

---

[*] A Punjabi folk tale relates that Heer loved Ranjha, a man of scant resources, but was forcibly married into the wealthy Khera family and lived in the luxurious **Khera mansions**, all the while longing to be reunited with Ranjha.

बानी तुलसी साहिब जी

बार बार बिनती करूँ
सतगुर चरन निवास॥
सतगुर चरन निवास
बास मोहिं दीन्ह लखाई।
नित नित करूँ बिलास
पास घर अपने आई॥
मैं अति पति मति हीन
दीन देखा मोहिं साँई।
लीन्हा अंग लगाय
कहूँ अस कौन बड़ाई॥
तुलसी मैं अति हीन हूँ
दीन्हा अगम अवास।
बार बार बिनती करूँ
सतगुर चरन निवास॥

बिपति कासे गाऊँ री माई।
जगत जाल दुखदाई॥ टेक॥
रात दिवस मोहि नींद न आवै।
जम दारुन जग खाई॥
पिय के ऐन बिन चैन न आवै।
हर दम बिरह सताई॥
जा दिन से पिय सुधि बिसराई।
भटक भटक दुख पाई॥
तुलसीदास स्वाँस सुख नाहीं।
पिय बिन पीर सताई॥

Bani Tulsi Sahib Ji

1 baar baar binati karoon
satgur charan nivaas.
2 satgur charan nivaas
baas mohen deenh lakhaa'i.
nit nit karoon bilaas
paas ghar apne aa'i.
3 main ati pati mati heen
deen dekha mohen saa'een.
leenha ang lagaaye
kahoon as kaun barraa'i.
4 Tulsi main ati heen hoon
deenha agam avaas.
baar baar binati karoon
satgur charan nivaas.[1]

1 bipati kaase gaa'oon ri maa'i,
jagat jaal dukh-daa'i. tek.
2 raat divas mohe neend na aavai,
jam daarun jag khaa'i.
3 piy ke ain bin chain na aavai,
har dam birah sataa'i.
4 ja din se piy sudhi bisraa'i,
bhatak bhatak dukh paa'i.
5 Tulsidas svaans sukh naahi,
piy bin peer sataa'i.[2]

Tulsi Sahib Ji

Again and again I pray that I may dwell at the Satguru's feet.   *1*

As I took shelter at the Satguru's feet   *2*
    he revealed the eternal abode to me;
    every day I rejoice because I have come
    nearer to my primal home.

Destitute and lacking in intellect, I am the lowest of the low,   *3*
    yet the Lord has blessed me with his merciful glance
    and embraced me – how can I extol his glory?

Says Tulsi: I am the lowest of the low,   *4*
    yet I was granted the unattainable abode –
    repeatedly I pray that I may dwell at the Satguru's feet.

The web of this world is horribly painful –   *1*
    to whom, O mother, can I tell my tale of woe?

I cannot sleep at night or during the day –   *2*
    dreadful Yama devours this world.

Without a glimpse of my Beloved, I am restless;   *3*
    pangs of separation torment me constantly.

From the day the Beloved ignored me,   *4*
    I have been in agony, wandering aimlessly.

Says Tulsidas: without the Beloved,   *5*
    the pain of separation torments me
    and my every breath is empty of joy.

ब्याकुल बिरह दिवानी,
झड़े नित नैनन पानी॥ टेक॥

1 byaakul birah divaani,
jharre nit naainan paani. tek.

हरदम पीर पिया की खटके,
सुधि बुधि बदन हिरानी॥

2 hardam peer piya ki khatke,
sudhi budhi badan hiraani.

होस हवास नहीं कुछ तन में,
बेदम जीव भुलानी॥

3 hos havaas nahi kuchh tan mein,
bedam jeev bhulaani.

बहु तरंग चित चेतन नाहीं,
मन मुरदे की बानी॥

4 bahu tarang chit chetan naahi,
man murde ki baani.

नाड़ी बैद बिथा नहिं जाने,
क्यों औषद दे आनी॥

5 naarri baid bitha nahin jaane,
kyon aushad de aani.

हिये में दाग जिगर के अन्दर,
क्या कहि दरद बखानी॥

6 hiye mein daag jigar ke andar,
kya kah darad bakhaani.

सतगुर बैद बिथा पहचानें,
बूटी है उनकी जानी॥

7 satgur baid bitha pahchaanen,
booti hai unki jaani.

तुलसी यह रोग रोगिया बूझे,
जिनको पीर पिरानी॥

8 Tulsi yah rog rogiya boojhe,
jinko peer piraani. [3]

मैं अति कुटिल कराल हूँ
बार बार सरनाय॥

1 main ati kutil karaal hoon
baar baar sarnaaye.

बार बार सरनाय
चरन धर धारू धूरी।

2 baar baar sarnaaye
charan dhar dhaaru dhoori.

सतगुर की बलिहारि
दीन सत गत मत पूरी॥

3 satgur ki balihaari
deen sat gat mat poori.

I am restless, anguished in separation   *1*
   and driven to insanity by love for my Beloved;
   from my eyes flows a constant stream of tears.
My heart hurts as I pine for my Beloved   *2*
   and I have lost awareness of my very existence.
Oblivious of my body,   *3*
   I have lost all sense and awareness.
I have become impervious to innumerable currents of passions;   *4*
   it is as if my mind were dead.
The physician knows not my malady –   *5*
   how can his remedy be of any avail?
This wound is deep within my heart –   *6*
   how can I describe my agony?
My Master, the physician, alone knows my pain,   *7*
   and he alone knows the remedy.
Only someone who is afflicted   *8*
   understands this malady, O Tulsi –
   only one who suffers the pangs of this anguish.

*E*xtremely devious and gruesome am I –   *1*
   again and again I beg for your refuge, O Master!
I anoint my forehead with the dust of your feet*   *2*
   and repeatedly implore you to give me refuge.
I sacrifice myself to the true Master,   *3*
   who has given me complete instructions
   for realizing Truth.

---

* Applying the dust of the feet of the Guru to one's forehead is an expression of deep reverence, humility and submission. Esoterically, it refers to the Guru's lotus feet, which the devotee experiences on a spiritual plane within.

आदि अंत गत मूल
फूल पत कँवल लखाई।

4   *aadi ant gat mool*
     phool pat kanval lakhaa'i.

कीन्हा अगम निवास
पाय घर अपने आई॥

5   *keenha agam nivaas*
     paaye ghar apne aa'i.

तुलसी निरख निहाल होय
परखा निज घर पाय।

6   *Tulsi nirakh nihaal hoye*
     parkha nij ghar paaye.

मैं अति कुटिल कराल हूँ
बार बार सरनाय॥

7   *main ati kutil karaal hoon*
     baar baar sarnaaye. [4]

मैं सतगुर की दासी,
अमरपुर केरी निवासी॥ टेक॥

1   *main satgur ki daasi,*
     amarpur keri nivaasi. tek.

मोरे पिया ने मोहिं पीहर पठाई,
बहुत दिवस रही पासी॥

2   *more piya ne mohen peehar pathaa'i,*
     bahut divas rahi paasi.

अब मोहिं नैहर नीक न लागे,
निस दिन रहूँ री उदासी॥

3   *ab mohen naihar neek na laage,*
     nis din rahoon ri udaasi.

मात पिता भैया भौजाई,
परी री प्रेम की फाँसी॥

4   *maat pita bhaiya bhaujaa'i,*
     pari ri prem ki phaansi.

माया मोह जाल बिध बाँधी,
बसी पास बुध नासी॥

5   *maaya moh jaal bidh baandhi,*
     basi paas budh naasi.

अब चित चैन मोर नहिं पावे,
बसूँ जाय पिया पासी॥

6   *ab chit chain mor nahin paave,*
     basoon jaaye piya paasi.

कहार भेज करि डोलिया पठावो,
आऊँ दीपक चढ़ि चासी॥

7   *kahaar bhej kari doliya pathaavo,*
     aa'oon deepak charrh chaasi.

तुलसीदास पिया बिन प्यारी,
ब्याकुल बिरह अबिनासी॥

8   *Tulsidas piya bin pyaari,*
     byaakul birah abinaasi. [5]

From the very beginning to the end,   *4*
  he has revealed the whole mystery
  as if he were explaining
  the roots, leaves and blossoms of a lotus.
Having arrived at my true home,   *5*
  I have gained residence in the inaccessible abode.
Tulsi has experienced supreme bliss on reaching   *6*
  and seeing the primal abode.
Extremely devious and gruesome am I –   *7*
  again and again I beg for your refuge, O Master!

O friend, I am a disciple of the Satguru   *1*
  who dwells in the eternal realm.
My Beloved sent me to the home of my parents,   *2*
  where I have stayed for a very long time.
Now my parents' home no longer pleases me –   *3*
  day and night I remain forlorn here, O friend!
My mother, father, brother and sister-in-law   *4*
  have fastened the noose of attachment around my neck.
I lie entrapped in the web of illusory attachments;   *5*
  caught in the snare, I have lost my sense of discrimination.
Now my heart finds no respite –   *6*
  it longs to dwell with the Beloved.
Please send bearers with a palanquin for me;   *7*
  guided by the light within,
  I shall enthusiastically climb aboard and travel home.
Says Tulsidas: without the eternal Beloved,   *8*
  the lover is anguished by the pangs of separation.

तुलसी ऐसी प्रीत कर,
जैसे चन्द चकोर।
चोंच झुकी गरदन लगी,
चितवत वाही ओर॥

उत्तम औ चंडाल घर,
जहँ दीपक उजियार।
तुलसी मते पतंग के,
सभी जोत इक सार॥

तुलसी कँवलन जल बसै,
रबि ससि बसै अकास।
जो जा के मन में बसै,
सो ताही के पास॥

मकरी उतरै तार से,
पुनि गहि चढ़त जो तार।
जा का जा से मन रम्यो,
पहुँचत लगै न बार॥

अज्ञाकारी पीव की,
रहै पिया के संग।
तन मन से सेवा करै,
और न दूजा रंग॥

भक्ति भाव बूझे बिना,
ज्ञान उदै नहिं होय।
बिना ज्ञान अज्ञान को,
काढ़ सकै नहिं कोय॥

1   Tulsi aisi preet kar,
    jaise chand chakor.

2   chonch jhuki gardan lagi,
    chitvat vaahi or.

3   uttam au chandaal ghar,
    jahan deepak ujiyaar.
    Tulsi mate patang ke,
    sabhi jot ik saar.

4   Tulsi kanvalan jal basai,
    rabi sasi basai akaas.
    ja ja ke man mein basai,
    so taahi ke paas.

6   makri utrai taar se,
    puni gahi charrhat jo taar.
    ja ka ja se man ramyo,
    pahunchat lagai na baar.

6   agyaa-kaari peev ki,
    rahai piya ke sang.
    tan man se seva karai,
    aur na dooja rang.

7   bhakti bhaav boojhe bina,
    gyaan udai nahin hoye.
    bina gyaan agyaan ko,
    kaarrh sakai nahin koye.[6]

O Tulsi, love your Beloved   1
   as the moonbird loves the moon.*

It twists its beak down to its neck   2
   to keep its gaze fixed only on the moon.

A moth sees all light as the same, O Tulsi,   3
   whether it comes from a lamp in a stately or modest home.

Says Tulsi: just as the lotus dwells in the water   4
   and the sun and the moon dwell in the sky,
   so also whoever dwells in one's mind
   is close to one's heart.

Just as a spider descends from the ceiling on its thread   5
   and climbs up again on the same thread,
   so also it does not take long to reach
   that in which one's mind is absorbed.

Someone who is obedient to the will of her beloved   6
   and who remains ever absorbed in him
   serves him with mind and body
   and is not dyed in any colour
   other than that of her beloved.

Without realizing the essence of love and devotion,   7
   no one can attain the light of knowledge,
   and without this knowledge, ignorance cannot be dispelled.

---

*The **moonbird** is a legendary bird that is in love with the moon. It watches the moon with such absorption that as the moon moves across the sky the moonbird keeps bending its head backwards until it touches its tail.

तुलसी मैं अति नीच निकामा।
मैं अनाथ गति बूझि न जाना॥

मैं अति कुटिल क्रूर कुबिचारी।
सत सत संत सरनि निरबारी॥

अब मैं अपना औगुन भाखी।
निरनय जी की कोइ नहिं राखी॥

अपनी चाल गती गुन गाऊँ।
मोहिं सों अधम और नहिं नाऊँ॥

संत दयाल दीन-हितकारी।
मोरे औगुन नाहिं बिचारी॥

संत सरल चित सब सुखकारी।
मो को पकरि हाथ निरबारी॥

कहँ लगि उनके गुन गति गाऊँ।
मोर अचेत लखी नहिं काहू॥

मोरी तपन ताप निज हेरा।
तुलसी नीच का कीन्ह निबेरा॥

कोटिन जिभ्या जो मुख होई।
तौ मैं बरनि सकौं नहिं सोई॥...

कहँ लग कहौं संत गति न्यारी।
मोरी मति गति नाहिं बिचारी॥...

संतन की गति कस कस गाऊँ।
अस कोइ देखि परै नहिं ठाऊँ॥

1 Tulsi main ati neech nikaama,
   main anaath gati boojhi na jaana.

2 main ati kutil koor kubichaari,
   sat sat sant sarani nirbaari.

3 ab main apna augun bhaakhi,
   nirnay ji ki koi nahin raakhi.

4 apni chaal gati gun gaa'oon,
   mohen son adham aur nahin naa'oon.

5 sant dayaal deen-hitkaari,
   more augun naahin bichaari.

6 sant saral chit sab sukh-kaari,
   mo ko pakari haath nirbaari.

7 kahan lagi unke gun gati gaa'oon,
   mor achet lakhi nahin kaahu.

8 mori tapan taap nij hera,
   Tulsi neech ka keenh nibera.

9 kotin jibhya jo mukh hoi,
   tau main barani sakaun nahin soi.

10 kahan lag kahaun sant gati nyaari,
   mori mati gati naahin bichaari.

11 santan ki gati kas kas gaa'oon,
   as koi dekhi parai nahin thaa'oon.[7]

Tulsi says: I was wretched, worthless and desolate,   *1*
   and did not comprehend Truth.

I was devious, cruel and had wicked thoughts –   *2*
   only surrender to the true Master has saved me.

Now I have disclosed all my faults to my Master   *3*
   and have done so without reservation.

I have told him the tale of my faults and failings –   *4*
   there was no one else as sinful as me.

My Master is merciful and gracious to the meek;   *5*
   he overlooked my failings.

The pure-hearted Master bestows bliss to all;   *6*
   taking hold of my hand, he has redeemed me.

Lacking awareness, I do not understand him –   *7*
   how can I sing of his glory and know his state within?

When he observed my pain and suffering,   *8*
   he relieved the lowly Tulsi from his misery.

Even if I had a million tongues,   *9*
   I still would not be able to describe his grace.

How can I describe the unique state of the Saints   *10*
   when I have neither the ability
   nor the capacity to understand it?

How can I praise the ways of the Saints?   *11*
Wherever I look I find no one to equal them.

बानी स्वामी जी महाराज

Baani Soami Ji Maharaj

बचन उन्नीसवाँ, शब्द इक्कीसवाँ

अब बही सुरत मँझधार।
गुरू बिन कौन लगावे पार॥
जकड़ कर पकड़ा इन संसार।
नाम बिन कौन करे निरवार॥
नाम का किया न कुछ आधार।
गुरू संग किया न अब के प्यार॥
कर्म का बहुत उठाया भार।
काल ने खाया सब को झाड़॥
साध कोइ किया न अपना यार।
देह में किया बहुत अहंकार॥
कुमति बस भरमें बारम्बार।
सुमति का किया न नेक विचार॥
देह संग रही न कुछ हुशियार।
हुई अब ग़ाफिल भोगन लार॥
बिछाया जग में मन ने जार।
पड़ी अब मन के क़ाबू हार॥
कहैं राधास्वामी तोहि पुकार।
पकड़ अब चरन सम्हार सम्हार॥

Bachan 19, Shabd 21

1 ab bahi surat manjhdhaar,
guru bin kaun lagaavai paar.

2 jakarr kar pakrra in sansaar,
naam bin kaun kare nirvaar.

3 naam ka kiya na kuchh aadhaar,
guru sang kiya na ab ke pyaar.

4 karm ka bahut uthaaya bhaar,
kaal ne khaaya sab ko jhaarr.

5 saadh koi kiya na apna yaar,
deh mein kiya bahut ahankaar.

6 kumati bas bharmen baarambaar,
sumati ka kiya na nek vichaar.

7 deh sang rahi na kuchh hushiyaar,
hui ab gaaphil bhogan laar.

8 bichhaaya jag mein man ne jaar,
parri ab man ke qaabu haar.

9 kahain radhasoami tohe pukaar,
pakarr ab charan samhaar samhaar.[1]

बचन तेंतीसवाँ, शब्द दूसरा

अब मैं कौन कुमति उरझानी।
देश पराया भई हूं बिगानी॥
अब की बार मोहिं लेओ सुधारी।
मैं चरनन पर निस दिन वारी॥

Bachan 33, Shabd 2

1 ab main kaun kumati urjhaani,
desh paraaya bhayi hoon bigaani.

2 ab ki baar mohen le'o sudhaari,
main charnan par nis din vaari.

Soami Ji Maharaj

Bachan 19, Shabd 21

The soul is drifting midstream –	1
except the Guru, who will ferry it across?	
People cling tightly to this world –	2
what other than Nam will liberate them?	
They have neither made Nam their mainstay	3
nor engendered love for the Guru in this life.	
They carry a heavy load of karmas;	4
Kal devours them all.	
They have not befriended any Saint	5
and have fostered ego while in the body.	
Influenced by the devious mind,	6
they repeatedly wander in delusion	
and do not foster any righteous thoughts.	
The soul is not vigilant in the human body –	7
engrossed in sensual pleasures, it has become negligent.	
Mind has spread a web of delusion in the world –	8
vanquished, the soul is now controlled by it.	
Radha Soami exhorts you:*	9
firmly hold on to the feet of the Master	
with complete dedication.	

Bachan 33, Shabd 2

I am a stranger in this alien land –	1
what foolishness am I embroiled in!	
Reform me this time, O Lord –	2
day and night I submit myself at your feet.	

---

* **Radha Soami** means Lord (*soami*) of the soul (*radha*); it is a name used by Soami Ji for the supreme Lord of the highest spiritual stage.

रहूं पछताय झुरूँ मन अपने।
कैसे लगूँ मैं संग पिया अपने॥
मैं धरती पिया बसें अकासा।
बिन पाये पिया रहूं उदासा॥
हे सतगुरु सुनो मेरी टेरा।
काल चक्र अब मारो घेरा॥
दीन दुखी होय करत पुकारी।
सुन स्वामी यह बिनती हमारी॥
तुम दयाल सब को देओ दाना।
मैं ही अभागिन भई दुख खाना॥
क्या कहुं मैं अब अपनी पीर की।
जस कोइ छेदत भाल तीर की॥
तब स्वामी ने दियो दिलासा।
प्रेम पंख ले उड़ो अकासा॥
दया हुई अब मिली पिया से।
हरी पीर दुख दूर जिया से॥

3 rahoon pachhtaaye jhuroon man apne,
   kaise lagoon main sang piya apne.
4 main dharti piya basen akaasa,
   bin paaye piya rahoon udaasa.
5 he satguru suno meri tera,
   kaal chakr ab maaro ghera.
6 deen dukhi hoye karat pukaari,
   sun swaami yah binati hamaari.
7 tum dayaal sab ko de'o daana,
   main hi abhaagin bhayi dukh khaana.
8 kya kahun main ab apni peer ki,
   jas koi chhedat bhaal teer ki.
9 tab swaami ne diyo dilaasa,
   prem pankh le urro akaasa.
10 daya hui ab mili piya se,
   hari peer dukh door jiya se.[2]

बचन इकतीसवाँ, शब्द दूसरा

छुटूं मैं कैसे इस मन से।
सुरत यह कहती निज मन से॥
जाल इन डाला बहु रस से।
छुटाया मोहिं धुर घर से॥
बँधी मैं आय इन दस से।
किया परपंच इन मुझ से॥
द्वार मैं आन नौ परसे।
गिराया मोहिं दस दर से॥
लगी अब लाग भोगन से।
छुटूं क्यों हाय इस फँद से॥

Bachan 31, Shabd 2

1 chhutoon main kaise is man se,
   surat yah kahti nij man se.
2 jaal in daala bahu ras se,
   chhutaaya mohen dhur ghar se.
3 bandhi main aaye in das se,
   keeya parpanch in mujh se.
4 dvaar main aan nau parse,
   giraaya mohen das dar se.
5 lagi ab laag bhogan se,
   chhutoon kyon haaye is phand se.

---

*The **ten** *indriyas* or faculties – the five senses and five motor faculties.

I am contrite and my mind laments in remorse – 3
  how can I unite with my Beloved?
I am in this world while my Beloved dwells in the heavens; 4
  unable to find the Beloved, I remain forlorn.
O Satguru, please listen to my humble request: 5
  destroy the snare of Kal now.
Humbled and distressed, I beseech you, O Master: 6
  listen to my plea!
You are merciful and generous to all – 7–8
  why am I the only one who is unfortunate and miserable?
It is as if I have been pierced by an arrow –
  how do I express my agony?
On hearing my plea my Master offered solace 9
  and told me to rise to the skies on the wings of love.
By his grace, I have now met my Beloved; 10
  all pain and sorrow have disappeared from my heart.

Bachan 31, Shabd 2

*H*ow can I free myself from the grip of this mind? 1
  soul asks the higher mind.
A vast net of countless pleasures was spread 2
  that separated me from my primal home.
On coming here the ten beguiled me* 3
  and tied me to themselves.
I was pulled down from the tenth portal 4
  and have become involved in this body of nine doors.†
Alas! I am engrossed in sensual pleasures; 5
  I do not know how to free myself from this net.

---

† The body has ten portals or doors; **nine doors** (eyes, ears, nostrils, mouth, lower openings) lead outward into the world and the **tenth portal** or door at the eye centre leads to the inner regions.

गुरू बिन कोइ नहीं दरसे।	6	*guru bin koi nahi darse,*
निकाले मोहिं इस बन से॥		*nikaale mohen is ban se.*
कांपती मैं फिरूं जम से।	7	*kaampti main phiroon jam se,*
छुड़ावे कौन इस डर से॥		*chhurrave kaun is dar se.*
पशू सम हो गई नर से।	8	*pashu sam ho gayi nar se,*
करी नहिं प्रीत मैं गुरु से॥		*kari nahin preet main guru se.*
डार ज्यों टूट गइ जड़ से।	9	*daar jyon toot gayi jarr se,*
पड़ी मैं दूर निज घर से॥		*parri main door nij ghar se.*
करूं फ़र्याद सतगुरु से।	10	*karoon faryaad satguru se,*
लगाओ मोहिं चरनन से॥		*lagaa'o mohen charnan se.*
दूर करो मैल सतसंग से।	11	*door karo mail satsang se,*
होय फिर भिन्न इस तन से॥		*hoye phir bhinn is tan se.*
मिले तब जाय सुन धुन से।	12	*mile tab jaaye sun dhun se,*
अमीरस पाय तब सरसे॥		*ameeras paaye tab sarse.*
शब्द से जाय कर परसे।	13	*shabd se jaaye kar parse,*
मिटे दुख फिर नहीं तरसे॥		*mite dukh phir nahi tarse.*
लगूं मैं आय राधा से।	14	*lagoon main aaye raadha se,*
करूँ मैं प्रीत स्वामी से॥		*karoon main preet swaami se.*
करो राधास्वामी तुम अपना।	15	*karo radhasoami tum apna,*
पड़ी मैं आय तुम सरना॥		*parri main aaye tum sarna.* [3]

बचन सत्ताईसवाँ, शब्द छठवाँ		**Bachan 27, Shabd 6**
चुनर मेरी मैली भई।	1	*chunar meri maili bhayi,*
अब का पै जाऊँ धुलान॥		*ab ka pai jaa'oon dhulaan.*
घाट घाट मैं खोजत हारी।	2	*ghaat ghaat main khojat haari,*
धुबिया मिला न सुजान॥		*dhubiya mila na sujaan.*

---

[*] **Sunn** is a term derived from *shoonya* (Sanskrit) meaning void, emptiness or vacuum. Here it refers to an inner spiritual region where the soul becomes free from the bondage of matter, mind and the three attributes (harmony, action and inertia).

[†] Mystically, **ambrosial nectar** is the spiritual nourishment that comes from contact with the divine inner music or sound, which takes the soul to eternity.

My fear of Yama sends shivers down my spine –   *6–7*
   who can help me overcome this fear?
Other than the Master I know of no one
   who can rescue me from this jungle.
While in the human form,   *8*
   I have not inculcated love for the Master,
   and my actions are like those of an animal.
Flung far from my real home,   *9*
   I am like a branch severed from a tree.
I beseech the Master to grant me refuge at his feet   *10–12*
   and cleanse me with satsang
   so that my soul can detach itself from this body
   and attach itself to the melody of Sunn.*
Only then shall I find contentment
   through the ambrosial nectar.†
When the soul attaches itself to Shabd   *13*
   all its troubles will end and it will not have any cravings left.
I shall then join with Radha   *14*
   and rejoice in my love for Soami.‡
Make me your own, Radha Soami –   *15*
   I have now taken refuge in you.

Bachan 27, Shabd 6

*M*y shawl has been soiled§ –   *1*
   where should I go to get it washed?
I have searched every washing place in vain   *2*
   but could not find a wise washerman.

---

‡ **Radha** refers to the soul that longs to join with her Lord, **Soami**.
§ Soami Ji is referring to his mind as a **shawl**, the covering of the soul that is full of the dirt of karmas.

नैहर रहुं कस पिया घर जाऊँ।
बहुत मरे मेरे मान॥

नित नित तरसूँ पल पल तड़पूँ।
कोइ धोवे मेरी चूनर आन॥

काम दुष्ट और मन अपराधी।
और लगावें कीचड़ सान॥

का से कहूं सुने नहिं कोई।
सब मिल करते मेरी हान॥

सखी सहेली सब जुड़ आई
लगीं भेद बतलान॥

राधास्वामी धुबिया भारी।
प्रगटे आय जहान॥

3   *naihar rahun kas piya ghar jaa'oon,*
bahut mare mere maan.

4   *nit nit tarsoon pal pal tarrpoon,*
koi dhove meri choonar aan.

5   *kaam dusht aur man apraadhi,*
aur lagaaven keecharr saan.

6   *ka se kahoon sune nahin koi,*
sab mil karte meri haan.

7   *sakhi saheli sab jurr aa'een,*
lageen bhed batlaan.

8   *radhasoami dhubiya bhaari,*
pragte aaye jahaan.[4]

बचन सत्ताईसवाँ, शब्द दूसरा

दर्द दुखी मैं बिरहिन भारी।
दर्शन की मोहिं प्यास करारी॥

दर्शन राधास्वामी
छिन छिन चाहूं।
बार बार उन पर बल जाऊं॥

वह तो ताड़ मार फटकारें।
मैं चरनन पर सीस चढ़ाऊं॥

निर्धन निर्बल क्रोधिन मानी।
औगुन अपने अब पहिचानी॥

स्वामी दीन दयाल हमारे।
मो सी अधम को लीन्ह उबारे॥

मैं ज़िद्दिन दम दम हठ करती।
मौज हुक्म में चित नहीं धरती॥

दया करो राधास्वामी प्यारे।
औगुन बख़्शो लेवो उबारे॥

Bachan 27, Shabd 2

1   *dard dukhi main birhin bhaari,*
darshan ki mohen pyaas karaari.

2   *darshan radhasoami*
chhin chhin chaahoon,
baar baar un par bal jaa'oon.

3   *vah to taarr maar phatkaaren,*
main charnan par sees charrhaa'oon.

4   *nirdhan nirbal krodhin maani,*
augun apne ab pahichaani.

5   *swaami deen dayaal hamaare,*
mo si adham ko leenh ubaare.

6   *main ziddin dam dam hath karti,*
mauj hukm mein chit nahi dharti.

7   *daya karo radhasoami pyaare,*
augun bakhsho levo ubaare.[5]

While living in my parents' home I have lost my dignity –   3
   how can I go to my Beloved's abode?
Every day I feel the yearning,   4
   every moment I remain tormented –
   I long for someone to come and wash my shawl.
Wicked passions and a culpable mind   5
   stain my soul with more mud and filth.
No one listens to me;   6
   everyone colludes to cause me harm –
   to whom shall I tell my tale of woe?
All my friends and companions have assembled –   7
   reveal the secret to me.
Radha Soami, the perfect washerman,   8
   has manifested himself in this world.

Bachan 27, Shabd 2

I am afflicted by the acute agony of separation   1
   and have an intense longing for his darshan.
Every moment I yearn for Radha Soami's darshan;   2
   again and again I sacrifice myself to him.
Although he rebukes, berates and scolds me,   3
   I bow my head at his feet.
I am poor, weak, irritable and arrogant;   4
   now I recognize my shortcomings.
My Lord is merciful to the meek;   5
   he liberates even lowly wretches like me.
I am obstinate and relentlessly exert my will,   6
   disregarding his will and command.
O beloved Radha Soami, have mercy on me;   7
   forgive my vices and liberate me.

बचन तेंतीसवा, शब्द इक्कीसवाँ

Bachan 33, Shabd 21

दर्शन की प्यास घनेरी।
चित तपन समाई॥

1 darshan ki pyaas ghaneri,
chit tapan samaa'i.

जग भोग रोग सम दीखें।
सतसंग में सुरत लगाई॥

2 jag bhog rog sam deekhen,
satsang mein surat lagaa'i.

गति अगम तुम्हारी समझी।
पर दरस बिन तिरपत नहिं आई॥

3 gati agam tumhaari samjhi,
par daras bin tirpat nahin aa'i.

गुरुमुखता बन नहिं पड़ती।
फिर कैसे प्रत्यक्ष पाई॥

4 gurmukhta ban nahin parrti,
phir kaise pratyaksh paa'i.

तुम गुप्त रहो जीवन से।
संग सब के दूर न भाई॥

5 tum gupt raho jeevan se,
sang sab ke door na bhaa'i.

बिन किरपा सतगुरु पूरे।
निज रूप न तुम दिखलाई॥

6 bin kirpa satguru poore,
nij roop na tum dikhlaa'i.

अब तरसूँ तड़पूँ बहु बिधि।
तुम निकट न होत रसाई॥

7 ab tarsoon tarrpoon bahu bidhi,
tum nikat na hot rasaa'i.

हो समरथ दाता सब के।
मुझ को भी खैंच बुलाई॥

8 ho samrath daata sab ke,
mujh ko bhi khainch bulaa'i.

मैं कैसे देखूँ तुम को।
कोई जतन न अब बन आई॥

9 main kaise dekhoon tum ko,
koi jatan na ab ban aa'i.

घट का पट खोलो प्यारे।
यह बात न कुछ कठिनाई॥

10 ghat ka pat kholo pyaare,
yah baat na kuchh kathinaa'i.

तुम चाहो तो छिन में कर दो।
नहिं जन्म जन्म भटकाई॥

11 tum chaaho to chhin mein kar do,
nahin janam janam bhatkaa'i.

अब दरस दिखादो जल्दी।
मैं रहूं नित्त मुरझाई॥

12 ab daras dikhaado jaldi,
main rahoon nitt murjhaa'i.

अब दया बिचारो ऐसी।
मैं रहूं चरन लौ लाई॥

13 ab daya bichaaro aisi,
main rahoon charan lau laa'i.

तुम बिन कोई और न जानूं।
तुमहीं से रहुं लिपटाई॥

14 tum bin koi aur na jaanu,
tumhi se rahun liptaa'i.

Bachan 33, Shabd 21

My longing for darshan is intense   1
   and pangs of yearning sear my heart.

Ever since I put my mind into satsang,   2
   worldly pleasures seem like afflictions.

I understand that your status is beyond comprehension,   3
   but without your darshan I cannot be content.

I am unable to achieve the state of true discipleship –   4
   how will I realize you within?

You are not far away –   5–6
   you are with all your souls, yet hidden from them,
   for without the grace of a perfect Master
   you never reveal your true form.

I yearn and writhe in agony   7
   because you are close at hand, yet out of reach.

O Almighty! You are benevolent to all –   8
   draw me also to yourself.

No amount of effort on my part bears fruit–   9
   how am I to see you?

Open the window of my heart, O Beloved –   10
   it cannot be that difficult.

Should you so will, you can do so in an instant;   11
   otherwise I will be lost in myriads of lives.

Please bless me with your darshan soon;   12
   without it I stay withered and dispirited.

Bestow such grace on me   13–14
   that I stay attached to your feet,
   that I hold you in my embrace and think of none but you.

यह आरत अद्भुत गाई।
सूरत मेरी शब्द समाई॥
राधास्वामी कहत सुनाई।
मैं दासन दास कहाई॥

15 *yah aarat adbhut gaa'i,*
soorat meri shabd samaa'i.

16 *radhasoami kahat sunaa'i,*
main daasan daas kahaa'i.[6]

बचन तेंतीसवाँ, शब्द अट्ठारहवाँ

घट का पट खोल दिखाओ॥ टेक॥
यह मन जूझ जूझ कर हारा।
लगे न एक उपाओ॥
तुम समरत्थ कहा नहिं तुम्हरे।
क्यों एती देर लगाओ॥
मैं दुख सुख में
खाऊँ झकोले।
क्यों न पड़ा मेरा
अब तक दाओ॥
अब ही दया करो मेरे दाता।
मन और सूरत गगन चढ़ाओ॥
मन तो दुष्ट बिरह नहिं लावे।
प्रेम प्रीत का दान दिवाओ॥
यह तो सुख झूठे ही चाहे।
सच्चे की परतीत न लाओ॥
भोग बिलास जगत के माँगे।
सुरत शब्द का रस नहिं पाओ॥
क्योंकर कहूँ
किस बिधि समझाऊँ।
गुरु का बचन न रिदे समाओ॥
इस मन की कुछ घढ़त अनोखी।
शब्द माहिं
कुछ प्रेम न भाओ॥

Bachan 33, Shabd 18

1 *ghat ka pat khol dikhaa'o. tek.*

2 *yah man joojh joojh kar haara,*
lage na ek upaa'o.

3 *tum samratth kaha nahin tumhre,*
kyon eti der lagaa'o.

4 *main dukh sukh mein*
khaa'oon jhakole,
kyon na parra mera
ab tak daa'o.

5 *ab hi daya karo mere daata,*
man aur soorat gagan charrhaa'o.

6 *man to dusht birah nahin laave,*
prem preet ka daan divaa'o.

7 *yah to sukh jhoothe hi chaahe,*
sacche ki parteet na laa'o.

8 *bhog bilaas jagat ke maange,*
surat shabd ka ras nahin paa'o.

9 *kyonkar kahoon*
kis bidhi samjhaa'oon,
guru ka bachan na ride samaa'o.

10 *is man ki kuchh gharrhat anokhi,*
shabd maahin
kuchh prem na bhaa'o.

I have now sung that wondrous song of devotion;   15
   my soul has merged in Shabd.
I have recited it to Radha Soami –   16
   I am now called a slave of his slaves.

Bachan 33, Shabd 18

Open the window of my heart   1
   and show me what lies within.
A hard struggle has left my mind exhausted;   2
   none of its efforts have met with success.
You are all-powerful – what is beyond you, why the delay?   3
I am buffeted by waves of pain and pleasure –   4
   why have I still not achieved my goal?
Be merciful to me now, my Lord,   5
   and raise my mind and soul to the inner skies.
My evil mind does not feel the separation –   6
   please grant it the gift of love.
It puts no faith in what is true and permanent   7
   but hankers after ephemeral pleasures.
It craves indulgence in carnal passion   8
   and has no taste for the nectar of Surat Shabd.*
How can I explain to the mind?   9
How can I make it understand?
It does not absorb the Master's message.
There is something peculiar in the make-up of this mind;   10
   it has neither love nor longing for Shabd.

---

* The path of **Surat Shabd** is the practice of joining the soul consciousness (*surat*) with the Lord's creative power, the Sound (*shabd*), and merging with it. Once the soul merges into Shabd, it is carried by the Shabd to its source, the Lord.

कैसे बचे पचे चौरासी।
यह नहिं चढ़ता गुरु की नाओ॥

संसारी के धक्के खावे।
फिर जमपुर में पिटता जाओ॥

ऐसे दुक्ख सहेगा बहुतक।
अब नहिं माने गया भुलाओ॥

सब घट में गुरु तुमहीं प्रेरक।
मुझ दुखिया को क्यों न बुलाओ॥

तुम बिन और न कोई मेरा।
चार लोक में तुमहिं दिखाओ॥

अब तो दया करो राधास्वामी।
जैसे बने तैसे घाट चढ़ाओ॥

बचन उनतीसवाँ, शब्द तीसरा

गुरू मैं गुनहगार अति भारी॥ टेक॥
काम क्रोध और छल चतुराई।
इन संग है मेरी यारी॥

लोभ मोह अहंकार ईर्षा।
मान बड़ाई धारी॥

कपटी लम्पट झूठा हिंसक।
अस अस पाप करा री॥

दुक्ख निरादर सहा न जाई।
सुख आदर अभिलाष भरा री॥

बिंजन स्वाद अधिक रस चाहे।
मन रसना यही चाट पड़ा री॥

धन और कामिन चित्त बसाये।
पुत्र कलित्तर आस भरा री॥

नाना बिधि दुख पावत पापी।
तो भी यह करतूत न छाँड़ी॥

यह मन दुष्ट काल का चेरा।
नित भरमावत निडर हुआ री॥

11	kaise bache pache chauraasi,
	yah nahin charrhta guru ki naa'o.
12	sansaari ke dhakke khaave,
	phir jampur mein pit'ta jaa'o.
13	aise dukkh sahega bahutak,
	ab nahin maane gaya bhulaa'o.
14	sab ghat mein guru tumhi prerak,
	mujh dukhiya ko kyon na bulaa'o.
15	tum bin aur na koi mera,
	chaar lok mein tumhin dikhaa'o.
16	ab to daya karo radhasoami,
	jaise bane taise ghaat charrhaa'o.[7]

Bachan 29, Shabd 3

1	guru main gunahgaar ati bhaari. tek.
	kaam krodh aur chhal chaturaa'i,
	in sang hai meri yaari.
2	lobh moh ahankaar eersha,
	maan barraa'i dhaari.
3	kapti lampat jhootha hinsak,
	as as paap kara ri.
4	dukkh niraadar saha na jaa'i,
	sukh aadar abhilaash bhara ri.
5	binjan svaad adhik ras chaahe,
	man rasna yahi chaat parra ri.
6	dhan aur kaamin chitt basaaye,
	putr kalittar aas bhara ri.
7	naana bidhi dukh paavat paapi,
	to bhi yah kartoot na chhaanrri.
8	yah man dusht kaal ka chera,
	nit bharmaavat nidar hua ri.

Trapped in birth and death, how can it be saved 11
    when it refuses to board the Master's ship?
It is punished and kicked around in the world 12
    and then gets a thrashing on the way to Yama's court.
It will have to endure numerous such miseries 13
    if it does not listen now and again goes astray.
You are the inspiration in every heart, O Master! 14
Why do you not call back this soul in distress?
No one but you is really mine; 15
    I see only you in the four planes of existence.*
Show me mercy now, Radha Soami – 16
    carry me across the ocean in any way that pleases you.

Bachan 29, Shabd 3

O Master, I am a terrible sinner – 1
    lust, anger, deceit and craftiness are my allies.
While desiring praise and fame, 2
    I have embraced greed, attachment, vanity and jealousy.
Addicted to hypocrisy and lies, lust and violence, 3
    I have committed many sins.
Pain and dishonour I cannot bear; 4
    pleasure and honour I crave.
I hunger for delectable delicacies; 5
    my mind is obsessed with the flavours of the palate.
My mind is preoccupied with wealth and women 6
    and filled with expectations of my wife and sons.
This sinner has to undergo various miseries, 7
    and even then he does not renounce his transgressions.
This wicked mind, the agent of Kal, 8
    has become fearless and constantly deludes me.

---

* The **four planes of existence** are physical, astral, causal and spiritual.

जब जब चोट पड़ी दुक्खन की।
तब डर डर कर भजन करा री॥

देखो दया मेहर सतगुरु की।
उसी भजन को मान लिया री॥

बुधि चतुराई बचन बनावट।
हार जीत की चरचा धारी॥

शेख़ी बहुत प्रीत नहिं अंतर।
भोले भक्तन धोख दिया री॥

नर नारी बहुतक बस कीन्हे।
मान प्रतिष्ठा भोग किया री॥

गुरु संग प्रीत कपट कुछ डर की।
कभी थोड़ी
कभी बहुत किया री॥

कहाँ लग औगुन बरनूँ अपने।
याद न आवत भूल गया री॥

चोर चुग़ल इन्द्री रस माता।
मतलब की सब बात विचारी॥

ख़ुद मतलबी निर्दई मानी।
बहुतन का अपमान किया री॥

कोटिन पाप किये बहुतेरे।
कहूं कहाँ लग वार न पारी॥

हे सतगुरु अब दया विचारो।
क्या मुख ले मैं करूँ पुकारी॥

नहिं परतीत प्रीत नहिं रंचक।
कस कस मेरा करो उबारी॥

मो सा कुटिल और नहिं जग में।
तुम सतगुरु मोहिं लेव सुधारी॥

जतन करूँ तो बन नहिं आवत।
हार हार अब सरन पड़ा री॥

यह भी बात कही मैं मुँह से।
मन से सरना कठिन भया री॥

9 jab jab chot parri dukkhan ki,
tab dar dar kar bhajan kara ri.

10 dekho daya mehar satguru ki,
usi bhajan ko maan liya ri.

11 budhi chaturaa'i bachan banaavat,
haar jeet ki charcha dhaari.

12 shekhi bahut preet nahin antar,
bhole bhaktan dhokh diya ri.

13 nar naari bahutak bas keenhe,
maan pratishtha bhog kiya ri.

14 guru sang preet kapat kuchh dar ki,
kabhi thorri
kabhi bahut kiya ri.

15 kahan lag augun barnu apne,
yaad na aavat bhool gaya ri.

16 chor chugal indri ras maata,
matlab ki sab baat vichaari.

17 khud matlabi nirdayi maani,
bahutan ka apmaan kiya ri.

18 kotin paap kiye bahutere,
kahoon kahaan lag vaar na paari.

19 he satguru ab daya vichaaro,
kya mukh le main karoon pukaari.

20 nahin parteet preet nahin ranchak,
kas kas mera karo ubaari.

21 mo sa kutil aur nahin jag mein,
tum satguru mohen lev sudhaari.

22 jatan karoon to ban nahin aavat,
haar haar ab saran parra ri.

23 yah bhi baat kahi main munh se,
man se sarna kathin bhaya ri.

When it suffers the blows of misfortune,   *9*
   only then, out of fear, does it meditate.

Look at the grace and mercy of the Master –   *10*
   he accepts even this meditation!

Intellectual cleverness, ostentatious display   *11*
   and discussions of winning and losing keep me engaged.

I am boastful and lack inner love;   *12*
   I have cheated innocent devotees.

Having subjugated many men and women,   *13*
   I savour honour and applause.

Based partly in fear, my love for the Master   *14*
   is merely a facade – at times it waxes, at times it wanes.

I cannot recount all my faults; my memory betrays me –   *15*
   how many should I list?

I am a thief and a gossip, and am absorbed in sensual pleasure;   *16*
   all my thoughts stem from self-interest.

Egoistic, cruel and conceited,   *17*
   I have subjected many to humiliation.

Innumerable sins have I committed –   *18*
   what can I say, there is no end to them!

O Master, have mercy on me now –   *19*
   with what face can I implore you?

I have no faith or love,   *20*
   but please redeem me somehow.

There is no one as devious as me in this world –   *21*
   O Master, reform me now!

All my efforts are worthless; thoroughly defeated,   *22*
   I have finally taken refuge in you.

But this surrender too is mere words –   *23*
   real surrender is a formidable task.

सरना लेना यह भी कहना।
झूठ हुआ मुँह का कहना री॥

24 sarna lena yah bhi kahna,
jhooth hua munh ka kahna ri.

तुम्हरी गति मति तुमहीं जानो।
जस तस मेरा करो उबारी॥

25 tumhri gati mati tumhi jaano,
jas tas mera karo ubaari.

मैं तो नीच निपट संशय रत।
लगे न चरनन प्रीत करारी॥

26 main to neech nipat sanshay rat,
lage na charnan preet karaari.

मेरे रोग असाध भरे हैं।
तुम बिन को अस करे दवा री॥

27 mere rog asaadh bhare hain,
tum bin ko as kare dava ri.

जब चाहो जब छिन में टारो।
मेहर दया की मौज निरारी॥

28 jab chaaho jab chhin mein taaro,
mehar daya ki mauj niraari.

बारम्बार करूँ मैं बिनती।
और प्रार्थना करूँ तुम्हारी॥

29 baarambaar karoon main binati,
aur praarthna karoon tumhaari.

तुम बिन और न कोई दीखे।
तुमहीं हो मेरे रखवारी॥

30 tum bin aur na koi deekhe,
tumhi ho mere rakhvaari.

बुरा बुरा फिर बुरा बुरा हूं।
जैसा तैसा आन पड़ा री॥

31 bura bura phir bura bura hoon,
jaisa taisa aan parra ri.

अब तो लाज तुम्हें है मेरी।
राधास्वामी खेवो बला री॥

32 ab to laaj tumhen hai meri,
radhasoami khevo bala ri.[8]

बचन तेंतीसवाँ, शब्द पन्द्रहवाँ

Bachan 33, Shabd 15

गुरू मोहि अपना रूप दिखाओ॥ टेक॥

1 guru mohe apna roop dikhaa'o. tek.

यह तो रूप धरा तुम सर्गुण।
जीव उबार कराओ॥

2 yah to roop dhara tum sargun,
jeev ubaar karaa'o.

रूप तुम्हारा अगम अपारा।
सोई अब दरसाओ॥

3 roop tumhaara agam apaara,
soi ab darsaa'o.

देखूँ रूप मगन होय बैठूँ।
अभय दान दिलवाओ॥

4 dekhoon roop magan hoye baithoon,
abhay daan dilvaa'o.

यह भी रूप पियारा मो को।
इस ही से उसको समझाओ॥

5 yah bhi roop pyaara mo ko,
is hi se usko samjhaa'o.

बिन इस रूप काज नहिं होई।
क्यों कर वाहि लखाओ॥

6 bin is roop kaaj nahin hoi,
kyon kar vaahi lakhaa'o.

Even my claim to have taken your refuge is not valid –   24
  my words prove false even as I say them.

You alone know your splendour and magnitude –   25
  save me, no matter what it entails.

I am ignoble, confounded by doubt   26
  and unable to nurture deep love for your feet.

I am full of incurable maladies –   27
  who except you can remove them?

Wondrous is your willingness to grant mercy and grace;   28
  the moment you will it, you bestow liberation.

Again and again I beg you and offer my prayers.   29

I perceive no one other than you –   30
  you are my sole protector.

I am bad, awfully bad and deplorable I remain;   31
  regardless, I have come and fallen at your door.

Now my honour lies in your hands –   32
  O Radha Soami, ferry me through my troubles.

Bachan 33, Shabd 15

Master, reveal your true form to me!   1

This physical form you have assumed to emancipate souls;   2–3
  now show me your other form –
  inaccessible and boundless.

When I see that form, may I be profoundly absorbed in it;   4
  pray grant me the gift of fearlessness.

This physical form is also very dear to me,   5
  but make me perceive that one through this one.

Without this form the true objective cannot be accomplished –   6
  that form cannot be revealed without this one.

ता ते महिमा भारी इसकी।
पर वह भी लखवाओ॥

वह तो रूप सदा तुम धारो।
या ते जीव जगाओ॥

यह भी भेद सुना मैं तुम से।
सुरत शब्द मारग नित गाओ॥

शब्द रूप जो रूप तुम्हारा।
वा में भी अब सुरत पठाओ॥

डरता रहूं मौत और दुख से।
निर्भय कर अब मोहि छुड़ाओ॥

दीनदयाल जीव हितकारी।
राधास्वामी काज बनाओ॥

7 ta te mahima bhaari iski,
par vah bhi lakhvaa'o.

8 vah to roop sada tum dhaaro,
ya te jeev jagaa'o.

9 yah bhi bhed suna main tum se,
surat shabd maarag nit gaa'o.

10 shabd roop jo roop tumhaara,
va mein bhi ab surat pathaa'o.

11 darta rahoon maut aur dukh se,
nirbhay kar ab mohe chhurraa'o.

12 deen-dayaal jeev hitkaari,
radhasoami kaaj banaa'o.[9]

बचन तेंतीसवाँ, शब्द तेरहवाँ

गुरू मोहि दीजे अपना धाम॥ टेक॥

मैं तो निकाम भर्म बस रहता।
तुम दयाल लो मोको थाम॥

ना जानूँ क्या पाप कमाये।
गहे न सूरत नाम॥

कैसी करूँ ज़ोर नहिं चाले।
मन नहिं पावे दृढ़ विश्राम॥

हे सतगुरु अब दया बिचारो।
मैं दुख में रहूं आठों जाम॥

ना सुर्त चढ़े न मन ठहरावे।
शब्द महातम नहिं पतियाम॥

संत मता ऊंचा सुन पकड़ा।
क्यों नहिं संत करें मेरी साम॥

Bachan 33, Shabd 13

1 guru mohe deeje apna dhaam. tek.

2 main to nikaam bharm bas rahta,
tum dayaal lo moko thaam.

3 na jaanu kya paap kamaaye,
gahe na soorat naam.

4 kaisi karoon zor nahin chaale,
man nahin paave drirrh vishraam.

5 he satguru ab daya bichaaro,
main dukh mein rahoon aathon jaam.

6 na surt charrhe na man thahraave,
shabd mahaatam nahin patiyaam.

7 sant mata ooncha sun pakarra,
kyon nahin sant karen meri saam.

This form is therefore supremely exalted,   7
    but please reveal your other form too!
That form is eternal,   8
    while you have assumed this physical form to awaken souls.
This secret also I have learned from your discourses   9
    on the path of Surat Shabd.
Now merge my soul in your Shabd Form* –   10
    that is your true form.
I live in constant fear of death and adversity –   11
    deliver me and make me fearless.
Merciful Radha Soami, benefactor of souls,   12
    help me realize my true objective.

Bachan 33, Shabd 13

Admit me into your primal home, O Master!   1
I am worthless, I live in the grip of delusion,   2
    but you are merciful – please hold me tight.
I know not what sins I have committed   3
    which keep my soul from attaching to Nam.
What should I do – I am powerless   4
    and my mind does not find lasting peace.
Be merciful to me now, dear Master –   5
    day and night I live in anguish.
My soul does not rise nor my mind hold still;   6
    I cannot put my faith in the greatness of Shabd.
Having heard of its supreme worth,   7
    I adopted the path of the Saints –
    I wonder why they do not help me on this path.

---

* The Master's **Shabd form** is his real inner radiant form, that of pure spirit.

संत मते को लज्जा आवे।
जो मेरा नहिं पूरन काम॥
अपनी मति ले करूँ पुकारा।
मौज तुम्हारी मैं नहिं जाम॥
बार बार मैं बिनय पुकारूँ।
जस जानो तस देओ निज नाम॥
राधास्वामी कहें निज नामी।
दर्दी को चहिये आराम॥

8   sant mate ko lajja aave,
     jo mera nahin pooran kaam.
9   apni mati le karoon pukaara,
     mauj tumhaari main nahin jaam.
10   baar baar main binay pukaaroon,
     jas jaano tas de'o nij naam.
11   radhasoami kahen nij naami,
     dardi ko chahiye aaraam.[10]

बचन उन्तीसवाँ, शब्द पन्द्रहवाँ

गुरु तारेंगे हम जानी।
तू सुरत काहे बौरानी॥
दृढ़ पकड़ो शब्द निशानी।
तेरी काल करे नहिं हानी॥
तू होजा शब्द दिवानी।
मत सुनो और की बानी॥
सब छोड़ो भर्म कहानी।
गुरु का मत लो पहिचानी॥
चढ़ बैठो अगम ठिकानी।
राधास्वामी कहत बखानी॥

Bachan 19, Shabd 15

1   guru taarenge ham jaani,
     tu surat kaahe bauraani.
2   drirrh pakarro shabd nishaani,
     teri kaal kare nahin haani.
3   tu hoja shabd divaani,
     mat suno aur ki baani.
4   sab chhorro bharm kahaani,
     guru ka mat lo pahichaani.
5   charrh baitho agam thikaani,
     radhasoami kahat bakhaani.[11]

बचन सत्ताईसवाँ, शब्द तीसरा

कैसी करूँ कसक उठी भारी।
मेरी लगी गुरू संग यारी॥
दम दम तड़पूँ
छिन छिन तरसूँ।
चढ़ रही मन में बिरह ख़ुमारी॥

Bachan 27, Shabd 3

1   kaisi karoon kasak uthi bhaari,
     meri lagi guru sang yaari.
2   dam dam tarrpoon
     chhin chhin tarsoon,
     charrh rahi man mein birah khumaari.

It would bring discredit to the path 8
  should I fail to accomplish my goal.
I can only pray to you with my limited intellect – 9
  I do not know what your will is.
So time and again I cry out in supplication: 10
  please give me your true Nam,
    as and when it pleases you.
Radha Soami, bestower of the true Nam, says: 11
  anyone who suffers the pain of separation shall be comforted.

Bachan 19, Shabd 15

Why are you confused and disheartened, dear soul – 1
  I know that the Master will ferry you across!
Kal cannot harm you 2
  if you hold tight to the banner of Shabd.
Become enthralled with Shabd 3
  and do not listen to others.
Ignore all misleading talk – 4
  recognize the path of the Master as true.
Rise up and establish yourself in the inaccessible realm, 5
  as Radha Soami has explained.

Bachan 27, Shabd 3

What can I do – a piercing ache wrenches my heart; 1
  I have fallen in love with my Master!
With every breath I am tormented, 2
  each moment I am tantalized –
    the ecstasy of separation is intensifying within me.

सुलगत जिगर फटत नित छाती।
उठन लगी हिये से चिनगारी॥

नैनन नीर बहत जस नदियाँ।
डूब मरी माया मतवारी॥

ठंडी आह उठे पल पल में।
छाय गई अब प्रीत करारी॥

तोड़ी न टूटे छोड़ी न छूटे।
काल करम पच हारी॥

सुरत निरत दोउ क़ासिद कीन्हे।
बिथा लिखूँ अब सारी॥

पतियाँ भेजूँ गुरु दरबारा।
अब लो ख़बर हमारी॥

नगर उजाड़ देश सब सूना।
तुम बिन जग अँधियारी॥

कौन सुने और कौन सम्हारे।
सब मोहिं दीन निकारी॥

बही जात नइया मँझधारा।
तुम बिन कौन उबारी॥

खेवटिया क्यों देर लगाई।
क्यों कर करूँ पुकारी॥

मैं मरी जाऊँ जिऊँ अब कैसे।
तुम मेरी सुधि न सम्हारी॥

डालो जान देवो सरजीवन।
मैं तुम पर बलिहारी॥

बचन सुनाओ दरस दिखाओ।
हरो पीर मेरी सारी॥

राधास्वामी सुनो हमारी।
मैं तुम्हरे आधारी॥

3   *sulgat jigar phatat nit chhaati,*
uthan lagi hiye se chingaari.

4   *nainan neer bahat jas nadiyaan,*
doob mari maaya matvaari.

5   *thandi aah uthe pal pal mein,*
chhaaye gayi ab preet karaari.

6   *torri na toote chhorri na chhoote,*
kaal karam pach haari.

7   *surat nirat do'u qaasid keenhe,*
bitha likhoon ab saari.

8   *pattiyaan bhejoon guru darbaara,*
ab lo khabar hamaari.

9   *nagar ujaarr desh sab soona,*
tum bin jag andhiyaari.

10   *kaun sune aur kaun samhaare,*
sab mohen deen nikaari.

11   *bahi jaat nayya manjh-dhaara,*
tum bin kaun ubaari.

12   *khevatiya kyon der lagaa'i,*
kyon kar karoon pukaari.

13   *main mari jaa'oon ji'oon ab kaise,*
tum meri sudhi na samhaari.

14   *daalo jaan devo sarjeevan,*
main tum par balihaari.

15   *bachan sunaa'o daras dikhaa'o,*
haro peer meri saari.

16   *radhasoami suno hamaari,*
main tumhre aadhaari.[12]

---

* The faculty of the soul to hear within is referred to as **surat** while **nirat** is the faculty of
the soul to see within.

My body is constantly in agony 3
    and sparks rise from my smouldering heart.
The flood of tears streaming from my eyes 4
    has drowned that seductive maya.
Each moment I heave deep sighs; 5
    profound love has overwhelmed me.
This love can be neither broken nor abandoned – 6
    Kal and karmas have given up in desperation.
With surat and nirat as my messengers,* 7
    I shall now write a complete account of my woes.
I will send letters to my Master's court – 8
    come see my plight now.
This city is deserted, and this country desolate – 9
    without you, O Master, the whole world is utter darkness.
No one cares and no one listens; 10
    I have been turned away from every door.
My boat is adrift midstream – 11
    who other than you will take me across?
Why this delay, O helmsman? 12
How do I call out to you?
I am dying – how can I live 13
    when you do not attend to my plight?
Restore my spirit with the water of life† – 14
    I sacrifice myself to you.
Bless me with your wisdom and darshan 15
    and take away all my pains.
Listen to me, Radha Soami – 16
    you are the sustenance of my life.

---

† The **water of life** is the nectar of Nam, which restores the soul and returns it to its true home.

बचन छठा, शब्द सातवाँ

Bachan 6, Shabd 7

करूँ आरती राधास्वामी,	1	karoon aarti radhasoami,
तन मन सुरत लगाय।		tan man surat lagaaye,
थाल बना सत शब्द का,		thaal bana sat shabd ka,
अलख जोत फहराय॥		alakh jot phahraaye.
हंस सभी आरत करें,	2	hans sabhi aarat karen,
सन्मुख दर्शन पाय।		sanmukh darshan paaye.
राधास्वामी दया कर,	3	radhasoami daya kar,
दीन्हाँ अगम लखाय॥		deenhaan agam lakhaaye.
अनहद धुन घंटा बजे,	4	anhad dhun ghanta baje,
संख बजे मिरदंग।		sankh baje mirdang.
ओंकार मँडल बँधा,	5	onkaar mandal bandha,
मेघनाद गरजंत॥		megh-naad garjant.
सुन्न मँडल धुन सारँगी,	6	sunn mandal dhun saarangi,
किंगरी बजे अनूप।		kingri baje anoop.
कोटि भान छबि रोम इक,	7	koti bhaan chhabi rom ik,
ऐसा पुरुष स्वरूप॥		aisa purush swaroop.
कँवलन की क्यारी बनी,	8	kanvalan ki kyaari bani,
भँवर करें गुंजार।		bhanvar karen gunjaar.
सेत सिंहासन बैठ कर,	9	set singhaasan baith kar,
देखें पुरुष सम्हार॥		dekhen purush samhaar.
बीन बाँसरी मधुर धुन,	10	been baansari madhur dhun,
बाजें पुरुष हुज़ूर।		baajen purush huzoor.
सुन सुन हंसा मगन होयँ,	11	sun sun hansa magan hoyen,
पिवें अमीरस मूर॥		piven ameeras moor.

---

*arti: A ritual of worship performed by waving a tray containing small oil lamps and other items such as incense and flowers in front of an image of a deity, accompanied by singing and the ringing of small bells. Esoterically, arti refers to the inner devotion of the soul, which brings the experience of inner light and music.

† **Alakh** is the Lord beyond perception.

‡ *mridang*: A type of drum.

§ **Onkar** is the lord of the second inner region, Trikuti.

Bachan 6, Shabd 7

O Radha Soami, in ardent devotion I perform your arti*   1
   with body, mind and soul.
The true Shabd is the offering tray;
   in it shimmers the flame of Alakh.†
All realized souls pay obeisance   2
   as they behold the Lord before them.
Radha Soami, by his grace, has revealed the inaccessible.   3
The unstruck melody of the bell resounds   4
   and the sounds of the conch and the *mridang* reverberate.‡
The realm of Onkar resonates§   5
   with the rumbling of thunder clouds.
The unsurpassed melodies of the *sarangi*   6
   and *kingri* fill the Sunn region.⁋
Every pore of the Radiant Form of that realm's sovereign   7
   has the brilliance of millions of suns –
   such is the splendour of his form!
Lotus beds are laid out and gentle sound   8
   like the humming of black bees fills the atmosphere.
Seated on a white majestic throne,   9
   the Lord watches and sustains all.
The sweet melodies of the veena and flute**   10
   resound in the Lord's presence.
The realized souls are enraptured with the melodies   11
   and drink the divine ambrosial nectar.

⁋ *sarangi* and *kingri*: Indian stringed instruments; the *sarangi* is played with a bow and *kingri* played with a bow or the index finger. Mystics have likened the sound of the *sarangi* to that of the divine music heard in the region of **Sunn**, where the soul is cleansed of its coverings of mind and matter.
** The **veena** is a multi-stringed musical instrument which produces a sound often compared to the melody of the Shabd heard in the fifth inner region.

रंग महल सत्तपुरुष का,
शोभा अगम अपार।

12 *rang mahal satt-purush ka,*
shobha agam apaar.

हंस जहाँ आनंद करें,
देखें बिमल बहार॥

13 *hans jahaan aanand karen,*
dekhen bimal bahaar.

अब आरत पूरन भई,
मन पाया बिसराम।

14 *ab aarat pooran bhayi,*
man paaya bisraam.

राधास्वामी चरन पर,
कोटि कोटि परनाम॥

15 *radhasoami charan par,*
koti koti parnaam. [13]

बचन सातवाँ, शब्द पहला

Bachan 7, Shabd 1

करूँ बेनती दोउ कर जोरी।
अर्ज़ सुनो राधास्वामी मोरी॥

1 *karoon benati do'u kar jori,*
arz suno radhasoami mori.

सत्त पुरुष तुम सतगुरु दाता।
सब जीवन के पितु और माता॥

2 *satt purush tum satguru daata,*
sab jeevan ke pitu aur maata.

दया धार अपना कर लीजे।
काल जाल से न्यारा कीजे॥

3 *daya dhaar apna kar leeje,*
kaal jaal se nyaara keeje.

सतयुग त्रेता द्वापर बीता।
काहु न जानी शब्द की रीता॥

4 *satyug treta dvaapar beeta,*
kaahu na jaani shabd ki reeta.

कलजुग में स्वामी दया विचारी।
परगट करके शब्द पुकारी॥

5 *kaljug mein swaami daya vichaari,*
pargat karke shabd pukaari.

जीव काज स्वामी जग में आये।
भौ सागर से पार लगाये॥

6 *jeev kaaj swaami jag mein aaye,*
bhau saagar se paar lagaaye.

तीन छोड़ चौथा पद दीन्हा।
सत्तनाम सतगुरु गत चीन्हा॥

7 *teen chhorr chautha pad deenha,*
satt-naam satguru gat cheenha.

---

*A **yuga** is an age or cycle of time. According to Hindu scriptures, there are four yugas which follow each other in endless recurring cycles: **Satyuga** (the Age of Truth or the Golden Age); **Tretayuga** (the Silver Age); **Dwaparyuga** (the Copper or Bronze Age); and the present age, **Kaliyuga** (the Dark or Iron Age).

The grandeur of the true Lord's blissful palace   *12–13*
   is indescribable and unrivalled;
   the realized souls remain in a state of pure ecstatic bliss,
   enjoying the pristine panorama.
Now my arti is complete   *14*
   and my mind has found eternal peace.
I bow millions of times at Radha Soami's feet.   *15*

Bachan 7, Shabd 1

With my hands joined in prayer   *1*
   I beseech you, Radha Soami: listen to my supplication!
You are the true Lord, my benevolent Master –   *2*
   you are the father and mother of all beings.
Be merciful to me, accept me   *3*
   and set me free from the snare of Kal.
The three yugas – Satyuga, Treta and Dwapar – have passed   *4*
   and no one understood the method of Shabd practice.
Now in Kaliyuga Radha Soami in his mercy*   *5*
   has openly proclaimed the secret of Shabd.
Radha Soami has come to this world   *6*
   for the benefit of souls –
   to carry them across the ocean of existence.
Passing by the first three realms,   *7*
   he takes them to the fourth,†
   where they realize that the status of the Master
   is that of the true Lord, Satnam.

---

† The first **three realms** or planes of existence are the physical, astral and causal planes; the **fourth** is the realm of pure spirit.

जगमग जोत होत उजियारा।
गगन सोत पर चन्द्र निहारा॥

8 *jagmag jot hot ujiyaara,*
gagan sot par chandr nihaara.

सेत सिंहासन छत्र बिराजे।
अनहद शब्द ग़ैब धुन गाजे॥

9 *set singhaasan chhatr biraaje,*
anhad shabd gaib dhun gaaje.

क्षर अक्षर नि:अक्षर पारा।
बिनती करे जहाँ दास तुम्हारा॥

10 *kshar akshar nih'akshar paara,*
binati kare jahaan daas tumhaara.

लोक अलोक पाऊं सुख धामा।
चरन सरन दीजे बिसरामा॥

11 *lok alok paa'oon sukh dhaama,*
charan saran deeje bisraama.[14]

बचन पन्द्रहवाँ, शब्द अट्ठारहवाँ

Bachan 15, Shabd 18

कुमतिया बैरन पीछे पड़ी।
मैं कैसे हटाऊँ जान॥

1 *kumatiya bairan peechhe parri,*
main kaise hataa'oon jaan.

सतगुरु बचन न माने कबही।
उन संग धरे गुमान॥

2 *satguru bachan na maane kab hi,*
un sang dhare gumaan.

काम क्रोध की सनी बुद्धि से।
परखा चाहे उन का ज्ञान॥

3 *kaam krodh ki sani buddhi se,*
parkha chaahe un ka gyaan.

सेवा करे न सरधा लावे।
उलट करावे उनसे मान॥

4 *seva kare na sardha laave,*
ulat karaave unse maan.

अपनी गति हालत नहिं बूझे।
कैसे लगे ठिकान॥

5 *apni gati haalat nahin boojhai,*
kaise lage thikaan.

लोभ मोह की सूखी नदियाँ।
ता में निस दिन रहे भरमान॥

6 *lobh moh ki sookhi nadiyaan,*
ta mein nis din rahe bharmaan.

संत मता कहो कैसे बूझे।
अपनी मति के दे परमान॥

7 *sant mata kaho kaise boojhe,*
apni mati ke de parmaan.

तिन से संत मौन होय बैठे।
सो जिव करते अपनी हान॥

8 *tin se sant maun hoye baithe,*
so jiv karte apni haan.

---

*Daswan Dwar** literally means tenth door or gate. It also refers to the inner region where the soul becomes free of the coverings of mind and matter.

The refulgence of a resplendent flame 8
  brightens one's heart within;
  then a moon is seen in Daswan Dwar.*
Further on, a magnificent white throne is set up 9
  under an elegant canopy, and there the hidden melody
  of the boundless Shabd resounds.
Beyond the regions of Trikuti, Sunn and Maha Sunn† 10
  your devotee stands in humble supplication.
Give me protection at your feet, O Lord, 11
  so that I may find peace in this world and in the world beyond.

Bachan 15, Shabd 18

Base thinking, my enemy, is haunting me – 1
  how do I save myself?
It never accepts the Master's advice, 2
  and instead displays arrogance towards him.
With an intellect swathed in lust and anger 3
  people try to test the wisdom of the Master.
Instead of serving the Master and having faith in him 4
  they expect recognition from him.
They do not realize the severity of their own situation – 5
  how will they ever reach their destination?
The streams of greed and attachment will run dry, 6
  yet people chase mirages day and night.
How can they comprehend the path of the Masters 7
  when they are always preoccupied
  with asserting their own opinions?
These people only harm themselves, 8
  for Saints simply withdraw from them and stay quiet.

---

† **Trikuti** and **Sunn** are inner regions. On entering Sunn, the soul becomes free from the bondage of matter, mind and the three attributes. **Maha Sunn** is a region of intense darkness between the third and fourth spiritual regions.

कुमति अधीन हुए सब प्रानी।
क्या क्या उनका करूँ बखान॥
जिन पर मेहर पड़े आ सरना।
वे पावें सतगुरु पहिचान॥
अपनी उक्ति चतुरता छोड़ें।
अपने को जानें अनजान॥
तब सतगुरु प्रसन्न होय कर।
देवें पता निशान॥
कुमति हटाय छुड़ावें पीछा।
सुरत लगावें शब्द ध्यान॥
बिना शब्द उद्धार न होगा।
सब संतन यह किया बखान॥
सोई गावें राधास्वामी। जो
कोइ मानें सोइ सुजान॥

9 kumati adheen huye sab praani,
   kya kya unka karoon bakhaan.
10 jin par mehar parre aa sarna,
   ve paaven satguru pahichaan.
11 apni ukti chaturta chhorren,
   apne ko jaanen anjaan.
12 tab satguru prasann hoye kar,
   deven pata nishaan.
13 kumati hataaye chhurraaven peechha,
   surat lagaaven shabd dhyaan.
14 bina shabd uddhaar na hoga,
   sab santan yah kiya bakhaan.
15 soi gaaven radhasoami,
   jo koi mane soi sujaan.[15]

बचन तेंतीसवाँ, शब्द बीसवाँ

लगाओ मेरी नइया सतगुरु पार।
मैं बही जात जग धार॥
तुम बिन नाहीं को कढ़ियार।
लगादो डूबी खेप किनार॥
सहेली मत तू मन में हार।
दिखाऊँ जग का वार और पार॥
चढ़ाऊँ सूरत उल्टी धार।
शब्द संग खेय उतारूँ पार॥
गुरू को धर ले हिये मँझार।
नाम धुन घट में सुन झनकार॥
तरंगें उठतीं बारम्बार।
भँवर जहाँ पड़ते बहुत अपार॥
मेहर से पहुंची दसवें द्वार।
राधास्वामी दीन्हा पार उतार॥

Bachan 33, Shabd 20

1 lagaa'o meri nayya satguru paar,
   main bahi jaat jag dhaar.
2 tum bin naahi ko karrhiyaar,
   lagaado doobi khep kinaar.
3 saheli mat tu man mein haar,
   dikhaa'oon jag ka vaar aur paar.
4 charrhaa'oon soorat ulti dhaar,
   shabd sang khey utaaroon paar.
5 guru ko dhar le hiye manjhaar,
   naam dhun ghat mein sun jhankaar.
6 tarangen uthteen baarambaar,
   bhanvar jahan parrte bahut apaar.
7 mehar se pahunchi dasven dvaar,
   radhasoami deenha paar utaar.[16]

They are all victims of their base thinking –   9
   how much should I tell you about them?
Only those who are blessed seek refuge   10
   and are able to recognize the true Master.
They abandon their cleverness and so-called wisdom   11
   and realize how ignorant they are.
Only then is the Master pleased and he reveals the path.   12
He rids them of their base thinking   13
   and guides their souls to contemplation on Shabd.
Every Saint has affirmed   14
   that without Shabd there is no salvation.
Radha Soami gives you the same teaching;   15
   wise is the one who accepts this message.

Bachan 33, Shabd 20

O Satguru, please ferry my boat across –   1
   I am drifting in the currents of this world.
Except you, there is no other saviour –   2
   please take my sinking boat ashore.
O friend, do not despair;   3
   I will show you this side and the other side of the creation.
I will raise your soul above the current   4
   and with Shabd I will ferry your boat across.
Enshrine the Guru within your heart   5
   and listen to the resounding melody of Nam within.
Waves rise one after another   6
   and countless whirlpools abound in this world.
By his grace, my soul has reached Daswan Dwar –   7
   Radha Soami has ferried me across!

बचन तेंतीसवाँ, शब्द ग्यारहवाँ

माँगूँ इक गुरु से दाना।
घट शब्द देव पहिचाना॥

मन साथ सदा भरमाना।
कर किरपा कर्म छुड़ाना॥

सुर्त चढ़े सुने धुन ताना।
मन मारो कर्म नसाना॥

सब छूटे बान कुबाना।
सत शब्द मिले दृढ़ थाना॥

अब कर दो नाम दिवाना।
मैं ताकूँ शब्द निशाना॥

कोइ करे न मेरी हाना।
मोहि तुम पर बल बल जाना॥

कल धारा मुझे न बहाना।
मोहि देना शब्द ठिकाना॥

मन हो गया बहुत निमाना।
अब राधास्वामी चरन समाना॥

Bachan 33, Shabd 11

1 maangoon ik guru se daana,
  ghat shabd dev pahichaana.

2 man saath sada bharmaana,
  kar kirpa karm chhurraana.

3 surt charrhe sune dhun taana,
  man maaro karm nasaana.

4 sab chhoote baan kubaana,
  sat shabd mile drirrh thaana.

5 ab kar do naam divaana,
  main taakoon shabd nishaana.

6 koi kare na meri haana,
  mohe tum par bal bal jaana.

7 kal dhaara mujhe na bahaana,
  mohe dena shabd thikaana.

8 man ho gaya bahut nimaana,
  ab radhasoami charan samana.[17]

बचन आठवाँ, शब्द सोलहवाँ

मैं कौन कुमति उरझाना।
गुरू दर्श छोड़ घर जाना॥

अब कौन जतन अस करिये।
गुरु चरन चित्त में धरिये॥

यह बचन कहां मैं पाऊँ।
मन खेती बीज जमाऊँ॥

निस दिन रहे चित्त उदासी।
क्यों छोड़ूँ चरन बिलासी॥

नर देह न बारम्बारी।
क्यों भौजल डूबे आ री॥

Bachan 8, Shabd 16

1 main kaun kumati urjhaana,
  guru darsh chhorr ghar jaana.

2 ab kaun jatan as kariye,
  guru charan chitt mein dhariye.

3 yah bachan kahaan main paa'oon,
  man kheti beej jamaa'oon.

4 nis din rahe chitt udaasi,
  kyon chhorroon charan bilaasi.

5 nar deh na baarambaari,
  kyon bhaujal doobe aa ri.

Bachan 33, Shabd 11

I ask my Guru for just one gift –   1
  to make me realize the Shabd within.
My association with the mind has perpetually deluded me –   2
  shower your grace and release me from my karmas.
Subdue my mind and destroy my karmas –   3
  may my soul ascend by hearing the divine melody!
Free me from my good and bad habits;   4
  let me find permanent refuge in the true Shabd.
Now make me ecstatic with Nam –   5
  I seek the mark of Shabd.
Let no one harm me;   6
  I sacrifice myself to you again and again.
Do not let me drift in the current of Kal;   7
  grant me eternal refuge in Shabd.
My mind has been greatly humbled –   8
  may I now merge in Radha Soami!

Bachan 8, Shabd 16

Oh, what folly confounded me –   1
  forsaking the Guru's darshan I walked away!
What do I do now   2
  to hold the Guru's feet in my heart?
Where will I find that instruction   3
  that nourishes the seed in the soil of my heart?
Day and night my mind is troubled –   4
  how could I forgo the bliss of those feet?
The human form will not be gained again and again –   5
  having received it, why drown in the ocean of existence?

सतगुरु संग कभी न छोड़ूँ।
मन तन से नाता तोड़ूँ॥

गुरु बल से करम निकारूं।
सतसंग से काल पछाड़ूँ॥

जो मेहर करें गुरु मुझ पर।
यह बात बने अति दुस्तर॥

मेरे मन में चाहत येही।
गुरु चरन न छोड़ूं कबही॥

गुरु से कोई अधिक न राखा।
पुनि संत बेद अस भाखा॥

गुरु महिमा सबहिन गाई।
मैं दीन अधीन जनाई॥

मेरी लाग लगी गुरु चरनन।
नख सोभा क्या करूँ बरनन॥

कोटिन रवि चन्द्र लजाई।
उस नख की गति नहिं पाई॥

यह तिमिर बाहरी खोवें।
वह अन्तर मोती पोवें॥

हिरदे में सदा उजारी।
गुरु नख पर जाऊँ बलिहारी॥

अब आरत उनकी करता।
मन चरन कंवल में धरता॥

सुर्त फेरो सतगुरु मेरी।
घर जाऊं करूँ फिर फेरी॥

राधास्वामी काटो बेड़ी।
यह बिनती सुनिये मेरी॥

मैं दासन दास तुम्हारा।
तुम बचन मोर निस्तारा॥

6   satguru sang kabhi na chhorroon,
    man tan se naata torroon.

7   guru bal se karam nikaaroon,
    satsang se kaal pachhaarroon.

8   jo mehar karen guru mujh par,
    yah baat bane ati dustar.

9   mere man mein chaahat yehi,
    guru charan na chhorroon kabahi.

10 guru se koi adhik na raakha,
    puni sant bed as bhaasha.

11 guru mahima sabahin gaa'i,
    main deen adheen janaa'i.

12 meri laag lagi guru charnan,
    nakh sobha kya karoon barnan.

13 kotin ravi chandr lajaa'i,
    us nakh ki gati nahin paa'i.

14 yah timir baahri khoven,
    vah antar moti poven.

15 hirde mein sada ujaari,
    guru nakh par jaa'oon balihaari.

16 ab aarat unki karta,
    man charan kanval mein dharta.

17 surt phero satguru meri,
    ghar jaa'oon karoon phir pheri.

18 radhasoami kaato berri,
    yah binati suniye meri.

19 main daasan daas tumhaara,
    tum bachan mor nistaara.[18]

I may sever my link with this mind and body,　　　　　　　6
　　but I will never withdraw from the Master's fold.
With the Guru's might I shall eliminate karma;　　　　　7
　　through his satsang I shall repulse Kal.
I can only accomplish this arduous task　　　　　　　　8
　　if the Master is merciful to me.
There is only one desire in my heart –　　　　　　　　9
　　that I never leave the Master's company.
Saints and scriptures have confirmed time and again　10
　　that there is no protector greater than the Master.
They have all sung the praises of the Guru　　　　　11
　　and made even a simple person like me understand.
I have fallen in love with the Master's feet –　　　　12–13
　　the splendour of even his toenail is beyond description –
　　its radiance puts to shame
　　the light of millions of suns and moons.
These only dispel external darkness,　　　　　　　14
　　but that radiance threads the pearls of inner light.
My heart is perpetually illumined with its radiance –　15
　　I sacrifice everything to that one nail of my Master.
Contemplating on his lotus feet,　　　　　　　　　16
　　I revere the Master now.
Turn my consciousness around, Master,　　　　　17
　　so that I can make my journey back home.
Listen to my plea, Radha Soami,　　　　　　　18
　　and cut the chains that keep me bound.
I am the slave of your slaves –　　　　　　　　19
　　in your command lies my emancipation.

बचन इकतीसवाँ, शब्द चौथा

मन चंचल कहा न माने।
मैं कौन उपाय करूँ॥

गुरु नित समझावें साध बुझावें।
सतसंग में चित जोड़ धरूँ॥

सुन सुन बचन बहुत पछताऊँ।
बहुर भुलावे भर्म रहूँ॥

अपनी सी बहु जुक्ति सम्हारी।
कैसे मन को मार मरूँ॥

सुरत शब्द का घाट न पाया।
फिर क्योंकर मैं गगन भरूँ॥

डावाँडोल रहे संशय में।
जगत आस से नाहिं टरूँ॥

सतगुरु सरन पकड़ कर बैठूं।
तो इस मन की व्याधि हरूँ॥

जगत जाल यह अति दुखदाई।
इसी अगिन में नित्त जरूँ॥

बिना मेहर कुछ काज न सरिहै।
अब राधास्वामी की सरन पड़ूं॥

Bachan 31, Shabd 4

1 man chanchal kaha na maane,
main kaun upaaye karoon.

2 guru nit samjhaaven saadh bujhaaven,
satsang mein chit jorr dharoon.

3 sun sun bachan bahut pachhtaa'oon,
bahur bhulaave bharm rahoon.

4 apni si bahu jukti samhaari,
kaise man ko maar maroon.

5 surat shabd ka ghaat na paaya,
phir kyonkar main gagan bharoon.

6 daavaan-dol rahe sanshay mein,
jagat aas se naahin taroon.

7 satguru saran pakarr kar baithoon,
to is man ki vyaadhi haroon.

8 jagat jaal yah ati dukh-daa'i,
isi agin mein nitt jaroon.

9 bina mehar kuchh kaaj na sarihai,
ab radhasoami ki saran parroon.[19]

बचन उनतीसवाँ, शब्द दूसरा

मेरी पकड़ो बाँह हे सतगुरु।
नहिं बह्यो धार भौ सागर॥

मैं बचूं जाल से क्योंकर।
तुम बिन कोई और न आसर॥

अब मिला अजायब औसर।
जम काल बड़ा है फनधर॥

Bachan 29, Shabd 2

1 meri pakrro baanh he satguru,
nahin bahyo dhaar bhausaagar.

2 main bachoon jaal se kyonkar,
tum bin koi aur na aasar.

3 ab mila ajaayab ausar,
jam kaal barra hai phan-dhar.

Bachan 31, Shabd 4

$\mathcal{M}$y restless mind does not listen to me –   1
    how do I deal with it?

I sit in satsang with an attentive mind   2
    while the Master unceasingly explains the method.

When I listen to his words I am deeply repentant,   3
    but my mind deludes me and I remain astray.

No matter how many ways I have devised   4–5
    to overpower this mind, how can I rise to the inner sky
    when I never even get to the threshold of Surat Shabd?*

My mind continues to waver and doubt –   6
    I am unable to let go of worldly ambitions.

I can be rid of the degeneracy of this mind   7
    if I take refuge in the perfect Master.

The web of this world is utter torment;   8
    it is in this fire that I constantly burn.

I now take the protection of Radha Soami,   9
    for nothing is accomplished without his grace.

Bachan 29, Shabd 2

$\mathcal{T}$ake hold of my arm, my Master, or I will be swept away   1
    by the currents of this ocean of existence.

I have no support other than you –   2
    how can I possibly escape from this net?

I have received a remarkable opportunity now,   3
    but I face the dreadful vipers of Yama and Kal.

---

*The path of **Surat Shabd** is the practice of joining the soul consciousness (*surat*) with the Lord's creative power, the Sound (*shabd*), and merging with it. Once the soul merges into Shabd, it is carried by Shabd to its source, the Lord.

कोइ मंत्र सिखाओ आ कर।
लो चरन ओट किरपा कर॥
मैं थका चौरासी फिर फिर।
अब कैसे मिले अमर घर॥
तब सतगुरु कहा दया कर।
अब सुरत चढ़ाओ गगन पर॥
वह घाटी है अति अड़बड़।
मन इन्द्री खैंच उधर धर॥
तब मिले शब्द तोहि अस्थिर।
तन मन धन आज अरप धर॥
गुरु प्रीत करो चित्त सम कर।
यह आरत करो अधर चढ़॥
राधास्वामी सरन तू दृढ़ कर।
फिर छोड़ न कभी उमर भर॥

4 koi mantr sikhaa'o aa kar,
   lo charan ot kirpa kar.

5 main thaka chauraasi phir phir,
   ab kaise mile amar ghar.

6 tab satguru kaha daya kar,
   ab surat charrhaa'o gagan par.

7 vah ghaati hai ati arrbarr,
   man indri khainch udhar dhar.

8 tab mile shabd tohe asthir,
   tan man dhan aaj arap dhar.

9 guru preet karo chitt sam kar,
   yah aarat karo adhar charrh.

10 radhasoami saran tu drirrh kar,
   phir chhorr na kabhi umar bhar.[20]

बचन अट्ठाईसवाँ, शब्द तीसरा

मोहिं मिला सुहाग गुरू का।
मैं पाया नाम गुरू का॥
मैं सरना लिया गुरू का।
मैं किंकर हुआ गुरू का॥
मेरे मस्तक हाथ गुरू का।
मैं हुआ गुलाम गुरू का॥
मैं पाया अधार गुरू का।
मैं पकड़ा चरन गुरू का॥
मैं सरबस हुआ गुरू का।
मैं हो गया अपने गुरू का॥

Bachan 28, Shabd 3

1 mohen mila suhaag guru ka,
   main paaya naam guru ka.

2 main sarna liya guru ka,
   main kinkar hua guru ka.

3 mere mastak haath guru ka,
   main hua gulaam guru ka.

4 main paaya adhaar guru ka,
   main pakrra charan guru ka.

5 main sarbas hua guru ka,
   main ho gaya apne guru ka.

Come and teach me some mantra   4
    and kindly take me under your protection.

I am exhausted by my wanderings   5
    in the cycle of eighty-four* –
    how can I return to my eternal home now?

In his mercy the Master then said: 6–7
    raise your consciousness to the sky within –
    the valley is formidable.

Withdraw your attention from the mind and senses
    and concentrate it there.

Surrender your mind, body and worldly possessions –   8
    only then will you find the eternal Shabd.

Love the Master with a steady mind;   9
    rise to the higher regions within and venerate him.

Take firm refuge in Radha Soami   10
    for the rest of your life, without giving up your resolve.

Bachan 28, Shabd 3

I have been blessed with divine union with the Master   1
    and have obtained Nam from him.

I have taken refuge in the Master   2
    and have become his slave.

The Master has placed his protective hand on my head   3
    and I have become his servant.

The Master has become my mainstay;   4
    I firmly hold on to his feet.

I belong to the Master completely –   5
    I have become totally his.

---

* The **cycle of eighty-four** is the cycle of 8,400,000 life forms into which souls keep reincarnating.

कोइ और न मुझसा गुरु का।
गुरु का मैं गुरु का गुरु का॥
राधास्वामी नाम यह धुर का।
मैं पाया धाम उधर का॥

6 koi aur na mujh sa guru ka,
guru ka main guru ka guru ka.

7 radhasoami naam yah dhur ka,
main paaya dhaam udhar ka.[21]

बचन तेंतीसवा, शब्द छठवाँ

Bachan 33, Shabd 6

नाम दान अब सतगुरु दीजे।
काल सतावे स्वाँसा छीजे॥

1 naam daan ab satguru deeje,
kaal sataave svaansa chheeje.

दुख पावत मैं निस दिन भारी।
गही आय अब ओट तुम्हारी॥

2 dukh paavat main nis din bhaari,
gahi aaye ab ot tumhaari.

तुम समान कोइ और न दाता।
मैं बालक तुम पित और माता॥

3 tum samaan koi aur na daata,
main baalak tum pit aur maata.

मो को दुखी आप कस देखो।
यह अचरज मोहिं होत परेखो॥

4 mo ko dukhi aap kas dekho,
yah achraj mohen hot parekho.

मैं हूं पापी अधम विकारी।
भूला चूका छिन छिन भारी॥

5 main hoon paapi adham vikaari,
bhoola chooka chhin chhin bhaari.

अवगुन अपने कहँ लग बरनूँ।
मेरी बुधि समझे नहिं मरमूँ॥

6 avgun apne kahan lag barnu,
meri budhi samjhe nahin marmu.

तुम्हरी गति मति नेक न जानूँ।
अपनी मति अनुसार बखानूं॥

7 tumhri gati mati nek na jaanoon,
apni mati anusaar bakhaanu.

तुम समरथ और अंतरजामी।
क्या क्या कहूं मैं सतगुरु स्वामी॥

8 tum samrath aur antarjaami,
kya kya kahoon main satguru swaami.

मौज करो दुख अंतर हरो।
दयादृष्टि अब मो पै धरो॥

9 mauj karo dukh antar haro,
daya-drishti ab mo pai dharo.

माँगूँ नाम न माँगूँ मान।
जस जानो तस देओ मोहिं दान॥

10 maangoon naam na maangoon maan,
jas jaano tas de'o mohen daan.

मैं अति दीन भिखारी भूखा।
प्रेम भाव नहिं सब बिधि रूखा॥

11 main ati deen bhikhaari bhookha,
prem bhaav nahin sab bidhi rookha.

There is no one else like my Master –   6
   I am his, only his, absolutely his.
Radha Soami is the primal Nam,   7
   whose abode I have attained.

Bachan 33, Shabd 6

Give me the gift of Nam, O Master!   1
Kal torments me as my life-breaths dwindle.
Having suffered deeply, day and night,   2
   I have come to take refuge in you now.
There is no giver as generous as you;   3
   I am your child and you are my father and my mother.
It perplexes me to think   4
   how you can bear to see me in such pain!
I am a sinner and a degenerate –   5
   time and again I have gone astray.
How can I describe my countless shortcomings?   6
My mind fails to understand how it all happened.
I have no understanding of your power or reach;   7
   I only speak from my own frame of mind.
You are all-powerful and all-knowing –   8
   what more can I say, O Lord Satguru?
Through your gracious will,   9
   take away the anguish of my heart;
   cast your merciful glance on me now.
I beg for your Nam, not the honour of the world –   10
   grant me this gift in any way you see fit.
I am an abject wretch, a craving beggar,   11
   without love and utterly dense.

कैसे दोगे नाम अमोला।
मैं अपने को बहु बिधि तोला॥
होय निरास सबर कर बैठा।
पर मन धीरज धरे न नेका॥
शायद कभी मेहर हो जावे।
तो कहूं नाम नैक मिल जावे॥
बिना मेहर कोइ जतन न सूझे।
बख़शिश होय तभी कुछ बूझे॥
किनका नाम करे मेरा काज।
हे सतगुरु मेरी तुमको लाज॥
अब तो मन कर चुका पुकार।
राधास्वामी करो उधार॥

12 kaise doge naam amola,
    main apne ko bahu bidhi tola.

13 hoye niraas sabar kar baitha,
    par man dheeraj dhare na neka.

14 shaayad kabhi mehar ho jaave,
    to kahoon naam naik mil jaave.

15 bina mehar koi jatan na soojhe,
    bakhshish hoye tabhi kuchh boojhe.

16 kin ka naam kare mera kaaj,
    he satguru meri tumko laaj.

17 ab to man kar chuka pukaar,
    radhasoami karo udhaar.[22]

बचन सत्ताईसवाँ, शब्द चौथा

पिया बिन कैसे जिउं मैं प्यारी।
मेरा तन मन जात फुका री॥
कोइ संत मिलें अब भारी।
जो पिया को मिलावें आ री॥
मैं चढ़ूँ गगन में सारी।
दिन रात लगे मेरी तारी॥
मैं बिरहिन लगी कटारी।
मैं घायल फिरूँ उजाड़ी॥
सतगुरु अब करें सम्हारी।
तब हिरदे घाव पुरा री॥
मोहिं नाम देहिं निज सारी।
यह मरहम नित्त लगा री॥
राधास्वामी करें दवा री।
मैं उन पै जाउं बलिहारी॥

Bachan 27, Shabd 4

1 piya bin kaise jeeyun main pyaari,
   mera tan man jaat phuka ri.

2 koi sant milen ab bhaari,
   jo piya ko milaaven aa ri.

3 main charrhoon gagan mein saari,
   din raat lage meri taari.

4 main birhin lagi kataari,
   main ghaayal phiroon ujaarri.

5 satguru ab karen samhaari,
   tab hirde ghaav pura ri.

6 mohen naam dehen nij saari,
   yah marham nitt laga ri.

7 radhasoami karen dava ri,
   main un pai jaa'oon balihaari.[23]

Having keenly assessed myself, I wonder how you can   *12*
  possibly bless me with your invaluable Nam.

Weary and despairing, I am now resigned to my lot,   *13–14*
  but my mind is not at peace –
  I still hope that grace may descend one day
  and I may somehow receive Nam.

Without grace there is no recourse;   *15*
  understanding dawns only with grace.

O Master, you are the protector of my honour –   *16*
  only a particle of your Nam
  will fulfil the purpose of my life.

With this I now conclude my supplication: *17*
  Deliver me, O Radha Soami!

Bachan 27, Shabd 4

O dear one, my body and mind are being consumed by fire –   *1*
  how can I live without my Beloved?

O how I wish I could meet a great Saint   *2*
  who would come and unite me with my Beloved!

I would soar to the skies within   *3*
  and remain absorbed day and night.

I am pierced by the dagger of separation –   *4*
  wounded, I wander in desolation.

If only the Satguru would take me under his care   *5*
  and heal my wounded heart!

If he would bestow the gift of the true Nam on me   *6*
  I would apply that balm daily.

I sacrifice myself to him – may Radha Soami cure me!   *7*

बचन सातवाँ, शब्द दूसरा

रोम रोम मेरे तुम आधार।
रग रग मेरी करत पुकार॥

अंग अंग मेरा करे गुहार।
बन्द बन्द से करूं जुहार॥

हे राधास्वामी अधम उधार।
मैं किंकर तुम दीन दयार॥

इन्द्री मन मेरे भरे विकार।
तन भी बंधा जगत की लार॥

मैं सब विधि बहता भौ धार।
तुमही पार उतारनहार॥

हे राधास्वामी सुख भंडार।
मैं अति दीन फंसा संसार॥

काढ़ि निकारो मोहिं दातार।
दात तुम्हारी अगम अपार॥

दया सिन्ध जीवन आधार।
तुम बिन कोइ न सम्हारनहार॥

हे राधास्वामी सरन तुम्हार।
गही आन मैं नीच नकार॥

सदा रहूँ तुम चरन अधार।
कभी न बिछड़ूँ यही पुकार॥

निस दिन राखूं हिये सम्हार।
चरन तुम्हार मोर आधार॥

हे राधास्वामी अपर अपार।
मोहिं दिखाओ निज दरबार॥

मम करनी कहिं करो विचार।
तो मैं ठहरन जोग न द्वार॥

तुम गंभीर धीर जग पार।
मैं डूबत हूँ भौजल वार॥

Bachan 7, Shabd 2

1 rom rom mere tum aadhaar,
   rag rag meri karat pukaar.

2 ang ang mera kare guhaar,
   band band se karoon juhaar.

3 he radhasoami adham adhaar,
   main kinkar tum deen dayaar.

4 indri man mere bhare vikaar,
   tan bhi bandha jagat ki laar.

5 main sab vidhi bahta bhau dhaar,
   tumhi paar utaaran-haar.

6 he radhasoami sukh bhandaar,
   main ati deen phansa sansaar.

7 kaarrh nikaaro mohen daataar,
   daat tumhaari agam apaar.

8 daya sindh jeevan aadhaar,
   tum bin koi na samhaaran-haar.

9 he radhasoami saran tumhaar,
   gahi aan main neech nakaar.

10 sada rahoon tum charan adhaar,
   kabhi na bichhrroon yahi pukaar.

11 nis din raakhoon hiye samhaar,
   charan tumhaar mor aadhaar.

12 he radhasoami apar apaar,
   mohen dikhaa'o nij darbaar.

13 mam karni kahin karo vichaar,
   to main thahran jog na dvaar.

14 tum gambheer dheer jag paar,
   main doobat hoon bhaujal vaar.

Bachan 7, Shabd 2

Every vein of my body proclaims   1
   that you sustain its every particle.

Every part of my body cries out to you;   2
   every bit meditates on you.

O Radha Soami, redeemer of the fallen,   3
   I am your slave and you are the benefactor of the meek.

My mind and senses are steeped in vice   4
   and my body is bound by the strings of the world.

I am hopelessly adrift in the currents of life –   5
   only you can ferry me across.

O Radha Soami, I am a miserable wretch   6
   entangled in the world.

Liberate me, O benevolent giver –   7
   unfathomable and boundless are your bounties.

An ocean of mercy, you support all life;   8
   besides you there is no other sustainer.

I am lowly and worthless –   9
   O Radha Soami, I have come to you for refuge.

May your feet always be my mainstay   10
   and may I never be separated from you –
   this is my sole entreaty.

May I cherish you in my heart day and night   11
   and make your feet my only anchor.

O Radha Soami, incomparable and infinite,   12
   please reveal your true court to me.

If you were to look at my deeds, you would find that   13
   I am not even worthy of standing at your door.

You are profound, serene and beyond this world;   14
   I am drowning in this ocean of existence.

हे राधास्वामी लगाओ किनार।
तुम खेवटिया सबसे न्यार॥

चोर चुग़ल बरतू अहंकार।
कपट कुटिलता बड़ा लबार॥

काम क्रोध और मोह पियार।
क्या क्या बरनूं भरा विकार॥

हे राधास्वामी छिमा सम्हार।
लीजे मुझ को अभी उबार॥

तुम महिमा का वार न पार।
शेष गनेश रहे सब हार॥

माया ब्रह्म नहीं औतार।
कर न सके बहे काली धार॥

हे राधास्वामी सब के पार।
इन सब के तुम्हीं आधार॥

मैं तुम चरन जाऊं बलिहार।
देख न सकूं रूप उजियार॥

तेज पुंज तुम अगम अपार।
चाँद सूर की जहाँ न शुमार॥

हे राधास्वामी तुम दीदार।
बिना मेहर को करे अधार॥

राधास्वामी राधास्वामी
नाम तुम्हार।
यही मेरा कुल और यही परिवार॥

राधास्वामी राधास्वामी
बारम्बार।
कहत रहूँ और रहूँ हुशियार॥

हे राधास्वामी मर्म तुम्हार।
तुम्हरी दया से पाऊं सार॥

15 he radhasoami lagaa'o kinaar,
   tum khevatiya sabse nyaar.

16 chor chugal bartu ahankaar,
   kapat kutilta barra labaar.

17 kaam krodh aur moh pyaar,
   kya kya barnu bhara vikaar.

18 he radhasoami chhima samhaar,
   leeje mujh ko abhi ubaar.

19 tum mahima ka vaar na paar,
   shesh ganesh rahe sab haar.

20 maaya brahm nahi autaar,
   kar na sake bahe kaali dhaar4.

21 he radhasoami sab ke paar,
   in sab ke tumhi aadhaar.

22 main tum charan jaa'oon balihaar,
   dekh na sakoon roop ujiyaar.

23 tej punj tum agam apaar,
   chaand soor ki jahaan na shumaar.

24 he radhasoami tum deedaar,
   bina mehar ko kare adhaar.

25 radhasoami radhasoami
   naam tumhaar,
   yahi mera kul aur yahi parivaar.

26 radhasoami radhasoami
   baarambaar,
   kahat rahoon aur rahun hushiyaar.

27 he radhasoami marm tumhaar,
   tumhri daya se paa'oon saar.

---

* In Hindu mythology **Shesh** is the king of all serpents. **Ganesh**, the Hindu deity of wisdom with the head of an elephant, is known as the remover of obstacles.

O Radha Soami, please take me to the other shore –   15
    you are the most unique boatman.

I am a thief, a gossip and a great liar; I behave egoistically   16
    and am full of deceit and guile.

I am engrossed in lust, anger, attachment and desire   17
    and am totally steeped in vice – what else can I say?

O Radha Soami, please grant me forgiveness   18
    and liberate me now.

Boundless is your grandeur –   19
    even Shesh and Ganesh fail to fathom it.[*]

Even Maya, Brahm and their incarnations cannot realize you;[†]   20
    all are adrift in the currents of Kal.

O Radha Soami, the One beyond all,   21
    you alone are their support.

I sacrifice everything unto your feet   22
    but am unable to behold your Radiant Form.

Fountainhead of radiance, you are inaccessible and boundless;   23
    the sun and moon are insignificant in comparison.

O Radha Soami, without your grace   24
    who can behold you and obtain refuge in you?

Radha Soami, Radha Soami!   25–26
    Your Nam is my clan and family –
    again and again I say it,
    remaining attentive I repeat it continuously.

O Radha Soami, by your grace I attain   27
    the essence of your mystery.

[†] **Maya** is the goddess of illusion. **Brahm** is the ruler of the three worlds (physical, astral and causal).

गुरु स्वरूप धर लिया औतार।
जीव उबारन आये संसार॥
नर स्वरूप धर किया उपकार।
तुम सतगुरु मेरे परम उदार॥
हे राधास्वामी शब्द दुवार।
खोल दिया तुम बज्र किवाड़॥
लीला तुम्हरी अजब बहार।
कह न सके कोइ वार न पार॥
जिसे दिखाओ सो देखनहार।
तुम बिन कोई न परखनहार॥
हे राधास्वामी गुरू हमार।
तुम बिन कौन करे निरवार॥

28 guru swaroop dhar liya autaar,
   jeev ubaaran aaye sansaar.
29 nar svaroop dhar keeya upkaar,
   tum satguru mere param udaar.
30 he radhasoami shabd duvaar,
   khol diya tum bajr kivaarr.
31 leela tumhri ajab bahaar,
   kah na sake koi vaar na paar.
32 jise dikhaa'o so dekhan-haar,
   tum bin koi na parkhan-haar.
33 he radhasoami guru hamaar,
   tum bin kaun kare nirvaar.[24]

बचन तेंतीसवाँ, शब्द नौवाँ

सतगुरु मेरी सुनो पुकार।
मैं टेरत बारम्बार॥
दुरमत मेरी दूर निकारो।
मुझे कर लो चरन अधारो॥
मोहिं भौजल पार उतारो।
मेरी पड़ी नाव मँझधारो॥
तुम बिन अब कोइ न सहारो।
अपना कर मुझे सम्हारो॥
मैं कपटी कुटिल तुम्हारो।
तुम दाता अपर अपारो॥
मैं दीन दुखी अति भारो।
जब चाहो तब निस्तारो॥

Bachan 33, Shabd 9

1 satguru meri suno pukaar,
   main terat baarambaar.
2 durmat meri door nikaaro,
   mujhe kar lo charan adhaaro.
3 mohe bhaujal paar utaaro,
   meri parri naav manjhdhaaro.
4 tum bin ab koi na sahaaro,
   apna kar mujhe samhaaro.
5 main kapti kutil tumhaaro,
   tum daata apar apaaro.
6 main deen dukhi ati bhaaro,
   jab chaaho tab nistaaro.

Incarnating as the Guru,   28
   you have come into this world to redeem souls.
Assuming human form,   29
   you have bestowed great kindness –
   O Satguru, you are supremely benevolent to me.
O Radha Soami, by your Shabd   30
   you have opened the rock-hard door.*
Wondrous are your ways –   31
   no one can fathom them.
Those whom you show – only they can see;   32
   other than you, no one decides.
O Radha Soami, my Master –   33
   except you, who can grant me emancipation?

Bachan 33, Shabd 9

O Satguru, please listen to my plea –   1
   I beseech you again and again.
Rid me of my evil thinking;   2
   make your feet the mainstay of my life.
My boat is caught in the currents –   3
   ferry me across the ocean of existence.
Besides you, I have no other support;   4
   accept me and take me under your care.
I am your insincere and deceitful disciple,   5
   but you are the unmatched benefactor.
I am utterly wretched and lowly –   6
   please liberate me whenever you wish.

---

* The **rock-hard door** refers to the tenth door or the eye centre. This door is difficult to open, but the Master imparts the wisdom of how to access the inner regions through it.

मैं आरत करूँ तुम्हारी।
तन मन धन तुम पर वारी॥
अब मिला सहारा भारी।
मैं नीच अजान अनाड़ी॥
घट भेद नाद समझाया।
मन बैरी स्वाद न पाया॥
दुख सुख में बहु भरमाया।
जग मान बड़ाई चाहा॥
उलटूँ मैं इसको क्यों कर।
बिन दया तुम्हारी सतगुरु॥
अब खैंचो राधास्वामी मन को।
मैं विनय सुनाऊं तुमको॥

7   *main aarat karoon tumhaari,*
tan man dhan tum par vaari.

8   *ab mila sahaara bhaari,*
main neech ajaan anaarri.

9   *ghat bhed naad samjhaaya,*
man bairi svaad na paaya.

10   *dukh sukh mein bahu bharmaaya,*
jag maan barraa'i chaaha.

11   *ultoon main isko kyon kar,*
bin daya tumhaari satguru.

12   *ab khaincho radhasoami man ko,*
main vinay sunaa'oon tum ko.[25]

बचन तेंतीसवाँ, शब्द बाईसवाँ

Bachan 33, Shabd 22

सोचत रही री बेचैन,
रैन दिन बहु पछतानी।
मेरी लगी न प्रीत संग शब्द,
कहन मेरी सभी कहानी॥
झुरत रहूं मन माहिं,
कौन से करूँ बखानी।
सुननहार नहिं सुने,
कहो मेरी कहा बसानी॥
मौज बिना क्या होय,
मौज की सार न जानी।
सबर न आवे चित्त,
दर्द में रैन बिहानी॥
दिवस करूँ फ़र्याद,
गुरू मेरे अन्तरजामी।

1   *sochat rahi ri bechain,*
rain din bahu pachhtaani.

2   *meri lagi na preet sang shabd,*
kahan meri sabhi kahaani.

3   *jhurat rahoon man maahin,*
kaun se karoon bakhaani.

4   *sunan-haar nahin sune,*
kaho meri kaha basaani.

5   *mauj bina kya hoye,*
mauj ki saar na jaani.

6   *sabar na aave chitt,*
dard mein rain bihaani.

7   *divas karoon faryaad,*
guru mere antarjaami.

I am lowly, ignorant and foolish,   *7–8*
   yet I have found the greatest support.
I venerate you and sacrifice
   my body, mind and wealth unto you.
You explained the secret of the inner Sound,   *9*
   but my hostile mind does not savour it.
It keeps me deluded in pain and pleasure;   *10*
   I desire worldly name and fame.
O Satguru, how can I reverse its course   *11*
   without your grace?
Listen to my humble plea, O Radha Soami –   *12*
   rein in my mind now.

Bachan 33, Shabd 22

I am restless; my mind is in turmoil   *1*
   and intense remorse consumes me day and night.
I have not cultivated love for Shabd   *2*
   and now everyone is speaking of my plight.
I keep lamenting within myself –   *3*
   to whom shall I tell the tale of my woe?
When the Listener does not listen to me,   *4*
   pray tell me, what control do I have?
I do not understand the mystery of his will,   *5*
   but what can happen without it?
My mind is impatient;   *6*
   my nights pass in anguish.
My days are spent imploring   *7*
   my all-knowing Guru.

अपनी चूक विचार,
रहूं मैं अति घबरानी ॥

दीना नाथ दयाल,
सुनो जल्दी मेरी बानी ।

चरन पकड़ हठ करूँ,
मेहर कर देवो दानी ॥

मैं तो अजान अभाग,
कुटिल मोहिं सब जग जानी ।

जो अपना कर लिया,
लाज अब तुम्हें समानी ॥

राधास्वामी कह रहे,
यह अचरज बानी ।

सौदा पूरा मिले,
होय नहिं तेरी हानी ॥

8   *apni chook vichaar,*
     rahoon main ati ghabraani.

9   *deena naath dayaal,*
     suno jaldi meri baani.

10   *charan pakarr hath karoon,*
     mehar kar devo daani.

11   *main to ajaan abhaag,*
     kutil mohen sab jag jaani.

12   *jo apna kar liya,*
     laaj ab tumhen samaani.

13   *radhasoami kah rahe,*
     yah achraj baani.

14   *sauda poora mile,*
     hoye nahin teri haani.[26]

बचन तेंतीसवाँ, शब्द दसवाँ   Bachan 33, Shabd 10

तुम धुर से चल कर आये ।
अब क्यों ऐसी ढील लगाये ॥

जल्दी से काज सँवारो ।
तुम दाता देर न धारो ॥

मैं आतुर तुम्हें पुकारूं ।
चित में कोइ और न धारूं ॥

मेरा जीवन मूर अधारा ।
जस सीपी स्वाँत निहारा ॥

अब मुक्ता नाम जमाओ ।
मेरे जी की आस पुराओ ॥

1   *tum dhur se chal kar aaye,*
     ab kyon aisi dheel lagaaye.

2   *jaldi se kaaj sanvaaro,*
     tum daata der na dhaaro.

3   *main aatur tumhen pukaaroon,*
     chit mein koi aur na dhaaroon.

4   *mera jeevan moor adhaara,*
     jas seepi svaant nihaara.

5   *ab mukta naam jamaa'o,*
     mere ji ki aas puraa'o.

When I reflect upon my folly,   8
  I become painfully anxious!
O merciful Lord, protector of the meek,   9
  please hear my plea; do not delay!
Clinging to your feet, I insist   10
  that you please be gracious and bless me.
I am ignorant, unfortunate and deceitful –   11
  the whole world knows it.
You have accepted me,   12
  and now it is up to you to uphold my honour.
With wondrous words Radha Soami has proclaimed: 13–14
  you shall receive the full benefit of the bargain
  and shall not suffer any loss!

Bachan 33, Shabd 10

You have come all the way from your eternal home –   1
  why this delay now?
Quickly accomplish this task, O Lord –   2
  please do not hold back.
Distraught, I cry out to you;   3
  I cherish no one other than you.
Just as an oyster thirsts for the Swati raindrop,*   4
  I am thirsting for the source of my life.
Now seed the pearl of Nam in my heart   5
  and fulfil my heart's cherished desire.

---

* According to legend, when the moon passes through the Swati Constellation, very special **Swati raindrops** fall. When they fall into an oyster shell, a pearl is formed.

मन सूरत अधर चढ़ाओ।
अब के मेरी खेप निबाहो ॥

भौसागर वार न पारा।
डूबे सब उसकी धारा ॥

है मिथ्या झूठ पसारा।
धोखे को सच सा धारा ॥

सतगुरु बिन धोख न जाई।
बिन शब्द सुरत भरमाई ॥

या ते तुम सरना ताकूँ।
सोवत मैं क्यों कर जागूँ ॥

बिन मेहर जतन सब थाके।
मैं कर कर बहु बिधि त्यागे ॥

बल पौरुष मोर न चाले।
मैं पड़ी काल जंजाले ॥

बिनती अब करूँ बनाई।
तुम सतगुरु करो सहाई ॥

मैं दीन अधीन तुम्हारी।
तुम बिन अब कौन सम्हारी ॥

कुछ करो दिलासा मेरी।
भरमों की पड़ी अँधेरी ॥

परकाश करो घट भाना।
मिटे भर्म तिमिर अज्ञाना ॥

तुम तज अब किस पै जाऊँ।
मैं कह कह तुम्हें सुनाऊँ ॥

जब चाहो तब ही देना।
तुम बिन मोहि किससे लेना ॥

मैं द्वारे पड़ी तुम्हारे।
धीरज धर रहूं सम्हारे ॥

6   *man soorat adhar charrhaa'o,*
    ab ke meri khep nibaaho.

7   *bhausaagar vaar na paara,*
    doobe sab uski dhaara.

8   *hai mithya jhooth pasaara,*
    dhokhe ko sach sa dhaara.

9   *satguru bin dhokh na jaa'i,*
    bin shabd surat bharmaa'i.

10 *ya te tum sarna taakoon,*
    sovat main kyon kar jaagoon.

11 *bin mehar jatan sab thaake,*
    main kar kar bahu bidhi tyaage.

12 *bal paurush mor na chaale,*
    main parri kaal janjaale.

13 *binati ab karoon banaa'i,*
    tum satguru karo sahaa'i.

14 *main deen adheen tumhaari,*
    tum bin ab kaun samhaari.

15 *kuchh karo dilaasa meri,*
    bharmon ki parri andheri.

16 *parkaash karo ghat bhaana,*
    mite bharm timir agyaana.

17 *tum taj ab kis pai jaa'oon,*
    main kah kah tumhen sunaa'oon.

18 *jab chaaho tab hi dena,*
    tum bin mohe kis se lena.

19 *main dvaare parri tumhaare,*
    dheeraj dhar rahoon samhaare.

Raise my mind and soul to the inner regions
   and this time bring an end to my journey.   6

Everyone is drowning in the tides
   of this shoreless ocean of existence.   7

They have taken as truth what is actually illusion –
   a vast expanse of falsehood.   8

Without the Satguru, this illusion is not removed;
   without Shabd, the soul remains deluded.   9

That is why I seek refuge in you –
   how else am I to wake up from my slumber?   10

I have tried and tested numerous ways –
   without grace all efforts are in vain.   11

My power is ineffectual;
   I am ensnared in Kal's net.   12

I earnestly pray to you, O Master –
   come to my aid.   13

Helpless, I am dependent on you –
   who else will protect me?   14

Please give me solace –
   the storm of delusion is raging.   15

Let the sun rise within me;
   dispel the darkness of ignorance and illusion.   16

Again and again I plead with you –
   where would I go if I left you?   17

Give me your grace whenever you wish –
   who else would I receive it from?   18

I have fallen at your door in submission
   and shall patiently persevere.   19

मन आतुर दुख न सहारे।
उठ बारंबार पुकारे॥
मैं सरन दयाल तुम्हारी।
कर जल्दी लो निस्तारी॥
घर तुम्हरे कमी न कोई।
कहिं भाग ओछ मेरा होई॥
यह भी सब तुम्हरे हाथा।
तुम चाहो करो सनाथा॥
अब कहँ लग करूँ पुकारी।
मैं हार हार अब हारी॥
तुम दाता दीन दयाला।
राधास्वामी करो निहाला॥
मैं आरत कीन्ह अधारी।
तुम राधास्वामी सब पर भारी॥

20   *man aatur dukh na sahaare,*
      uth baarambaar pukaare.

21   *main saran dayaal tumhaari,*
      kar jaldi lo nistaari.

22   *ghar tumhre kami na koi,*
      kahin bhaag ochh mera hoi.

23   *yah bhi sab tumhre haatha,*
      tum chaaho karo sanaatha.

24   *ab kahan lag karoon pukaari,*
      main haar haar ab haari.

25   *tum daata deen dayaala,*
      radhasoami karo nihaala.

26   *main aarat keenh adhaari,*
      tum radhasoami sab par bhaari.[27]

My distraught mind can no longer endure the pain;   20
   again and again it cries out for help.
I seek your protection, O merciful Lord –   21
   make haste and deliver me.
Nothing is lacking in your house –   22
   my destiny must be wanting if I go away empty-handed.
Even this is in your hands –   23
   you can take me under your shelter if you so wish.
How much more can I entreat you?   24
I am completely defeated.
O Lord, merciful to the meek,   25
   exalt me, Radha Soami!
I am relying on this prayer,   26
   for you, Radha Soami, are the greatest of all.

Endnotes

PREFACE

1. *Philosophy of the Masters*, vol. 3, p. 130.

SANT NAMDEV JI

1. Adi Granth, p. 1196.
2. Adi Granth, p. 727.
3. Adi Granth, p. 873–874.
4. *Sant Namdev ki Hindi Padavali*, 155.
5. *Sant Namdev ki Hindi Padavali*, 51.

SANT TUKARAM JI

1. *Sri Tukaram Bavanchya Abhanganchi Gatha*, 2527.
2. *Sri Tukaram Bavanchya Abhanganchi Gatha*, 1031.
3. *Sri Tukaram Bavanchya Abhanganchi Gatha*, 2256.
4. *Sri Tukaram Bavanchya Abhanganchi Gatha*, 648.
5. *Sri Tukaram Bavanchya Abhanganchi Gatha*, 4113.
6. *Sri Tukaram Bavanchya Abhanganchi Gatha*, 1867.
7. *Sri Tukaram Bavanchya Abhanganchi Gatha*, 565.
8. *Sri Tukaram Bavanchya Abhanganchi Gatha*, 3808.

SANT KABIR JI

1. *Kabir Granthavali*, p. 69.
2. *Kabir Granthavali*, p. 156.

3. Adi Granth, p. 856.
4. *Kabir Sahib ki Shabdavali*, vol. 1. p. 6–7.
5. *Kabir Granthavali*, p. 122.
6. Adi Granth, p. 484.
7. *Kabir Sahib ki Shabdavali*, vol. 2, p. 64.
8. Adi Granth, p. 856.
9. Adi Granth, p. 337.
10. Adi Granth, p. 1106.
11. *Kabir Sahib ki Shabdavali*, vol. 2, p. 72–73.
12. *Kabir Sahib ki Shabdavali*, vol. 1, p. 12.
13. *Kabir Sahib ki Shabdavali*, vol. 1, p. 10.
14. *Kabir Granthavali*, p. 138–139.
15. *Kabir Sakhi-Sangrah*, p. 96–98.

DHANI DHARAMDAS JI

1. *Dhani Dharamdasji ki Shabdavali*, p. 19–20.
2. *Dhani Dharamdasji ki Shabdavali*, p. 17.
3. *Dhani Dharamdasji ki Shabdavali*, p. 20–21.
4. *Dhani Dharamdasji ki Shabdavali*, p. 26.
5. *Dhani Dharamdasji ki Shabdavali*, p. 18.
6. *Dhani Dharamdasji ki Shabdavali*, p. 23.
7. *Dhani Dharamdasji ki Shabdavali*, p. 10.

GURU RAVIDAS JI

1. *Sant Guru Ravidas-Vani*, 66.
2. Adi Granth, p. 1106.
3. *Sant Guru Ravidas-Vani*, 109.
4. Adi Granth, p. 694.
5. Adi Granth, p. 658–659.
6. *Raidasji ki Bani*, p. 23.
7. *Sant Guru Ravidas-Vani*, 73.
8. Adi Granth, p. 345.
9. *Sant Guru Ravidas-Vani*, 116.
10. *Sant Guru Ravidas-Vani*, 151.
11. Adi Granth, p. 486.
12. *Sant Guru Ravidas-Vani*, 93.

MIRABAI JI

1. *Mirabai ki Shabdavali*, p. 28.
2. *Miran Sudha-Sindhu*, p. 338.
3. *Miran Sudha-Sindhu*, p. 322.
4. *Mirabai ki Shabdavali*, p. 20.
5. *Miran Sudha-Sindhu*, p. 351.
6. *Mirabai ki Shabdavali*, p. 4.
7. *Miran Brihatpdavali*, vol. 1, 109.
8. *Miran Sudha-Sindhu*, p. 171.
9. *Miran Sudha-Sindhu*, p. 359.
10. *Miran Sudha-Sindhu*, p. 328.
11. *Mirabai ki Shabdavali*, p. 29.
12. *Miran Brihatpdavali*, 407.
13. *Miran Brihatpdavali*, 487.
14. *Miran Brihatpdavali*, 278.
15. *Miran Sudha-Sindhu*, p. 842.
16. *Miran Sudha-Sindhu*, p. 471.
17. *Mirabai ki Shabdavali*, p. 31.
18. *Mirabai ki Shabdavali*, p. 31.

SANT SURDAS JI

1. Belvedere Press, *Santbani Sangrah*, vol. 2, p. 55.
2. Belvedere Press, *Santbani Sangrah*, vol. 2, p. 56.
3. Belvedere Press, *Santbani Sangrah*, vol. 2, p. 58.
4. Belvedere Press, *Santbani Sangrah*, vol. 2, p. 56–57.
5. Belvedere Press, *Santbani Sangrah*, vol. 2, p. 54–55.
6. *Sur-Vinay-Patrika*, 269.
7. Belvedere Press, *Santbani Sangrah*, vol. 2, p. 54.

GOSWAMI TULSIDAS JI

1. *Vinay-Patrika*, 223.
2. *Vinay-Patrika*, 81.
3. *Vinay-Patrika*, 101.
4. *Vinay-Patrika*, 160.
5. *Vinay-Patrika*, 245.
6. *Vinay-Patrika*, 269.
7. *Vinay-Patrika*, 79.
8. *Vinay-Patrika*, 242.
9. *Vinay-Patrika*, 273.
10. *Vinay-Patrika*, 103.

SANT DADU DAYAL JI

1. Belvedere Press, *Santbani Sangrah*, vol. 2, p. 82.
2. *Dadu Dayal ki Bani*, vol. 2, 85.
3. *Dadu Dayal ki Bani*, vol. 2, 132.
4. *Dadu Dayal ki Bani*, vol. 2, 146.
5. *Dadudayal Granthavali*, p. 481.
6. *Dadu Dayal ki Bani*, vol. 2, 14.
7. *Dadu Dayal ki Bani*, vol. 2, 178.
8. *Dadu Dayal ki Bani*, vol. 1, p. 234–241.

JAGJIVAN SAHIB JI

1. *Jagjivan Sahib ki Bani*, vol. 2, p. 50.
2. *Jagjivan Sahib ki Bani*, vol. 1, p. 12.
3. *Jagjivan Sahib ki Bani*, vol. 1, p. 10–11.
4. *Jagjivan Sahib ki Bani*, vol. 1, p. 11–12.
5. *Jagjivan Sahib ki Bani*, vol. 2, p. 50.
6. *Jagjivan Sahib ki Bani*, vol. 1, p. 15.
7. *Jagjivan Sahib ki Bani*, vol. 1, p. 18.
8. *Jagjivan Sahib ki Bani*, vol. 1, p. 20.
9. *Jagjivan Sahib ki Bani*, vol. 1, p. 17.
10. *Jagjivan Sahib ki Bani*, vol. 1, p. 6.

11. *Jagjivan Sahib ki Bani*, vol. 1, p. 17–18.
12. *Jagjivan Sahib ki Bani*, vol. 1, p. 14.
13. *Jagjivan Sahib ki Bani*, vol. 1, p. 21–22.
14. *Jagjivan Sahib ki Bani*, vol. 1, p. 11.
15. *Jagjivan Sahib ki Bani*, vol. 2, p. 105.

SANT PALTU JI
1. *Paltu Sahib ki Bani*, vol. 3, 14.
2. *Paltu Sahib ki Bani*, vol. 1, 159.
3. *Paltu Sahib ki Bani*, vol. 3, 72.
4. Belvedere Press, *Santbani Sangrah*, vol. 1, p. 201.

SANT DARIYA JI OF BIHAR
1. *Dariya Granthavali*, vol. 1, p. 117.
2. Belvedere Press, *Santbani Sangrah*, vol. 2, p. 130–131.

SANT CHARANDAS JI
1. *Sri Bhakti Sagar*, p. 388–389.
2. *Charandasji ki Bani*, vol. 1, p. 13.
3. *Charandasji ki Bani*, vol. 1, p. 46.
4. Belvedere Press, *Santbani Sangrah*, vol. 2, p. 158.
5. *Charandasji ki Bani*, vol. 1, p. 45.
6. *Charandasji ki Bani*, vol. 1, p. 41.
7. *Charandasji ki Bani*, vol. 1, p. 43.
8. *Charandasji ki Bani*, vol. 1, p. 45.
9. *Charandasji ki Bani*, vol. 1, p. 44.

SAHJOBAI JI
1. *Sahjobai ki Bani*, p. 57.
2. *Sahjobai ki Bani*, p. 48.
3. *Sahjobai ki Bani*, p. 56–57.

MALUKDAS JI
1. *Malukdasji ki Bani*, p. 23–24.
2. *Malukdasji ki Bani*, p. 2.

DHARNIDAS JI
1. *Dharnidasji ki Bani*, p. 21.
2. *Dharnidasji ki Bani*, p. 16.
3. *Dharnidasji ki Bani*, p. 16.
4. *Dharnidasji ki Bani*, p. 24–25.
5. *Dharnidasji ki Bani*, p. 23.
6. *Dharnidasji ki Bani*, p. 45.

GARIBDAS JI
1. Belvedere Press, *Santbani Sangrah*, vol. 2, p. 171–172.

SHEIKH FARID JI
1. Adi Granth, p. 1378–1384.

SAIN BULLEH SHAH
1. *Sain Bulleh Shah*, p. 222.
2. *Sain Bulleh Shah*, p. 219.
3. *Sain Bulleh Shah*, p. 220.
4. *Sain Bulleh Shah*, p. 29.
5. *Kulliyat Bulleh Shah*, 80.
6. *Sain Bulleh Shah*, p. 287.
7. *Sain Bulleh Shah*, p. 291.
8. *Sain Bulleh Shah*, p. 277.
9. *Sain Bulleh Shah*, p. 229.
10. *Sain Bulleh Shah*, p. 257.
11. *Sain Bulleh Shah*, p. 300.
12. *Sain Bulleh Shah*, p. 303.
13. *Sain Bulleh Shah*, p. 30.
14. *Sain Bulleh Shah*, p. 31.
15. *Sain Bulleh Shah*, p. 325.
16. *Sain Bulleh Shah*, p. 275.

HAZRAT SULTAN BAHU
1. *Hazrat Sultan Bahu*, 70.
2. *Hazrat Sultan Bahu*, 71.
3. *Hazrat Sultan Bahu*, 11.
4. *Hazrat Sultan Bahu*, 134.
5. *Hazrat Sultan Bahu*, 173.
6. *Hazrat Sultan Bahu*, 186.
7. *Hazrat Sultan Bahu*, 106.
8. *Hazrat Sultan Bahu*, 107.

GURU NANAK DEV JI
1. Adi Granth, p. 750.
2. Adi Granth, p. 790.
3. Adi Granth, p. 25.

GURU AMAR DAS JI
1. Adi Granth, p. 1284.
2. Adi Granth, p. 666.
3. Adi Granth, p. 853.
4. Adi Granth, p. 1333–1334.
5. Adi Granth, p. 244–245.
6. Adi Granth, p. 917.

GURU RAM DAS JI
1. Adi Granth, p. 527–528.
2. Adi Granth, p. 667–668.
3. Adi Granth, p. 450.
4. Adi Granth, p. 799.
5. Adi Granth, p. 799.
6. Adi Granth, p. 861–862.
7. Adi Granth, p. 171–172.
8. Adi Granth, p. 10.
9. Adi Granth, p. 757–758.
10. Adi Granth, p. 1321.
11. Adi Granth, p. 310.
12. Adi Granth, p. 527.
13. Adi Granth, p. 735.
14. Adi Granth, p. 169–170.

GURU ARJUN DEV JI
1. Adi Granth, p. 828.
2. Adi Granth, p. 828.
3. Adi Granth, p. 533.
4. Adi Granth, p. 829.
5. Adi Granth, p. 389.
6. Adi Granth, p. 742.
7. Adi Granth, p. 704.
8. Adi Granth, p. 218.
9. Adi Granth, p. 675.
10. Adi Granth, p. 613.
11. Adi Granth, p. 1120.
12. Adi Granth, p. 761.
13. Adi Granth, p. 749–750.
14. Adi Granth, p. 780.
15. Adi Granth, p. 204.
16. Adi Granth, p. 882–883.
17. Adi Granth, p. 701–702.
18. Adi Granth, p. 1301.
19. Adi Granth, p. 738.

20. Adi Granth, p. 713.
21. Adi Granth, p. 396.
22. Adi Granth, p. 802.
23. Adi Granth, p. 724.
24. Adi Granth, p. 96.
25. Adi Granth, p. 673.
26. Adi Granth, p. 749.
27. Adi Granth, p. 1220.
28. Adi Granth, p. 820.
29. Adi Granth, p. 716.
30. Adi Granth, p. 809.
31. Adi Granth, p. 205–206.
32. Adi Granth, p. 99–100.
33. Adi Granth, p. 713.
34. Adi Granth, p. 746.
35. Adi Granth, p. 801–802.
36. Adi Granth, p. 547.
37. Adi Granth, p. 714–715.
38. Adi Granth, p. 810–811.
39. Adi Granth, p. 893.
40. Adi Granth, p. 1218.
41. Adi Granth, p. 739.
42. Adi Granth, p. 103.
43. Adi Granth, p. 193.
44. Adi Granth, p. 662–663.
45. Adi Granth, p. 1144.
46. Adi Granth, p. 389.
47. Adi Granth, p. 547.
48. Adi Granth, p. 268.
49. Adi Granth, p. 749.
50. Adi Granth, p. 206–207.
51. Adi Granth, p. 673–674.
52. Adi Granth, p. 563.

GURU TEGH BAHADUR JI
1. Adi Granth, p. 685.
2. Adi Granth, p. 411.
3. Adi Granth, p. 1231.
4. Adi Granth, p. 703.
5. Adi Granth, p. 1008.
6. Adi Granth, p. 632.
7. Adi Granth, p. 1008.
8. Adi Granth, p. 632–633.
9. Adi Granth, p. 902.

GURU GOBIND SINGH JI

1. *Sri Dasam Granth Sahib*, vol. 2, p. 672.

TULSI SAHIB JI

1. *Tulsi Sahib ki Shabdavali*, vol. 1, p. 40.
2. *Ghat Ramayan*, vol. 2, p. 119.
3. *Tulsi Sahib ki Shabdavali*, vol. 2, p. 107.
4. *Tulsi Sahib ki Shabdavali*, vol. 1, p. 40.
5. *Tulsi Sahib ki Shabdavali*, vol. 2, p. 106–107.
6. Belvedere Press, *Santbani Sangrah*, vol. 1, p. 211–212.
7. *Ghat Ramayan*, vol. 1, p. 71.

SOAMI JI MAHARAJ

1. *Sar Bachan Sangrah*, 19:21.
2. *Sar Bachan Sangrah*, 33:2.
3. *Sar Bachan Sangrah*, 31:2.
4. *Sar Bachan Sangrah*, 27:6.
5. *Sar Bachan Sangrah*, 27:2.
6. *Sar Bachan Sangrah*, 33:21.
7. *Sar Bachan Sangrah*, 33:18.
8. *Sar Bachan Sangrah*, 29:3.
9. *Sar Bachan Sangrah*, 33:15.
10. *Sar Bachan Sangrah*, 33:13.
11. *Sar Bachan Sangrah*, 19:15.
12. *Sar Bachan Sangrah*, 27:3.
13. *Sar Bachan Sangrah*, 6:7.
14. *Sar Bachan Sangrah*, 7:1.
15. *Sar Bachan Sangrah*, 15:18.
16. *Sar Bachan Sangrah*, 33:20.
17. *Sar Bachan Sangrah*, 33:11.
18. *Sar Bachan Sangrah*, 8:16.
19. *Sar Bachan Sangrah*, 31:4.
20. *Sar Bachan Sangrah*, 29:2.
21. *Sar Bachan Sangrah*, 28:3.
22. *Sar Bachan Sangrah*, 33:6.
23. *Sar Bachan Sangrah*, 27:4.
24. *Sar Bachan Sangrah*, 7:2.
25. *Sar Bachan Sangrah*, 33:9.
26. *Sar Bachan Sangrah*, 33:22.
27. *Sar Bachan Sangrah*, 33:10.

Glossary

Note that the dates of birth and death of the mystics cannot always be reliably identified, so the dates given here are often approximate.

Adi Granth   Primal (*aadi*) book or scripture (*granth*); also called the Granth Sahib; the name given to the scripture that brings together the poetry of the first five Gurus and the ninth Guru in the line of Guru Nanak, as well as numerous mystics from various parts of the Indian subcontinent. The Adi Granth, one of India's most sacred scriptures, is a mosaic of esoteric poetry by Saints from various religious, cultural, vocational and geographic backgrounds whose teachings emphasize the oneness of God, the path of the Word, the equality of all people and the pursuit of truth. The Adi Granth was compiled by Guru Arjun, the fifth Guru, and completed in 1604. The hymns of Guru Tegh Bahadur, the ninth Guru, were added by Guru Gobind Singh, the tenth Guru.

Ajamil   The story of the brahmin Ajamil is narrated in the Bhagavata Purana. Ajamil led a sinful life, but at the time of his death he piteously called out the name of his favourite son, Narayan, which is also a name of the Lord. Hearing the call, the Lord was moved with compassion and extricated him from the hands of the messengers of death. This episode is frequently referred to in devotional literature to indicate the great compassion of the supreme Lord and the power of repeating the divine Name. *See also* Nam.

Amar Das, Guru (1479–1574)   Guru Amar Das was the third Guru in the line of Guru Nanak. Born in the Punjab, he came to his Master, Guru Angad, late in life and became Guru at the age of seventy-three. He is credited with starting the institution of the langar (free community kitchen). He compiled the works of his two predecessors, to which he added his own poetic works of 907 shabds. This collection became the basis of Guru Arjun's later compilation, the Adi Granth.

ambrosial nectar   *See* nectar.

Anand   Peace or bliss; a state of inner poise and equanimity in which one is freed from all suffering. Anand is also the name of a composition of Guru Amar Das in which he says that eternal bliss will only be found when we repeat the sacred Nam and listen to the purifying Shabd under the direction of a true Guru.

Arjun, Guru (1563–1606)   Guru Arjun Dev was the son of Guru Ram Das, the fourth Guru in the line of Guru Nanak, and became the fifth Guru in that line. Born in Goindwal, Punjab, he became Guru at the age of eighteen and designed and supervised the building of the Golden Temple in Amritsar. Guru Arjun Dev collected, classified, compiled and edited the writings of the first four Gurus as well as over two thousand of his own hymns along with those of other mystics from all over the Indian subcontinent for the Adi Granth.

astpadi   A canto or poetic work of eight stanzas. The Adi Granth contains numerous astpadis in various ragas. For example, the Sukhmani, a composition in the Adi Granth composed by Guru Arjun Dev, consists of twenty-four astpadis, each of which has eight stanzas that follow and expand upon an introductory couplet (slok). *See also* slok.

bachan   Word or words, speech, teachings, instructions, commands, sayings. In *Sar Bachan Poetry*, Soami Ji's shabds are arranged into forty-two sections called bachans. Mystically, bachan also refers to the Word, Nam or Shabd.

Bahu, Hazrat Sultan (1629–1691)   Hazrat Sultan Bahu, a disciple of Shah Abdul Qadir Jilani, was one of the great Sufi Saints of India. He was not formally educated, but is said to have written more than a hundred works in Persian and Arabic. However, it is his poems in the Punjabi language that live on and remain popular among the people of the Punjab. Hazrat and Sultan are honorifics – Sultan is an Islamic title of authority which conveys Bahu's spiritual strength, power and nobility, while Hazrat is a term of veneration used for Muslim religious leaders and other socially and spiritually exalted persons.

bani   Sound, utterance, hymns; holy texts or devotional compositions by Saints; also may refer to Nam or Shabd.

bhakti   Devotion, worship, adoration; a spiritual discipline undertaken to please God, a deity or other revered being. Guru bhakti is devotion to the Guru – following a path of spiritual discipline in accordance with the Guru's instructions.

Bhanwar Gupha   *See* inner regions.

Brahm   The ruler of the three realms (*triloki*) – the physical, astral and causal worlds; the universal mind. Saints explain that whatever is subject to change and death falls within the realm of Brahm. The seat of Brahm is Trikuti, which is also the home of the mind and the seedbank of all karma. Brahm is also sometimes used as the name of the supreme Lord. *See also* karma, three realms.

Brahma   The god of creation in the Hindu triad of Brahma the creator, Vishnu the sustainer and Shiva the destroyer. *See also* Vishnu, Shiva.

Bulleh Shah, Sain (1680–1758)   Born into an aristocratic Muslim family, Bulleh Shah grew up in Kasur, near Lahore, where he was educated in Arabic and Persian. He received spiritual light from Shah Inayat Qadiri of Lahore and incurred severe disapproval from his family and community for becoming a disciple of this simple low-born gardener. Bulleh Shah attained fame for his songs containing deep esoteric truths, many of which are still recited and sung in India and Pakistan. He is called Sain as a sign of respect.

castor plant   A weed that seeds itself and grows rampantly in most conditions.

Charandas (1703–1782)   Sant Charandas was born at Dehra, a village in Mewar, Rajasthan. Originally known as Ranjita, he was given the name Shyam Charandas by Sukdev Ji, his Guru, but he commonly referred to himself as Charandas, which is how he is known today. From early childhood Charandas displayed a spiritual bent, and at the age of nineteen he became a disciple of Sukdev Ji. He meditated for twelve years with great dedication and then began expounding spiritual teachings. He spent the later part of his long life in Delhi. Many of his writings are collected in *Bhaktisagar*, which includes poems as well as stories.

chaupada   A poem with four verses generally consisting of two verses of thirty-two syllables (*matras*) each and containing one or two pauses in each verse.

chhant   Literally, song of praise. This is the name given to a certain type of composition of unique rhythmic style. It is often a long hymn composed of two, four or six verses.

cycle of birth and death/eighty-four/transmigration   The endless round of incarnation and reincarnation in various forms of life which the soul has to undergo due to the consequences of performing actions. The soul moves from one of the 8,400,000 life forms to another, reaping the harvest of seeds it has sown in previous lives. *See also* karma, transmigration.

Dadu (1544–1603)   Born into a family of cotton carders in Ahmedabad in the state of Gujarat, Dadu was only eleven when he was initiated by Sri Vriddhananda. At the age of nineteen, following the command of his Master, he started teaching the practice of Nam in Jaipur and other parts of Rajasthan, accepting both Muslims and Hindus as disciples, but insisting on vegetarianism and abstention from alcohol. He came to be known as Dadu Dayal, Dadu the Merciful, for his compassionate nature. He wrote more than five thousand verses, hymns and aphorisms in Hindi on spiritual and philosophical themes, all characterized by their forthright language, often challenging the orthodox views of the day.

Dariya of Bihar (1674–1780)   Dariya Sahib was born at Dharkanda in district Rohtas, Bihar. His father was born a Hindu but converted to Islam to protect his brothers. Dariya Sahib himself attached no importance to religious and caste distinctions; he openly declared that Saints have no caste or religion and accepted disciples regardless of religion or caste. At a very early age he began to show signs of detachment from the world. His writings disclose that he had received enlightenment by the age of twenty and by the age of thirty he started initiating people into the spiritual path. His well-known works are *Dariya Sagar* and *Gyan Dipak*.

darshan   Sight, vision, seeing, having a glimpse of someone; looking at someone or something with admiration, love and reverence; looking at the Master or an image of a deity with such absorption that one forgets everything else, even his own body, and loses the sense of his separate existence, merging into oneness with the object of darshan. The mystics generally use the term for inner darshan of the radiant form of the Master. This darshan elevates the soul to spheres of higher consciousness and is attained through a process of deep inner contemplation. *See also* radiant form.

Daswan Dwar   *See* inner regions.

Dharamdas, Dhani (1420–1532)   A rich merchant and banker at Band-hogarh in Uttar Pradesh, Dhani Dharamdas showed a devotional bent of mind from early childhood. He believed in traditional rites, rituals and idol worship until he met Kabir, who initiated him into the practice of the Word. As he was one of the successors of Kabir, he also taught the doctrine of the Word. Some of his poems are printed under the title *Dhani Dharamdasji ki Shabdavali*. Dhani is an honorific meaning one who is wealthy and generous.

Dharmrai   The lord (*rai*) of justice (*dharma*); the dispenser of justice. Also called Kal or Yama. Dharmrai dispenses justice according to the karmic law or dharma, administering reward or punishment after death according to the karma of the individual. Based on its karmic account, the soul is sent to a heaven or a hell, or reborn in a different form which is best suited to clear its karmic obligations. A soul initiated by a perfect Master is not under the jurisdiction of Dharmrai, because the Master himself administers the karma of his disciples, tempering justice with mercy. *See also* Kal, Yama.

Dharnidas (born 1616)   Sant Dharnidas was a poet-Saint born in Manjhi, Bihar, who practised the path of Shabd. He composed *Prem Prakash* and *Satya Prakash*, giving mystic teachings and praising the emi-nence of Saints in Bhojpuri, a Bihari language spoken in Bihar and Uttar Pradesh.

Dhruva   Dhruva was the son of the mythological king Uttanapada. As a child he was pushed away by his stepmother Suruchi when he attempted to share his father's lap with her son Uttam. Dhruva's mother advised him that he had no chance to succeed to the throne because the king's deep affection for Suruchi assured that Uttam would be the heir apparent. Dhruva vowed that he would seek no honour other than that which his own actions would bring him. He left home to take up the path of devotion to God. It is said that he was initiated into the path of devotion by Narad, one of the seven legendary sages and a devoted disciple of Vishnu. Dhruva applied himself to bhakti so assiduously that Vishnu, pleased with his steadfast devotion, appeared to him and raised him to the heavens as the pole star (known in India as the Dhruva star), the symbol of stability, determination, unwavering faith and commitment. *See also* bhakti, Narad.

divine nectar   *See* nectar.

doha   Poetry written in the form of couplets in which each line is a sentence, the meaning of which is complete in itself.

dupada   A hymn with a measure of two verses.

dust of the feet   In the bhakti tradition, bathing in the dust of the Guru's or Saint's feet, or applying the dust of the Guru's feet to one's forehead is deemed to be an act of deep reverence and an expression of humility and submission. Esoterically, the dust of the Guru's feet does not refer to physical dust, but represents the misty radiance emanating from his inner feet, also called the lotus feet, which the devotee experiences on a spiritual plane within and which brings light to inner darkness. The term also may be used to denote humility in general, as in 'becoming the dust of the feet of all'. *See also* feet of the Master, lotus feet.

Dwaparyuga   *See* yugas.

eight supernatural powers   In Hinduism the eight supernatural powers (*ashta siddhi*) are: reducing one's body to the size of an atom, expanding the size of one's body infinitely, becoming infinitely heavy, becoming weightless, having access to all places, realizing all of one's desires, controlling nature, and controlling others.

eye centre   *See* tenth door.

Farid, Sheikh (1173–1265)   Sheikh Farid, or Baba Farid, a Muslim Saint whose verses are preserved in the Adi Granth, was the earliest-known mystic poet who wrote in Punjabi. Born near Multan (now in Pakistan), Farid undertook rigorous self-discipline and physically punishing methods in his attempt to achieve his goal of God-realization. Eventually he was advised to go to Khwaja Qutubuddin Bakhtiar Kaki of Delhi, who revealed to him the path of God-realization.

feet of the Master   In India bowing at someone's feet or washing their feet indicates respect. Thus this expression connotes the respect and devotion that the disciple feels for the Master, as well as the shelter and protection of the Master for the disciple. To surrender at the Master's feet is an expression of humility and submission. The Master's feet are also referred to as lotus feet which, in an esoteric sense, means the radiant form of the Master as seen within at the eight-petalled lotus on the astral plane. Similarly, clinging to the feet of the Lord or laying one's heart at his feet can signify meeting the Lord, who is one with the Master within. *See also* lotus feet, radiant form.

five elements   Indian philosophy describes all life forms in terms of five vital elements (*tattwas*): earth, water, fire, air and ether. The number of active elements in any life form determines its place on the scale of evolution. In human beings all five elements are active. It is the etheric element that gives us discrimination and makes us conscious of our origin in God. Thus in a mystical sense, human beings are the highest form of life.

five enemies/passions/vices/adversaries/robbers/demons   Lust, anger, greed, attachment and pride; five modes of destructive mental action which beset human beings and provide motives for performing actions. Action, which is an expression of ego, is also the compulsion of life because no one can live without constantly performing actions, but every new action further complicates our entanglement in the karmic maze, which prevents the soul from experiencing union with the Lord. *See also* karma.

Ganges   A sacred river in India. Many places of pilgrimage are situated on the banks of this river. Bathing in the Ganges is believed by some to be spiritually purifying. In the verses of the mystics, the Ganges is sometimes used as a metaphor for purification.

Garibdas (1717–1778)   Mahatma Garibdas was born into an agricultural family in the village of Chhurani in the District of Rohtak in Haryana. He subsequently established his spiritual centre in Chhurani. Some of his poems are published under the title *Garibdas Ji ki Bani*.

Gobind Singh, Guru (1666–1708)   Guru Gobind Singh, son of Guru Tegh Bahadur, was the tenth Guru in the line of Guru Nanak. He was born in Patna, Bihar, and became a Guru when he was only nine years old. He wrote inspiring poetry in Punjabi and is known for founding the Khalsa (pure of faith) and organizing his followers into a military force. His best-known compositions are contained in the *Dasam Granth* (Book of the Tenth Master).

Goswami Tulsidas   *See* Tulsidas, Goswami.

Guru   Dispeller (*ru*) of darkness (*gu*); one who brings light into darkness; a spiritual teacher or Master; a spiritual guide who gives new birth to the soul through initiation into spiritual life. *See also* Master, Saint, Satguru.

Hazrat Sultan Bahu   *See* Bahu, Hazrat Sultan.

holy feet   *See* dust of the feet, lotus feet.

inner regions   Realms of existence or consciousness are described either as four planes – three of creation and one of spirit – or as a physical region and five inner regions above the physical realm that the soul crosses on its journey to God-realization: (1) Sahasdal Kamal – the thousand-petalled lotus or the astral region; (2) Trikuti – the 'three peaks' or the causal region; (3) Daswan Dwar – the region where the soul becomes free from mind and matter, sometimes referred to as Sunn; (4) Bhanwar Gupha – the revolving cave or the region where the soul first recognizes its identity with God, but is still separate from him; (5) Sach Khand – the realm of truth, the region of pure spirit where the soul merges into eternal oneness with the Lord, its source. *See also* three realms.

Jagjivan (1682–1750)   Jagjivan Sahib was born in Sarhada, District Barabanki, in Uttar Pradesh. He was a disciple of Bulla Sahib, who taught the path of the Word. His books include *Gyan Prakash* (Light of Knowledge), *Maha Pralaya* (Grand Dissolution), *Pratham Granth* (The First Book) and *Shabd Sagar* (Ocean of Shabd).

jauhar/jauhari   In Rajasthan, when a fort was besieged and the defenders realized that it could not be further defended, the able-bodied men and women evacuated the rest of the people and remained behind. The men armed themselves, put on saffron-coloured robes and bid farewell to their wives. The women, dressed in their wedding clothes and fine ornaments, would send off their husbands, reminding them that death in battle is preferable to defeat. Immediately after the departure of the men they would prepare a huge pyre, singing songs of love and valour, and enter it to be burnt to ashes while the men fought to the end. This was known as *jauhar*. It was believed that when husbands died defending their freedom and wives perished in *jauhar*, they would meet in heaven and live together in bliss. Rajput women looked upon such a death as a matter of great honour and glory and would mount the pyre with a fervour hard to describe or understand. When the Saints speak about *jauhar*, they are not condoning the practice, but describing the intensity of devotion that allows a devotee to accept even death rather than be parted from the Beloved.

Ji   An honorific used after a name to show respect.

Jilani, Shah Abdul Qadir (1077–1166)   Shah Abdul Qadir Jilani was one of the great Sufi Masters. He lived in Baghdad and was reverently called the Master of Masters (*piran-i-pir*), the Master who holds his disciple's hand (*pir dastgir*) and the Great Redresser of Complaints (*ghaus-ul-a'zam*). Shah Jilani was Hazrat Sultan Bahu's Master, and Bulleh Shah and his Master Inayat Shah came from the Qadiri order, which takes its name from Shah Jilani. His best-known books are *Al-fatah-al-Rabbani* (The Sublime Revelation) and *Fatuh-al-Ghaib* (Revelations of the Unseen).

Kabir (1398–1518)   Kabir Sahib, or Sant Kabir, was a Saint and poet from Varanasi (Benares) who was a contemporary of Guru Nanak and Guru Ravidas. Legends surround his birth, life and death, and both Hindus and Muslims claim him as their own. He taught that the one God can be reached through the practice of Nam and emphasized the central importance of the Guru, the reality of the law of karma and the equality of all human beings in the eyes of God. He condemned rites, rituals and all external observances. Tradition has it that Kabir appeared in earlier incarnations as Karunamay (in the Dwaparyuga or Copper Age), Munindra (in the Tretayuga or Silver Age) and Sat Sukrit (in the Satyuga or Golden Age). A selection of his poems is included in the Adi Granth, and his writings are still widely quoted in daily life throughout India, having become a part of folk music and culture.

kafi   Derived from the Arabic word *kafa*, which means a group, kafi is a classical form of Sufi poetry in which the first or the second line, or both lines together, serves as the refrain. Kafi is chanted like a song and is often used a metaphor for mystical truths and spiritual longing for God.

Kal   Time or death; the ruler of the three worlds who administers justice strictly according to the law of karma. Dependent for all power on the Supreme Being, Kal is universal mind, known also as the god of death (Yama) or Dharmrai. The domain of Kal is the whole creation up to the top of Trikuti, the second inner region, which includes the physical, astral and causal worlds. *See also* Dharmrai, karma, three realms, Yama.

Kaliyuga   *See* yugas.

karma   The law of cause and effect, of action and reaction; the fruits or result of past thoughts, words and deeds. There are three types of karma: *pralabdh* – that portion of our karma that is allotted to this life and is responsible for our present existence, also called fate or destiny; *kriyaman* – new actions performed during the present life; and *sinchit* – the balance of unpaid karmas from all our past lives, the store of karmas. *See also* cycle of birth and death.

lord of death   *See* Yama.

lotus feet   The significance of the lotus feet is greatly emphasized in the bhakti tradition, which emphasizes that devotion to the Name leads a devotee's consciousness to the Guru's or the Lord's lotus feet or radiant reality within. The Lord as well as the Guru in his true Shabd form are not physical entities. The appearance of their feet in a lotus or in the form of a lotus occurs when the disciple's attention is concentrated at the astral plane; it marks an advanced state of inner revelation, the radiant inner reality of the Guru leading to the Lord and uniting the devotee with the Divine. *See also* bhakti, dust of the feet, feet of the Master.

Malukdas   Malukdas was a seventeenth-century Saint who lived in Kara, on the right bank of the River Ganga in Uttar Pradesh. He was widely venerated and counted among his admirers and followers both Muslims and Hindus. He knew about Guru Nanak and his spiritual lineage, and when Guru Tegh Bahadur met him in 1666, Malukdas received instruction and initiation and became one of the Guru's most devoted followers.

mantra   Literally, tool for thinking; sacred word or formula; a word, phrase or sound repeated to aid concentration in meditation. *See also* simran.

Master   True spiritual teacher; a Saint, Sant or Satguru who is ordained to take certain marked souls back to God by initiating them into the path of the sound current, Surat Shabd Yoga, also known as the path of Nam. *See also* Guru, radiant form, Saint, Satguru, Surat Shabd.

maya   Illusion, delusion, unreality; the phenomenal universe. Maya denotes everything that comes and goes, that is transient. The entire creation (the physical, astral and causal worlds) is described as illusory or false because it is impermanent, in contrast to Satnam, the supreme reality that alone is permanent, eternal and true. *See also* three realms.

Mirabai (1498–1563) Mirabai Ji was a Rajput princess and devotee of Lord Krishna until she met her Guru, Ravidas, and was initiated by him. Persecuted by her family for following a cobbler Saint, Mira eventually left her home and wealth, living as a penniless wanderer. Her songs of devotion, love and longing are still popular today.

Nam In the language of the mystics, Nam, also called the Name, represents the dynamic power of God that created and sustains the universe and can unite souls with God. Nam can also refer to the initiation mantra given by a perfect Master. *See also* mantra, Shabd, simran.

Namdev (1270–1350) A tailor and calico printer by profession, Sant Namdev was initiated into the path of the Word by Visoba Khechar. Namdev was born at Narsi Bamni in the Satara District of Maharashtra and lived in Pandharpur in Maharashtra during the early years of his life. Namdev travelled extensively throughout India for about thirty-five years, giving satsangs and teaching the bhakti path. Namdev settled in the Punjab, where he spent his last twenty-five years. Namdev spoke various languages from many parts of India and wrote thousands of devotional poems in Marathi, Hindi and Punjabi. His writings are preserved in *Namdev Gatha*, and some are included in the Adi Granth.

Nanak, Guru (1469–1539) Born in Talwandi (now in Pakistan), Guru Nanak Dev travelled widely in India and nearby countries to spread the doctrine of Nam. At a time when there was no mechanized form of transport, legend says that he went as far as the south of India, Sri Lanka, Mecca in Arabia as well as Tibet and China. He endeavoured to transform the prejudices and superstitions of the people, emphasizing that ritualistic practices and external forms of worship keep the seeker of God away from the truth. He was the first Guru in the line of the ten Gurus whose teachings are recorded in the Adi Granth. He appointed his disciple, Bhai Lehna, as his successor, whom he renamed Guru Angad.

Narad Literally, wisdom (*naara*) giver (*da*). Narad is one of the seven divine sages and is revered for his devotion to Lord Vishnu. He practised bhakti yoga meditation, the path of devotion taught to him by the saintly priests he and his mother had served, in order to attain enlightenment. Vishnu appeared to Narad in his meditation and told Narad he would not see Vishnu's divine form again until death, that he had been given this one vision in order to inspire others and fuel his desire to see Vishnu again. Thereafter Narad was focused on meditation and devotion to Vishnu, chanting and singing the Lord's Name and spreading bhakti yoga teachings. *Bhagavata Mahapurana* mentions that he is actually an incarnation of Vishnu. *See also* bhakti, Dhruva.

nectar   In classical mythology, the food of the gods; in mystic terms, spiritual nourishment that comes from contact with Nam (Shabd), which absorbs the listener in its bliss and carries the soul to eternity. *See also* Nam, Shabd.

nine treasures (*nau nidh*)   Ancient Indian scriptures enumerate nine worldly treasures: family and precious metals; precious stones and jewels; delicious food; skill in the use of arms and ability to rule others; clothing and food; dealing in gold; trading in precious gems and jewels; mastery of the fine arts; riches of all kinds. The Saints, however, use the term to describe the wealth of Nam, through which one attains the spiritual treasure God has placed within all beings: faith; attachment to God; contentment; detachment from worldly possessions, family and friends; acceptance of and surrender to God's will; mental equipoise; lasting and permanent happiness; ecstasy achieved by overcoming ego; seeing everything as coming from God rather than from one's own efforts. *See also* Nam.

ocean of existence   Also described as the ocean of dread or ocean of phenomena, the ocean of existence is used as a metaphor for the three worlds (physical, astral and causal), where the soul 'drowns' under the weight of its karma. *See also* three realms.

Paltu (1710–1780)   Paltu Sahib was born in Nanga-Jalalpur in Uttar Pradesh near Ayodhya, a town sacred to Hindus and a place of pilgrimage. A grocer by profession, Sant Paltu later lived in Ayodhya, where he spread the teachings of Nam. A disciple and successor of Gobind Sahib, Paltu fearlessly denounced the rituals and customs of organized religion. For his bold utterances he was persecuted and burnt alive by the enraged orthodoxy. His poems, which convey his message directly to the hearts of his readers, are published under the title *Paltu Sahib ki Bani*.

Pandavas   The five sons of King Pandu are called the Pandavas; they fought their cousins, the Kauravas, in the great war of the Mahabharata and with the help of Lord Krishna regained their kingdom. One of the Pandavas was Arjuna, who engaged in a dialogue with Krishna about the moral dilemmas he faced on the battlefield. Lord Krishna instructed Arjuna to do his duty as required, without any expectation of reward. This dialogue is known as the Bhagavad Gita (Song of the Lord) and forms a part of the epic Mahabharata.

passions, five *See* five enemies/passions/vices/adversaries/robbers/demons.

philosopher's stone A mythical stone much sought after by alchemists, who believed it had the power to turn base metals into gold and to grant eternal youth. Mystically, the Master is referred to as the philosopher's stone, as he transforms his disciples from sinners into Saints.

powers, eight supernatural *See* eight supernatural powers.

Puranas Literally, the old or ancient ones, the Puranas are ancient scriptures which consist of religio-mythological stories dealing with aspects of ancient Indian history, legend and theology and describing the lives and deeds of the gods, heroes and great kings. There are eighteen principal and eighteen secondary Puranas, composed at different times, most of them dealing with theories of the creation, destruction and renewal of the universe. They are a kind of encyclopaedia of Hindu religious forms and their countless traditions.

Radha Soami The Lord (*swami*) of the soul (*radha*); the supreme Lord, the Lord of the highest spiritual stage; also the name of the stage itself.

radiant form Light form; astral form. At the time of initiation the Master projects his radiant form within the disciple from the Word or Shabd, which is the real and ultimate form of the Master; also called the Shabd form. *See also* Master, Shabd.

raga Literally colour, hue, also beauty, melody; an arrangement of musical notes in Indian classical music which is said to evoke a specific mood and tone such as love, inspiration or longing. Each raga has an organization of five to seven notes and a specific rhythm. Almost all of the hymns in the Adi Granth are composed in a particular raga, for example, Raga Asa, Bilawal, Gauri, Ramkali. There are thirty-one different ragas and the name of the raga is given at the start of the hymn. The Adi Granth is organized by raga.

Raidas An alternate spelling of Ravidas. *See* Ravidas, Guru.

Ram Das, Guru (1534–1581)   Guru Ram Das was the fourth Guru in the line of succession of Guru Nanak. Born into humble circumstances at Lahore (now in Pakistan), he became the son-in-law of Guru Amar Das, who appointed him as his successor. Guru Ram Das founded the city now known as Amritsar and composed more than six hundred of the verses in the Adi Granth, including the Lavan, which is recited in the Sikh wedding ceremony.

Ranjha   In Punjabi folklore, Ranjha is tormented by intense love for the beautiful unavailable Heer, who had been married to another man against her will. Heartbroken, he wanders the countryside and eventually either becomes a yogi or takes on the guise of a yogi in order to meet Heer, depending on the version of the story recounted. Several versions of this story exist, with some people saying that it had a happy ending; the most popular version ends unhappily. Mystically, the story symbolizes the quest of the soul for union with God.

Ravidas, Guru (1414–1532)   Guru Ravidas was a well-known Saint who was born in Uttar Pradesh, lived in Kashi (present-day Varanasi) and travelled widely across Rajasthan and other parts of India teaching the path of devotion to the Word. He was a contemporary of Kabir and Guru Nanak and is believed to have been a disciple of Swami Ramanand. He supported himself as a cobbler, and in spite of this profession, which in his time was viewed as having low status, he had a great impact on the many people who came to him for spiritual guidance, including Mirabai, princess of Mewar, and Raja Pipa, a Rajput king. Some of his writings are preserved in the Adi Granth.

realms, three   *See* three realms.

regions   *See* inner regions.

Sahjobai   An eighteenth-century Saint of Rajasthan, Sahjobai Ji was known for her selfless devotion to her Master, Sant Charandas. Sahjobai composed *Sahaj Prakash* (Light on the Natural State), a collection of poems that are simple and direct in expression and filled with love and devotion for her Master.

Sain Bulleh Shah   *See* Bulleh Shah, Sain.

Saint   Mystic of the highest order. In mystical literature the Hindi term *sant* denotes a God-realized mystic who has attained the region of pure spirit (Sach Khand). Sant is often translated into English as 'Saint' and the two words are used interchangeably. Mystics also sometimes address their audience as 'Saints' because of the potential which they see in all human beings to become true God-realized Saints through love and devotion. *See also* Guru, Master, Satguru.

Sant   *See* Saint.

Satguru   True (*sat*) spiritual teacher (*guru*); a Master who has access to Sach Khand, the fifth inner region. A Satguru is a Saint who is ordained to take certain allotted souls back to God by initiating them into the path of Nam, Shabd or the sound current. *See also* Guru, Master, Saint.

satsang   The company (*sang*) of truth (*sat*); association with truth. Satsang ordinarily means the company of Saints or advanced souls, or a gathering of devotees held under the auspices of a Saint, where a discourse on God, Shabd, meditation and the Master is presented; the discourse itself is also called a satsang. Satsang also has a deeper sense, meaning internal satsang, the association or union of the soul with Shabd.

Satyuga   *See* yugas.

Shabd   Sound, voice, word, hymn; esoterically, the underlying current of divine energy that created and sustains the universe, which is also called Word, Name, Holy Spirit, sound current, unstruck melody, unstruck music, the music of the spheres and so forth. It was through Shabd, the eternal power of God, that souls were sent down from their original home to inhabit the creation, and it is through the same power that they must retrace their journey homewards. However, no one but a living true Master can reveal the secret of Shabd and connect the disciple's consciousness to it. A shabd is also a song, a hymn, a religious or spiritual poem. *See also* Master, Nam, Surat Shabd.

Shabri   Shabri was a member of the Nishadha tribal community. She was initiated by Sage Matanga, serving him with love and devotion. Before his death he told her that because of her devotion Lord Ram would give her darshan. Shabri picked berries in anticipation of Ram's visit, tasting each one to make sure it was sweet, not thinking that this might defile them. When Ram finally visited, he went only to Shabri because of her earnest longing, even though many other yogis were waiting. When Shabri offered him the berries, his companion Lakshman mentioned that they were already partly eaten and so not fit for Ram, but Ram replied that they were offered with such love and devotion that they were without equal. He then gave a discourse on ninefold devotion to Shabri. Because of her devotion, she was granted liberation.

Shah Jilani Abdul Qadir   *See* Jilani, Shah Abdul Qadir.

shah   A title given to the lords and rulers in the Indian subcontinent; thus also a term of veneration.

Sheikh Farid   *See* Farid, Sheikh.

sheikh   A Muslim scholar or priest who lives by the Muslim religious code; a term of respect.

Shiva   God of destruction in the Hindu trinity of creator, preserver and destroyer (Brahma, Vishnu and Shiva). *See also* Brahma, Vishnu.

simran   Remembrance, recollection, repetition of holy names. Simran is the first part of the spiritual practice taught by the Sant Mant Masters; its technique is given to the disciple at the time of initiation. The holy names that a perfect Master gives are charged with his power; when disciples repeat the names with love and one-pointed attention the soul currents are withdrawn from the body to the eye centre, also called the third eye or tenth door, from where the real spiritual journey begins. *See also* mantra, tenth door.

slok   A hymn of praise, a couplet, a saying; an epic stanza traditionally composed of two half-verses of sixteen syllables each. The Adi Granth uses numerous forms of sloks varying in the number of syllables and lines.

Soami Ji (1818–1878)   Seth Shiv Dayal Singh, referred to as Soami Ji Maharaj by his followers, was born in Agra. He was associated with Tulsi Sahib of Hathras right from his birth, as his parents were Tulsi Sahib's disciples, and began meditating at a very early age. After about seventeen years of intense meditation, he started teaching Surat Shabd Yoga in 1861. He is the author of *Sar Bachan Poetry* and *Sar Bachan* (Prose).

Sri   Used in the Indian subcontinent as a polite form of address or a title of veneration.

Sukdev   Little is known about the life of Sukdev Ji, an eighteenth-century Saint. In his poetry, Sant Charandas mentions Sukdev as his Guru.

Sultan Bahu   *See* Bahu, Hazrat Sultan.

Sunn A term derived from *shoonya*, a Sanskrit word meaning void, emptiness or vacuum. Saints have used Sunn with a variety of meanings. Soami Ji uses Sunn to refer to the third spiritual region, Daswan Dwar, where the soul becomes free from the bondage of matter, mind and the three attributes.

Surat Shabd The union of soul or consciousness (*surat*) with Word (*shabd*); the merging of the soul with its essence. Surat Shabd Yoga is the path to God-realization taught by the Masters, through which the consciousness is applied to the hearing of the Shabd within. Once the soul merges into the Shabd, it is carried by the Shabd to its source, the Lord. *See also* Master, Shabd, yoga.

Surdas (born 1478) A blind poet, musician and mystic renowned for his devotional songs, Sant Surdas was born near Faridabad, Haryana. When Surdas, whose name means 'slave of melody', met his Guru, Shri Vallabharacharya, it was the turning point in his life. Surdas is the author of *Sur Sagar* (Ocean of Melody).

Tegh Bahadur, Guru (1621–1675) The ninth Guru in the line of Guru Nanak, Guru Tegh Bahadur was born in Amritsar and was the youngest son of Guru Hargobind, the sixth Guru. Guru Tegh Bahadur lived an austere lifestyle and travelled extensively, teaching the philosophy of one God, the need for the true Guru and practice of Nam. He contributed many hymns to the Adi Granth. Because of his refusal to renounce his beliefs, Guru Tegh Bahadur was beheaded by the Mughal emperor Aurangzeb in 1675.

ten directions East, west, north, south, northeast, northwest, southeast, southwest, above and below, indicating everywhere.

tenth door/portal The eye centre or third eye, referred to as the tenth door because it is through this door that the soul enters the inner regions when the attention is concentrated here and withdrawn from the nine doors of the body through which the soul energy spreads into the world (two eyes, two ears, two nostrils, mouth and the two lower apertures). *See also* simran.

third eye *See* tenth door.

three realms The three realms – physical, astral and causal – are divisions of the creation which are mixed with mind and matter. The physical is the lowest, consisting of gross matter with just enough mental and spiritual substance to give it life and motion. It is a reflection of the astral, from which it was created. The astral, which includes all the heavens and paradises, is a reflection of and created from the causal realm, the home of universal mind, from which all individual minds are derived. There are four realms in all. The highest, Sach Khand, is the region of pure spirit, Nam, from which everything emanated, and is the source of the soul. *See also* inner regions, ocean of existence, web of illusion.

transmigration   The endless round of incarnating and reincarnating in different life forms, which the soul has to undergo due to the consequences of karma, reaping the positive and negative consequences of actions performed in previous lives. Also called the wheel of eighty-four. *See also* cycle of birth and death, karma.

treasures, nine   *See* nine treasures.

Tretayuga   *See* yugas.

Trikuti   *See* inner regions.

Tukaram (1598–1650)   Born into a well-to-do family of traders in Dehu in the District of Pune, Sant Tukaram's early life was comfortable and enjoyable. However, when he was still in his teens, he lost his parents, wife, children and his business. Disillusioned, he turned towards God and was blessed with initiation by Babaji Raghava Chaitanya in 1619. Tukaram became a mystic adept, composing thousands of poems denouncing all outward forms of worship. His poems, which remain popular even today, are published under the titles *Saarth Shri Tukaramachi Gatha* and *Shri Tukaram Bavanchya Abhanganchi Gatha*.

Tulsi Sahib (1763–1843)   The great poet-Saint of Hathras and author of the *Ghat Ramayana* was born in the princely family of the Peshwas. Tulsi Sahib began to show signs of a devotional trend of mind at an early age and had no desire for worldly pleasures and pursuits. When he was appointed as the royal successor, he fled from the court and settled in Hathras near Agra, where he was known as Dakkhini Baba.

Tulsidas, Goswami (1536–1623)   The mystic poet Goswami Tulsidas was born into a very poor family and lived and died in Varanasi (Benares) in Uttar Pradesh. He was a disciple of Baba Narhari Das. His epic poem *Ramcharitmanas* (Sacred Lakes of the Acts of Ram) describes the path to Ram, the one Lord. Based on the ancient story of the Ramayana, it is still a popular and revered Hindi classic. Goswami Tulsidas is considered one of the greatest devotional poets of medieval India, and thus was given the honorific Goswami, a Sanskrit term meaning 'master of the senses'.

twenty-five tendencies   According to Hindu philosophy, human beings have twenty-five tendencies (*prakritis*) that are manifestations of the five elements that make up the human body: earth, air, fire, water and ether. These tendencies project themselves in various emotions and actions through the interaction among the five passions or vices of lust, anger, greed, attachment and pride or ego. *See also* five elements, five enemies.

var   A popular genre of Punjabi poetry that generally depicts the exploits of a folk hero and showers praise on him. Mystically, this verse form is used to depict the struggle of the soul to overcome adversity and reunite with the Lord.

Vedas   Literally, knowledge. The four earliest scriptures of Hinduism (Rig Veda, Sam Veda, Yajur Veda, Atharva Veda), the Vedas are said to have been directly revealed rather than of human origin. The Vedas deal with spiritual matters, the divine powers of gods, sacred formulas (mantras) and the problems of life in the world. The Vedas reveal that some of their transcribers knew about the Word of God, which they called *naad* (Sound) or *vaak* (Word). The term also refers to Vedic literature in general, including the Upanishads and various interpretive texts.

Vishnu   God of preservation in the Hindu trinity of creator, preserver and destroyer (Brahma, Vishnu and Shiva). *See also* Brahma, Shiva.

web of illusion/attachments/delusion/the world   Illusion or maya that envelops the phenomenal universe; denotes everything that comes and goes, that is transient. Souls are caught in the belief that this web is real. The entire creation (the physical, astral and causal worlds) is described as illusory or false because it is impermanent, in contrast to Satnam, the Supreme Being, which alone is permanent, eternal and true. *See also* maya.

Yama   The lord of death and divine justice, also known as Dharmrai, who takes charge of the soul at the time of death. Those souls who do not have the protection of a true Master are said to undergo different kinds of punishment at the hands of Yama for their misdeeds and are trapped in the cycle of birth and death. *See also* cycle of birth and death, Dharmrai, Kal, karma, transmigration.

yoga From the Sanskrit *yog*, meaning 'to yoke or join'; union. One of the six systems of Indian philosophy, yoga is believed to have been founded by the sage Yajnavalkya and later codified by Patanjali in his *Yoga Sutra*. In the broader context, yoga is any system, including spiritual exercises and meditation, meant to lead the human soul to union with God.

yugas The four ages or cycles of time. According to Hindu scriptures, the yugas follow each other in endlessly recurring cycles: Satyuga, the Golden Age; Tretayuga, the Silver Age; Dwaparyuga, the Copper Age; and Kaliyuga, the Iron Age or Dark Age. Kaliyuga, the age of strife and discord, is the present and last yuga of the cycle through which the universe passes.

Bibliography

ENGLISH

Adi Granth. *Gurbani Selections 1: Jap Ji, Asa ki Var, Sidh Gost, Barah Maha.* Translated by Shiv Singh Dhatt. Beas, Punjab: Radha Soami Satsang Beas, 2011.

———. *Gurbani Selections 2: Anand, Barah Maha, Sukhmani, Slok Mahla 9, Selected Hymns.* Translated by Shiv Singh Dhatt. Beas, Punjab: Radha Soami Satsang Beas, 2011.

Bahu, Sultan. *Sultan Bahu.* Compiled, translated and introduced by J. R. Puri and K. S. Khak. (1st ed. 1998) 2nd ed. Mystics of the East Series. Beas, Punjab: Radha Soami Satsang Beas, 1999.

Bulleh Shah. *Bulleh Shah.* Compiled, translated and introduced by J. R. Puri and T. R. Shangari. (1st ed. 1986) 3rd ed. Mystics of the East Series. Beas, Punjab: Radha Soami Satsang Beas, 2010.

Dadu Dayal. *Dadu: The Compassionate Mystic.* Compiled, translated and introduced by K. N. Upadhyaya. (1st ed. 1979) 4th ed. Mystics of the East Series. Beas, Punjab: Radha Soami Satsang Beas, 2010.

Dariya Sahib of Bihar. *Dariya Sahib: Saint of Bihar.* Compiled, translated and introduced by K. N. Upadhyaya. (1st ed. 1987) 2nd ed. Mystics of the East Series. Beas, Punjab: Radha Soami Satsang Beas, 2006.

Kabir. *Kabir: The Great Mystic.* Compiled, translated and introduced by Isaac A. Ezekiel. (1st ed. 1966) 6th ed. Mystics of the East Series. Beas, Punjab: Radha Soami Satsang Beas, 2002.

———. *Kabir: The Weaver of God's Name.* Compiled, translated and introduced by V. K. Sethi. (1st ed. 1984) 3rd ed. Mystics of the East Series. Beas, Punjab: Radha Soami Satsang Beas, 1998.

Namdev. *Saint Namdev.* Compiled, translated and introduced by J. R. Puri and V. K. Sethi. (1st ed. 1977) 3rd ed. Mystics of the East Series. Beas, Punjab: Radha Soami Satsang Beas, 2001.

Nanak, Guru. *Guru Nanak: His Mystic Teachings.* Compiled, translated and introduced by J. R. Puri. (1st ed. 1982) 4th ed. Mystics of the East Series. Beas, Punjab: Radha Soami Satsang Beas, 2004.

Paltu. *Saint Paltu: His Life and Teachings.* Compiled, translated and introduced by Isaac A. Ezekiel. (1ˢᵗ ed. 1978) 4ᵗʰ ed. Mystics of the East Series. Beas, Punjab: Radha Soami Satsang Beas, 2009.

Ravidas. *Guru Ravidas: The Philosopher's Stone.* Compiled, translated and introduced by K. N. Upadhyaya. (1ˢᵗ ed. 1982) 4ᵗʰ ed. Mystics of the East Series. Beas, Punjab: Radha Soami Satsang Beas, 2009.

Sawan Singh. *Philosophy of the Masters.* Vol. 3. (1ˢᵗ ed. 1965) 5ᵗʰ ed. Beas, Punjab: Radha Soami Satsang Beas, 1996.

Soami Ji (Seth Shiv Dayal Singh). *Sar Bachan Poetry (Selections).* Selected and translated by Shiv Singh Dhatt. Beas, Punjab: Radha Soami Satsang Beas, 2002.

Tukaram. *Tukaram: The Ceaseless Song of Devotion.* Compiled, translated and introduced by Chandravati Rajwade. (1ˢᵗ ed. 1978) 3ʳᵈ ed. Mystics of the East Series. Beas, Punjab: Radha Soami Satsang Beas, 2004.

Tulsi Sahib. *Tulsi Sahib: Saint of Hathras.* Compiled, translated and introduced by J. R. Puri and V. K. Sethi. (1ˢᵗ ed. 1978) 3ʳᵈ ed. Mystics of the East Series. Beas, Punjab: Radha Soami Satsang Beas, 1995.

Tulsidas, Goswami. *The Teachings of Goswami Tulsidas: A Spiritual Perspective.* Compiled, translated and introduced by K. N. Upadhyaya. Mystics of the East Series. Beas, Punjab: Radha Soami Satsang Beas, 2008.

HINDI AND MARATHI

Adi Granth. *Sri Guru Granth Sahib (Santha Sainchiyan).* 2 vols. Amritsar: Shiromani Gurdwara Prabandhak Committee, 2004, 2005.

Avasthi, Achariya Bacchulal. *Tulsi Shabd-Kosh.* Vol. 1. Delhi: Books 'n' Books, 1991.

Bahu, Sultan. *Hazrat Sultan Bahu.* Compiled and introduced by J. R. Puri and Kirpal Singh Khak. Beas, Punjab: Radha Soami Satsang Beas, 2000.

Belvedere Press. *Santbani Sangrah.* 2 vols. 6ᵗʰ ed, 5ᵗʰ ed. Allahabad: Belvedere Printing Works, 1970, 1975.

Bulleh Shah. *Sain Bulleh Shah.* 9ᵗʰ ed. Compiled and introduced by J. R. Puri. Beas, Punjab: Radha Soami Satsang Beas, 2002.

Charandas. *Charandasji ki Bani.* Vol. 1. 7ᵗʰ ed. Allahabad: Belvedere Printing Works, 1978.

———. *Sri Bhakti Sagar.* Jaipur: Albeli Madhuri Sharan, Samvat 2056 (1999).

Dadu Dayal. *Dadu Dayal ki Bani.* 2 vols. Reprint (original c. 1911). Allahabad: Belvedere Printing Works, 1963, 1974.

———. *Dadudayal Granthavali.* Edited by Parshuram Chaturvedi. Varanasi: Nagari Pracharini Sabha, Samvat 2023 (1966).

Dariya Sahib of Bihar. *Dariya Granthavali (Pratham Granth).* Edited by Dharmendra Brahmchari Shastri. Patna: Bihar Rashtrabhasha-Prishad, Samvat 2011 (1954).

Dharamdas, Dhani. *Mahatma Dhani Dharamdasji ki Shabdavali.* Allahabad: Belvedere Printing Works, 1997.

Dharnidas. *Dharnidasji ki Bani.* 3rd ed. Allahabad: Belvedere Printing Works, 1976.

Jagjivan. *Jagjivan Sahib ki Bani.* 2 vols. 5th ed, 3rd ed. Allahabad: Belvedere Printing Works, 1990, 1972.

Kabir. *Kabir Granthavali.* 13th ed. Compiled and edited by Shyamsunder Das. Varanasi: Nagari Pracharini Sabha, Samvat 2032 (1975).

———. *Kabir Sahib ki Shabdavali.* 2 vols. Reprint (original c.1902). Allahabad: Belvedere Printing Works, 1998, 2000.

———. *Kabir Sakhi Sangrah.* 2 vols. 10th ed. Allahabad: Belvedere Printing Works, 1996.

Malukdas. *Malukdasji ki Bani.* 6th ed. Allahabad: Belvedere Printing Works, 1997.

Mirabai. *Mirabai ki Shabdavali.* 13th ed. Allahabad: Belvedere Printing Works, 2000.

———. *Miran Brihatpadavali.* Compiled and edited by Harinarayan Purohit. Jodhpur: Rajasthan Prachayavidiya Pratishthan, 1968.

———. *Miran Sudha-Sindhu.* Compiled and edited by Anand Swarup. Bhilwara: Sri Miran Prakashan Samiti, Samvat 2014 (1957).

Namdev. *Sant Namdev ki Hindi Padavali.* Edited by Bhagirath Mishr. Puna: Puna Vishav Vidiyalay, 1964.

Paltu. *Paltu Sahib ki Bani.* Vol. 1, 3. 13th ed, 9th ed. Allahabad: Belvedere Printing Works, 1993.

Ravidas / Raidas. *Raidasji ki Bani.* 12th ed. Allahabad: Belvedere Printing Works, 1997.

———. *Sant Guru Ravidas Vani.* Compiled by B. P. Sharma. Delhi: Surya-Prakashan, Samvat 2035 (1978).

Sahjobai. *Sahjobai ki Bani.* 12th ed. Allahabad: Belvedere Printing Works, 1977.

Soami Ji (Seth Shiv Dayal Singh). *Sar Bachan Sangrah.* 15th ed. Beas, Punjab: Radha Soami Satsang Beas, 2008.

Surdas. *Sur-Vinay Patrika.* 2nd ed. Gorakhpur: Geeta Press, Samvat 2012 (1955).

Tukaram. *Sant Tukaram.* 2nd ed. Compiled and introduced by Chandravati Rajwade. Beas, Punjab: Radha Soami Satsang Beas, 2010.

———. *Shri Tukaram Bavanchya Abhanganchi Gatha.* Vol. 2. Edited by Vishnu Parshuram Shastri Pandit. Mumbai: Indu Prakash Press, 1950.

Tulsidas. *Vinay-Patrika.* 17th ed. Gorakhpur: Geeta Press, Samvat 2015 (1958).

Tulsi Sahib of Hathras. *Ghat Ramayan.* 2 vols. 9th ed, 15th ed. Allahabad: Belvedere Printing Works, 1973, 1999.

———. *Tulsi Sahib ki Shabdavali.* 2 vols. Allahabad: Belvedere Printing Works, 1973.

URDU

Bulleh Shah. *Kafian Bulleh Shah*. Edited by Abdul Majid Bhatti. Islamabad: Lok Virse da Qaumi Idara, 1975.

———. *Kalam Bulleh Shah*. Compiled by Nazir Ahmad. Lahore: Pakistan International Printers, 1976.

———. *Kulliyat Bulleh Shah*. Edited by Muhammad Faqir. Lahore: Punjabi Adabi Academy, 1970.

———. *Qanune Ishaq*. Edited by Anvar Ali Rohatki. Lahore: Navalkishore Press, n. d.

Index of Transliterated First Lines

Index of Translated First Lines

Subject Index

Addresses for Information and Books

INDIAN SUB-CONTINENT

INDIA
The Secretary
Radha Soami Satsang Beas
Dera Baba Jaimal Singh
District Amritsar, Punjab 143204

NEPAL
Mr. S.B.B. Chhetri
Radha Soami Satsang Beas
Gongabu 7 P.O. Box 1646,
Kathmandu
☎ +977-01-435-7765

PAKISTAN
Mr. Sadrang Seetal Das
Lahori Mohala
Larkana, Sindh

SRI LANKA
Mrs. Maya Mahbubani
Radha Soami Satsang Beas
No. 47/1 Silva Lane
Rajagiriya, Colombo
☎ +94-11-286-1491

SOUTHEAST ASIA

Mrs. Cami Moss
RSSB-HK
T.S.T., P.O. Box 90745
Kowloon, Hong Kong
☎ +852-2369-0625

GUAM
Mrs. Rekha Sadhwani
625 Alupang Cove
241 Condo Lane, Tamuning 96911

HONG KONG
Mr. Manoj Sabnani
Radha Soami Satsang Beas
27th Floor, Tower B
Billion Centre
1 Wang Kwong Road
Kowloon Bay
☎ +852-2369-0625

INDONESIA
Mr. Ramesh Sadarangani
Yayasan Radha Soami Satsang Beas
Jl. Transyogi Kelurahan Jatirangga
Pondok Gede 17434
☎ +62-21-845-1612

Yayasan Radha Soami Satsang
Jalan Bung Tomo
Desa Pemecutan Raya
Denpasar, Bali 80118
☎ +62-361-438-522

JAPAN
Mr. Jani G. Mohinani
Radha Soami Satsang Beas
1-2-18 Nakajima-Dori
Aotani, Chuo-Ku
Kobe 651-0052
☎ +81-78-222-5353

KOREA
Mr. Haresh Buxani
Science of the Soul Study Group
638, Hopyeong-Dong
R603-1 & 604 Sungbo Building
Nam Yangju, Gyeong Gi-Do
☎ +82-315-117-008

MALAYSIA
Mr. Bhupinder Singh
Radha Soami Satsang Beas
29 Jalan Cerapu Satu, Off Batu 3 ¼
Jalan Cheras, Kuala Lumpur 56100
☎ +603-9200-3073

PHILIPPINES
Mr. Kay Sham
Science of the Soul Study Center
9001 Don Jesus Boulevard
Alabang Hills, Cupang
Muntinlupa City, 1771
☎ +63-2-772-0111 / 0555

SINGAPORE
Mrs. Asha Melwani
Radha Soami Satsang Beas
19 Amber Road
Singapore 439868
☎ +65-6447-4956

TAIWAN, R.O.C.
Mr. Haresh Buxani
Science of the Soul Study Group
Aetna Tower Office
15F., No. 27-9, Sec.2,
Jhongjheng E.Rd.
Danshuei Township, Taipei 25170
☎ +886-2-8809-5223

THAILAND
Mr. Harmahinder Singh Sethi
Radha Soami Satsang Beas
Foundation Bangkok
58/32 Thaphra Ratchadaphisek Road,
Soi 16, Wat Thapra,
Bangkok Yai District, Bangkok 10600
☎ +66-2-868-2186 / 2187

ASIA PACIFIC

AUSTRALIA
Mrs. Jill Wiley
P.O. Box 1256
Kenmore 4069, Queensland

Science of the Soul Study Centre
1530 Elizabeth Drive
Cecil Park, New South Wales 2178
☎ +61-2-9826-2564

NEW ZEALAND
Mr. Tony Waddicor
P.O. Box 5331, Auckland

Science of the Soul Study Centre
80 Olsen Avenue, Auckland
☎ +64-9-624-2202

CANADA & UNITED STATES

CANADA
Mr. John Pope
5285 Coombe Lane, Belcarra,
British Columbia V3H 4N6

Science of the Soul Study Centre
2932 -176th Street
Surrey, B.C. V3S 9V4
☎ +1-604-541-4792

Mrs. Meena Khanna
149 Elton Park Road
Oakville, Ontario L6J 4C2

Science of the Soul Study Centre
6566 Sixth Line, RR 1 Hornby
Ontario L0P 1E0
☎ +1-905-875-4579

UNITED STATES
Mr. Hank Muller
P.O. Box 1847
Tomball, TX 77377

Dr. Vincent P. Savarese
2550 Pequeno Circle
Palm Springs, CA 92264-9522

Dr. Douglas Torr
P.O. Box 2360
Southern Pines, NC 28388-2360

Dr. Frank E. Vogel
275 Cutts Road
Newport, NH 03773

Science of the Soul Study Center
4115 Gillespie Street
Fayetteville, NC 28306-9053
☎ +1-910-426-5306

Science of the Soul Study Center
2415 Washington Street
Petaluma, CA 94954-9274
☎ +1-707-762-5082

MEXICO & CENTRAL AMERICA

Dr. Servando Sanchez
16103 Vanderbilt Drive
Odessa, Florida 33556 USA

MEXICO
Mr. Carlos Vega Perez
Radha Soami Satsang Beas
Efrain Gonzalez Luna
2051 Col. Americana
Guadalajara, Jalisco 44090
☎ +52-333-615-4942

Radha Soami Satsang Beas
Circuito Universidad S/N
Lomas Del Progreso EL Pitillal
Puerto Vallarta, CP 48290
☏ +52-322-299-1954

BELIZE
Mrs. Milan Hotchandani
4633 Seashore Drive
P.O. Box 830, Belize City

PANAMA
Mr. Ashok Tikamdas Dinani
P.O. Box 01000
Zona Libre, Panama 0302

SOUTH AMERICA

ARGENTINA
Ms. Fabiana Shilton
Leiva 4363 Capital Federal
C.P. 1427 Buenos Aires

BRAZIL
Mr. Guillerme Almeida
RUA Jesuino Arrvda 574/51
Sao Paulo 04532-081

CHILE
Mr. Vijay Harjani
Pasaje Cuatro No. 3438
Sector Chipana, Iquique

Fundacion
Radha Soami Satsang Beas
Av. Apoquindo 4770,
Oficina 1504, Las Condes, Santiago

COLOMBIA
Mrs. Emma Orozco
Asociacion Cultural
Radha Soami Satsang Beas
Calle 48 No. 78A-30
Medellin 49744
☏ +574-234-5130

ECUADOR
Mr. Miguel Egas H.
Radha Soami Satsang Beas
Calle Marquez de Varela
OE 3-68y Avda. America
P.O. Box 17-21-115, Quito
☏ +5932-2-555-988

PERU
Mr. Carlos Fitts
Asociacion Cultural
Radha Soami Satsang Beas
Av. Pardo #231, 12th Floor
Miraflores, Lima 18

VENEZUELA
Mrs. Helen Paquin
Radha Soami Satsang Beas
Av. Los Samanes con
Av. Los Naranjos Conj
Res. Florida 335
La Florida, Caracas 1012

CARIBBEAN

Mr. Sean Finnigan
Science of the Soul Foundation
P.O. Box 978, Phillipsburg
St. Maarten, Dutch Caribbean

Mrs. Jaya Sabnani
1 Sunset Drive South
Fort George Heights
St. Michael BB111 02
Barbados

BARBADOS, W.I.
Mr. Deepak Nebhani
Science of the Soul Study Center
No. 10, 5th Avenue, Belleville
St. Michael BB11114
☏ +1-246-427-4761

CURACAO
Mrs. Hema Chandiramani
Science of the Soul Study Centre
Kaya Seru di Milon 6-9
Santa Catharina
☏ +599-9-747-0226

ST. MAARTEN
Mr. Prakash Daryanani
Science of the Soul Study Centre
203 Oyster Pond Road
St. Maarten, Dutch Caribbean
☏ +1-721-547-0066

GRENADA, W.I.
Mr. Ajay Mahbubani
P.O. Box 820, St. Georges

GUYANA
Mrs. Indu Lalwani
155, Garnette Street
Newtown Kitty, Georgetown

HAITI, W.I
Ms. Monique Finnigan Pierre
Route de Camp Perrin
Lamartiniere, HT 8140

JAMAICA, W.I.
Mrs. Reshma Daswani
17 Colombus Height
First Phase, Ocho Rios

ST. THOMAS
Mrs. Hema Melwani
P.O. Box 600145
US Virgin Islands
VI00801-6145

SURINAME
Mr. Ettire Stanley Rensch
Surinamestraat 36, Paramaribo

TRINIDAD, W.I.
Mr. Chandru Chatlani
20 Admiral Court
Westmoorings-by-Sea
Westmoorings

EUROPE

AUSTRIA
Mr. Hansjorg Hammerer
Sezenweingasse 10
A-5020 Salzburg

BELGIUM
Mr. Piet J. E. Vosters
Driezenstraat 26
Turnhout 2300

BULGARIA
Mr. Deyan Stoyanov
Foundation
Radha Soami Satsang Beas
P.O. Box 39, 8000 Bourgas

CYPRUS
Mr. Heraclis Achilleos
P.O. Box 29077
1035 Nicosia

CZECH REPUBLIC
Mr. Vladimir Skalsky
Maratkova 916
142 00 Praha 411

DENMARK
Mr. Tony Sharma
Sven Dalsgaardsvej 33
DK-7430 Ikast

FINLAND
Ms. Anneli Wingfield
P.O. Box 1422
00101 Helsinki

FRANCE
Mr. Pierre de Proyart
7 Quai Voltaire
Paris 75007

GERMANY
Mr. Rudolf Walberg
P.O. Box 1544
D-65800 Bad Soden

GIBRALTAR
Mr. Sunder Mahtani
RSSB Charitable Trust
15 Rosia Road,
Gibraltar GX11 1AA
☏ +350-200-412-67

GREECE
Mr. Themistoclis Gianopoulos
6 Platonos Str.
17672 Kallithea, Attiki

ITALY
Mrs. Wilma Salvatori Torri
Via Bacchiglione 3
00199 Rome

NETHERLANDS
Mr. Henk Keuning
Kleizuwe2
3633 AE Vreeland

Radha Soami Satsang Beas
Middenweg 145 E
1394 AH Nederhorst den Berg
☏ +31-294-255-255

NORWAY
Mr. Manoj Kaushal
Langretta 8
N - 1279 Oslo

POLAND
Mr. Vinod Sharma
P.O. Box 59
Ul. Szkolna 15
05-090 Raszyn

PORTUGAL
Mrs. Sharda Lodhia
CRCA Portugal
Av. Coronel Eduardo Galhardo
No. 18 A-B, Lisbon 1170-105

ROMANIA
Mrs. Carmen Cismas
C.P. 6-12, 810600 Braila

SLOVENIA
Mr. Marko Bedina
Brezje pri Trzicu 68
4290 Trzic

SPAIN
Mr. J. W. Balani
Fundacion Cultural RSSB
Fca Loma del Valle S/N
Cruce de Penon de Zapata
Alhaurin De la Torre
Malaga 29130
☎ +34-952-414-679

SWEDEN
Mr. Lennart Zachen
Norra Sonnarpsvägen 29
SE-286 72 Asljunga

SWITZERLAND
Mr. Sebastian Züst
Weissenrainstrasse 48
CH 8707 Uetikon am See

UNITED KINGDOM
Mr. Narinder Singh Johal
Science of the Soul Study Centre
Haynes Park, Haynes
MK45 3BL Bedford
☎ +44-1234-381-234

AFRICA

BENIN
Mr. Jaikumar T. Vaswani
01 Boite Postale 951,
Recette Principale Cotonou 01

BOTSWANA
Dr. Krishan Lal Bhateja
P.O. Box 402539
Gaborone

DEM. REP. OF CONGO
Mr. Prahlad Parbhu
143 Kasai Ave.
Lubumbashi

GHANA
Mr. Murli Chatani
Radha Soami Satsang Beas
P.O. Box 3976, Accra
☎ +233-242-057-309

IVORY COAST
Mr. Veerender Kumar Sapra
Avenue 7, Rue 19, Lot 196
Trechville, 05 BP 1547 Abidjan 05

KENYA
Mr. Amarjit Singh Virdi
Radha Soami Satsang Beas
P.O. Box 15134
Langata 00509, Nairobi
☎ +254-20-890-329

LESOTHO
Mr. Sello Wilson Moseme
P.O. Box 750
Leribe 300

MADAGASCAR
Mrs. I. Rakotomahandry
BP100 Airport d'Ivato
Antananarivo 105

MAURITIUS
Dr. I. Fagoonee
Radha Soami Satsang Beas Trust
69 CNR Antelme /Stanley Avenues
Quatre Bornes
☎ +230-454-3300

MOZAMBIQUE
Mr. Mangaram Matwani
Av Josina Machei, 1st floor No. 376
Maputa 190

NAMIBIA
Mrs. Jennifer Carvill
P.O. Box 449
Swakopmund 9000

NIGERIA
Mr. Nanik N. Balani
G.P.O. Box 5054, Marina
Lagos

RÉUNION
Ms. Marie-Lynn Marcel
5 Chemin 'Gonneau, Bernica,
St Gillesles Hauts 97435

SIERRA LEONE
Mr. Kishore S. Mahboobani
82/88 Kissy Dock Yard,
P O Box 369, Freetown

SOUTH AFRICA
Mr. Gordon Clive Wilson
P.O. Box 1959
Randpark Ridge
Gauteng 2156

Science of the Soul Study Centre
Bush Hill
24 Kelly Road
Bush Hill, Johannesburg
☎ +27-11-025-7655

SWAZILAND
Mr. Mike Cox
Green Valley Farm
Malkerns

TANZANIA
Mr. Manmohan Singh
99 Lugalo Street
Dar-Es-Salaam 65065

UGANDA
Mr. Sylvester Kakooza
Radha Soami Satsang Beas
P.O. Box 31381, Kampala

ZAMBIA
Mr. Surinder Kumar Sachar
2922 Mutondo Crescent
Copperbelt, Kitwe 212

ZIMBABWE
Mr. Gordon Clive Wilson
P.O. Box 1959
Randpark Ridge
Gauteng 2156, South Africa

MIDDLE EAST

BAHRAIN
Mr. Sameer Deshpande
Flat No. 55, Bldg No. 781
Rd. No. 3630, Block 336
AL Adliya, Manama

ISRAEL
Mr. Michael Yaniv
Moshav Sde Nitzan 59
D.N. Hanegev 85470

KUWAIT
Mr. Jayakara Shetty
P.O. Box 22223
13083 Safat

U.A.E.
Mr. Daleep Jatwani
P.O. Box 37816, Dubai
☎ +971-4-339-4773

Books on Spirituality

RSSB TRADITION

Sar Bachan Prose – Soami Ji Maharaj
Sar Bachan Poetry – Soami Ji Maharaj

Spiritual Letters – Baba Jaimal Singh

The Dawn of Light – Maharaj Sawan Singh
Discourses on Sant Mat, Volume I – Maharaj Sawan Singh
My Submission – Maharaj Sawan Singh
Philosophy of the Masters (5 volumes) – Maharaj Sawan Singh
Spiritual Gems – Maharaj Sawan Singh

Discourses on Sant Mat, Volume II – Maharaj Jagat Singh
The Science of the Soul – Maharaj Jagat Singh

Die to Live – Maharaj Charan Singh
Divine Light – Maharaj Charan Singh
Light on Saint John – Maharaj Charan Singh
Light on Saint Matthew – Maharaj Charan Singh
Light on Sant Mat – Maharaj Charan Singh
The Path – Maharaj Charan Singh
Quest for Light – Maharaj Charan Singh
Spiritual Discourses (2 volumes) – Maharaj Charan Singh
Spiritual Heritage – Maharaj Charan Singh
Spiritual Perspectives (3 volumes) – Maharaj Charan Singh

Call of the Great Master – Daryai Lal Kapur
Heaven on Earth – Daryai Lal Kapur
Honest Living – M. F. Singh
In Search of the Way – Flora E. Wood
The Inner Voice – C. W. Sanders
Liberation of the Soul – J. Stanley White
Life Is Fair: The Law of Cause and Effect – Brian Hines
Living Meditation – Hector Esponda Dubin
Message Divine – Shanti Sethi
The Mystic Philosophy of Sant Mat – Peter Fripp
Mysticism: The Spiritual Path – Lekh Raj Puri
The Path of the Masters – Julian P. Johnson
Radha Soami Teachings – Lekh Raj Puri
A Soul's Safari – Netta Pfeifer
A Spiritual Primer – Hector Esponda Dubin
Treasure beyond Measure – Shanti Sethi
With a Great Master in India – Julian P. Johnson
With the Three Masters (3 volumes) – Rai Sahib Munshi Ram

MYSTIC TRADITION

Bulleh Shah – J. R. Puri and T. R. Shangari
Dadu: The Compassionate Mystic – K. N. Upadhyaya
Dariya Sahib: Saint of Bihar – K. N. Upadhyaya
Guru Nanak: His Mystic Teachings – J. R. Puri

Guru Ravidas: The Philosopher's Stone – K. N. Upadhyaya
Kabir: The Great Mystic – Isaac A. Ezekiel
Kabir: The Weaver of God's Name – V. K. Sethi
Mira: The Divine Lover – V. K. Sethi
Saint Namdev – J. R. Puri and V. K. Sethi
Sant Paltu: His Life and Teachings – Isaac A. Ezekiel
Sarmad: Martyr to Love Divine – Isaac A. Ezekiel
Shams-e Tabrizi – Farida Maleki
Sultan Bahu – J. R. Puri and K. S. Khak
The Teachings of Goswami Tulsidas – K. N. Upadhyaya
Tukaram: The Ceaseless Song of Devotion – C. Rajwade
Tulsi Sahib: Saint of Hathras – J. R. Puri and V. K. Sethi

MYSTICISM IN WORLD RELIGIONS
Adventure of Faith – Shraddha Liertz
Buddhism: Path to Nirvana – K. N. Upadhyaya
The Divine Romance – John Davidson
The Gospel of Jesus – John Davidson
Gurbani Selections (Volumes I, II)
The Holy Name: Mysticism in Judaism – Miriam Caravella
Jap Ji – T. R. Shangari
The Mystic Heart of Judaism – Miriam Caravella
The Odes of Solomon – John Davidson
One Being One – John Davidson
The Prodigal Soul – John Davidson
The Song of Songs – John Davidson
Tales of the Mystic East
A Treasury of Mystic Terms,
    Part I: The Principles of Mysticism (6 volumes) – John Davidson, ed.
Yoga and the Bible – Joseph Leeming

VEGETARIAN COOKBOOKS
Baking Without Eggs
Creative Vegetarian Cooking
The Green Way to Healthy Living
Meals with Vegetables

BOOKS FOR CHILDREN
The Journey of the Soul – Victoria Jones
One Light Many Lamps – Victoria Jones

MISCELLANEOUS THEMES
Empower Women: An Awakening – Leena Chawla

For Internet orders, please visit: www.rssb.org

For book orders within India, please write to:
Radha Soami Satsang Beas
BAV Distribution Centre, 5 Guru Ravi Dass Marg
Pusa Road, New Delhi 110 005